M000019299

HANDBOOK OF INSTRUCTIONAL PRACTICES FOR LITERACY TEACHER-EDUCATORS

Examples and Reflections From the Teaching Lives of Literacy Scholars

Edited by

Joyce E. Many
Georgia State University

 LAWRENCE ERLBAUM ASSOCIATES, PUBLISHERS

2001   Mahwah, New Jersey   London

Copyright © 2001 by Lawrence Erlbaum Associates, Inc.
All rights reserved. No part of this book may be reproduced in any
form, by photostat, microfilm, retrieval system, or any other means,
without prior written permission of the publisher.

Lawrence Erlbaum Associates, Inc., Publishers
10 Industrial Avenue
Mahwah, NJ 07430

Cover design by Kathryn Houghtaling Lacey

Library of Congress Cataloging-in-Publication Data

Handbook of instructional practices for literacy teacher-educators :
Examples and reflections from the teaching lives of literacy scholars /
edited by Joyce E. Many.
      p. cm.
    Includes bibliographical references and index.
    ISBN 0-8058-3110-X (pbk. : alk. paper)
  1. English teachers—Training of—Handbooks, manuals, etc.
  2. English philology—Study and teaching—Handbooks, manuals, etc.
  I. Many, Joyce E.
PE66 .H36 2000
428'.0071—dc21   00-029365
                                        CIP

Books published by Lawrence Erlbaum Associates are printed on acid-
free paper, and their bindings are chosen for strength and durability.

Printed in the United States of America
10 9 8 7 6 5 4 3 2 1

Contents

IV   EMERGENT LITERACY

V   CONTENT AREA LITERACY

VI   LITERACY ASSESSMENT AND INSTRUCTION

VII   LANGUAGE AND LITERACY IN A DIVERSE SOCIETY

VIII   LITERACY AND TECHNOLOGY

IX   INQUIRIES INTO LITERACY, THEORY, AND CLASSROOM PRACTICE

Annotated Contents

This elementary language arts methods course was designed to be team taught by Donna Cooner and cooperating teachers from a professional development school and Donna Wiseman or another professor from the university. Approximately 120 students enroll in the course, take a weekly class from the professor, participate as reading/writing buddies to children in the professional development school, and discuss their experiences in breakout sessions after school with the classroom teachers.

In this course, JoBeth creates an inquiry community where teachers are enabled to construct their own knowledge about whole language teaching based on their individual needs, questions, experiences, and explorations.

Nancy's English/Language arts methods course was designed for middle and secondary preservice teachers. While taking this course, students are concurrently doing their first semester of student teaching. Therefore, they are able to integrate the coursework into their classroom work, and the classroom provides a rich context for questions and issues to bring back to the university methods class. Special emphases include interdisciplinary curriculum, teaching in multicultural classrooms, technology use in teaching and learning, and action research (student-teacher-as-researcher).

Peter has designed this course to focus on methods of teaching high school English. Strands of the course (a) require that students draw on their prior knowledge from previous course work focusing on cultural diversity, media and technology, adolescent psychology, and language development as they consider instructional issues, (b) engage students in designing instructional units, and (c) involve students in field experiences in secondary classrooms.

In this graduate course, Peggy emphasizes the ways that talking and writing contributes to learning in middle grades classrooms by examining current theories, research, and instructional practices.

David shapes this course in a way that ensures prospective teachers of writing have the opportunity to read various theories of teaching writing while also writing themselves and struggling with it as they expect their students to do. Prospective teachers also create demonstrations based on their expertise and share these projects with their colleagues.

III   LITERATURE AND THE TEACHING OF LITERATURE

Kathy and Cheri designed this course so that teachers and librarians could explore art and illustration as meaning-making processes. Educators study art as a semiotic process, examine and respond to picture books, and create art in studio experiences. A complex interplay of experiences with interpreting and composing visual images form the context of the course focus on visual literacy and the essential role of illustrations in picture books.

This course involves teachers in analyzing culturally diverse children's literature and in exploring models of literature-based instruction. Lee integrated book sharings, literature study sessions, and individual projects into her course in order to introduce students to new children's books and as a way to model good teaching practices.

Pat developed this summer seminar for graduate students and practicing teachers who are interested in reading current multicultural literature and raising questions regarding the theories and practices of selecting and mediating representations of self and others in K–8 classrooms.

In this contribution, Violet incorporated excepts from her syllabi across the years to illustrate how she guides students to an understanding of multicultural literature, its role as a literary product, and its position in relation to social, historical, political, or other issues.

Using a reader-response approach, Bob and his students discuss novels, drama, short stories, and poetry that are relevant to the needs, values, and interest of adolescents.

IV EMERGENT LITERACY

In this course, Lesley differentiates assignments to meet the needs of students seeking initial certification, teachers working toward a master's degree in early childhood or reading, and doctoral students who can all be in the same section of the course. In addition to studying theories and varied accepted strategies and practices, she emphasizes current issues such as early intervention programs, teaching skills in a developmentally appropriate manner, achieving standards, and balancing guided or explicit instruction as well as constructivist approaches appropriate for young children.

Mona shares an in-process course record for an Early Childhood Master's Program rather than a syllabus in the traditional sense. Rather than outlining future course experiences, the course record documents ongoing work and describes strategies that the class has identified as important to ensure the course goals are met. One goal is to enhance understanding of the tools and language of action research and the second is to organize the course experiences around constructivist principles.

Using a dialogue format, David and two graduate students (Angela and Camille) reflect on a semester in a doctoral seminar focusing on the developmental and conceptual foundations of literacy growth in young children from sociohistorical, constructivist, and critical perspectives. In doing so, the authors provide personal, realistic accounts of the course's design, content, tensions, and highlights.

V   CONTENT AREA LITERACY

In this course, Carol integrates specific practices related to reading and writing in content areas with broader concerns of meaningful, relevant learning. Preservice teachers are asked to expand their perceptions of the role of texts in secondary classrooms and to continue to evaluate what it means to be literate in their endorsement areas.

Victoria developed this course to emphasize the connection between literacy and learning in all content areas. Content area reading is taught concurrently and shares a field experience with required content specific methods courses. The course emphasizes reflective practice through the use of learning logs and their analysis, a course *Listserve*, on which Victoria posts her professional journal entries, and student responses to those journal posts.

Tom's approach to this master's degree course includes modeling literacy practices and strategies that can be used in the content areas. Teachers also read and discuss literature that can be integrated into the content areas and use Web sites to gather information applicable to science, math, social studies, and English classrooms.

VI LITERACY ASSESSMENT AND INSTRUCTION

Penny shares her syllabus for the first course in a three-course sequence
in which teachers tutor a child across a year. Teachers discuss research,
theory, and instructional practices in a seminar setting, closely track
their child's responses, and integrate tutoring experiences and course
assignments.

This course syllabus covers a class in the assessment and instruction of
children with reading problems. Participants learn to work with children
with reading problems by working with children through the university's
reading clinic. Steve noted that this approach makes the topics addressed
in the class more meaningful for the students and the tutoring has been
highly successful for the children who have been served.

This course undergraduates in exploring assessment from multiple perspectives—in terms of assessment's relationship to school and society, the
ethics of assessment, social justice and assessment, ways of knowing,
school reform and assessment—as well as examining specific assessment
practices. Students are involved in an internship as they explore issues and
refine their own repertoire of assessment strategies.

VII LANGUAGE AND LITERACY IN A DIVERSE SOCIETY

This undergraduate course is focused on literacy as it is situated in a low
income, minority community. Preservice teachers explore the challenges
and opportunities associated with literacy in this particular context. The
major goal of the course is to provide students with a perspective on literacy that reaches beyond the traditional walls of the classroom or the
school.

IX   INQUIRIES INTO LITERACY, THEORY, AND CLASSROOM PRACTICE

participants were afforded a place to initiate and continue conversations and the syllabus became dynamic—a living object that changed as interests and needs shaped the course.

Joyce created this issues course around the national trend toward balanced instruction. As part of the course, teachers chose a specific focus area (such as the teaching of phonics, early reading instruction, literature-based instruction, comprehension instruction, or writing) and created a CD-Rom/Web site resource focusing on balanced instruction within that area.

Preface

THE NEED FOR THIS BOOK

At first glance, being a researcher in literacy education may seem to require that a person lead two lives, those of a researcher and a teacher. In any given semester, we immerse ourselves in inquiry and we teach, prepare conference proposals and give feedback to our students, reflect on our data and prepare for class, make conference handouts and support students' learning in field experience settings, edit research manuscripts and evaluate student portfolios, and then we leave for conferences. When we arrive at conferences, it may appear that many of us take time out from juggling our research/teaching hats and take the opportunity to foreground our research selves. For days, we immerse ourselves in learning what colleagues have done in their lives as researchers. We stay up late into the night talking about ideas we heard in sessions, articles we are writing, or new inquiries we are planning. Hearing about each other's research invigorates us and we often leave for home exhilarated, our brains electric with the impulses of possibilities. Arriving back at our universities, it may seem that we resume our split personalities and begin again the balancing act with our two loves, research and teaching. However, for the literacy scholars who have agreed to contribute to this volume, the split between research and teaching is actually a false dichotomy. We return from conferences pondering how we might incorporate ideas we have heard into our next semester's syllabus. We contemplate how our colleagues' findings might relate to the problems our student teachers are having. We reconsider how the content of our courses might be revised to be more consistent with our increased understanding of how literacy develops. In such ways, our teaching reflects our scholarship. Our research and teaching lives intertwine.

Unfortunately, although we personally weave together the strands of our lives as researchers and teachers, seldom within the profession do we have opportunities to celebrate our own teaching. The ways in which we personally draw on knowledge of literacy development, literacy processes, and literacy education to craft our own approaches to undergraduate and graduate instruction is not typically the focus of our conferences nor has it frequently been the focus of our writing. The purpose of the *Handbook of Instructional Practices for Literacy Teacher-Educators* is to provide such an opportunity. In this work, literacy researchers reflect on their own lives, experiences, and lessons learned as teachers as they share an approach they have used in one of their courses.

Overview

This handbook is organized by cognate areas within literacy: methods of teaching reading; methods of teaching the English language arts (including language arts in elementary and middle school, secondary English education, and the teaching of writing); literature and the teaching of literature; emergent literacy; content area literacy; literacy assessment and instruction; literacy in a diverse society; literacy and technology; and inquiries into literacy, theory, and classroom practice. The authors, who were invited to discuss their approaches to a specific course in each of these areas, teach in a variety of universities, programs, and settings. Consequently (as the reader can see by scanning the annotated table of contents), the contributions encompass a breadth of professional development experiences including graduate and undergraduate preparation, field-based and university-based settings, team-taught courses, and course experiences ranging from practicums that continue across an entire year to an intense week-long summer workshop.

Authors introduce their syllabi through personal reflections, giving the reader a sense of the theories, prior experiences, and influential authors who have shaped their own thoughts and approaches. In addition to describing the nature of their students and the program in which the course is taught, many authors also share key issues with which they have grappled over the years while teaching their course. Others discuss considerations that were relevant during the preparation of this particular syllabus or describe how their syllabus evolved in light of student input.

For Whom is This Book Written?

Although we recognize this book would be invaluable to those just entering literacy teacher-education, it became clear as we, the contributors, worked on this book that professionals at every stage of their career would find this text of interest. Across our careers, we frequently find ourselves teaching courses not directly related to our areas of expertise. At times, we may also be assigned to teach a course we have not taught in many years or be asked to work with a course we have never taught. More importantly, most of us continually reflect on how we address the courses we teach regularly. Across the time we were working on this project, contributors continually asked for copies of one another's chapters so they could get a feel for what other people were doing in a particular course. As literacy teacher-educators, it was clear that we were eager to incorporate the innovative ideas, fresh approaches, and thought-provoking material that is found in this handbook. We grew excited reading about each other's teaching lives and we now are eager to share this resource with others.

Web Site for This Book

After enjoying the stories these literacy scholars have to share regarding their teaching lives, we urge the reader to also turn to the Web site that is a companion to this handbook. This online resource provides additional information regarding the authors' courses including complete syllabi, recommend readings, grading rubrics, and/or sample assignments the authors have used in their courses. The creation of this accompanying Web site allowed authors to furnish a breadth of support information that individual readers may find beneficial. The address for the Web site is: http://msit.gsu.edu/handbook.

ACKNOWLEDGMENTS

The idea for this book came to me in the middle of a night when I had awakened from a deep sleep. With the miracle of technology at my disposal, by the following evening I had already contacted and received replies from countless literacy professionals across the country. My sincere appreciation goes to the contributors who were willing to carve out time from their overloaded schedules to pause and reflect on the art of their teaching. Next, I would like to recognize the assistance of Susan Henderson, my graduate research assistant, colleague, and friend, who contacted and followed up with authors during the revision and editing of individual contributions. The reflections and advice of the three reviewers: Janet Richards, University of Southern Mississippi; Marcia Popp, Southern Illinois University–Edswardsville; and Elizabeth K. Wilson, The University of Alabama, also guided the development of this resource in important ways. Finally, my love and gratitude go to my husband, Steve, and my children Victoria and Kaleb, who share the stories of their lives with me on a daily basis, and in doing so, bring meaning to my world.

—*Joyce E. Many*

I

READING

1

Two Views Presentations:
Demonstrating the Differences Between Theoretical Orientations in Reading Instruction

Donna L. Wiseman
Northern Illinois University

Conversations about theoretical orientation in reading instruction are important for future elementary teachers. One outcome of conversations about theoretical orientation is an awareness that there is more than one way to teach reading. Even beginning reading methods courses should help future teachers understand that some teachers view reading as the identification of words, yet other teachers view reading as a way to construct meaning (Weaver, 1994). As with their experienced counterparts in schools, future teachers will develop personal definitions of reading that fall on a continuum. The continuum runs between a strong emphasis on phonics and the recognition of words to an emphasis on literature and writing as one way to learn about words and letter/sound patterns.

What is the best way to facilitate future teachers' understandings about the different approaches to reading instruction? How can they be encouraged to critically analyze and reflect on differences between major approaches and frame current discussions about reading methodology? The issues related to theoretical approaches to reading instruction are complex (Sebesta, 1997). Discussions about reading methodology are more than an instructional issue and can be emotionally charged. They include elements of critical pedagogy, race and culture, educational philosophy, and standards and testing. Reading instruction can even be politically charged. Several states such as North Carolina, Ohio, Wisconsin, California, and Texas are legislating teacher training and public school curriculum with a singular instructional approach (Johns & Elish Piper, 1996).

Teacher educators are accused regularly of being out of touch with public views about reading instruction. I have become increasingly sensitive to criticisms leveled at teacher-preparation programs. The criticism has made me spend more time planning how to present a balanced approach to my students (Johns & Elish-Piper, 1996). I invite teachers into my classroom who hold differing perspectives, require my students to read articles that present different views, and offer opportunities for debates within my classroom. I want to encourage my students to think about the instructional strategies they will use to teach reading, make explicit their own views, and develop their personal rationale. The *Two Views* assignments in my reading methods classes provide one way for students to explore the differences in theoretical approaches and review the impact those differences have on classroom instruction.

The Graduate Class

The idea to present *Two Views* of reading instruction was developed one semester when I was planning for a graduate class. The class was an advanced reading methodology course for the master's and doctoral programs and all the students were experienced, practicing teachers. I began to think about how I could get the students to take charge of their discussions and use their own experiences to contrast theories and approaches. As I read sources such as Donald Graves' *Build a Literate Classroom* (1991) to get ideas for class, the idea of presenting two approaches for a similar instructional objective took form.

I planned and organized the *Two Views* presentations in the following way. First, students selected a partner and each pair was assigned a basic reading topic such as phonics, early reading instruction, testing, or comprehension instruction. The pair developed a very simple instructional objective for their topic such as: "The students will learn the beginning 'B' sound." Then, each one of the pair developed a research-based lesson that would meet the instructional objective. One member of the pair planned a literature-based, integrated language arts lesson and the other planned a skills-based, direct instruction lesson. They reviewed the literature and supported their lessons with five research studies and two theoretical essays.

The research and lessons completed by each pair served as the basis of a series of class presentations that followed whole class readings and discussions on the same topic. During the presentation, each pair presented the theory and research related to their lessons. Then they taught the two lessons one right after another. The illustrations of the two theoretically different lessons teaching a single instructional objective were quite dramatic. The graduate students could hardly suppress their thoughts and ideas until the lessons were completed. Immediately after the lessons, the class launched into discussions and considered the subtle messages about teaching reading from a particular perspective. Following class discussions, each student wrote a reaction to the lessons. The next class session, they shared their reaction papers with partners who provided written feedback about their ideas.

Experiencing the two lessons had a powerful impact on the class. The graduate students admitted that, in most cases, they kept their original views of reading instruction, but they were able to understand and appreciate differing perspectives. When the students reported changes in their ideas, they usually moved toward a more balanced view of reading instruction. The discussions seemed to build a class community, too. The class formed a bond that still exists and students often remind me about the *Two Views* presentations and what an impact that simple exercise had on their own learning.

The Undergraduate Class

This technique was such a success at the graduate level, that I decided to adapt it for my undergraduate class. The reading class, Elementary School Developmental Reading Programs, served as an introductory course for most of the students in our undergraduate programs. They were not ready to develop their own lessons so I had to think of another way to introduce the two views. The class enrollment of the undergraduate class was 35 students instead of the class of 12 graduate students enrolled in the graduate class. Their lack of experience and the size of the class required modifications when planning for the undergraduates.

A basic understanding of the theoretical approaches to reading instruction was first developed through small group discussions of shared readings, class lectures, and discussions. I identified four topics—phonics, comprehension, early reading instruction, and assessment and testing—as the basis of the *Two Views* presentations. The *Two Views* presentations served as an introductory activity for each of the topics. I planned the two lessons and provided lesson plans for the students. As the remainder of the class watched, I presented the two mock lessons to a small group who role played elementary students' behaviors.

The mock lessons were followed by small group discussions that focused on identifying differences in the lessons. A whole class discussion summarized the benefits and challenges of each approach. The undergraduates were asked to produce written reactions to the two lessons. An outline guided them to describe both lessons, list the pros and cons of both approaches, and identify the lesson that would be easiest for them to teach. On the day that they handed their papers to me, one of their peers provided written feedback to their *Two Views* paper.

At first my students were enthusiastic about the approach. They discussed the lessons in depth, disagreed about basic philosophies, and talked about definitions of reading. By the fourth mock lesson, their enthusiasm was greatly reduced. They no longer attacked the discussions with such enthusiasm. During the exiting portfolio interview with me, half of the students identified the *Two Views* activity as impacting their learning. Even so, I knew they didn't enjoy the activity nearly as much as the graduate students.

Reflecting On My Own Teaching

I should not have been surprised that the undergraduate experiences were not as dynamic as the graduate experiences. The undergraduate *Two Views* presentation was almost entirely teacher- driven. I planned the lessons, guided the discussions, and evaluated the written reactions. I should know better! In contrast, graduate students developed their own lessons and were ready to unpack experiences, illustrate their points with their own teaching, and talk about successes they experienced in their own classrooms. The undergraduate *Two Views* presentations lacked the needed link between theory and practice. The students could not maintain the momentum just from role playing reading lessons. They needed more real experiences.

There are a couple of ways to link theory and practice. The most effective method of presenting the *Two Views* presentation would be a closely linked clinical experience in which the undergraduates would observe and participate in classroom reading instruction. Listening to real teachers talk about their instructional choices would also provide needed real-life experiences. A combination of observations in real classrooms and input of practice teaching could freshen up the role-playing activities associated with *Two Views* presentations.

The *Two Views* presentations have potential for presenting different ideas about reading instruction to graduates and undergraduates. It is one way to help them describe and talk about their own views and to analyze how different approaches affect classroom decision making. The impact of the strategy is sure to be impacted by linking real-life decision making with university coursework. The next time I use it with undergraduates, I will make needed changes so that undergraduates will experience same vibrant learning opportunities that the graduate students experienced.

REFERENCES

Graves, D. H. (1991). *The reading/writing teachers' companion: Build a literate classroom.* Portsmouth, NH: Heinemann.

Johns, J. L., & Elish-Piper, L. (Eds.). (1996). *Balanced reading instruction: Teachers' visions and voices.* Dubuque, IA: Kendall/Hunt.

Sebesta, S. L. (1997). Having my say. *The Reading Teacher, 50,* 542–549.

Weaver, C. (1994). *Reading process and practice: From socio-psycholinguistics to whole language.* Portsmouth, NH: Heinemann.

Sample Syllabus

Course Focus

This course will provide opportunities for future teachers to develop understandings about reading and reading instruction in elementary schools. Discussions, readings, activities, and reflections will familiarize class participants with reading and language processes, children's literature, instructional materials and procedures, classroom activities, and organizational matters associated with teaching of reading in elementary schools. The course will focus on the interrelationship between reading and writing and the impact of classroom diversity on approaches to elementary school reading instruction.

Tentative Topics

Week 1	The Cornerstone of Authentic Reading/Integrated Literary Theories and Approaches to Reading

Week 2	Reading and Writing Connections
	Reading Material: Literature-Based Instruction
	    Children's Literature
	    The Basal Reader
	    Student-Authored Texts

Week 3	An Overview of Classroom Reading Instruction: A Case Study of Reading Instruction
Week 4	Reading and Language Development Emergent Literacy Development
Week 5	Two Views Presentation I: Beginning Reading Instruction Organizing for Reading Instruction Major Focus: Grouping and Tracking
Week 6	Peer Response to Two Views Presentation I Thematic Approach and Interdisciplinary Planning Use of Literature in the Classroom
Week 7	Two Views Presentation II: Comprehension The Process of Comprehending Instructional Frameworks for Fostering Comprehension
Week 8	Comprehension, continued Peer Response to Two Views Reactions II * Exam
Week 9	Two Views Presentation III: Skills Decoding and Word Identification Word-Study Teaching Strategies Vocabulary The Role of Writing in Word Study Discussion: What do we mean when we say "Back to the Basics?
Week 10	Peer Response to Two Views Presentation III Experimenting With Technology

Week 11	Two Views Presentation IV: Assessment and Evaluation
	Assessment and Evaluation:
	    Tests and Formal Procedures
	    Portfolios, Alternative-Authentic Assessment
	    Monitoring Emergent Literacy
	    Using the Assessment Results

Week 12	Peer Response to Two Views Presentation IV
	Reading in Content Areas
	Methods
	Interdisciplinary Approaches
	Textbooks and Literature
Week 13	Reading and Families: Including Families and Community in Literacy
	Development
	Focusing on Diversity
	Personal Growth
	Make Appointment for Conference with Wiseman
Week 14	Interviews—No formal class
Week 15	Current Issues and Trends and the Politics of Reading Instructions
Finals Week	Final (Whew! We made it!) Exam

Class Logistics

1. *Two Views Reactions:* After each *Two Views* presentation, you should prepare a 1- to 3-page reaction paper to the class discussions. A classmate will provide feedback during the next class session. I will read and respond to your reaction papers at least once during the term. You must hand in all four papers on April 28 and each must have feedback from class members or myself to receive credit. In addition, to receive full credit on the reaction papers you must have reflective, well thought-out ideas that link your own learning with class discussions. The topics of the four short papers will be: (1) Beginning Reading Instruction, (2) Comprehension, (3) Skills, and (4) Assessment and Evaluation.

2. *Discussion Activities:* Seven activities are designed to provide you insights into literacy. Each of these activities will be completed during small group activities during class. In most cases, there will be no opportunity to make up group work if you are absent from class.

3. *Reading Log:* You will keep a log of children's literature that you read this semester. Occasionally, you will work with children's books in class or discussion groups, but most of this reading must be done independently. You will need to record the author, title, pages read, and a short statement indicating your opinion of the book. This will be due on April 28 with your reaction papers. The number of books will be the basic factor involved in the number of points that you can earn. In addition, in order to receive all the points for this activity, your book list should include only children's literature and represent a variety of high quality books: 10 picture books and 3 children's novels = 15 points; 5 picture books and 2 children's novels = 10 points; and 5 picture books and 1 children's novel = 5 points.

4. *Two Exams:* There will be two exams based on lecture notes and textbook readings. The dates of the exams are in your semester schedule.

5. *Final: Evaluation of Personal Growth.* Review your responses to the required activities and provide a self-evaluation. You may use one activity to illustrate your growth.

You will need to identify areas where you feel confident and those that you would like to know and understand more. Illustrate with specific examples of class activities, assignments, and observations. A protocol will be provided to guide your evaluation. (You may want to make copies of your reaction papers and reading log as it will be handed in before the end of the term.) You will discuss your personal growth during an interview with me and then provide a written evaluation that will be handed in anytime during the last 2 weeks of the semester.

Points for quizzes, final, and other classroom activities:

Four Reaction Papers	40
Seven Discussion Activities	35
Reading Logs	15
Two Exams	200
Evaluation of Personal Growth	10
Total Points	300

A = 270–300; B = 240–267; C = 210–239

Extended absences will eventually affect your grade. Please remember that group activities completed in class cannot be made up for full credit. If there is a reason for any absences from class, please be sure to talk to me about your situation.

Activate your e-mail account as soon as possible. Some class participation will involve the use of e-mail. The class will plan and organize one entire class session to be delivered through e-mail.

2

Matching Standards With Substance:
Preparing Preservice Teachers to Teach Literacy

Susan L. Pasquarelli
Rachel L. McCormack
Roger Williams University

Students enrolled in our year-long literacy education course are preparing to become elementary classroom teachers. Although our students' goals are similar, their backgrounds are diverse. Some of our students are undergraduates matriculating with a major in Elementary Education as well as in other liberal arts fields. In our evening division, adults, many working full time jobs and possessing degrees in other disciplines, are seeking teacher certification. The rigorous, two-semester literacy course is the first course these students take in a series of elementary methods courses. Recently revised to align with the Rhode Island (RI) Standards for Beginning Teachers, the course is divided into two seamless segments: (a) Literacy I, with a focus on the teaching of reading, speaking, and listening; and, (b) Literacy II, with a focus on the teaching of writing and literacy performance assessment. In this chapter, we present the substance of this literacy course through a description of its context, syllabus, principles, and components.

THE CONTEXT OF LITERACY EDUCATION

Our Teacher Education Program mirrors the elementary school curriculum. Each course has two strands: a university classroom strand and a field-based strand. In the past year, we have modified the content and requirements for each course to comply with the RI Standards for Beginning Teachers. In accordance with these new Standards, our department designed and implemented a performance-based assessment system. The system has two parts: (a) a "Preparing to Teach" portfolio, which includes documentation from course work, and (b) a "Performance in the Classroom" portfolio, which documents students' practicum and student teaching experiences.

Beginning with Literacy I, students plan, develop, and experiment with instructional approaches in both the university classroom and the public school setting. Evidence of their work is placed in their "Preparing to Teach" portfolio containers. Many of the assignments given in the course syllabus (see Tables. 2.1 and 2.2) become the artifacts for their portfolios. As the students proceed through preliminary course work and build their program portfolios, they self-assess their pedagogical knowledge and set goals to achieve the RI Standards. The "Preparing to Teach" portfolio becomes the evidence used to gain entry into the next level of the program: internship experiences.

Field internship experiences include 100 hours of practicum and one semester of full-time student teaching. Both experiences are evaluated by cooperating teachers and university faculty. Student teachers also enroll in an accompanying "lab" to assist them in preparing the documentation needed for their "Performance in the Classroom" portfolio. After completion of the internship experiences, the students, with evidence in hand, may then apply for state licensure.

The Course Syllabus

Overview

Because Literacy I and II are both parts of a continuum of literacy instruction, they share common course purposes and texts. After presenting the course purposes and textbooks, we provide detailed documentation of course assignments for each semester in Tables. 2.1 and 2.2.

Course Purposes

1. To provide a knowledge base that will lead to competency in designing literacy instructional practices and contexts for a diverse elementary population.
2. To provide instruction and experiences that lead to competence in the ongoing evaluation and successful intervention of children's (Grades 1–6) literacy development.

Required Course Books

1. Cooper, J. D. (1997). *Literacy: Helping children construct meaning, 3rd edition.*
2. Cunningham, P. (1995). *Phonics they use.*
3. Johnston, P. (1997). *Knowing literacy: Constructive literacy assessment.*

TABLE 2.1
Literacy I Course Assignments

1: Understanding an Ethnic Culture—Field & Research Experience—25%
Choose one ethnic group from the variety of populations represented in Rhode Island Public Schools. Examples—Portuguese, Dominican, Mexican, Japanese, Cambodian, Vietnamese, etc. Learn about this chosen ethnic culture by examining the country's language, ways of life, traditional customs, food, religion, gender roles, celebrations, dress, implied stereotypes, etc. In addition, interview and observe children from that country by visiting a public school of your choice. Prepare a written report presenting your research findings and integrating the school interview and observation information. Include a bibliography of children's books that depict your chosen peoples in their homelands and in America. Please use American Psychological Association (APA) format for research reports.

2: Graphic Organizers—15%
Create graphic organizers for one higher level (Grades 4–6) expository tradebook and one lower level (Grades 1–2) narrative tradebook. Be sure to set a clear purpose that will help students concentrate on a specific comprehension focus during reading.

3: Comprehension Lesson Plans—25%
Design two comprehension lesson plans—one for narrative text and one for expository text.

(1) The expository lesson plan will be designed to teach a specific comprehension strategy using a strategic instructional model.

(2) The narrative lesson plan will focus on the content of the book only. You will assume that the comprehension strategy the students apply within the lesson was already taught and the students are simply practicing applying the strategy to glean content knowledge from the storybook.

4: Word Identification lesson—25%
Design a word identification strategy lesson plan using your narrative tradebook or another chosen for teaching beginning reading. Because we never teach word identification strategies in isolation, you must also design a comprehension focus for students to derive meaning from the text.

(All assignments may be used as "Preparing to Teach" portfolio artifacts)

5: Class Participation—10%

6: Final Examination—0%
The final examination for this course is an assessment of your own phonological awareness. According to RWU's assessment system based on the RI Standards for Beginning Teachers, we require that you pass this assessment with an 80 or above prior to your student teaching field experience.

TABLE 2.2
Literacy II Course Assignments

1: Reading Journal (Home & Field Experience)—20%

The primary text for this course is P. Johnstons's Knowing literacy: Constructive literacy assessment. The beginning of each class period will be devoted to discussing the day's text assignment and any other articles that are listed as readings for the day. To help prepare for these discussions, you will maintain a reading journal. For each chapter/article assigned, I would like you to record the following information in your journals:

(1) Summary of main points and your reflections
(2) Questions that remain after reading the chapter/article
(3) Important points to remember while assessing children

During the course, I would also like you to:

(1) interview an elementary school teacher about her/his current classroom assessment methods, and
(2) observe this teacher while engaged in a classroom assessment event. Summaries of the interview and observation are to be recorded in your reading journals.

2: Reading Performance Assessment (Field Experience)—20%

Students will assess a Grade 3 students' word identification, comprehension, and self-monitoring performance using a reading assessment we design together in class. Your Johnston textbook will provide valuable background material to aid your implementation and interpretation of this assessment. This assignment will become one of your "Preparing to Teach" portfolio artifacts.

3. A personal narrative—20%

Students will plan, draft, revise, edit, and publish one personal narrative. During the last two classes, from the author's chair, you will share your story.

4: Grammar Editing Assignments—0%

Short grammar editing exercises will be assigned. This editing practice will help you to relearn English grammar—an essential component to writing instruction. These assignments will become "Preparing to Teach" portfolio artifacts.

5: A writing mini-lesson—20%

This lesson will include declarative, procedural, and conditional knowledge of a grammar editing strategy. This may become one of your "Preparing to Teach" portfolio artifacts.

6: A writing performance assessment—20%

In a collaborative team of two students, you will design a performance writing task (example: personal narrative, persuasive essay), valid evaluation criteria for that task, and a matching scoring scale (rubic). This will become one of your "Preparing to Teach" portfolio artifacts.

7: Final Exam—0%

The final examination for this course is an English language arts conventions performance assessment. According to RWU's assessment system based on the RI Standards for Beginning Teachers, we require that you pass this assessment with an 80 or above prior to your student teaching field experience.

GUIDING PRINCIPLES FOR COURSE INSTRUCTION

Our department has two primary goals for the literacy course. First, we want to ensure that our students remain grounded in theory and current views of practice in the literacy field. Therefore, as each topic is presented, we begin with the theoretical foundation. For example, when we present grouping practices, we begin with Vygotsky's (1978) Zone of Proximal Development Theory. We then discuss heterogeneous and flexible grouping practices for literacy instruction (Paratore & McCormack, in press).

Our second goal is to make certain that our own instruction reflects "best practice." It is often the case that students are relearning a literacy skill in order to be able to teach it. Therefore, our instruction must be explicit and direct. We do this by modeling many of the teachers' instructional actions associated with strategic teaching (Roehler & Duffy, 1991). For example, we typically begin by identifying what we are teaching and why it is important. Then, we model an instructional action, provide many opportunities for guided practice, and invite students to evaluate the effectiveness of what they are learning. Finally, we ask the students to determine when to use the instructional action in an elementary classroom. Course assignments, including work in the field, become independent practice.

In the sections that follow, we describe the components of our literacy instructional program. Each component is accompanied by sample literature citations that help us connect theory with practice. Additional readings can be found on the Web site that accompanies this resource.

COURSE COMPONENT DESCRIPTIONS

Speaking and Listening Instruction

In Literacy I, we begin with a simple investigation. We ask our students to reflect on their own literacy development and what they already know about how children learn to be literate beings. As students bring their beliefs and biases to the surface, we place them in schools with diverse populations. For many of our students, this experience becomes critical in preparing them to teach in the 21st century.

The students' personal reflections and field experiences typically yield exploratory talk. These discussions become a segue to investigating classroom speaking and listening events. We depart from the typical Initiation–Response–Evaluation (IRE) participation structure by facilitating student talk. In this way, the students explore the give and take of effective classroom discussion. As part of that exploration, we review and talk about social learning theories (Vygotsky, 1978). We also compare our own elementary school experiences with current practices regarding closed versus open participation structures (Au & Mason, 1983), productive classroom speaking and listening events (Cazden, 1988), peer talk (McCormack, 1997) and homogeneous versus heterogeneous grouping procedures (Paratore & McCormack, in press).

After reflecting on the ways they learned to speak and listen in classrooms, the students are presented with research on beginning reading instruction. Contrary to the obsolete concept of reading/writing readiness, they learn that effective literacy programs help children develop literacy naturally by using what they already know about print. The ensuing discussions often lead students to contemplate: When does literacy actually begin? What kinds of reading and writing do young children do? How can a literacy program help children to develop? Finally, after sharing their responses, students are ready to understand the bridges that exist between emergent literacy theory and practice.

Reading Comprehension & Response Instruction

We begin our work on comprehension by reviewing current theory. Topics include schema theory, theories about metacognition including executive control, and self-regulated learning (Anderson & Pearson, 1984; Garner, 1987; Zimmerman, 1989). Discussions follow about how these theories impact instruction for both the emergent and the developing reader and writer.

From theory level, we proceed to classroom practice by investigating ways in which expert readers use comprehension strategies such as activating prior knowledge and setting purposes for reading (Pearson, 1985). Next, we review comprehension strategies for expository and narrative text. Finally, we look at reader response theory and practice by examining the work of Rosenblatt (1938) and other response theorists.

The students demonstrate their understanding by designing guided reading lessons that employ pre-, during reading , and postreading comprehension and/or response strategies. When we feel that they understand how to teach a guided reading lesson, our next task is to instruct how to teach a literacy strategy.

Strategic Reading Instruction

Our forays into strategic reading instruction begin by asking students to recall how they learned to ride a bike, tie their shoes, and drive a car. From students' testimonies, we are able to identify modeling, verbal explanation, practice, observation, trial and error, and coaching as important teaching/learning tools. We also show how a combination of these instructional actions create a cognitive model that is based on Paris's (1991) three clusters of metacognitive knowledge: declarative, procedural, and conditional.

By the end of this introduction, we make certain that our students understand that a strategic instructional model includes: (a) explaining what the strategy is and why one should learn it, (b) modeling and thinking aloud the procedure for applying the strategy, (c) providing a heuristic of cognitive processes for procedural application, (d) providing guided and independent practice of the strategy, and (e) giving students opportunities to evaluate the effectiveness of the strategy in multiple contexts (Paris & Winograd, 1990; Pasquarelli, 1997).

Using the same model, we demonstrate extensively how to carry out a strategy lesson. For example, peer dyads practice modeling and thinking aloud the cognitive steps of a literacy strategy. Next, the concept of student mediation is considered through Pearson and Gallagher's Gradual Release of Responsibility Model (1983). Our discussions are extensive in the areas of scaffolded instruction and student coaching. Finally, students are required to write a scripted comprehension lesson plan as independent practice.

In Literacy I, we devote many hours of class time to this instructional model because we feel it is the cornerstone of best literacy practice.

Word Identification Instruction

As students begin to conceptualize how literacy processes can be taught strategically, we progress to word identification instruction. Using what our students know, we help them to reconstruct a picture of emergent readers' struggles to "break the code." After reviewing the concept that reading is for meaning, we guide students in identifying three components in word identification instruction: phonological awareness, structural analysis, and sight vocabulary (Cunningham, 1995).

Students are taught two ways to teach word identification: (a) shared reading with predictable text, and (b) direct instruction in phonemic analysis. In many cases, students need to relearn phoneme/grapheme relationships. Modeling these strategies within an authentic context of real books and stories is critical to the success of our instruction. While students are increasing metacognitive awareness about their own phonemic knowledge, they are learning how to teach it. Following our lead, students then design a word identification lesson using authentic children's texts.

Teaching the Writing Process

When we designed the writing segments for Literacy II, we began by identifying three essential elements: (a) the writing process, (b) the types and forms of writing, and (c) the English language arts conventions. In order to teach all of these aspects of writing in one semester, we decided to teach the class workshop style. In other words, the students participate as writers and teachers of writers while we model the teaching. Over several class sessions, we ask them to compose a personal narrative, and we meticulously walk them through the writing process. For example, while we demonstrate instruction in revision, the students not only revise their own writing, they learn how they can apply the instruction in their own classrooms (Calkins, 1991). As a culminating activity, students design an editing mini-lesson that can be used in an elementary classroom.

We have found this course framework to be successful for two reasons. First, the students are more engaged in the instruction because they have to apply it immediately to their own writing. Second, the students change their perceptions about themselves as writers over the course of the semester. When students take the author's chair to share their personal narratives, they truly view themselves as writers.

Exploring Literacy Assessment and Portfolios

We spend a great deal of time and effort throughout both semesters helping our students understand, design, and practice administering simple performance task assessments and portfolio systems. On our assessment agenda is teaching students the links that exist between instruction and assessment, the difference between standardized and informal assessment, the guiding principles that help establish our current assessment practices, and the knowledge essential to the implementation of performance-based assessment (Johnston, 1997; Winograd, Paris, & Bridge, 1991). When we observe our student teachers assessing children's literacy knowledge in some fairly sophisticated ways, we know they are on their way to making informed decisions about meeting the needs of all children.

CONCLUSION

Much of our work with preservice teachers is centered around the new, and more rigorous, RI Standards for Beginning Teachers and our companion performance assessment system. The teacher education faculty is apprised of the fact that we have "raised the bar" in both the substance of our instruction and the quality and quantity of course assignments. Our students are well aware that becoming an elementary school teacher means taking ownership of the very literacy processes that they are being asked to teach. They learn that this takes perseverance, hard work, and hours and hours of preparation.

We still have miles to go. One of our goals is to work toward consistent application of the scoring scales (rubics)that we recently designed for our common program assignments such as lesson plans, units, and case studies. Another goal is to simply continue to amend our syllabi every semester as the student assessment system renders valuable feedback about our own teaching. For now, we have chosen to continue to test the waters with a system uniquely designed to match substance with high standards.

REFERENCES

Anderson, R., & Pearson, P. D. (1984). A schema-theoretic view of basic processes in reading. In P. D. Pearson (Ed.), *Handbook of reading research, Vol. I* (pp. 255–292). New York: Longman.

Au, K., & Mason, J. (1983). Cultural congruence in classroom participation structures: Achieving a balance of rights. *Discourse Processes, 6,* 145–167.

Calkins, L. M. (1991). *Living between the lines.* Portsmouth, NH: Heinemann.

Cazden, C. (1988). *Classroom discourse: The language of teaching and learning.* Portsmouth, NH: Heinemann.

Cooper, J. D. (1997). *Literacy: Helping children construct meaning.* New York: Houghton Mifflin.

Cunningham, P. (1995). *Phonics they use.* New York: Harper Collins College Publishers.

Garner, R. (1987). *Metacognition and reading comprehension.* Norwood, NJ: Ablex.

Johnston, P. (1997). *Knowing literacy: Constructive literacy assessment.* York, ME: Stenhouse.

McCormack, R. L. (1997). Eavesdropping on second graders' peer talk about African trickster tales. In J. R. Paratore & R. L. McCormack (Eds.), *Peer talk in the classroom: Learning from research* (pp. 26–44). Newark, DE: International Reading Association.

Paratore, J. R., & McCormack, R. L. (in press). Responding to research in grouping: Flexible grouping in the middle grades. In K. Wood & T. Dickinson (Eds.), *Promoting literacy in the twenty-first century: A handbook for teachers and administrators in grades 4–8.* Needham, MA: Allyn & Bacon.

Paris, S. G. (1991). Portfolio assessment of young readers. *The Reading Teacher, 44,* 680–681.

Paris, S. G., & Winograd, P. N. (1990). How metacognition can promote academic learning and instruction. In B. Jones & L. Idol (Eds.), *Dimensions of thinking and cognitive instruction* (pp. 15–51). Mahwah, NJ: Lawrence Erlbaum Associates.

Pasquarelli, S. L. (1997). What is strategic reading instruction? Addressing the Rhode Island English language arts frameworks. *Rhode Island Reading Review, 14,* 8–13.

Pearson, P. D. (1985). Changing the face of comprehension instruction. *The Reading Teacher, 38,* 724–738.

Pearson, P. D., & Gallagher, G. (1983). The gradual release of responsibility model of instruction. *Contemporary Educational Psychology, 8,* 112–123.

Roehler, L., & Duffy, G. (1991). Teacher's instructional actions. In P. D. Pearson, R. Barr, M. Kamil, & P. Mosenthal (Eds.), *Handbook of reading research, Vol. II* (pp. 861–884). New York: Longman.

Vygotsky, L. S. (1978). *Mind in society.* (M. Cole, V. John-Steiner, S. Scribner, & E. Souberman, Eds.). Cambridge, MA: Harvard University Press.

Winograd, P. N., Paris, S. G., & Bridge, C. (1991). Improving the assessment of literacy. *The Reading Teacher, 45,* 108–116.

Zimmerman, B. (1989). Models of self-regulated learning and academic achievement. In B. Zimmerman & D. Schunk (Eds.), *Self regulated learning and academic achievement* (pp. 1–26). New York: Springer-Verlag.

3

Social Foundations as a Foundation for Literacy Instruction:
An Effort in Collaboration

Sally M. Oran
Northern Arizona University

Kathleen Bennett deMarrais
Jamie B. Lewis
University of Georgia

Our Instructional Contexts

The literacy block of courses we describe in this chapter is taught within the unique context of Northern Arizona—a vast rural region that includes a large portion of the Navajo Nation as well as the entire Hopi Reservation. Northern Arizona University (NAU), the primary teacher education institution in the state, serves many Native communities (Apache, Zuni, Navajo, Hopi) through statewide distance education programs. We have the privilege to work with Native students as well as Anglo students in our elementary education programs. Consequently we teach our literacy course to preservice education students who are markedly different from one another in their life experiences and cultural backgrounds.

Due to our unique geographical context, Northern Arizona University offers a wide variety of teacher education options including: (1) several school-based programs that emphasize content-area themes; (2) programs on the Navajo Reservation that combine special education and elementary education degrees and allow students to continue their work as instructional aids in reservation schools; (3) programs on the main Flagstaff campus for returning students who need scheduling flexibility because they have jobs and families; (4) cohort classes on the main campus for students in a small group who complete their program together; and (5) programs at statewide sites where students can get their education classes via Interactive Instructional Television, with statewide faculty. These programs each draw a fairly predictable collection of students. We teach this block of literacy courses to students in three of the programs: (1) the Piñon Preparation Program on the Navajo Reservation; (2) the campus-based "traditional" or flexible schedule program; and (3) the campus-based cohort program. Our course outline is used in whole or part by other NAU literacy instructors in these various programs.

Our classes range in size from 10 to 32 students. Our instruction is designed to weave theory, current research, reflection, and teaching so that our students experience best practice as both teachers and learners. Because we believe in an integrated curriculum for elementary students, this course[1] combines reading and language arts methods in a 9-hour block of classes that includes a weekly practicum in elementary classrooms. Our students begin to experience how reading and language arts instruction are central to and can be incorporated across the entire elementary curriculum.

Our Collaborative Style

Our collaboration is active and systematic. Although we teach different populations of students, we create lessons and course materials together. We share regularly with one another the status of our students' learning. This includes the successful lessons and the unsuccessful ones. We depend on one another to critique the instructional strategies we design. When schedules allow, we combine classes to provide a team-teaching model for our students. We actively reflect on our teaching in this course and share those reflections in class. Projects our students complete are shared with all of our classes, effectively raising the standards of students' professional presentations. Learning differences that seem to be a result of our various student populations are shared with all our students, thus challenging them to consider new perspectives. We share instructional files, the journal articles we read, and our creative visions for preservice teachers. When problems arise, we share insights with one another and look for guidance in current research. An important demonstration of our collaboration is the multicultural children's literature collection we share. Although the books are stored in each of our offices, our students and colleagues are encouraged to borrow books to use in their teaching. Our intent is to offer a model of active, professional collaboration and reflection within our teacher education program.

---

[1]The Literacy Block consists of the following courses: ECI 301—Decoding; ECI 303—Reading Instruction for the Elementary Grades; ECI 304—Language Arts for the Elementary Grades; and ECI 308—Practicum. The students sign up for all of these courses at one time and we simply treat them as one course.

Major Ideas That Have Influenced our Work

The composition of a course nearly always reflects the experiences and passions of those who construct it. This literacy education course situates effective practices in language development and literacy education within a sociocultural context. The field of Social Foundations as well as the Social Foundations Standards presented by the Council of Learned Societies in Education (1996) heavily inform our work. Our primary purpose is to engage our preservice teachers in critical reflection of the varied contexts in which literacy instruction takes place. Our particular concern is with equity issues through examinations of language diversity, race, ethnicity, social class, and gender. Based on our collective background and expertise areas, we bring the following experiential and research perspectives to our literacy course: many years of public school teaching, ethnographic research in inner-city schools, anthropology of education, gender issues in elementary schools, training in literacy education, educational law, and advocacy for students usually labeled "at risk." As we work and write together, we realize our experience, knowledge, and continuing professional inquiry stimulate our energy to provide teacher preparation in literacy that is engaging, relevant, and equitable for diverse student populations. The course we present in this chapter represents our collaborative work as literacy educators for preservice teachers.

Our course is based on the work of researchers who have explored the cultural socialization children receive around language/literacy and social justice issues in schools. Shirley Brice Heath's work (1983) and Allyssa McCabe's research (1996), coupled with research on how children gain knowledge of text conventions (Clay, 1992), signal an urgency for preservice teachers to understand the nature of children's language and literacy development. Too often, teachers understand only their own cultural perspective regarding the status, acquisition, and application of literacy skill and fail to recognize other cultural traditions that give impetus and form to literacy development. Heath's and McCabe's work remind us that all children's early experiences with story are shaped by culture. We believe teachers need an understanding of how they can use those traditions to effectively foster literacy development for every child.

The real task is to present to our university students content and experiences that assist them to understand how children acquire literacy skill. Central to this task is our use of quality, multicultural children's literature. Students are required to examine and acquaint themselves with current, multicultural books for children of all ages. They learn to use these books to plan and deliver engaging literacy lessons for children each week in schools. They learn to select books that are rich in content and support literacy skills in developmentally appropriate ways. We intend for our students to use quality multicultural children's literature to invigorate their own learning about storytelling styles across cultures and to provide bridges to the prior knowledge children outside the dominant culture offer. With quality multicultural children's literature as the focus for lessons, we extend learning by engaging our university students in context-specific activities that provide opportunities for them to read, write, speak, and listen in real, meaningful ways. Our purpose is for these lessons to model the goals, designs, and types of engagement we intend for them to provide for their own students.

Issues We Considered When Designing the Literacy Block

We believe that an understanding of language and literacy development alone cannot insure effective literacy instruction in today's diverse school populations. Consequently, our instruction includes historical and current sociocultural issues as well as effective literacy practices. Our students examine their own schooling and educational perspectives. Part of teacher education is for novices to understand "the way schools work" (Bennett deMarrais & LeCompte, 1995). For us, that means critiquing the instructional strategies, materials, curricula, and school structures surrounding literacy education (Edelsky, 1991; Freire, 1970, 1987; Nieto, 1996; Spring, 1995). We provide instruction to illuminate why teachers do things certain ways, why students are frequently blamed for their lack of achievement, and how some instructional practices actually deter literacy acquisition. Central to our instruction are the educational standards provided by national professional organizations, state guidelines, and local school districts. Through reflective practice around a variety of educational issues, students learn to evaluate their professional standards, their developing practice as teachers, and their ethical standards regarding literacy education for diverse learners.

Tensions in Teaching the Literacy Block

We find ourselves balancing a variety of tensions as we teach this literacy course. One that continues to be troublesome is the resistance our students demonstrate toward multicultural literature and education. Mainstream, dominant culture students are those most likely to reflect conservative political views and offer the most resistance to multicultural issues. Classes made up of nontraditional students and students of color offer less resistance to such issues. We continue to explore ways to help preservice teachers understand the need for instruction that welcomes cultural diversity and recognizes its value in an effective literacy program.

A particular challenge is changing preservice teachers' notions about effective literacy instruction. For most of our university students, their own views about effective literacy instruction are obstacles at the beginning of our course. For some students, these views remain problematic throughout the semester, reinforcing the voices of researchers who report that most teachers teach as they have been taught. For a few students whose desire to read and write was effectively stifled by poor literacy instruction, the challenge is to change their attitudes toward literacy so that they can begin to learn sound instructional strategies. Coupled with these tensions, is the lack of knowledge many of our students have about child development. As their understanding of child development is limited, it is difficult for them to devise lessons that are effective and developmentally appropriate. For many of our students, it is easier to employ strategies their own elementary teachers used. The practicum experience that is a part of this course becomes a series of trial and error attempts to learn how to engage children to support their developing literacy skills. It is not uncommon for the practicum to convince students that their own educational experiences were harmful to their literacy acquisition.

An additional tension we experience is supporting students' transition from full-time students to part-time professionals. We believe that professional attitudes and behaviors can be taught and assessed. We have devised various ways for our students to measure their developing professionalism. However, it is hard for our students to maintain professional standards that affect their learning during this course and their practicum experience when they view themselves as university students, not members of the teaching profession. We continue to search for ways to successfully negotiate behaviors that evidence appropriate professional development during the term of this literacy course.

A SAMPLE OF SUCCESSFUL LITERACY INSTRUCTION ACTIVITIES

The Literacy Block

The following activities and assignments represent ones we have developed apart from the usual instruction in reading and language arts methods. We hope you will find them helpful in understanding how we have shaped our course to reflect literacy education in the context of social justice issues in school settings.

Cultural Autobiography

Students write a short essay describing who they are in terms of their cultural background. They are asked to include descriptions of: ethnicity/heritage, family traditions, geographical influences, gender socialization, critical school experiences, and social class influences and how these shaped their experiences, goals, and the person they are today. They are asked to reflect on ways their cultural values influence their beliefs and behaviors as teachers. The cultural autobiography assists us to know them and is used from time to time to illustrate students' diversity and commonalties.

Learning to Read/Write Memoirs

Students write a short essay describing their memories of learning to read and write. They are asked to focus on experiences inside and outside of school during their preschool and elementary years. Students choose their most vivid positive and negative memories related to learning to read and write, paying careful attention to the details of their experiences and feelings. They are asked to include a reflection of how their experiences inform their preparation for becoming reading/writing teachers.

Survey of Learning to Read/Write Themes

Over the course of several years, we have devised a 60-item survey of events learners encounter in learning to read and write. These events are derived from a qualitative analysis of students' Learning to Read/Write Memoirs. Students complete the survey, marking items that reflect their personal experiences and compile the results of the entire class. Particular attention is given to the class demographic information (number of students, ethnicities represented, age ranges, gender distribution, etc.). Class results are compared with other classes with varying demographic profiles. Class discussion focuses on differences in literacy education experiences for children.

Emergent Literacy Timeline

Learning History

The class constructs an illustrated timeline that evidences their emergent literacy experiences. Using colored chalk on a chalkboard (or butcher paper) that spans the front of the class, the class works together to write or illustrate the play activities, rhythms, songs, games, riddles, codes, and so forth that children use as they practice language in early childhood. The timeline, marking the first 10 years of life, soon becomes a mural of activities children engage in around language. The more diverse the class, the more students are likely to see that every culture and every family is an exciting arena for children's early language development. This activity often points out common and different experiences across socioeconomic and ethnic groups.

Weekly Lessons

A practicum accompanies this nine-credit literacy block and provides students an opportunity to work with students in real school settings. Our students work individually or in pairs to construct engaging, high quality literacy lessons for elementary students. They use a lesson plan format that is modeled during the first weeks of class to prepare their lessons. A checklist of lesson components supports their lesson plan writing. This checklist and their lesson plan is submitted for approval prior to teaching it in the schools.

Child Literacy Study

During the first 3 weeks of their practicum, students complete a series of literacy assessments on one young child. Specific instructions for these assessments are explained and modeled in class. At the end of the 3-week period, students write a complete report of their findings. Literacy assessments include but are not limited to: a modified concepts of print test; letter recognition; sight word assessment; interest and attitude inventories; environmental word recognition; sound/symbol relationships; story retelling. This study enables students to construct a detailed literacy profile of a child and share that information with the child's teacher.

Professional Growth Assessments

Professional growth criteria around the themes of reliability, initiative, credibility, collaborative skill, reflective skill, academic skill, personal wellness, and respect are presented at the beginning of the course pack and explained during the first class meetings (see expanded version on Web site). These criteria represent ways we expect students to evidence their growth toward becoming professional educators. Each class meeting, with its discussion, small group participation, reflection and practice activities gives students opportunities to demonstrate their professional growth. At midsemester and at the end of the semester, students are asked to evidence and assess their professional growth progress.

Big Book and Multicultural Read-Alouds

Students select a Big Book to read aloud to the class. Criteria for this assignment are given in the course pack and modeled before this assignment is due. They are also responsible for selecting a multicultural picture book that fits criteria for high quality children's literature. Students prepare and read this book for their peers as a way to develop engaging skills as readers.

ABC Book

Students select a theme and compose, illustrate, and produce an ABC book. Text and illustrations must be original. The book is evaluated on richness of content, creativity, and professional presentation. Students find this to be a time-consuming, but rewarding and creative project that is later shared with family members and friends.

Author/Illustrator Display

Working in a small group, students select an author or illustrator of multicultural books for children. After reading the author's (or illustrator's) work, they design and present a display center that illustrates an overview of information about that person. Students are encouraged to incorporate activities for children that will engage them in further study of the chosen works.

Annotated Bibliography of Children's Books

Students read 30 *multicultural* children's books, 25 picture books and 5 chapter books (two of which are required reading for two other assignments, the Reader's Response project and the Literature Circles project). At least half (15) of the books must be award winners or "placers" (Newbery, Caldecott, Coretta Scott King, Horn Book, ALA, etc.). Annotations include correct citation, award/year, suggested grade level/purpose (i.e., read aloud, independent reading), a brief summary, an analysis of the art work, and a list of the content the book offers for instructional purposes. The bibliography may be presented in any attractive, usable format such as a file box, ring holder, notebook, and so forth. Some very good books are not recommended because they represent books required by other courses and popular reading that students may have already done. Our intent is to be sure students read new, excellent, multicultural books that contain a large amount of content about multicultural issues.

Reader-Response Project

Students read chapter books such as *Sing Down the Moon* by Scott O'Dell, *Racing the Sun* by Paul Pitts, *Crossing the Starlight Bridge* by Alice Mead, *The Eternal Spring of Mr. Ito* by Sheila Garrigue, and/or *The Watsons Go to Birmingham—1963* by C. P. Curtis. They select one book for their reader-response project, a personal exploration of a topic central to the book's theme. Students submit a proposal for the reader-response project that includes criteria listed in the course pack. Students prepare and present a center explaining their topic and providing engaging learning activities for children to do.

Literature Circles

Students choose one of the books listed previously for their literature circle project. During class time, they meet with small groups of peers in a literature circle where they discuss the book thoroughly. We ask students to choose roles from the following list to assist in the literature circle discussion.

Word Keeper.   This role explores vocabulary, phonics, derivations, word analysis, jargon, or other interesting ways words are used in the book. The word keeper's job is to construct interesting ways to explore and learn more words in the book.

Illustrator.   The illustrator's job is to illustrate the book's major themes or unique messages. This role may incorporate various artistic ways to create a visual response to the book.

Historian.   The historian explores historic themes presented in the book. The historian traces the major events of each chapter or creates a representation of historical events and themes.

Geographer.   The geographer is responsible for constructing an activity that represents geographical themes in the book. The geographer draws a map and creates symbols, logos, place markers, and text to support the geographic content of the book.

Character Analyst.   This role focuses on the book's characters. The character analyst studies one of the characters in-depth or compares and contrasts characters, and displays this knowledge in interesting ways.

Questioner.   The questioner designs engaging questions about the book. The questions should require factual knowledge, an analysis of the story, a synthesis of information, and answers beyond yes or no. The questioner devises ways to display student-centered responses to expand the group knowledge about the book. We have added new roles to enrich the literature circles and provide students options for engaging in discussions about book in creative ways. These roles include playwright, poet, musicologist, and journalist. We suggest that the reader continue to expand this list of roles.

Service Learning Project

Students submit a proposal for a personal service learning project to complete during the semester. Suggested activities include reading to children at a community food center, assisting with tutoring in after-school programs, listening to children read aloud at local schools or community centers. Six hours of service and a reflection about the experience is required for completion of this project.   *over internet*

Personal Writing Portfolio

Students choose any three of the following genres: personal journal, story, simulated journal, poetry, essay, informational/nonfiction (hiking guide, how-to, etc.). They write a piece for each genre that is original, current, and reflects their growth as emerging writers. Students participate in some group editing activities with their portfolio pieces during class. They choose one piece to share with the class during the Literacy Celebration at the end of the semester.

Literacy Celebration

Students present a selection from their personal writing portfolio to read aloud to the whole class. The literacy celebration is a special event scheduled at the end of the semester. It includes refreshments, room decorations, invited guests, and a written program provided by student committees.

FINAL REFLECTIONS

We find our creative and collaborative efforts challenge us to constantly reflect on our own growth as literacy professionals as we discuss what is working effectively and what is not working as well as we would like. Throughout the last 3 years, our course has undergone tremendous change as we learn more ourselves and refine our practices. We are able to support each other and engage in an energizing process that results in more engaging and authentic work for our preservice teachers. For us, the challenge and intense nature of collaboration is certainly worth the personal and professional growth we have experienced and have observed in our students.

REFERENCES

Bennett deMarrais, K., & LeCompte, M. D. (1995). *The way schools work: A sociological analysis of education*. New York: Longman.

Clay, M. M. (1992). *Becoming literate: The construction of inner control*. Portsmouth, NH: Heinemann.

Edelsky, C. (1991). *With literacy and justice for all: Rethinking the social in language and education*. London: Falmer Press.

Freire, P. (1970). *Pedagogy of the oppressed*. New York: Continuum.

Freire, P. (1987). *A pedagogy for liberation*. South Hadley, MA: Bergen and Garvey.

Heath, S. B. (1983). *Ways with words: Language, life and work in communities and classrooms*. New York: Cambridge University Press.

McCabe, A. (1996). *Chameleon readers: Teaching children to appreciate all kinds of good stories*. New York: McGraw-Hill.

Nieto, S. (1996). *Affirming diversity: The sociopolitical context of multicultural education*. New York: Longman.

Spring, J. (1995). *The intersection of cultures: Multicultural education in the United States*. New York: McGraw-Hill.

The Council of Learned Societies in Education. (1996). *Standards for academic and professional instruction in foundations of education, educational studies, and educational policy studies, Second Edition*. Council of Learned Societies in Education.

4

Comprehension of Text:
The Reader–Text Relationship

Victoria Purcell-Gates
Michigan State University

This course was originally titled "Reading Comprehension", and it began many years ago as a methods course for reading teachers within a skills-based paradigm for reading instruction. The name change reflects the broader discourse-based scope of the content and brings writing into the picture through an added emphasis on the role of *text* and thus the author of the text. The course's primary mission is to serve both masters and doctoral students within the Language and Literacy Program in the Harvard Graduate School of Education (HGSE), and this has guided its design.

CONCEPTUAL INFLUENCES

My conceptualization of what content comprises a course in "comprehension," was influenced to a large degree by my experiences during graduate school in the Language and Literacy Program at the University of California at Berkeley, particularly the required course I took on "Reading Comprehension." It so happened that the year during which I took this course, two of my professors, Herb Simons and Sarah Freedman decided to team teach and combine two courses: Reading Comprehension and Discourse Analysis. The result of this was a confluence in my mind of comprehension and textual features, a paradigm that has guided my thinking, teaching, and research to this day! During those years, schema theory dominated the research literature on comprehension, and the work emanating from the Center for the Study of Reading, under the directorship of Richard Anderson, shaped our thinking about comprehension.

Several years later, however, my thinking about how to think about comprehension was elaborated upon by the work of Judith Langer, who was conducting research on 'making meaning' from literature under the sponsorship of the Center for the Learning and Teaching of Literature, of which she was co-director with Arthur Applebee. Langer's work was situated within a reader response frame, drew upon the work of literary criticism, and invoked such authors as Bakhtin, Fish, and Iser. After conducting a small study within this frame, I found that I included it whenever I thought about 'reading comprehension'.

DILEMMAS

The major issue I grappled with in designing this course was how to serve both the masters and doctoral students, two groups with very different needs and goals. The masters students are spending only one year at HGSE before entering or returning to the field. They need practical information on how to teach and improve the text comprehension abilities of their students. While theory and research are important pieces of this, they should not be the only ones. Language and Literacy doctoral students, on the other hand, at HGSE are preparing for participation in the world of literacy research. Thus, these students need to understand the theoretical landscape of the study of comprehension, the significant questions waiting to be answered in the field, and to acquaint themselves with the ways in which people are researching the issues.

My solution to this problem was to approach the course from theory and issues and then to explore instruction within this frame. Furthermore, I established different requirements for each group: while all students were to complete a take-home exam, the project for the masters' students was to be a comprehension lesson prepared and then taught to the class while the project for the doctoral students was a literature review of research on a topic of interest.

A related challenge for me was the fact that the field of comprehension of text was currently strongly influenced by more than one theoretical frame. This, plus the fact that all of the students—masters and doctoral—were challenged conceptually by the ways in which "theory" was related to research and instruction as well as the concept of a "theoretical frame," led me to begin the course with several classes devoted to the major theoretical frames in the field and to explicitly teach/explain/demonstrate the ways in which theories are "theories" and not "facts", and how they influence research and instruction.

I do this by bringing in three different toy lenses (small, plastic kaleidoscope-types of toys). Each one is a different color and each one has a different pattern to the lens. I pass these around and ask each person to look at the same object in the room through each lens. These are my metaphors (or manipulatives, if you will) for theories. I follow this with some representative readings for each of the following theoretical frames: schema theory, transactional theory, literary criticism, and perspectival theory, accompanied by lectures and group discussions of how they each are looking at 'comprehension of text', they each are looking at the reader/text relationship, they each have slightly different lenses and how these differences are reflected in the issues they emphasize and their implications for instruction, and so on. Of course, this is all updated each time I teach the course to reflect new work. For example, the syllabus presented here reflects my picking up the introduced but yet to be elaborated "perspectival theory" which links to schema theory with a more postmodern slant. Throughout the remainder of the course, I refer both research studies and instructional strategies which are read and discussed by the class back to the theories which frame them.

After the 2 to 3 days devoted to theories, I structure the class around topics, using the advance organizer of *reader/text relationships* as the frame. One topic is devoted to textual factors that can make comprehension easy or difficult as well as readers' acquisition of the knowledge of texts that interact with these factors. Other topics include vocabulary, cultural aspects of reader and texts that are integral to comprehension, strategies, reader response, and motivation and engagement, reflecting the latest work from the National Reading Research Center. One inclusion I make is probably relatively unique and reflects my own work on text. During the focus on textual factors, I bring in the linguistic research on oral and written language differences (Chafe & Danielewicz, 1987) and the research done by me and others (Purcell-Gates, McIntyre, & Freppon, 1995) on what we have learned about how children acquire different register knowledge of books, both narrative and expository. This rounds out the discussion on texts, I believe, from the more typical focus on only text structure, which I also include.

Related to the needs of the masters' students, the readings for the course include both articles and textbooks written for teachers. In my experience, masters' students are less well-served by a collection of readings which reflect disparate, seemingly disconnected bits of information than by a conceptually organized text that synthesizes for the students the field of interest. Further, the texts are much more useful for the masters students when they return to the field and can refer back to them for instructional and assessment strategies as needed. The doctoral students will be more interested in the articles and will, by virtue of conducting a literature review, begin to amass research reports related to their own impending research.

Because it is important to me that the students in the course actually read the assigned readings, and to model ways to ensure deeper processing and comprehension of texts, I include a take-home exam (included) as part of the requirements of the course. To model theory and instruction related to comprehension of text, I hand out the exam at the beginning of the course as an advanced organizer. The questions on the exam are designed to require synthesis across readings and lectures and to allow for individual interpretations of the material to the extent appropriate to the goals of the course.

REFERENCES

Adams, M. J., & Collins, A. (1977). *A schema-theoretical view of reading*. Cambridge, MA: Bolt, Beranek & Newman.

Beck, I. L., McKeown, M. G., & Worth, J. (1995). Giving a text voice can improve students' understanding. *Reading Research Quarterly, 30*, 220–238.

Bulgren, J., & Scanlon, D. (1997). Instructional routines and learning strategies that promote understanding of content area concepts. *Journal of Adolescent and Adult Literacy, 41*, 292–302.

Chafe, W., & Danielewicz, J. (1987). Properties of spoken and written language. In R. Horowitz & S. J. Samuels (Eds.), *Comprehending oral and written language* (pp. 83–113). San Diego, CA: Academic Press.

Dole, J. A., Brown, K. J., & Trathen, W. (1996). The effects of strategy instruction on the comprehension performance of at-risk students. *Reading Research Quarterly, 31*, 62–88.

Fish, S. (1980). Introduction, or how I stopped worrying and learned to love interpretation. In S. Fish *Is there a text in this class?* (pp. 1–17). Cambridge, MA: Harvard University Press.

Gaskins, R. W. (1996). "That's just how it was": The effect of issue-related emotional involvement on reading comprehension. *Reading Research Quarterly, 31*, 385–405.

Guthrie, J. T. (1996). Educational contexts for engagement in literacy. *The Reading Teacher, 49*, 432–445.

Halliday, M. A. K., & Hasan, R. (1976). Introduction. In M. A. K. Halliday & R. Hasan, *Cohesion in English* (pp. 1–30). London: Longman.

Iser, W. (1978). Rudiments of a theory of aesthetic response. In W. Iser *The art of reading: A theory of aesthetic response* (pp. 20–50). Baltimore, MD: Johns Hopkins Press.

Katims, D. S., & Harris, S. (1997). Improving the reading comprehension of middle school students in inclusive classrooms. *Journal of Adolescent and Adult Literacy, 41*, 116–123.

Lee, C. D. (1995). A culturally based cognitive apprenticeship: Teaching African American high school students skills in literacy interpretation. *Reading Research Quarterly, 30*, 608–630.

Norris, S. P., & Phillips, L. M. (1994). The relevance of a reader's knowledge within a perspectival view of reading. *Journal of Reading Behavior, 26*, 391–412.

Pritchard, R. (1990). The effects of cultural schemata on reading processing strategies. *Reading Research Quarterly, 25*, 273–295.

Purcell-Gates, V. (1991). On the outside looking in: A study of remedial readers' meaning-making while reading literature. *Journal of Reading Behavior, 23*, 235–253.

Purcell-Gates, V., McIntyre, E., & Freppon, P. A. (1995). Learning written storybook language in school: A comparison of low-SES children in skills-based and whole language classrooms. *American Educational Research Journal, 32*, 659–685.

Rosenblatt, L. M. (1989). Writing and reading: The transactional theory. In J. Mason (Ed.), *Reading and writing connections* (pp. 153–176). Boston: Allyn & Bacon.

Stein, N. L. (1982). The definition of a story. *Journal of Pragmatics, 6*, 487–507.

Todorov, T. (1984). Theory of the utterance. In T. Todorov *Mikhail Bakhtin: The dialogical principle* (pp. 41–59). Minneapolis: University of Minnesota Press.

Turner, J. C. (1995). The influence of classroom contexts on young children's motivation for literacy. *Reading Research Quarterly, 30*, 410–441.

Weaver, C. (1985). Parallels between new paradigms in science and in reading and literary theories: An essay review. *Research in the Teaching of English, 19*, 298–316.

Comprehension of Text
Sample Syllabus

Required Texts

Blachowicz, C. & Fisher, P. (1996). *Teaching vocabulary in all classrooms.* Englewood Cliffs, NJ: Merrill.

Conley, M. W. (1992). *Content reading instruction: A communication approach.* New York: McGraw-Hill.

Langer, J. A. (1995). *Envisioning literature: Literary understanding and literature instruction.* New York, NY: Teachers College Press.

(Additional readings are also on reserve for students.)

Recommended Texts

Pittelman, S. D., Heimlich, J. E., Berglund, R. L., & French, M. P. (1991). *Semantic feature analysis: Classroom applications.* Newark, DE: International Reading Association.

Wood, K. D., Lapp, D., & Flood, J. (1992). *Guiding readers through text: A review of study guides.* Newark, DE: International Reading Association.

Course Objectives

This course will look at the topic of comprehension of text with the underlying assumption being that comprehension is the result of an active search for meaning by a reader who is situated in a sociocultural context. Three main theoretical positions will underlie the ways in which comprehension is studied: (1) Schema Theory; (2) Transactional Theory; and (3) Literary Criticism–Reader Response. The theoretical foundations of each of these theories will be explored and then sample research and practice stemming from these theories will be examined. The course content will include theory, research, and implications for practice.

Course Requirements

1. Regular class attendance and completion of readings.
2. Take-Home Final Exam / Synthesis Activity (See Table 1)
3. Project:

Masters and CAS Students.   Prepare a 30-minute comprehension lesson with topic and text of choice and present to the class. You may do this in pairs. You must be prepared to discuss the link between your lesson and theory and research. This must also be written up and turned in on the day of the presentation. If the lesson is done in pairs, only one written version is to be turned in. Each member of the pair will receive the same grade. The written version should have the following sections: (a) Rationale for lesson (i.e., what are you trying to teach and why); (b) Theory and Research on which this lesson is based; (c) Lesson Plan; (d) Copies of, or samples of, materials which you will use for this lesson. The writeups are due the day you give the lesson to the class.

EdD Students.   Research paper which focuses on an issue in understanding the nature of comprehension of text. You must clear your topic with me before beginning. This paper should not exceed 30 pages, double-spaced, and must rely on the theoretical and/or research literature. APA 4th style is required.

Grades

Your final grade will be computed in the following way: (a) Take-Home Exam will be worth 40%; (b) final Project will be worth 40%; (c) Class attendance, participation, and evidence of having read the assigned readings by their due dates will be worth 20%.

Late Policy

All assignments are due *in class* on the date indicated on the schedule. Any assignment turned in after this deadline will be graded one-third grade lower in all cases.

Originality, Cooperation, Plagiarism

All written work must be your own unless otherwise referenced in the text. For the Take Home Exam, you may discuss and share information/ideas with each other. However, the written version must be original to you. For the Comprehension Lesson Project, if it is done in pairs, the written version will be assumed to be a combined, cooperative venture and be attributable to two authors. The Research Paper, although based on referenced sources, must be original both for ideas and writing.

Tentative Schedule

Topic	*Readings/Due*
Overview of Course & Requirements	————————
Foundations: Schema Theory & Transactional Theory	Adams, M. J., & Collins, A. (1997) Rosenblatt, L. M. (1989) Weaver, C. (1985)

Foundations: Perspectival Theory & Literary Criticism/ Reader Response Theory	Norris, S. P., & Phillips, L. M. (1994) Iser, W. (1978) Fish, S. (1980) Todorov, T. (1984) (Bakhtin)
Text Issues	Stein, N. L. (1982) Halliday, M. A. K. & Hasan, R. (1976) Chafe, W. & Danielewicz, J. (1987) Purcell-Gates, V., McIntyre, E., & Freppon, P. (1995)
Assessing Texts	Conley Book: Ch. 2
Instructing on Text Factors	Conley Book: pg. 198–204 Recom: Pittelman et al. Book Wood et al. Book
Vocabulary Learning	Blachowicz & Fisher Book: Ch. 1–3
Envisioning Literature	Langer Book: Ch. 1–6
Problems Envisioning Literature	Langer Book: Ch. 7 Purcell-Gates, V. (1991) Blachowicz & Fisher Book: Ch 4 & 8
Strategies	Dole, J. A., Brown, K. J., & Trathen, W. (1996) Katims, D. S. & Harris, S. (1997) Bulgren, J. & Scanlon, D. (1997)
Content Area Comprehension	Conley Book: Ch. 1 & 7 Beck, I. L., McKeown, M. G. & Worthy, J. (1995)
Content Area Vocabulary	Conley Book: Ch. 6 Blachowicz & Fisher Book: Ch. 5
Cultural Influences	Lee, C. D. (1995) Pritchard, R. (1990)
	Take Home Exam Due
Synthesis	Research Papers Due

Take-Home Exam

Your answers to the following questions must be based upon the class lectures and the collections of readings for this course and the Blachowicz & Fisher, Conley, and Langer texts. It is not necessary to go to outside sources. However, you may draw upon experience for examples and for lessons if you wish. Each answer should be no less than two pages and no more than five pages in length of typed, double-spaced text.

I. Discuss "comprehension" of text from the perspectives of (1) schema theory; (2) transactional theory; (3) literary criticism/reader response theory;

and (4) perspectival theory. Your discussion should include (a) definition of "comprehension" from each theoretical stance; (b) respective roles of reader and text within each.

II. Describe one classroom comprehension lesson that would fit within each theoretical lens from #1. Choose your own grade level and subject matter.

III. Identify, briefly describe, and discuss (a) two effective *prereading* comprehension activities; (b) two effective *reading* comprehension activities; and (c) two effective *postreading* comprehension activities. Your discussion should include (a) why the activity might be effective in facilitating comprehension of text; (b) which theoretical lens(es) the activity reflects.

IV. Discuss three ways in which oral language differs from written. Give examples. Explain why we think this is important to comprehension of text issues.

V. How might text structure affect comprehension of text? Discuss in light of (a) reader characteristics and (b) text characteristics.

VI. What is (are) the relationship(s) between vocabulary knowledge and comprehension of text?

VII. Identify and discuss/describe three vocabulary building activities which teachers can use.

VIII. Why is it important to understand and know about the sociocultural contexts from which our students and texts come, as this regards comprehension of text? Discuss in light of schema theory implications.

IX. Discuss the ways engagement and motivation are involved in the comprehension process. Which of our four theoretical lenses could accommodate engagement and motivation best (can be more than one). Explain.

X. Drawing on our readings and class discussions, hypothesize the ways in which a biliterate child would comprehend text utilizing two languages and cultures. Would this child utilize different comprehension strategies than the monolingual/monocultural child? What are the cultural and linguistic resources that this child would bring to text? What are the challenges to comprehension of text for this child?

XI. How do 'remedial' readers differ from 'normal' readers in terms of stances toward comprehension/envisioning? What do these differences imply for comprehension instruction for these remedial readers?

5

Book Club Workshop:
Learning About Language and Literacy Through Culture

Taffy E. Raphael

Center for the Improvement of Early Reading Achievement,
Oakland University

This course grew out of a line of research about literature-based instruction that I began as a professor at Michigan State University and a line of research on developing teachers' understandings of culture, begun by Susan Florio-Ruane, my colleague and friend at MSU. Susan and I had offices next door to each other, and over the years, became sounding boards for each other's work. We shared an interest in conversation-based learning approaches and teachers' professional development, applying our interest to our individual lines of research from 1991 through 1995. In 1995, we began to work together to explore how my research on Book Club (Goatley, Brock & Raphael, 1996; McMahon & Raphael, 1997; Raphael, Brock, & Wallace, 1998) and her research on the Future Teachers' Autobiography Club (Florio-Ruane, 1994, 1997; Florio-Ruane & deTar, 1995) could be connected. We currently codirect a project within the Center for the Improvement of Early Reading Achievement and this course has resulted from our collaboration. In this work, we began by unpacking challenges associated with literacy education today. We then created professional development contexts to support teachers' attempts to address these challenges, one of which is the Book Club Workshop course. Most recently, we have begun to explore how teachers who participated in these professional development contexts have changed their own beliefs about culture, literacy, and their sense of themselves as professional; and how such changes have influenced the curriculum they create and related literacy instruction.

Challenges Facing Literacy Educators

In our individual and joint research, Susan and I had been concerned about three challenges to literacy educators today: (a) challenges that arise from the lack of connection between literacy in school and literacy in the world outside of school, (b) challenges in terms of conflicting ideas about what we should be teaching, often phrased as a question of balance, and (c) challenges that stem from the wide range of diversity within the students we teach.

Innovations Connecting Literacy In and Out of School.   Consider the first challenge—connecting school practice to actual reading experiences. We've all experienced reading something great and giving it to a friend or family member to read; or we've gotten a good book someone else has recommended. In subsequent conversations about the now-shared reading experience, I predict that never have we asked or been asked, "Who was the main character? What was the setting? What happened first?" Yet, in school literacy instruction, this is all too often the only talk students experience around stories they've read. Unfortunately, simply expecting teachers today to teach using conversation-based approaches (e.g., book clubs/literary circles, process writing) may be unrealistic since innovations related to changing talk about text are complex, and teachers themselves have not experienced these innovations either in their own role as students, or in their teacher preparation programs. Such innovations to school practice include:

- changes in textual materials (e.g., moving from commercially prepared short stories and text excerpts as a basis for instruction to using original literature),
- changes in curriculum organization (e.g., moving from isolated instruction in reading, writing, language, and subject matter to intra- and interdisciplinary teaching),
- changes in teachers' roles (e.g., moving from teacher control over topics and turns to teachers assuming multiple roles, including direct teaching, modeling and scaffolding, facilitating and participating),
- and changes in students' roles where students are asked to assume more responsibilities for selecting books, initiating discussion topics, and evaluating their progress.

Burbules (1993) has written that status quo professional education practice encourages teachers to support learning that is dialogic in nature and aimed at framing and solving complex problems, but it rarely provides teachers opportunities to experience directly such teaching and learning. At best, this creates challenges for today's teachers; worse, it leads to frustration and even disenchantment for teachers, students, administrators, and parents.

Balance in the Literacy Curriculum.   The second area where teachers face challenges relates to today's emphasis on the need for balance, as if balance were a single phenomenon (see Pearson & Raphael, 2000). The problem is, balance isn't simply one dimension. There is balance in the *content* of what gets taught, such as balancing skill and strategy instruction with opportunities to engage in more authentic activities reading, writing, and talking about books. There's balance in *teachers' and students' roles* (see Au & Raphael, 1998). There's also a need to balance and integrate *language and literacy experiences*, where teachers connect students' reading, writing, and discussion opportunities through intradisciplinary units (Gavelek, Raphael, Biondo, & Wang, 2000; Lipson, Valencia, Wixson, & Peters, 1993).

Diversity Between Teachers and Students and Among Students.   The third challenge stems from students' diversity, which plays out in two important ways: relationships among teachers and students; and curriculum focus for struggling readers.

First, most of the teachers with whom we work—and typical in the profession as a whole (National Center for Educational Statistics, 1995)—are Euro-American, monolingual speakers of English, female, middle income, and in their twenties and thirties. They are rather naive with respect to their own cultural practices and beliefs, and how these have influenced their own learning and the way they approach teaching. Many work with students who do not share their economic, racial, ethnic, or linguistic backgrounds. These teachers face challenges relating to their students, their literacy backgrounds and their cultural experiences. Culture—because of differences among teachers and students in this case—may serve as a barrier to students' school learning. In contrast, other teachers work with students who are so similar to themselves that culture becomes transparent, something that is not visible in their lives and thus not recognized or discussed. Instead, a false sense of sameness can pervade school interactions, doing little to prepare youngsters to live and work in an increasingly diverse society. Thus, one of our goals was to help teachers come to understand themselves as cultural beings, to understand literacy as cultural practice, and to extend these understandings to their curriculum development and instructional practices.

Second, diversity plays out in terms of students' academic achievements, especially our concern for students who aren't reading at grade level. Because of our focus on struggling readers, we often lose sight of the importance of (a) children who may know how to read, but choose not to and (b) struggling readers who never are asked to think critically about books that are age-appropriate. This doesn't mean we stop worrying about helping them build skills and strategies, but students who are in upper grade levels need to be asked to think critically about books written for their age levels, not just practice decoding and other skills with texts more appropriate for early elementary students.

Helping Teachers Develop as Professional Literacy Educators.   Susan had created a Future Teachers' Autobiography Club in which six young women preparing to become teachers engaged in six monthly discussions, each one centered on one of six autobiographies Susan had selected. These autobiographies represented stories of white teachers who chose to work with students from diverse backgrounds (Paley's *White Teacher;* Rose's *Lives on the Boundary*), of immigrants who left their homelands voluntarily to seek new educational and financial opportunities (Hoffman's *Lives in Translation;* Conway's *Road from Coorain*), and immigrants or descendents of immigrants who were forced to leave their homeland due to slavery or economic deprivation (Rodriguez's *Hunger of Memory;* Angelou's *I Know Why the Caged Bird Sings*). As a result of this experience, students had a heightened awareness of themselves as cultural beings, but struggled to talk about race, culture and gender. Susan was looking for a way to create a context in which she would have a more clearly defined role as instructor, while still emphasizing conversation-based learning.

I had been working with teachers in Book Club who were using dialogic methods to teach literacy, but who indicated their own discomfort from never having experienced book clubs themselves. Thus, I was looking for a substantive set of issues that teachers teaching with Book Club could read, write, and talk about in their own book clubs. The combination of the two lines of work seemed, to us, to be perfect. We began our joint research by studying what teachers felt they gained from participating in book clubs where the focus was on literacy, culture, and autobiography. We studied the impact this participation had on teachers' own professional development, and on the way they planned their curriculum and taught their students.

Why *autobiography* and why use the *Book Club* model? Jerri, one of our teacher participants, once said, "I was one of those people in the beginning who (thought) I had no culture. There's nothing to me. I've had no experiences." Getting culture "on the table" for discussion was an important first step. One means for doing so is through engaging one another in dialogue about rich textual material (Vygotsky, 1978; Harré, 1984; Gavelek & Raphael, 1996). However, in our practice which tends to emphasize social scientists discussions of culture, this dialogue reflects a limited range of voices. By drawing on autobiographies, written by authors of diverse social, cultural, racial, and linguistic backgrounds, as well as representing both genders, we could bring a broader range of voices to the table for discussion. Jerri described the reading of autobiographies as providing "experiences even though I haven't (had them). It's given me a better understanding for some of those things."

Another observation Jerri offered, after participating on the project for several months, was that, "one of the most important (reasons for participating) for me was mostly as a teacher actually because it gave me a feeling for what the kids are trying to do in the classroom.... Whenever I participate in things my kids do, it gives me a lot more insight as to what they're trying to do, ... more ideas." Hannah, another teacher, noted that "for me it was an excellent, excellent experience because I use book clubs in my classroom. So it was terrific for me to be able to participate in something that I ask my students to participate in." Jerri's and Hannah's comments reflect our second focus, using autobiography with adult book clubs. They were members of the first course for practicing teachers that combined Susan's research on autobiography with my research on Book Club. Susan taught the course and I worked as participant observer, primarily maintaining field notes, gathering students' course assignments as artifacts for later study, and so forth. Two research assistants worked with us, also as participant observers, and one of these research assistants interviewed the teachers. We read the same six autobiographies Susan had used in the Future Teachers' Club, but we embedded their discussions within a model of instruction based on the students' Book Club Program (see Florio-Ruane, Raphael, Glazier, McVee, & Wallace, 1997).

After the course, the teachers wanted to stay together, so we formed the Literary Circle, a voluntary group. We initially met at Susan's home, and everyone from the course participated. Since each of the authors had written a second book, at least, we decided to continue with the same group of authors. Over subsequent years (the next two, and continuing today), we moved our meetings from Susan's home to a private room at a local coffee shop/book store; we take turns recommending a book we've read in advance that fits our theme of literacy and culture; we broadened our text selection to include not only biography, but autobiographical fiction such as Amy Tan's *Kitchen God's Wife* and Nora Zeale Hurston's *Their Eyes Were Watching God*; and books such as Peggy Orenstein's *School Girls* that explore related issues—in this case, gender examined through a series of case studies.

In the masters' course I created when I moved from MSU to Oakland University, I decided to build on the autobiography and culture focus and created the Book Club Workshop. In this course, teachers engage in three types of activities. First, I continued the autobiography book club tradition. We read four in the course, each one over two nights. From this experience, teachers reported many of the same responses as did Hannah and Jerri. Second, I drew on Jane Hansen and Kathy Au's insights of the importance of uncovering our own literacy histories. Each student develops three entries that related to how literacy had played roles in our own lives. Third, each teacher creates a Book Club unit she could use in her own teaching. For example, Karen Damphousse, a middle-school teacher, emphasizes cultural practices as students explore different cultures ways of coping with grief and death, centered around author study of Cynthia Rylant and key book, *Missing May*, but drawing on poetry, essays, and other genres in their study.

The course has been taught Fall and Winter semesters since 1997. From this course has emerged a small group of teachers who have formed an adult book club to continue reading and discussing books that examine our storied lives (e.g., Coles [1989] *Call of Stories*). How long we will continue or what direction we take is yet to be determined. What its existence says to me is that there is a need to have opportunities as professionals to examine our own lives, our own literacy practices, and to do so in a context that helps connect these experiences to our roles as teachers and learners.

ACKNOWLEDGMENTS

The report described herein was supported in part under the Educational Research and Development Centers Program, PR/Award Number R305R70004, as administered by the Office of Educational Research and Improvement, U.S. Department of Education. However, the contents of the described report do not necessarily represent the positions or policies of the National Institute on Student Achievement, Curriculum, and Assessment or the National Institute on Early Childhood Development, or the U.S. Department of Education, and you should not assume endorsement by the Federal government.

REFERENCES

Au, K. H., & Raphael, T. E. (1998). Curriculum and teaching in literature-based programs. In T. E. Raphael & K. H. Au (Eds.), *Literature-based instruction: Reshaping the curriculum* (pp. 123–148). Norwood, MA: Christopher-Gordon Publishers.

Burbules, N. (1993). *Dialogue in teaching: Theory and practice.* New York: Teachers College Press.

Coles, R. (1989). *Call of stories.* Boston, MA: Houghton Mifflin.

Florio-Ruane, S. (1994). The future teachers' autobiography club: Preparing educators to support literacy learning in culturally diverse classrooms. *English Education, 26*(1), 52–66.

Florio-Ruane, S. (1997). To tell a new story: Reinventing narratives of culture, identity, and education. *Anthropology and Education Quarterly, 28*, 152–162.

Florio-Ruane, S., & de Tar, J. (1995). Conflict and consensus in teacher candidates' discussion of ethnic autobiography. *English Education, 27*(1), 11–39.

Florio-Ruane, S., Raphael, T. E., Glazier, J., McVee, M., & Wallace, S., (1997). Discovering culture in discussion of autobiographical literature: Transforming the education of literacy teachers. In C. K. Kinzer, K. A. Hinchman, & D. J. Leu (Eds.), *Inquiries in literacy theory and practice: Forty-sixth yearbook of the National Reading Conference* (pp. 452–464). Chicago, IL: National Reading Conference.

Gavelek, J. R., & Raphael, T. E. (1996). Changing talk about text: New roles for teachers and students. *Language Arts, 73*, 182–192.

Gavelek, J. R., Raphael, T. E., Biondo, S. M., & Wang, D. (2000). Integrated literacy instruction. In M. Kamil, P. Mosenthal, P. D. Pearson, & R. Barr (Eds.), *Handbook of reading research* (Vol. III). Mahwah, NJ: Lawrence Erlbaum Associates.

Goatley, V. J., Brock, C. H., & Raphael, T. E. (1995). Diverse learners participating in regular education "Book Clubs." *Reading Research Quarterly, 30*, 352–380.

Harré, R. (1984). *Personal being.* Cambridge, MA: Harvard University Press.

Lipson, M. Y., Valencia, S. W., Wixson, K. K., & Peters, C. W. (1993). Integration and thematic teaching: Integration to improve teaching and learning. *Language Arts, 70*, 252–263.

McMahon, S. I., & Raphael, T. E. (1997). *The Book Club connection: Literacy learning and classroom talk.* New York: Teachers College Press.

National Center for Educational Statistics (1995, January 7, 1996). Female and far from diverse. *The New York Times Education Life,* p. 22.

Pearson, P. D., & Raphael, T. E. (2000). Toward a more complex view of balance in the literacy curriculum. In W. D. Hammond & T. E. Raphael (Eds.), *Literacy Instruction for the New Millennium* (pp. 1–21). MI: Center for the Improvement of Early Reading Achievement & Michigan Reading Association

Raphael, T. E., Brock, C. H., & Wallace, S. (1998). Encouraging quality peer talk with diverse students in mainstream classrooms: Learning from and with teachers. In J. R. Paratore & R. McCormack (Eds.), *Peer talk in the classroom: Learning from research.* Newark, DE: International Reading Association.

Vygotsky, L. S. (1978). *Mind in society: The development of higher psychological processes.* (M. Cole, V. John-Steiner, S. Scribner, & E. Souberman, Trans.). Cambridge, MA: Harvard University Press.

The Book Club Workshop: Learning About Literacy and Culture Through Autobiography Sample Syllabus

Students can expect to develop a conceptual and practical grasp of literature-based instruction, including (1) social constructivism and reader response theory, (2) teacher as reader, (3) teachers' roles in literacy education, (4) literacy curriculum, (5) written responses to literature, (6) literature discussions, (7) classroom organization and management, and (8) assessment; and a deeper understanding of literacy as a cultural practice and each of us as cultural beings.

Expectations for Participation

1. Attend all classes and participate actively in class discussions and activities. Attendance and participation affect your grade.
2. Come to class prepared. Do the assigned readings before class. Due dates are indicated on the class calendar and in handouts. Readings are needed as background. You should come to class with questions, comments, or concerns from the readings. You are responsible for the information in the readings even if it is not covered in class.
3. Maintain a literature-response log, capturing your responses to the autobiographies. Your written responses are the basis for your sharing in literature discussions. Your log is to be turned in on the date indicated in the class calendar.
4. Consider your own literacy histories as you read about the lives of others. Develop at least 3 vignettes based on an artifact you have saved or can replicate to share in class. These vignettes serve as a basis for your Literacy History portfolio.
5. Ask for clarification about activities, projects, and lectures as needed. I'm happy to provide assistance, but it is your responsibility to let me know if you need help. Please contact me by phone or by email to set up an appointment.

Required Texts: Textbooks

McMahon, S. I., & Raphael, T. E (with Goatley, V. J. & Pardo, L. S.), (1997). *The book club connection: Literacy learning and classroom Talk.* NY: Teachers College Press.

Raphael, T. E., & Au, K. H. (1998). *Literature-based instruction: Reshaping the curriculum.* Norwood, MA: Christopher-Gordon Publishers.

Required Texts: Autobiographies/Autobiographical Fiction
(Selections change each time the course is offered.)

Angelou, M. (1969). *I know why the caged bird sings.* NY: Bantam Books.
Conway, J. K. (1989. *The road from Coorain.* New York: Vintage.
Tan, A. (1983). *Kitchen god's wife.* New York: Ballantine Books.
Welty, E. (1991). *One writer's beginning.* MA: Harvard University Press.

Optional Resource Materials

Raphael, T. E., Pardo, L. S., Highfield, K., & McMahon, S. I. (1997). *Book club: A litera-ture-based curriculum.* Andover, MA: Small Planet Communication. (A Teachers' Guide—see www.smplanet.com, or 1-800-475-9486).
Raphael, T. E., & Hiebert, E. H. (1996). *Creating an integrated approach to literacy instruc-tion.* Orlando, FL: Harcourt Brace College Publishers.

Course Overview

Each class is divided into two parts: (a) curriculum content focusing on Book Club, Culture, and Literacy Instruction and (b) Book Club thematic unit focusing on cul-ture and literacy through the genre of autobiography. Part A, the curriculum con-tent, includes lecture/discussions on the Book Club Program and literacy instruction. Part B is Book Club during which we will read, write and talk about a series of autobiographies, thematically related in terms of their focus on the immi-grant experience—reflected across generations within families, as well as in terms of the genre itself. For a weekly list of assignments, activities, and discussion topics, see Table 5.1.

Course Assignments/Evaluation

Grades derive from written assignments, discussion leadership, book club participa-tion, and class participation. Because weekly assignments and papers relate to class discussions and participation, no late papers are accepted.

(1) Book Club Unit. Each participant will develop, teach, and evaluate a unit designed along the Book Club model, thematically-oriented, and based in quality literature. The unit assignments are divided into three parts: Phase 1) Iden-tifying your organizing framework for your unit; Phase 2) Developing the curricular focus; and Phase 3) Accountability issues. (Readers are invited to see the accompa-nying Web site for complete guidelines for the Book Club Assignment.)

(2) Reading Log and Reflective Writing.   For each of the books you are reading, you should write your reflections in a reading log to prepare for the book club discussions during class. Your reflections should include questions the text raises for you, personal response to the text, connections among the books you are reading, connections between your experiences as a book club member and the teaching practices you are attempting, and so forth.

(3) Literacy History Portfolio.   Three entries required. Identify three areas of influence in your own literacy development. Talk with your family members, examine your "treasure boxes" as well as your own memories. In the past, students have examined early reading experiences, early writing experiences, family stories of literacy among parents and grandparents, holiday traditions within their family and related literacy activities, and so forth. For each entry, select or create a representative artifact or a set of artifacts. Then, write a one-page essay explaining its or their significance. Try to select, over the course, three different categories of entries to write about. You will have the opportunity to share each entry and hear others' during the course. (See the accompanying Web site for a sample of my own Literacy History based on a series of artifacts I have collected related to communications among members of my family.)

(4) Participation.   Participation includes contributions to whole class and book club discussions; support for peers when interacting within small groups; presentations throughout the semester.

TABLE 5.1
Weekly Plan

Week	Topics	Readings/Activities
1	Course Orientation: Book Club Framework Theoretical Basis	Introductions and Course Overview BOOK CLUB: Essays from Yamanaka's *Wild Meat and the Bully Burgers*
2	Theoretical Bases for Literature-Based Instruction: • Why Literature? • Response to Literature [See website for sample activity]	Required Reading: McMahon & Raphael, Chapter 1, M & R Sipe, Chapter 3, R & A Book Club—*The Cat in the Hat*
3	Framing the Curriculum: Themes, Genres and Topics	Required Reading: Valencia & Lipson, Chapter 5, R & A Highfield & Folkert, Chapter 13, M & R BOOK CLUB: *Road from Coorain*

(Continues)

TABLE 5.1 (Continued)

Week	Topics	Readings/Actvities
4	The Curriculum for Literature-Based Instruction: An Overview	Required Reading: Au & Raphael, Chapter 6, R & A Highfield, Chapter 8, R & A
		BOOK CLUB: *Road from Coorain*
5	Book Club: Community Share	Required Reading: Raphael & Goatley, Chapter 2, M & R
		BOOK CLUB: Portfolio Entries #1
6	Book Club: Supporting Reading and Reader Response	Required Reading: McMahon, Chapter 3, M & R Brock & Gavelek, Chapter 4, R & A
		BOOK CLUB: *I Know Why the Caged Bird Sings*
7	Book Club: The Writing Component Sustained Writing Activity	Required Reading: Raphael & Boyd, Chapter 4, M & R Denyer & Florio-Ruane, Chapter 7, R & A
		BOOK CLUB: *I Know Why the Caged Bird Sings*
8	Book Club Discussion Groups	McMahon, Chapter 5, M & R (upper elementary) [OR] Scherer, Chapter 12, M & R (early elementary) AND Grattan, Chapter 13, M & R (grade 1)
		BOOK CLUB: Portfolio Entries #2
9	Literature Selection • Race and Literature Selection • Early Literacy Learners • Upper Elementary Grades	Required Reading: Harris, Chapter 2, R & A Hiebert, Chapter 9, R & A Pardo, Chapter 10, R & A
		BOOK CLUB: *Kitchen God's Wife*
10	Assessment in Literature-Based Instruction: Part 1	Bisesi et al., Chapter 11, R & A Bisesi & Raphael, Chapter 9, M & R
		BOOK CLUB: *Kitchen God's Wife*
11	Assessment, Part 2 Tracking Progress through Portfolios	Wong-Cam, Chapter 14, R & A McMahon, Chapter 13, R & A
		BOOK CLUB: Portfolio Entries #3

TABLE 5.1 (Continued)

Week	Topics	Readings/Activities
12	Teacher Observation for Tracking Students' Progress: The Role of Teacher Research	Required Reading: Pardo, Chapter 11
		Select One
		Goatley (special education) in M & R
		Brock (second language learners) in M & R
		Boyd (high school students who struggle) in M & R
		Scherer or Grattan (early elementary) in M & R
		Wong-Cam (conferences/portfolios) in R & A
		Highfield (upper elementary) in R & A
		BOOK CLUB: *One Writer's Beginnings*
13	Book Club from Students' Perspectives	Required Reading: Vance, Ross, & Davis, Chapter 10, M & R
		BOOK CLUB: *One Writer's Beginnings*
14	Literature-Based Instruction: Future	Essays 1–8: Read and presented within groups

II

ENGLISH/LANGUAGE ARTS

6

Teaching of Communication Arts

Jane West
Agnes Scott College

"Teaching of Communication Art" is one of the courses I most enjoy teaching. It is the language arts course in which my students and I get to know each other through our writing in ways that rarely happen in other courses. The course usually comes early in the students' education programs. Most of our students take this course in their junior year after having taken at least a children's literature course and an introduction to education course. Because there is a separate course in the teaching of reading, the primary focus in the language arts course is on composition. The class meets twice weekly for approximately 15 weeks, and, in addition, each student has one hour of field experience in an elementary classroom each week.

I teach in a very small liberal arts college for women. My students are undergraduates who are majoring in other disciplines and completing the early childhood (K–5) teacher education program in addition to their majors. An average class has approximately 10 students in it (although that is changing with the college's recent rapid growth) who are majoring, for example, in anthropology, religious studies, art, music, English, history, and (most often) psychology. The students who complete our early childhood program, which is almost 40 semester hours, along with their majors, tend to be highly motivated and enthusiastic.

The class meets twice weekly for 75 minutes, which is a sufficient block of time for incorporating experiences such as writing workshop. I like to begin each class session by reading aloud and discussing a children's book. I choose books based on their excellence as children's literature and their potential to generate interesting discussion and to spur our thinking about our own writing. A recent semester, for example, began with the reading of *The Watsons Go to Birmingham—1963* (Curtis, 1995) and continued with picture books like *When I Was Young in the Mountains*

(Rylant, 1982) and *My Great Aunt Arizona* (Houston, 1992). Concurrently, we began our reading of *The Art of Teaching Writing* (Calkins, 1994) with the chapter on memoir. This combination of reading about memoir and reading examples of memoir and memoir-like fiction inspired most of the class members to work on their own memoirs in writing workshop. We frequently referred to books in our collection of published memoirs as we wrote, and our talk about writing focused largely on the ways authors write in that genre.

KEY ISSUES

Major issues I consider each time I construct a syllabus for this course include how best to use our time in class, how to balance our attention among all the language arts, how to involve my students in inquiry-based learning, how to integrate the disciplines within our teacher education curriculum, and how to introduce issues of social justice.

Fitting It All In

Making time in class for the shared experiences of writing workshop and reading aloud is not easy. I have tried a couple of different approaches for scheduling writing workshop: setting aside about 3 weeks solely for writing (in the beginning or middle of the semester), or, as in the syllabus provided here, using 1 day a week for workshop. I continue to tinker with the balance among class discussion, writing workshop, and reading aloud. The writing and reading occupy much of the time I have with my students and, obviously, take away time that might otherwise be spent in discussion and other enterprises. However, I am committed to the idea that the kinds of shared literacy experiences provided by the workshops and read-alouds are vital. Many of my students have not had these kinds of experiences elsewhere, and I believe that first-hand participation in these enterprises is essential for their success as teachers of language and literacy.

Emphasizing Oral Language

Another issue related to allocation of time is the study of oral language processes. Although focused study of oral language occupies a very small percentage of our attention, my students and I spend a large portion of our time together engaged in discussion. We are explicit about what it means to participate in a discussion, to contribute productively, and to listen actively. I introduce by example a variety of strategies for both small group and whole-class discussion. We read articles about oral language on topics such as linguistic diversity, drama, questioning, discussion, and storytelling. Yet, our focus on oral language is always secondary to our focus on written language learning. I still search for the appropriate balance and degree of integration of our study of the language processes.

Modeling Inquiry

Third, I want my students to experience curriculum as inquiry. My ideas about inquiry are most strongly influenced by the work of Dewey (1938) and of Short and her colleagues (e.g., Short, Schroeder, Laird, Kauffman, Ferguson, & Crawford, 1996), who conceive of curriculum as a continuous cycle of inquiry growing from students' interests and experiences. My students and I read about inquiry-based learning and observe in inquiry-based classrooms; yet, as with writing workshops, I believe that my students must experience inquiry learning for themselves. As a result, I find that my syllabi are becoming less directive and more student-generated. In the coming semester, for example, I plan to present students with only a skeleton syllabus on the first day of class. After a few days of browsing an array of college and K–5 textbooks, other professional books, and curriculum guides and observing language and literacy instruction in classrooms, the students will pose questions and identify themes and topics they need to study in order to be prepared as language arts teachers. Those themes and topics will become the syllabus outline and will guide the class' decisions about readings and other assignments as they undertake whole-class and small-group inquiry into the teaching and learning of language arts. I have used this procedure successfully in other classes and am eager to do so with language arts. (Not surprisingly, language arts, the course for which I feel the greatest ownership, is the last course I have been willing to "give up" to student decision-making in this way.)

Integrating the College Curriculum

On a broader plane, I have been uncomfortable with a curriculum that separates reading from language arts and both of those from other areas of the school curriculum such as science, math, social studies, and the arts. We are now changing that segmented approach by weaving together our reading and language arts courses into a new two-semester, integrated language and literacy sequence. In turn, the first of those two language and literacy courses is fully integrated with a course in the teaching of social studies, and the second with science.

Our department has completed two year-long sequences in this fashion, and we are now planning for the third year. The greatest difficulty seems to be finding the appropriate balance between, for example, an integrated science and language arts experience, and a substantive consideration of the distinctive content, approaches, and research in each of those two areas. Despite the managerial and conceptual difficulties, the integrated courses highlight common principles of teaching and learning across subject areas, more closely approximate what our students see in the field, and are enjoyable and rewarding for both instructors and students.

In the new, integrated version of the course, students register both for this course and for social studies. The courses are scheduled back-to-back and treated as one extended class, and the social studies instructor and I team teach them. We spend part of our workshop time on writing and part on social studies inquiry (an exploration of religion in public schools or of issues in building classroom communities, for example), and discussion and texts often highlights issues common to both areas.

Educating for Democracy in My Classroom and My Students' Classrooms

Finally, I am committed to raising issues of social justice and education for democracy. Part of the reason I entered education in the first place was the desire to effect social change. My students are no longer urban children from low-income communities; instead, they are teacher candidates in a private college. Thus, my way of helping to make children's lives better is through my students. My thinking about issues of democracy and social justice in education has been shaped by the work of a group of Athens, Georgia teachers who meet regularly in a study and problem-solving group called Literacy Education for a Democratic Society (Allen, 1999). I participated in the group in its beginnings, and learned much from those committed teachers about the ways these weighty social issues manifest in the lives of children.

Asking my students to read Edelsky's (1994) "Education for Democracy" or some other writing about democratic education (see list of Course Readings) is a good way to begin a conversation about these issues. I like to discuss some such text during the first week of a semester and use it as a touchstone throughout the term as we consider the teaching and learning of language arts. In addition to reading and talking about issues of democracy and social justice, I encourage my students to consider those issues in reflecting on their field experiences and in completing other class assignments. Often, even the writing my students do in our workshops continues this theme; because we are in a women's college, issues of gender are often paramount in their writing. Again, the issue of balance surfaces: I must be cautious about imposing this agenda on a captive audience of students at the expense of their needs and interests.

REFERENCES

Allen, J. (Ed.) (1999). *Class actions: Teaching for social justice in elementary and middle school.* NY: Teachers College Press.
Curtis, C. P. (1995). *The Watsons Go to Birmingham—1963.* New York: Delacorte.
Dewey, J. (1938). *Experience and education.* New York: Macmillan.
Houston, B. (1992). *My Great Aunt Arizona.* New York: HarperCollins.
Rylant, C. (1982). *When I was young in the mountains.* New York: Dutton.

Sample Syllabus

Required Texts

Calkins, L. M. (1994). *The art of teaching writing.* Portsmouth, NH: Heinemann.
Graves, D. H., & Sunstein, B. S. (1992). *Portfolio portraits.* Portsmouth, NH: Heinemann.

Wilde, S. (1992). *You kan red this!: Spelling and punctuation for whole language classrooms, K–6.* Portsmouth, NH: Heinemann.

Goals of the Course

In this course, we will read and talk and learn about how children become adept at using spoken and written language and how we as teachers can facilitate that process. You should expect to learn about current trends and issues in the teaching of language arts, with particular attention to constructivist approaches to teaching, learning, and assessment. The class will operate as a model so that by semester's end you will have participated in reading workshops, writing workshops, and other structures for language and literacy learning.

Class Format

Here's the format we'll be trying his semester: Tuesdays will be set aside for discussion of reading assignments and field experience; always bring the text to be discussed and your response to it. Thursdays will be workshop days when we will write, or you will work in small groups on portfolios, class presentations, and other projects.

Requirements

1. *Learning Log (20%).* Each week as you do your reading, write down your ideas, questions, responses. Keep your log entries together in a notebook and bring them to class on the discussion date for that reading; these learning logs will guide our discussions. I will collect your entries each day, read and respond to them, and return them on the next class day.

2. *Portfolio (40%).* We'll talk extensively about these throughout the semester and work on them in workshops. Your portfolio should create a picture of you as a reader/writer/learner/ teacher. How you organize it is up to you; we will read and talk about several organizational models to get your thinking started. Most of the items in your portfolio are up to you, as well. There are a few that everyone must have: (1) One piece of writing created in our writing workshop and taken to finished, polished form; (2) a literacy autobiography; (3) a letter of introduction that describes your goals for the portfolio and the decisions you've made in designing it; (4) an explanation of each item included and your rationale for its inclusion. These four items are *minimal*; you must augment them with others of your choosing to present a well-rounded picture of your accomplishments, processes, and learning. Present your portfolio in a neat, professional form; when appropriate, items in your portfolio should be typed and proofread. (Of course, rough drafts, jottings, early writing, etc. not need not be typed.) A portfolio is not a finished product, but a work in process that represents your learning at a given point in time. Neither is it a resource file in which you place useful items collected from other sources, but rather, it is a tool for self-evaluation and reflection and for presenting your learning to others. Think of your portfolio as a collection of snap-

shots that tell the story of you as a language user, reader, writer, learner, and teacher. I'll read them at midterm and give you some feedback.

3. *Participation (20%)*.

In class. We must all be prepared for each class. On discussion days, that means we come having read the assigned material and written notes, reflections, and questions, and we participate actively in discussions. On workshop days, bring whatever materials you will need for that day's workshop project. Use the workshop time well. When someone is making a presentation or reading aloud, participation means actively listening, showing attention and interest. Get involved and make the class work for you.

Field experience. Participation in field experience includes developing a sense of professionalism. That means being on time and staying at least as long as you're supposed to, establishing good rapport with the classroom teachers and with the children, honoring any responsibilities the teacher extends to you, making good use of your time there, and dressing appropriately (follow the teachers' examples). I will provide you with a list of suggestions for ways you might participate in the field.

4. *Teaching journal (20%)*. Keep a journal in which you record how you spend your field experience time and what you're learning. The latter is more important; think about connections between what you're seeing in the classroom and what we've read and discussed in our class. What are you learning about the children, the classroom environment, the teaching, or yourself? You can use your journal to raise questions/concerns you'd like your partner or me to respond to. Using the format I will provide, e-mail your teaching journal to your journal partner each Monday and forward a copy to me. Each week, you'll get feedback from your partner along with her journal entry. I'll get copies of everything and participate in the conversation as needed. If there is some particular issue you would like me to respond to, note it as such. I'm always happy to offer my two cents' worth! The best journals reflect depth and thoughtfulness rather than being superficial and cursory.

Explanation of Assignments and Evaluation

The *learning logs* serve several purposes: They provide an opportunity for students to develop their thinking about a text before we discuss it in class, they are my window into the students' thinking, and they encourage everyone to keep up with the reading. I collect the logs at the end of each class, read them, and respond with my own brief comments as I try to nudge each student toward deeper understanding. To keep the process simple, each entry receives a plus, a check, or a suggestion for improving. Logs which, for example, raise substantive questions, make connections with other texts or with field experience, or reflect a critical stance receive a plus.

An important component of this course is the weekly hour of *field experience* in an elementary classroom. There are no specific teaching requirements; I simply ask the students to decide, in collaboration with their mentor teacher, what would make the most sense for them to do. Most begin with some observation and quickly move to working with individual children or small groups and finally the whole class (usually by reading aloud, teaching a mini-lesson, or leading book discussions).

Each week when the students return from the field, they make a *teaching journal* entry describing the field experience and reflecting on it. The dialog journals are delivered to a classmate/journal partner via campus e-mail. I read the entries weekly and respond, most often by commenting on the nature of the dialog, but sometimes by entering the dialog myself. The dialog journals are rated with the same plus, check, or suggestion system as the learning logs.

The "big assignment" for this course is the *portfolio*. The students have wide latitude as to how they construct their portfolios and what goes into them. I often require one or two specific entries, such as a literacy autobiography and a "published" piece of writing from our workshop. I always require an introductory letter and rationale statements describing the significance of each item chosen for inclusion. Careful decision-making and the illustrative purposes of portfolio contents, rather than quantity of items, are the goals.

Rather than a numerical scale or other rubric, my response to the portfolio is narrative. I have developed the following list of questions for portfolio evaluation: (1) Goals: Are they clearly articulated and appropriate? Does the portfolio demonstrate work toward them? (2) Rationales for individual items: Are they well reasoned? Do they indicate a reflective and goal-directed selection process? (3) Required items: Have you included them? Do they reflect an appropriate level of thought and effort? (4) Other contents: Is a range of language modes represented? Have you adequately represented any other aspects of yourself included in your goals (e.g., teaching, learning)? (5) Presentation: Does the portfolio look professional? Is it neat and attractive? Is it organized logically? Are items presented in appropriate form (polished and edited when necessary)? For each portfolio, I write my answers to these questions, providing plenty of explanation as well as reader response to individual items.

Occasionally, I also make other assignments, such as asking students or pairs of students to open our writing workshop with mini-lessons. Or, we divide the class into groups, and each group "teaches" one of Calkins' chapters on writing in different grade levels. Another frequent group assignment is to choose a topic not addressed in-depth in class, gather some information through reading, observation, teacher interviews, and so forth, and make a presentation to the class.

Course Readings

For additional readings to enrich the common primary texts, students often choose from among books and articles in my collection or our college library. Following are some commonly used resources:

Bibliography

Alvermann, D. G., Dillon, D. R., & O'Brien, D. (1987). What discussion is and is not. *Using discussion to promote reading comprehension* (pp. 1–8). Newark, DE: International Reading Association.

Bigelow, B., Christensen, L, Karp, S., Miner, B., & Peterson, B. (Eds.). (1994). *Rethinking our classrooms: Teaching for equity and justice.* Milwaukee, WI: Rethinking Schools, Ltd.

Butler, M. A., & Members of the Committee on College Composition and Communication Language Statement. (1974). *Students' right to their own language.* Urbana, IL: National Council of Teachers of English.

Cox, C. (1996). *Teaching language arts: A student- and response-centered classroom* (2nd ed.). Boston: Allyn & Bacon. (Particularly good on drama/arts.)

Delpit, L. D. (1986). Skills and other dilemmas of a progressive Black educator. *Harvard Educational Review, 56*(4), 379–385.

Delpit, L. D. (1988). The silenced dialogue: Power and pedagogy in educating other people's children. *Harvard Educational Review, 58*(3), 280–298.

Edelsky, C. (1994). Education for democracy. *Language Arts, 71,* 252–257.

Galda, L., Cullinan, B. E., & Strickland, D. S. (1997). *Language, literacy, and the child.* (2nd ed.). Fort Worth: Harcourt Brace. (Very good assessment chapter.)

Graves, D. H. (1994). *A fresh look at writing.* Portsmouth, NH: Heinemann. (I like his description of his own portfolio.)

Pappas, C. C., Kiefer, B. Z., & Levstik, L. S. (1995). *An integrated language perspective in the elementary school: Theory into Action* (2nd ed.). New York: Longman. (Great on thematic approaches.)

Putnam, L. (1991). Dramatizing nonfiction with emerging readers. *Language Arts, 68,* 463–469.

Routman, R. (1994). *Invitations: Changing as teachers and learners K–12.* Portsmouth, NH: Heinemann. (Very practical; helpful for students in their field experiences.)

Shannon, P. (1992). *Becoming political: Readings and writings in the politics of literacy education.* Portsmouth, NH: Heinemann.

Short, K. G., Schroeder, J., Laird, J., Kauffman, G., Ferguson, M. J., & Crawford, K. M. (1996). *Learning together through inquiry: From Columbus to integrated curriculum.* York, ME: Stenhouse.

Teaching Tolerance. Southern Poverty Law Center. (Magazine issued twice a year by the Southern Poverty Law Center; promotes racial and cultural understanding in schools.)

7

Writing Buddies:
Linking School and University Teachers in Language Arts Methodology Instruction[1]

Donna Cooner
Colorado Partnership for Educational Renewal

Donna L. Wiseman
Northern Illinois University

Recently a group of classroom teachers, working at an elementary schools where we place preservice teachers for field experiences, became concerned with the mismatch between how they were currently teaching language arts in the classroom, and how we were teaching preservice teachers to teach language arts in our methods classes. Preservice teachers would enter their classrooms for field experiences and observations with a completely different view of how language arts instruction should look in practice, and quickly grew frustrated with the perceived gulf that existed between the theory being expounded on in our university classes and the practice they saw being lived out before their eyes in the elementary school—a familiar, and often debated, concern in the language arts. However, this time, the discussions that grew out of the frustrations eventually led to a collaborative approach to teaching language arts methodology involving both the expertise of university faculty and experienced classroom teachers. The syllabus at the end of this description is a concrete representation of several years of work and many contributions. If the entire story is told, it would include happenings and results that went beyond the focus of language arts instruction and began a partnership that is still dynamic 5 years later.

---

[1]We developed this course while on faculty at Texas A&M University.

The discussions between the school and university faculties began around the learning needs of the students at each institution. Elementary school teachers were concerned about the low writing abilities of their students and the lack of teacher time available to conference regularly with students concerning their writing. University professors knew their students needed the real-world experience of working with real children in authentic reading and writing situations, but were failing to assist these preservice teachers in connecting the content of the methods courses to the classrooms they observed. As we began meeting to discuss the perceived differences, and needs, an idea began to take shape to redesign the language arts course to meet the needs of both institutions.

The course began with one university professor and five teacher volunteers. The traditional 3-hour contact hours for the course were divided up with 2 hours allocated to the professor on campus, for delivery of theory and content, in a large lecture hall with 125 students. Students enrolled in the class attended lecture classes 2 days during the week. The lectures were traditionally presented and accompanied by assigned textbook readings (see syllabus, Part I, RDNG 467). The other hour was allocated to a small lab discussion groups, of about 20 to 25 students, which met in the teachers' classrooms on the elementary campus immediately after school (see syllabus, Part II, sample schedule of topics). During the lab time, the classroom teacher demonstrated, through examples of student work and activities, how the theory learned that week in lecture could be translated into practice. A course syllabus was developed based on topics traditionally included in the course content, and 14 lab activities were planned to accompany university classroom lectures.

In addition to the weekly 3-hour combination of lecture and lab groups, university students also became a "writing buddy" for one additional hour a week with an assigned small group of elementary students. The university students met with their small writing group one hour a week throughout the semester—preparing lessons, conducting writing conferences, and building writing portfolios. Before leaving the classroom each week, preservice teachers reflected about their time spent with the students and corresponded with the supervising classroom teacher through written comments and questions. Questions in this reflective journal often dealt with classroom management issues or concerns for individual student needs, and because the journals were left with the teacher at the end of the writing buddy time and not picked up again until the beginning of writing buddy time the next week, supervising teachers were able to respond individually and thoughtfully to each journal without interrupting classroom instruction time.

After experimenting with several formats and structures, supervising teachers eventually began requesting four or five writing buddies to come to their classroom at the same time. During that hour, elementary students were divided up into small writing groups of four or five and preservice teachers met with these collaborative groups in various locations throughout the classroom, leaving the supervising teacher free to move about the room and monitor the groups in progress.

The lab group leaders spent a portion of the after school time each week helping preservice teachers plan for their writing buddy time, providing age appropriate sample lessons and materials, therefore maximizing their initial success with real students. Teachers who volunteered to have writing buddies in their classrooms were pleasantly surprised to find these preservice teachers entering their classrooms already prepared with meaningful, child-centered lessons, based on the theory discussed in the language arts methods course, and needing little intervention on their part other than assistance with classroom management techniques.

Communication was a constant challenge in this complex partnership. The first vital communication link was between the university professor and the lab leaders. Each week, lecture notes were faxed out to the elementary campus to keep teachers informed on the pace and content of the campus-based lectures and these notes were added to a notebook that became the reference for lab activities. The university professor and the teachers also met regularly to discuss what was happening in the class and the discussion groups. Constant adjustments were made in lecture and labs to make the content as meaningful and connected as possible. Lab teachers also communicated regularly with writing buddy supervisors, gathering important feedback on preservice teachers' success and preparedness for dealing with real students during writing buddy time and again making adjustments as needed in the content of the labs to provide more support as needed.

Time and resources were also problems. Lab teachers were employed full-time during the day as regular classroom teachers, so labs and planning meetings had to be held after school hours, resulting in long work days for those participating. Each discussion leader was paid a small stipend for their teaching, but the extra resources needed for this collaborative teaching arrangement were often provided by grants, and were not institutionalized into the university budget.

To those participating in the partnership, however, the benefits far outweighed the challenges. It was clear from student journals, university students valued the embedded practical experience in the "real world" of language arts instruction and learned a great deal based on their interactions with the teachers and the elementary students. Through the collaboration, the classroom teachers involved felt they had a voice in the teacher education program at the university and made important contributions to the profession beyond their own classroom walls (Wiseman & Cooner, 1996). And finally, and perhaps most importantly, the course not only met the needs of teachers, but benefited the children at the collaborating school as well. The teachers and the principal believed the test scores of the children improved as a result of the writing activities planned for individuals and small groups. All were beginning to understand that teacher education can have a strong impact on the quality of teaching when there is a clear link between coursework and subsequent experiences in classrooms (Zeichner & Tabachnik, 1981).

What started out as a familiar debate over the "right" way to teach language arts, resulted in a model of delivering a method course that provided for relevant and meaningful field experiences for a large number of students in a cost-effective way. Everyone involved would probably all agree the process, with so many layers of communication necessary for success, is not the easiest way to deliver a university class, but it is one that results in simultaneous renewal and benefits for all.

REFERENCES

Wiseman, D. L., & Cooner, D. (1996). Discovering the power of collaboration: The impact of a school–university partnership on teaching. *Teacher Education and Practice, 12*(1), 18–27.

Zeichner, K. M., & Tabachnik, B. R. (1981). Are the effects of teacher education "washed out" by school experience? *Journal of Teacher Education, 32*(3), 7–11.

Sample Syllabus Part I: Rdng 467
Reading and the Language Arts

Robb, L. (1994). *Whole language, whole learners.* New York: William Morrow.

Learning the language arts requires sharing, interaction, and collaboration and involves relationships between adults and children. Language arts instruction should reflect the learning that goes on in natural situations in which children are very successful at communicating their ideas, dreams, and needs. Teacher can easily facilitate language arts growth by implementing classroom activities that are purposeful and communicate meaningful and important ideas. Future teachers should develop abilities to plan activities that encourage children to become effective language learners. To help you understand some of your responsibilities in the area of language arts, we will focus on the development of the following concepts:

1. An awareness of the role of language arts in today's elementary classrooms.
2. An understanding of the importance of the adult role in children's acquisition of reading, writing, listening, and speaking.
3. The ability to understand concepts associated with language arts instruction (e.g., meaning-centered, child-focused, integrated curriculum, thematic units, and literature-based).
4. An appreciation of the importance of using children's literature in language arts.
5. The ability to recognize the differences between teaching language arts skills and facilitating children's language development.
6. The ability to view language arts as an integrated language process.

Your Work and Class Expectations

Your lab instructor will be evaluating your work and grading in labs may differ based on requirements established in your section. Your grade for this class will be determined by your involvement and productions as a result of the following activities:

1. Readings:	(a)	Review at least 20 children's books during the semester. At least three must be novels appropriate for upper grades and the rest can be picture books. You will need to respond to the books based on your lab instructor's requirements.
	(b)	Be familiar with your textbook by the end of the semester. Usually you will be assigned specific readings, but don't be afraid to find unassigned parts of the text that will help clarify what we are discussing in class.
2. Book guides:		Complete five book guides: They are discussed on page 85 of your text.
3. Published Writing:		As a result of your participation in the writing process during your lab activity, you will publish a piece of your writing. The writing can be a poem, a children's book, a memoir, or any other text. Your lab instructor will guide you through the activity. (By the way, if you plan this right, your publication can be a great gift for a special person in your life. Have you done your Christmas shopping, yet?)
4. Writing Buddy:		Each of you will be assigned a writing buddy at South Knoll. You will be asked to keep a journal that will be a form of communication between you and your writing buddy's teacher. The journal will keep record of your participation in this activity. In addition, in one section of your self evaluation, you will use your writing buddy's behaviors to describe your own learning. This evaluation will be used at that time of the due date for lab discussions. You are expected to meet regularly with your writing buddy. Any unexcused or unexplained absences will result in loss of total points.
5. Self-Evaluation:		In addition, to the writing buddy description, select at least one lab activity, class lecture, or writing buddy incident to help describe changes in your thinking regarding language arts. This should be handed in with your final.
6. Tests		There will be two tests during the semester and a final. One test will be given in lab on October 13, the second will be given in lecture on November 22, and you will have the option to take your final the week of December 8 during your lab time or the time associated with the MW 8:00 lecture.
7. Participation:		Several activities are built into both lab and lecture that will result in participation points. In most cases, it will not be possible to make-up these points.

Syllabus, Part II: Sample Schedule of Topics

Date	Topics for Lectures	Topics for Labs
August 31	Introductions Course Logistics	
September 1	Definition of Language Arts or How to tell a language arts when you see one	Introductions (Writing Inventory) Review the Syllabus Language Arts Lesson
September 6	Language Development How do we learn language?	
September 8	Language Arts Instruction Language Based Whole Language Language Arts Routines	Writing Buddies Literature Circles
September 13	Reading and Writing Connections How does writing impact reading and visa versa?	
September 15	Writing Development Little Kids and Writing	Writing Process Classroom Implementation: • Getting Started • Sharing Common Experiences • Literature • Selecting Topics
September 20	Writing Process How do I describe my own writing process?	
September 22	Writing as a Process Conferencing and Record- Keeping	Writing Process Classroom Implementation: • Encouraging Writing • Rough Drafts • In-process conferences—peer conferences
September 27	Writing as a Process Integrating Skills Instruction: Spelling Grammar and the Like	
September 29	Student-Authored Text in Language Arts Language Experience, Journals, Publishing	Writing Process Classroom Implementation: • Continuing the Writing • Peer Editing • Conferencing
October 4	Authentic Writing	

Date	Topics for Lectures	Topics for Labs
October 6	Using literature to integrate the language arts	Writing Process Classroom Implementation: • Publishing and Sharing
October 11	Methods of Literature Response Oral and Written Presentation of Picture Books Activities	
October 13	Talking and Listening in the classroom	Test # 1
October 18	Talking and Listening in the classroom	
October 20	Using the Literature: Oral and Written Drama	Rotating Sessions: Special Topics 1) Critical Response and Journals (Ms. Rankin) 2) Author Studies (Ms. Fluth) 3) Authentic writing in first grade (Ms. Kelly)
October 25	Thematic Units and Integration	
October 27	Language Arts in the Content Areas How to use science, social studies, and math to teach language arts.	Repeat: Rotating Sessions
November 3	Evaluating the growth of language arts	Repeat: Rotating Sessions
November 8	Evaluating the growth of language arts: Portfolios	
November 10	Standardized Testing	Evaluating Children's Writing **What am I learning from my writing buddy?**
November 15	Cooperative Learning	
November 17	Managing Integrated Blocks of Time	
November 22	Test # 2	
December 6	Grouping and Diverse Classrooms	
December 8	Major Issues in the Language Arts	

8

Whole Language Teaching in Elementary and Middle School

JoBeth Allen
University of Georgia

My goals for Whole Language Teaching in Elementary and Middle School, which you will find on the first page of the letter to colleagues (as included in the syllabus) are based on the following beliefs that ground me as an educator:

1. Human beings construct knowledge from their own needs, questions, experiences, and explorations through interactions with others in both immediate and extended inquiry communities.
2. My role as a critical educator is to understand, critique, and extend progressive educational practices to raise issues of equity and social justice, and to situate language and literacy in sociopolitical contexts.
3. Whatever we read, theorize, research, or write should have a direct and positive impact on the literacy and language opportunities for the students we teach.

The people who take this course include first-year masters students who have not taught, doctoral students, and novice as well as veteran teachers; they often have experience and interests ranging from preschool to adult education, and increasingly include those interested in not only English language arts but also Teaching English as a Second Language. Enrollment ranges from 15 to nearly 30. I usually teach the course one night a week, from 4:30–9:00 p.m., both to accommodate teachers with busy week-night schedules (and long commutes) and to incorporate a variety of learning structures (literacy workshop, theme immersion committees, book study groups, individual conferences, and whole group discussions). Although most class members arrive after teaching a full day, we find that by incorporating these structures that involve moving, interacting with different people, and a range of learning activities (including "Dinner Theater," when we watch a topic-relevant video and eat whatever that evening's dinner committee has provided), we remain actively engaged.

The course, like its undergraduate counterpart that I teach in a similar manner, is constantly evolving; it changes each time I teach it based on the needs and expertise of those enrolled, and it changes because the members and I critique it midway and at the end. There are aspects that I am not satisfied with. Although members do have a great deal of ownership in building the curriculum (e.g., they establish their own goals, learning activities, due dates, and points), I have not found an effective way, nor the time, to incorporate the kind of self-assessment that I believe would enhance continued growth. Some students, especially those from Asian countries, have pointed out in evaluations that they expect more lecture from me as the professor, and some are uncomfortable with so much self-direction in their learning. Another issue is how free students feel to critique the whole language philosophy; although I encourage such investigation and reflection, and am fairly familiar with current critiques, my recommended readings, shared readings, and experiences as a researcher all reflect my strong belief that instructional decisions based on a whole language philosophy lead to the most effective language and literacy learning. This leads to the occasional criticism that I am not presenting an objective, unbiased set of viewpoints and encouraging students to make their own choices.

While I admire colleagues who co-construct the entire syllabus with class members, I have not found that to be very workable with only 10-week quarters. I do order books for whole class reading (they change every time I teach the course). I always use books that are written by or include many teacher voices. For the Teacher Study Groups (TSG), members select topics of particular interest, skim a range of books I have "book talked" as well as others they know about, and divide into groups of three to five; I then order the various titles so that each group member has his/her additional book. Some TSG topic choices have included literacy instruction for speakers of second languages, making connections between home and school, authentic assessment, incorporating drama, and culturally relevant instruction of African American children.

On the first evening of class, we engage in a literacy workshop (sometimes reading, sometimes writing, sometimes an extended workshop linking the two) before I ever say a word about the class. I feel I am demonstrating what is valued by beginning there rather than with requirements. Next, we go over the Course Structure and Opportunities you will read in the next section, and we begin that night identifying the critical issues, study group readings, and possible resources (I bring a book cart to each meeting, with over 200 books, journals, and articles). After a brief lecture/discussion on beliefs, critiques, interpretations, and classroom incarnations of whole language instruction, we conclude the evening with a letter exchange. I give them a letter telling them about my life, family, teaching experiences, research, and personal reading and writing. I invite them to write me a personal letter, share my belief that personal relationships are central to learning, and give them time to write. I use the information to establish individual relationships, and in an activity the following week that helps the class to become a closer community. For example, in the last class we learned that

- "Home anchors me—I'm from the country, the seventh of eight children."
- "The first 2 years of my career my students were underprivileged.... For the past 2 years, I have taught ... over-privileged children.... I have loved both ..."
- "We are expecting an addition to the family in August!"
- "After teaching book-bound reading, English, and spelling to fifth-, sixth-, and seventh-graders in the early 70s, I was a passionate, stay-at-home, carpool driving, sports-ballet-Girl Scout mom ..."
- "I created a special ed. department for a middle-class high school in Augusta. I taught a K–2 resource/self-contained special ed. class in an inner city school, and I taught third grade in an affluent elementary school ..."

I love to talk about my teaching with others, learn of books that classes have found particularly valuable, and find out about ways other professors incorporate and model theoretically-based curriculum and teaching. I hope the sharing of one way of teaching opens many such dialogues.

Sample Syllabus
Whole Language Teaching and Learning
in Elementary and Middle School
Course Structure and Opportunities for EEN 642

Dear Colleagues,

Welcome to EEN 642, a class on whole language teaching in elementary and middle schools. This is one of my favorite classes to teach, and I hope it will become one of your favorites. I have several goals for the class; you will develop your personal and professional goals as well. My goals include:

a) that each of us grows as a literate adult,
b) that we become more effective teachers through exploring areas of personal literacy needs and interests,
c) that we model as much as possible in our own class setting what you will be doing in your present and future classrooms, including

    (1) generating our own curriculum,
    (2) designing our own evaluation process,

(3) assuming dual roles as teachers and students.

I have found several learning structures to be particularly helpful. I look forward to designing new ones based on the needs of this class. We will each participate in the following ways:

Learning by Reading

Whole Class Readings

Theme Immersion: Inquiry-Based Curriculum in Elementary and Middle Schools, by Maryann Manning, Gary Manning, and Roberta Long

Portraits of Whole Language Classrooms: Learning for All Ages, edited by Heidi Mills and Jean Anne Clyde

Building Communities of Learners: A Collaboration Among Teachers, Students, Families, and Community, by Sudia Paloma McCaleb

We'll determine areas of interest for study groups; each group will order one or more books as needed. In addition, there will be many books and articles available for extended reading, based on your specific interests.

Learning by Connecting Reading and Writing

We will have Reading Workshop the first 5 weeks, and Writing Workshop the last 5 weeks. You will read and write in **Literacy Groups** each class period. We'll form groups based on the kind of reading and writing we wish to develop this quarter (e.g., realistic fiction, children's literature, mystery, informational). Loose-leaf folders are best for personal writing; you may want spiral or sectioned notebooks for the other writing. During Literacy Group time, we'll have literature discussion and write on topics of personal interest. You will be sharing your writing (but only when you want to) as well as your literacy processes with the class regularly; this writing will not be graded, because I believe that your evaluation of your own growth is more important. There will also be ample opportunity for Professional Writing (continue reading!)

Learning by Talking

Each class session, we will also meet in Teacher Study Groups to discuss issues, projects, and readings related to a group-selected focus, for example, students placed at risk, or ESL education. Most of our class interaction will be based on our response to the professional readings. It is critical that each of us comes to class having read the common readings (and any individual readings you have chosen) and having written about them. Your note-taking style is up to you. What you need to add for this class is questioning the texts. Write questions about things you can't understand, things that make you think of your own learning, and especially, things that you relate to your own teaching. These questions will be the core of our discussions, so highlight them in your notes in some way. Group members will help each other learn from the readings, and will raise issues for whole-class discussion.

Learning by Investigating

We will all be involved in a Theme Immersion (TI) with a focus on a critical educational issue; we will form TI Committees. Each of you will also develop an individual learning contracts that is based on your personal and professional literacy goals. Some of these projects would be great team or partner collaborations, so talk with each other as you develop your contracts. Here are several options for active, personalized learning; I hope you will think of others:

MENU OF POSSIBLE INVESTIGATIONS FOR EEN 642

(* projects that your Teacher Study Group might develop individually or together, related to your area of inquiry)

*1. *Classroom Research*. Teacher research begins with a question, or a curiosity, and includes a systematic and intentional collection of data that provides insights into your question. Data collection may include a teaching journal, interviews, surveys, observational notes, taped and transcribed student discussions or conferences, numerical analyses, or comparisons. You may design a whole-class study, a small group study, a cross-class study, or an individual case study.

*2. *Literacy Research/Practice Review*. There may be an area of particular interest to you, such as spelling development, bilingualism, bidialectualism, ESL, portfolios, revision processes, literacy assessment, emergent literacy, assessment, intergenerational literacy, or reading/writing connections that you would like to research. You may wish to take the stance of a researcher, a practitioner, or both. A good review paper includes important works in a given area, analyses each article/book included in the review, and then synthesizes what the writer has learned.

*3. *Instructional Resource*. As you examine your actual or anticipated teaching practices, you may find particular areas you wish to develop more fully. You may wish to create materials for yourself and others that provide specific examples of such things as books that model particular aspects of writing, a connected series of mini-lessons (for example on topic choice, topic development, exploring genres such as memoir or fantasy, etc.), plans and guidelines for literacy conferences, home–school connections, spelling programs, instructional units on picture books or memoirs, evaluation tools and strategies, portfolios, or an author study. Teachers in past classes have developed a classroom newspaper; a school publishing center; plans for teaching science, math, social studies through literature; etc.

You will probably develop these resources from your readings, from interviewing and/or observing other teachers, and from talking with each other to develop your own ideas. Each instructional resource should be field tested, modified accordingly, and shared with an interested group of colleagues, preferably other teachers at your school.

*4. *Literacy Involvement with Children.* Those of you who have classrooms may want to focus on implementation of ideas we study. Others may volunteer in a classroom (possibly one of your class colleague's), or work through an agency such as Athens Tutorial (call Stephanie Caywood, 354-1653) or the Clarke County Mentoring Program (call Trudy Bradly). Develop plans based on our readings; then keep a careful journal of each session, including what you planned, what actually happened (with the focus on specific child response, development, etc.), and what you learned. This could be a "major" project extended by analysis that draws in readings from class and/or integrates relevant outside readings.

*5. *School Observations.* This would be a good option for those who do not have a classroom this year, and would like to observe writing teachers and students at work. Observations might focus on the roles and responsibilities of teacher, students, and classroom environment. Ideally, you might find someone from class who would like to have you in her/his classroom, and you could develop a combined project. The observations might include interviews with teachers about how they help children become literate, or with children about how they become literate.

6. *Literacy Portfolio.* Collect, Select, Reflect! Select a variety of artifacts to show yourself as a writer and a teacher of writing, including some of the following options:

a) You may include pieces of your writing through the years; comment on what you now "see" in these writing samples (e.g., an early note to your dad, a story from first grade, a report from middle school, etc.).

b) Include samples of your writing this quarter, with reflection on what they demonstrate about you as a writer (risks, accomplishments, etc.), and literature connections.

c) Include your goals, progress towards your goals, and reflections on your personal literacy processes.

d) In order to make the transfer from your experience to your teaching, you may want to write a section such as, "What did I learn about myself as a reader and writer that has made me a better teacher?"

e) You might include an annotated bibliography of books and/or articles about literacy teaching and learning.

f) It can be very enlightening to write your Reading (and/or) Writing Autobiography.

g) How can you show yourself as a reader? We'll discuss options including book lists, response journal excerpts, etc.

h) Portfolio readings—include at least three sources *about* developing portfolios that you read before and during your own process. Pts. 5–10 per well-developed section.

7. *Professional Conference*. Need a good excuse to travel? You can attend any local, state, or national conference on literacy (e.g., GCTE at Calloway Gardens in February). Pts. write-up of at least two sessions, 10; five or more sessions, 20.

8. *Published Piece*. Take something from our writing workshop through revision and editing to published form, with a specific audience in mind. Attach all drafts, notes, etc. Pts. 10 max.

9. *Outside Readings*. Please feel free to borrow books from me all quarter, or to find related readings on your own. The write-up should include key points, and how what you read might impact your teaching. Pts. 10 each, up to 30.

10. *Increased Technology Competence*. There are wonderful computer classes and labs available to develop your computer expertise. Learn something new, then apply it on at least one of your projects using the computer (word processing, data base, graphics, World Wide Web). Attach a brief (½–1 page) explanation of your computer skills, what you've learned recently, what you'd like to learn. Pts. 10–20.

11. *Theme Immersion Demonstration*. Everyone will be involved in this with your team. Pts. 20.

12. *Your ideas* ...

After you have decided what would be the *best set of learning experiences for you* based on your goals, please write up a contract. I'll review and sign, or we'll negotiate if necessary. We will have small group meetings in class to learn more about various project areas, for example, portfolios. I look forward to learning with each of you.

Goals, Learning Experiences, and Evaluation

My goals for participating in EEN 709 are the following:

_____

_____

_____

_____

_____

The learning experiences (usually 3–5) I've planned to help me meet my goals are the following:

Learning Activity and Plan (please elaborate)	Points	Due
1. Theme Immersion Demonstration	20	3/19
2.		
3.		
4.		
5.		

Note: I realized the last time I taught this (Winter 1997, the syllabus included in this chapter)—that because I believe that teachers who do what they ask their classes to do have more insight and credibility, I should also do a contract. The following is what I shared with students, and what I actually did (I followed through on all with the exception of the technology goal, where my learning was minimal).

JoBeth's Goals, Learning Experiences, and Evaluation

Goals:

1. To revise [this course] to include a social action component.
2. To move a little farther out of the technological dark ages.
3. To keep time for my own literacy engagement.
4. To learn how to help Shawn develop the literacy she'll need in middle school next year (work with Dorsey, Barbara).
5. To get both books FINISHED and IN THE MAIL.

Learning Activities	Points/Time	Due
1. Theme Immersion: develop as integral part of 642. Create lesson plans throughout quarter. Have class members evaluate process, revise for next class.	4 hours	end of quarter
2. Conferences: Lisa Delpit intro. Kansas IRA, workshop on home & school connections; develop into day-long, interactive workshop	8–10 hours preparation; 6 hours in workshop	1/10

3. Technology: develop and USE ability to access web sites for research; create web site for NCRLL; interface WP and e-mail	10–12 hours?	end of quarter
4. Book Club: Read, jot notes, and participate in discussions (next two books, *Little Altars Everywhere* and *The Laughing Place*)	(I've already read the books); 4–6 hours	2/15
5. Reading with Shawn weekly at 4th Street; provide books for class; develop strategies	1–2 hours per week	end of quarter
6. Finish writing/editing Engaging Teachers, LEADS book	20 hours	1/27

BIBLIOGRAPHY

Maryann Manning, Gary Manning, & Roberta Long (1994). *Them Immersion: Inquiry-Based Curriculum in Elementary and Middle Schools.* Portsmouth, NH: Heinemann.

Heidi Mills & Jean Anne Clyde (Eds.). (1990). *Portraits of Whole Language Classroom: Learning for All Ages.* Portsmouth, NH: Heinemann.

Sudia Paloma McCaleb (1995). *Building communities of Learner: A Collaboration Among Teachers, Students, Families, and Community.* New York: St. Martin's Press.

9

Teaching and Learning
in the English Language Arts

Nancy Farnan
San Diego State University

PROGRAM BACKGROUND
AND PARTICIPANTS

Teaching and Learning in the English/Language Arts (TE 914), better known in the vernacular as a methods course, is designed as part of the fifth-year, Single Subject credential program in the School of Teacher Education at San Diego State University. Teacher preparation in California requires completion of a 1-year, postbaccalaureate credential program (approximately 30 semester units, half of which must be fieldwork). Students enrolled in California's Single Subject programs have undergraduate degrees in a content area (e.g., science, math, English, physical education) and have decided they want to teach that content at the middle or secondary level. Some of them are recent college graduates. Others are career-change individuals who, for a variety of reasons, decide they want to become teachers.

I began teaching the English/language arts methods course 8 years ago and, in my initial planning, was immediately reminded of what I experienced personally in years before as a middle and secondary English/language arts teacher: that there is so much to learn, to know, and to do in the English/language arts classroom. As a teacher educator, the questions I grappled with as I designed and taught this course for the first time (and continue to grapple with) center on how to provide, within the confines of a three-unit semester course, content that will best prepare preservice teachers for their careers as teachers of English/language arts.

THE COURSE DESIGN

The course described in this syllabus represents its latest permutation. Based on my own reading and study, on conversations—both face-to-face and electronic—with colleagues, and on students' feedback over the years, the course is in a continual state of development and refinement. Although some of the initial premises underlying the course have remained unchanged (e.g., basic learning theories upon which the instructional foundation rests), others have changed and are still in development (e.g., a shifting focus to include more attention to classrooms comprised of highly diverse learners). Then, there are others that were not even part of the course early on (e.g., the technology component).

One of the basic premises of this course is captured in Fosnot's quote found at the beginning of the syllabus, and is also reiterated in the Course Description section. It refers to the idea that individuals must invent themselves as teachers. They must construct a philosophy, reflect on their beliefs, and create a knowledge base with which to make informed decisions about teaching and learning. Alan Purves (1990) expressed this constructivist concept in a statement that strikes me as elegant in its simplicity: "Knowledge is inside people, information is external to them" (p. 3). Over the years, my goal has been for the English/language arts course to provide experiences and information that preservice teachers can convert to a dynamic knowledge base for the purpose of helping them become expert and effective teachers. One of the ways I attempt to accomplish the goal of promoting their knowledge construction and reflection is through an action research project (described in the Course Requirements). Over the years, I have found that the teacher–researcher model represents one of the most effective ways to help students become reflective practitioners. In this case, the model is student-teacher-as-researcher (STAR) (Farnan & Fearn, 1992). Through action research, students ask questions and, as a result, look closely at certain issues and problems. Then, by conducting research and examining the results, they reflect directly and thoughtfully on outcomes and their implications.

Another premise that is critical to the design of this course is my attempt to illustrate connections between theory and practice, the *why*, as well as the *what* (i.e., what to teach and how to teach it). Although, understandably, preservice teachers have an urgent need to have the *what* question addressed, my experience has convinced me that without understanding *why* they are using certain curricular elements and instructional processes, it will be nearly impossible for them to make the kinds of informed decisions that teachers must make in order to ensure their students' success and learning. For example, Rosenblatt's transactional theory (reader-response theory) has guided much of my thinking about literature and literature instruction. I have come to believe that teachers cannot *teach* literature, but that, instead, the task is to design classrooms and instructional processes that provide opportunities for reading, that guide students through a reading, and that support students in processes of meaning construction and interpretation. That theory, then, has direct instructional implications for literature in the classroom.

As I work with the preservice teachers, I share my thinking with them. I provide readings and discussions through which they are asked to grapple with issues of *why* literature, *what* literature, and *how* to bring the experience of literature to their classrooms. As we discuss various literary theories, I want them to wrestle with what theories shape their beliefs about literature and literature instruction. I want them to be informed about theories that help educators understand reading comprehension and learning. I also make immediate connections, via instructional applications, of these theories to classroom practices and provide evidence of how those practices can affect students and their learning.

I also place a high priority on the teaching of writing and introduce students to the idea of program development in writing, which includes attention to environments for writing, relationships between writing and learning, self-reports of practicing writers, writing in a variety of genres, writing processes, and direct instruction based on assessments of students' abilities and needs.

Other issues that are becoming increasingly relevant to teachers of English include skills and competencies associated with workforce literacy, the teaching of English in an interdisciplinary setting, and the role of technology in teaching and learning in the English/language arts classroom. In the syllabus for this course, I present the foundational premises and issues as objectives around which the course is structured. These objectives are intended as guides for students throughout the course, as they were a guide for me in developing the syllabus.

Much of the discussion surrounding these issues comes from a collections of readings for the course, which is comprised of such things as journal articles, sample handouts, and samples of exemplary lesson and unit plans. We also read Atwell's (1987) text *In the Middle*. Although many excellent texts have been written that describe classroom models of reading, literature, and writing curriculum and instruction, I continue to use Atwell's book because preservice teachers find it straightforward and accessible and because, in my opinion, it offers a clear description of reading and writing workshops that can be easily adapted in a variety of ways to address various classroom configurations and diverse student needs.

REFERENCES

Atwell, N. (1987). *In the middle: Writing, reading, and learning with adolescents.* Upper Montclair, NJ: Boynton/Cook.

Farnan, N., & Fearn, L. (1992). A teacher researcher model in preservice education. *Action in Teacher Education, 14,* 50–54.

Purves, A. (1990). *The scribal society: An essay on literacy and schooling in the information age.* New York, NY: Longman.

Sample Syllabus
Teaching and Learning in the English/Language Arts
Teacher Education 914

... knowledge is constructed in the process of reflection, inquiry, and action, by learners themselves.... (Fosnot, C. T. (1989). *Enquiring teachers, enquiring learners: A constructivist approach for teaching*. New York: Teachers College Press.)

COURSE DESCRIPTION

This course is one element in your teacher preparation program and has one overriding purpose: to prepare you as thoroughly as possible for teaching English in middle and secondary school classrooms. The purpose of TE 914 is to offer you new ideas and perspectives, and may, perhaps, affirm ones you already hold. Your instructor's expectation is that these ideas and perspectives will provide a foundation upon which to add information and insights as your teaching career unfolds. If the foundation is a good one, you will have a broad base from which to work; and it is your instructor's intent that the course will make you more effective as a student teacher than you would have been without it. However, the larger goal is to prepare you for your career as a teacher.

There is a reason for making the larger picture, your life as a teacher, top priority. As a teacher, one of your most useful talents will be your ability to problem-solve, making decisions from an informed position that is built on a strong knowledge base. Therefore, the purpose of this course is not to provide an unlimited "bag of tricks" designed simply to help you survive student teaching, although you most certainly will take some "tricks" away with you. Instead, the intent is to help you develop understandings about how the discipline of English can be transformed into curriculum and instruction that will ensure your students will be successful learners. Crucial to this outcome are the following:

- being committed to the belief that all students can learn;
- knowing your subject content, as well as how to teach it to someone else (something Lee Schulman referred to as Pedagogical Content Knowledge [PCK], the intersection where content knowledge and effective instruction converge to promote learning);
- being a reflective practitioner with the ability to make informed judgments, based on your own and your students' experiences, about the effectiveness of your classroom; and
- participating regularly as a member of a professional teaching community. (Joining professional organizations is a not a requirement for this course. However, you will receive applications for membership in local, state, and national organizations in English/language arts; and you are urged to join

your professional community by taking advantage of this opportunity to receive reduced-rate student memberships.)

To these ends, this class will actively engage you in conversations and activities. Your role must be an interactive one; for basic learning theory tells us that we learn not what someone has taught, but what we do. You are responsible for creating yourself as a teacher. No one can do that for you. Only *you* can create the meanings (i.e., knowledge, beliefs, and perspectives) which will guide your teaching. You must be open to ideas, yet at the same time skeptical and questioning. Your perseverance, determination, and engagement are crucial variables; and, of course, these are all characteristics over which you hold absolute control.

This course is Part I of a 2-part sequence of courses. Next semester you will take a one-unit course, the Methods Seminar. Because you will be creating your professional portfolio in the seminar, you need to begin collecting artifacts this semester (e.g., sample lessons, assignments that highlight your technology expertise, interdisciplinary units, management plan, philosophy statement, and so forth). As this semester progresses, we will be talking more about this process.

TE 914 has been developed thoughtfully and organized to meet the course goals, and the course outline reflects an approximate topical organization for the semester. However, the professor reserves the right to make adjustments along the way if professor/student interest or need or class dynamics dictates a restructuring of the order of topics or a rethinking of the topics themselves.

COURSE OBJECTIVES

- To begin development of a philosophical foundation to guide your teaching of English/language arts
- To understand current language arts curriculum philosophies and their specific application in the *California English/Language Arts Framework*
- To understand current influences on language arts curriculum and instruction, such as
  – theories and applications relevant to an integrated and interdisciplinary approach to language arts instruction
  – current theories associated with reading and understanding literature, with specific focus on reader response theory
  – perspectives regarding integration of workforce skills and competencies into the curriculum
- To develop a knowledge of literature in a variety of genres appropriate to middle and secondary students
- To plan lessons around curriculum and instruction that will meet the needs of students with diverse and multicultural backgrounds and a wide range of skills and abilities

- To integrate technology into the classroom as support for teacher planning and student learning
- To develop an understanding of traditional and alternative assessment methods appropriate to teaching English/language arts
- To participate in and debrief instructional simulations that promote thinking and learning in the English/language arts classroom
- To engage in reflection concerning teaching and learning in English/language arts

COURSE OUTLINE

[In this section of the syllabus, I give students a fairly detailed description of the weekly class sessions, as in Session 1 here. However, for the purposes of this book, I have simply listed the general topics covered in Sessions 2–16.]

Session 1	Introduction to course—Read and discuss syllabus
	Getting Started in English Class: Using a syllabus in your classroom
	Teacher-as-Researcher Model—Why teacher research? Brainstorming questions....
	Assignments: For next week, read "English/Language Arts Framework" section in Issues in English Education (IEE). Read Chapters 1 and 2 in Atwell. Begin Reflection Log entries.
Session 2	Understanding the Framework and Designing Units/Planning Objectives
Session 3	Goals of a Literature-Based Program
Session 4	Response-Based Instruction—A Reader Response Approach
Session 5	Multicultural Literature/Multiethnic Classrooms
Session 6	Electronic Lesson Planning
Session 7	Technology in the English/Language Arts Classroom
Session 8	Poetry in the Classroom: Not Just a Poetry Unit, but Poetry Throughout the Curriculum
Session 9	Problem-Based Learning and Real-World Literacy: Implications for Interdisciplinary Curriculum
Session 10	Journals and Logs: Why, When, and How to use Journals
Session 11	Vocabulary Development
Session 12	A Writing Program—Craft, Process, and Genre
Session 13	A Writing Program and Writers' Workshops
Session 14	Assessment and Evaluation: Portfolios/Rubrics/Grading
Session 15	Film in the Classroom
Session 16	Draft of Philosophy Statement (This will be further discussed and revised next semester.) Portfolio Development: An Update

COURSE REQUIREMENTS

1. *Texts*:

a. (Optional) *English/Language Arts Framework*. California State Department of Education. Although *Issues in English Education* contains information about the framework, I encourage you to purchase your own copy of the entire document.

b. (Required) *Issues in English Education: A Collection of Readings* (at bookstore)

c. (Required) Atwell, N. (1987). *In the Middle: Writing, Reading, and Learning with Adolescents*. Portsmouth NH: Heinemann.

2. *Reflection Log*: A loose-leaf or spiral notebook is probably the best way to keep these writings. On a weekly basis, you will write reflections from your readings. Treat the readings in Atwell and your *Issues in English Education* separately. In other words, whenever you are reading from both texts, write an entry in your Reflection Log for each *set* of readings. Read and then write your reflections. Just sit and write—for approximately 5–7 minutes—reflections that are honest and thoughtful. Please, do not summarize; your instructor has read the readings. The objective is not to tell *what* you read, but to write your *response* to the reading (e.g., your insights, what you found interesting, what was confusing, questions that arose, and so forth). Logs will be used weekly in discussions and will be turned in on Session 15. At the time they are handed in, please (*) two entries you think are particularly interesting or insightful or important for your instructor to read. In addition, she will choose one or two other entries at random to read.

3. *Classroom Action Research*: For this assignment you will become a teacher-researcher. What questions do you have about classrooms, teachers, teaching, learning, learners, etc.? We will brainstorm lists of questions and listen to each other's ideas. Over the first two sessions, the task will be to develop a question that you can research over the course of this semester. Your data collection may occur through observations, interviews, informal surveys, or a combination of methods. You will find at least two articles related to your question and write a short summary of them, including the bibliographic citations. So that others can benefit from what you discovered in relation to your question, in Session 11 you will report your research in the following format briefly to the class: 1) report your question; 2) briefly describe your sample; 3) give a brief description of what you did in your research (how you collected your data and analyzed it); and 4) report your results and conclusions.

The following is an example of a research question that preservice teachers have researched in the past. If you find this question interesting, you can pursue it, alone or in collaboration with others, in which case you would prepare a collaborative report.

Sample Question and Research Methodology

What are students' perceptions of reading and literature and of writing? The first part of this assignment is to find two articles that deal with students' perceptions, interests, attitudes, and motivations regarding reading. Summarize those articles on no more than one page and include the bibliographic citations. This will become part of your research write-up.

The second part of the assignment is to interview six students, preferably all from the same grade level but not necessarily from the same class. You will need to indicate who each student is (e.g., high achievers, average achievers, less effective learners, second language students, etc.) Your Master/Guide Teacher can help you describe your interviewees. I recommend you tape record the interviews so that you can transcribe students' responses accurately. In your interviews include the following questions, adding any others you think are relevant:

Why do we (people in general) read literature?

What has gone on in school to help you become a better reader?

Why do you think writing is important?

What has gone on in school to help you become a better writer?

First, set your interviewees at ease. Do not give them answers. As an interviewer, you may ask such things as "Can you think of anything else?" or "What else do you think about that?" and so forth—only general, encouraging prompts.

The last part of this work is to write up your research. In this write-up, include the article summaries, describe your sample (the students), transcribe their responses (your research results), and then, in no more than two pages, draw conclusions from your interview—conclusions about the students, the curriculum, schooling in general, and so on.

4. *Lesson Plan*: One objective of this course is that you will learn and apply effective ways of making curriculum choices and designing instruction. In Session 16, you are to bring to class a hard copy of the lesson that you have designed and taught. (This write-up is of one lesson, not an entire unit.) Your lesson will be created in the software planning program called PLANalyst, and it will contain the following basic components:

- Rationale for content (Why are you teaching this lesson?)
- Grade level and course for which the lesson is designed
- Materials used
- Lesson objectives
- Anticipatory set
- Instructional sequence (the design of the lesson itself)
- Closure

In addition to developing the lesson in PLANalyst, in no more than two pages include the following: (1) a short explanation of what you did *explicitly* in this lesson to ensure that it addressed the needs of the diverse students in today's classrooms (How was it designed to ensure that all students would be successful?); and (2) a critique of the lesson (Did it work? What would you change next time, and why? What was most and least effective?)

5. *Annotated URL*: Explore one web site relevant to teaching and learning in English/language arts and write a description of that site as an annotation. (See the Appendix explanations and sample URL annotations.) You will present your site to the class during either Session 12 or 13.

6. *Class Participation and Attendance*: Students will be expected to participate actively in all class sessions. You will notice that a portion of each class has been set aside for discussion. These discussions will center on your assigned readings, your classroom experiences, and course content.

GRADING

Attendance and Participation	15 points
Journal	20 points
Classroom Action Research	25 points
Lesson Plan and Presentation	25 points
Annotated URL	15 points
Professional Credit (extra)	3 points

Because of the importance of conferences offered by such organizations as California Reading Association (CRA), Greater San Diego Reading Association (GSDRA), California Teachers of English and others, additional credit will be given for those who attend one or more conferences and who write a short (no more than two pages) summary about that conference.

Performance Standards.   As prospective teachers, specifically teachers of English/language arts, your instructor has high expectations for the level of your literacy skills (literary skills, also, but that's a different matter). What that means for this course is that each assignment will be evaluated according to high standards for oral and written skills. In addition, as responsibility, including timely attention to a variety of significant matters such as posting grades, is a primary requisite for teaching, it is a reasonable expectation of this course that you will meet your commitments as stipulated. It will be possible to get full credit on an assignment only if it is completed as designated in the Requirements section of the syllabus. Credit will not be given for papers handed in after the last class of the semester unless you have negotiated an Incomplete with your instructor.

APPENDIX 9.1:
EXPLANATION OF URL ACTIVITY

I have collected bookmarks for interesting web sites, using my Netscape Navigator 3 web browser. To date, I have collected approximately 75 bookmarks related to teaching English/language arts, school-to-career, interdisciplinary curriculum and instruction, technology in education, and others. I save those bookmarks on a disk and take them into the technology lab, where my students access them, save them to the individual computers in the lab, and also save them to their own disks if they choose to do so. I ask my students to visit several of my bookmarks, which specifically include such sites as those listed here.

Some students may not have experience with using the Internet and "surfing" the Web, so I do a brief tutorial for those students regarding terminology (e.g., URLs, web browser, Internet, web sites, bookmarks, and so forth) and processes of finding information on the Web. I give them a sample URL annotation and ask them to find a site related to the course, to explore the site and some of its links, and then to write a short description (annotation) of it. (See the sample URL annotation for the *English Journal* Homepage.)

Bookmarks Related to Teaching English/Language Arts

http://www.sdcoe.k12.ca.us/score/cyberguide.html
  This site has a wealth of teacher-created "supplementary units of instruction based on core works of literature, designed for students to use on the World Wide Web."
http://www.ucalgary.ca/~dkbrown/awards.html
  This is the site of the Children's Book Awards, described as "the most comprehensive guide to English-language arts children's book awards on the Internet." You will find links to national and international awards, Children's Choice Awards, Best Book of the Year Awards, and others.
http://interact.uoregon.edu/MediaLit/HomePage
  Titled "The Media Literacy Online Project," this site offers numerous links to resources about various media and ideas for helping students achieve media literacy.
http://edweb.sdsu.edu/courses/EDTEC596/edtec596.html
  This is the site of an interdisciplinary course that integrates technology into teaching and learning at middle and secondary levels. Most interesting are links to Course Projects, Final Projects, where interdisciplinary units created by preservice teachers are available.
http://home1.gte.net/patem/yalit/
  This is the "Young Adult Literature Homepage." It offers links to many sites that are intended for teachers and media specialists/librarians (e.g., links to

works by African-American writers, Kathy Schrock's Guide for Educators: Literature, and others, including numerous newsgroups).

SAMPLE URL ANNOTATION
English Journal Homepage
URL: http://DIGIT.soe.vcu.edu/EJ/

This web site offers the latest news from NCTE, what's upcoming in the *English Journal*, and more. At one particular site on this homepage, there is an interesting list of Web sites for English teachers. You can access this list by clicking on the link "Recent *English Journal* Software Columns" and then on "More Internet Resources for the English Teacher."

There is a link to NCTE, where you can find such things as enrollment information for NCTE; journal information; and an overview of the English/language arts standards, which address the question: What should English language arts students know and be able to do? There is a Professional Summary of the standards that gives background on their development, a rationale for having standards, an in-depth discussion of two of the 12 standards, and a classroom scenario. There is also an interesting link to "Teaching Ideas/Resources" that offers sample lessons in the areas of writing, reading and literature, critical thinking, interdisciplinary lessons in language arts, and others.

NOTE: If you are a member of NCTE and not on the NCTE listserv, you might want to join. Send e-mail to the following address:

listproc@itc.org

In the body of the message (Don't put anything in the "subject" line), write

(Your first name) (Your last name) subscribe NCTE-talk

Don't use any parentheses in your message. I just put them to clarify the writing of your first and last names. Warning: You will get lots of e-mail, but you will also get an opportunity to correspond with fellow English teachers and eavesdrop (lurk) on conversations among English language arts types all over the United States.

10

Preservice Secondary Language Arts Teaching Methods[1]

Peter Smagorinsky
University of Georgia

The syllabus included here is the most recent one I have used in the course known as "the methods course" in the secondary English Education program for preservice teachers at the University of Oklahoma. I have taught this class eight times in the last 7 years, with revisions almost every time I have taught it. The iteration of the syllabus that I present here was written during a time of change, being developed during a major program revision, the publication of the NCTE/IRA standards and related books, the completion of a study I helped to do of preservice methods classes (Smagorinsky & Whiting, 1995), and my own continuing efforts to provide a course that both builds on the prior classes and experiences in our departmental program and prepares preservice teachers for happy and successful early career experiences.

Before presenting the syllabus itself, I'd like to review what I feel are the most significant influences on my development of this syllabus (keeping in mind that in a few years it will probably look different): my own background, my methods class study, the programmatic context for the class, and the cultural context our teachers enter.

---

[1]The syllabus described in this chapter was developed when I taught in the English Education program at the University of Oklahoma; my methods course at Georgia has been redesigned to fit with the new programmatic context. Readers are invited to see Web site accompanying this book for a current version of a syllabus he uses when teaching Secondary Language Arts Methods.

PERSONAL BACKGROUND

My own preservice training still strongly influences the way in which I teach the methods class. In 1976 to 1977 I got my MAT from the University of Chicago, studying under George Hillocks. George's program focused on instructional principles that still form the core of my approach to teaching the methods class. In George's methods class, he impressed on us the importance of thinking of instruction in terms of thematically organized units of 4 to 8 weeks. A thematic emphasis, he believed, provided coherence and purpose to instruction and also helped to lay schematic foundations through which students could develop scripts for learning how to read literature. As he stated in the textbook we used, *The Dynamics of English Instruction, Grades 7–12* (Hillocks, McCabe, & McCampbell, 1971), "One of the most important things that any literature unit can do is to provide a conceptual matrix against which the student can examine each new work he reads. Insights into any given work are partly the result of experience in reading others because concepts grow by comparison and contrast" (p. 254). Conceptual growth is at the heart of this approach, facilitated by teacher scaffolding, student activity, and collaborative learning projects. When I completed George's program and began my first job, I was always surprised to hear that the other first-year teachers were staying up past midnight every night trying to figure out what to do the next day. My training in planning extended units always gave me a long-term plan that, while continually being adjusted, never left me wondering where to go or what to do next. Through the methods class, I hope to provide the same conceptual and pedagogical tools I learned from George for the teachers I work with. I try to model these instructional principles through explicit attention to scaffolding, frequent group activities, and instruction designed to provide extended conceptual growth toward a specific end: the development of a thematic unit of instruction that is designed for use during student teaching.

METHODS CLASS STUDY

A few years after I arrived at the University of Oklahoma (OU), I decided to get a better sense of how other people taught the methods class. The idea mushroomed and soon I solicited methods course syllabi from over 300 other universities, ultimately receiving over 80 to study along with Melissa Whiting, at the time a doctoral student and research assistant at OU. We learned quite a bit from seeing how other people organized the course (see Smagorinsky & Whiting, 1995, for the complete study). We were somewhat disheartened to find that a number of people taught the class as a *survey*; that is, as a broad effort to cover a very wide range of teaching issues, inevitably covering each superficially and often assessing students through factual exams. What was especially ironic about such courses was that the textbooks that they used (and tested students on) typically argued *against* broad coverage of surface information and instead stressed conceptual development and constructivist approaches to teaching and learning.

Other course organizations, however, proved to be very informative. In classifying the syllabi we found, in addition to the survey, courses that we called *workshops*, *experience-based*, *theoretical*, and *reflective*. My own course was primarily a workshop, one that set aside significant class time for students to do hands-on work applying concepts from the course readings. My methods class required students to develop a unit of instruction for its main project outside class (with the option of doing it in teams), and much of the in-class work was spent developing additional units under my supervision. The class itself therefore provided experiences of the type that they would go through in developing their own units, thus scaffolding their conceptual understanding of how to think in terms of units. Because the class involved a lot of collaboration and sharing, it also potentially provided each student with a number of units to take out into the field to make their first years of teaching less stressful.

When Melissa and I read the syllabi from the methods class study, we found new ways to make the workshop more effective. In particular, the *experience-based* courses provided an excellent approach that coincided with a programmatic development. Our program had previously required a minimum of 30 hours of field experiences for each of two departmental core courses. Following a program revision, in addition to these 60+ hours of field experiences, each methods class was required to be accompanied by 30 to 40 hours of field observations. The experience-based courses we identified in the study put preservice teachers out into the field for extensive observations, often requiring some sort of field log, case study, or teaching plans to be developed. I borrowed some ideas from these courses and, for the new field experience requirement in my methods class, gave the students a set of options that they could choose from for their field experience assessment. They could develop teaching plans, perhaps in conjunction with their supervising teacher. Or, they could do some sort of study of the classroom through a reflective log, an analysis of the textbooks and how they were taught, a case study of a student or set of students, or other type of classroom analysis. Any of these options would help prepare them for the final requirements of their preservice program: their student teaching and the complementary action research course taken during their ninth semester.

The *theoretical* and *reflective* influences also came into play, though less structurally. Following George's lead, I always tried to provide a theoretical grounding for any teaching methods I presented, using various NCTE Theory and Research Into Practice (TRIP) books over the years (e.g., Kahn, Walters, & Johannessen, 1984) as well as textbooks that had a clear theoretical foundation. The reflective syllabi that we studied made personal reflection the central activity of the class, requiring literacy autobiographies, analyses of personal learning styles, and so forth, as the primary means of assessment. With all of the other course demands, I could not include these assignments in the methods class, although some of the observation logs end up being personally reflective. Instead, I began requiring literacy autobiographies in one of the courses they took during their junior years, the course in the teaching of grammar. Our study of methods classes, then, had a great effect on my methods class syllabus.

PROGRAMMATIC CONTEXT

The program revision made the methods course the official capstone course of the preservice English Education program, taken during the final semester of the senior year. Ideally, the prior coursework would provide a strong foundation for the content area methods classes. The departmental curriculum requires courses in school and culture, computer/media, adolescent psychology, and instructional technology. English Education students, in addition to these departmental courses, begin their program through a course in the teaching of grammar. This class provides background in cultural issues of language development, engagement in a discussion of the politics of standard language, and initial instruction in the development of lesson plans related to language usage. The course also includes a mentoring component in which the students join a student affiliate of NCTE, subscribe to a professional electronic listserve discussion, and become acquainted with professional issues through guest appearances by local teachers. From this course, the students move as a cohort through a class in basic issues in literacy, a class in the teaching of adolescent literature, and then to the methods class, which itself serves as the final preparation for student teaching and the accompanying action research class (both taken for graduate credit).

The movement toward the cohort group and student affiliate are designed to give students a sense of community and continuity that has been missing in the past. Previously, two students could conceivably go through the program at the same time, never meet, and have different professors for key courses. Our goal with the new program is that when they come to the methods class the students will have a common language, similar conceptual understandings, and a cohesion and camaraderie that helps give them a distinct identity as students in our program. Overall, we hope for the program as a whole to provide rigorous instruction and experiences in the discipline that lead to the *shared ordeal* that Lortie (1975) argues provides a professional identity for doctors, lawyers, and other professionals but is lacking among teachers.

CULTURAL CONTEXT

One final consideration in the development of the methods class is attention to the cultural context of teaching. Many of our students leave the university and go out to teach in small, conservative communities. One of our graduates lost her job because during her first year, at a time that American troops were building their forces in Kuwait prior to the Gulf War, she refused to put her hand over her heart during the daily recitation of the Pledge of Allegiance. In the academy, we can easily become insulated from the values of many of the communities that we send our graduates out to teach in; university professors are rarely natives of the areas in which they teach and often espouse a more liberal and relatively radical philosophy than would sit well with local residents. Our program stresses student-, response-, and activity-oriented methods and inclusive attitudes towards diverse students. Yet, our students often find when they interview that local school administrators take a dim view of our progressive ideals, believing that real education begins through experience in the real world of schools.

The methods course is attentive to the situations that students will find themselves in and urges students to contextualize their instruction so that it approximates the instruction that they might ultimately provide. For instance, several earnest, high-minded, methods class students were designing instruction centered on the theme of war and peace, with their literary selections all having an antimilitary theme. We discussed what would happen if they taught this unit in the community where the teacher lost her job during the Gulf War, a community that included a great number of proud and patriotic military veterans who were highly respected citizens due to their honorable service to their country. The discussion helped the students see the political stance behind their literary selections and the disrespect it would show to the parents, siblings, and other relatives of many of their students. Adjusting instructional decisions to specific school settings is a critical lesson learned in the course.

THE SYLLABUS

Following is the syllabus I used in the spring, 1997 methods class, taking into account these various influences. One thing I should point out is that I use several texts that I have written. Using my own books has both advantages and disadvantages. On the positive side, the students get a pretty clear idea of how I see things and so there's little ambiguity about the values behind my classes. I also write my practice-oriented pieces so that they will work well in methods classes, and so they tend to match my own approach to the course pretty well. On the negative side, students are reluctant to be critical of my books when we discuss them, so the discussions probably lack the edge they might have in someone else's class. I am not sure where the best solution to this problem lies.

For this course, I start out with two books from the NCTE Standards in Practice series, one for middle school and one for high school. These books acquaint students with the issue of standards, illustrate the distinction between the middle school and high school models of curriculum and faculty structure, illustrate how teachers adapt to local contingencies, and provide an abundance of practical teaching ideas. The Beach and Marshall book serves as the source for designing thematic units of instruction and occupies several weeks of the course. Other books then deal with issues of multiple intelligences, classroom discourse, and vocabulary instruction, all of which fit within the thematic units that the students design. As noted, the class is taught to model the instruction that it advocates, and for the most part students say that it works in that regard.

REFERENCES

Hillocks, G., McCabe, B. J., & McCampbell, J. F. (1971). *The dynamics of English instruction, grades 7–11*. New York: Random House.

Kahn, E., Walters, C., & Johannessen, L. (1984). *Writing about literature*. Urbana, IL: National Council of Teachers of English.

Lortie, D. C. (1975). *Schoolteacher: A sociological study*. Chicago: University of Chicago Press.

Smagorinsky, P., & Whiting, M. E. (1995). *How English teachers get taught: Methods of teaching the methods class*. Urbana, IL: Conference on English Education and National Council of Teachers of English.

Sample Syllabus
Teaching English in the High School:
English Education Capstone Course

Texts

Beach, R., & Marshall, J. (1991). *Teaching literature in the secondary school*. San Diego: Harcourt Brace Jovanovich.

Marshall, J. D., Smagorinsky, P., & Smith, M. W. (1995). *The language of interpretation: Patterns of discourse in discussions of literature*. NCTE Research Report No. 27. Urbana, IL: National Council of Teachers of English.

Nagy, W. E. (1988). *Teaching vocabulary to improve reading comprehension*. Urbana, IL, and Newark, DE: National Council of Teachers of English and International Reading Association.

Smagorinsky, P. (1991). *Expressions: Multiple intelligences in the English class*. Urbana, IL: National Council of Teachers of English.

Smagorinsky, P. (1996). *Standards in practice, grades 9–12*. Urbana, IL: National Council of Teachers of English.

Wilhelm, J. (1996). *Standards in practice, grades 6–8*. Urbana, IL: National Council of Teachers of English.

Course Projects

You are responsible for completing one project (with the option of a second) from the coursework and readings, and one from your field experience. Following are descriptions of each project.

    Project 1A.   Either individually or in collaboration with one other student, you will prepare a teaching unit encompassing about 6 to 8 weeks to be used in student teaching. The unit will organize literature around some specific theme or principle and be derived from theories of learning and teaching. The unit will include:

1. Rationale
2. Objectives/Competencies/Outcomes
3. Materials
4. Specific lessons and activities
5. Means of evaluation through several types of intelligence

The unit should allow for a variety of means of expression, including writing, and other activities such as oral work, art, dance, film-making and whatever else you feel will promote understanding. The lessons in the unit should enable students to learn to construct meaning in subsequent independent undertakings.

The development of this unit will parallel the issues explored as the course progresses.

Project 1B.   This class is designed as a workshop to teach you how to satisfy Project 1A's requirements. The class sessions themselves will engage you regularly with a group of 3 to 4 students of fixed membership. (You will select your own group mates.) With this group you will develop a unit of instruction meeting the same requirements as those of the unit you design for Objective 1A. The unit you develop in class will be different, however, in that its primary intent is to provide you a supportive environment in which to learn how to plan instruction under risk-conducive conditions.

Field Experience

You may do one of the following projects to synthesize what you learn during your field experience.

1. Keep a log of your impressions during your field experience. This log should be a serious, detailed effort to relate what you observe in the school classroom to what you learn about teaching through the course readings and class discussions.
2. Conduct a focused study of one student, or a small set of students in the class you observe.
3. If you are observing more than one teacher—or if you are observing one teacher teaching two very different types of classes—write an analysis of the two types of teaching you observe.
4. Contrast the teaching and learning you observe in the classroom with the teaching and learning you have observed in another setting, such as a sport, an extracurricular activity, a university class, an out-of-school setting such as church or work, or other learning environment.
5. Conduct a rigorous critique of the teaching materials used by the teacher.
6. Other project of your choice, with my approval.

11

Oral and Written Communication[1]

Peggy Albers
Georgia State University

Oral and written communication is a masters' level course that examines current theories, research, and instructional practices pertaining to teaching and assessment of oral and written communication skills. In particular, this course emphasizes the ways that talking and writing contribute to learning in middle level classrooms. This is an elective offered in our language and literacy program for students who are working toward a reading specialist and/or literacy masters' degree. Many of the students who enroll in this course are practicing teachers who bring their classroom experiences into their understanding and analysis of the course readings and demonstrations.

I joined the GSU faculty in January, 1997, and EDLA 746 "Oral and Written Communication for Middle Childhood Education" was the first course that I taught at this inner-city university. Several issues factored into my construction of this course. First, I wondered whether the ideas I had used in my undergraduate classes at Indiana University would be of interest to and could be applied to Atlanta city classrooms. Second, I did not know my future students, their knowledge of holistic reading and writing theory, and the level of discussion I could expect. And, third, I hoped that the assignments that I chose would be of use to teachers in their classrooms. With these considerations, I selected books that I believed offered insights into teaching writing at all levels, were firmly grounded in theory, and also offered

---

[1]This course was developed for the quarter system. Our Reading, Language, and Literacy Education coursework was recently redesigned when our university moved to a semester system.

insights into the writing and oral communication needs of middle school students. Although this course focuses on middle school literacy, I wanted my master's students to think beyond just their present middle school classrooms and understand how these strategies could work with older students. As a former middle and high school teacher, I understand that it is important for students to develop good strategies as they deal with more complex text structures and content material.

For me, the interplay of theory, practice, and beliefs is essential. Yet, I always wonder if the strategies we work through will offer students ways to work with their own and others' texts. As such, I continue to emphasize the connections between reading and writing in middle school literacy classes. Several questions were instrumental in my development of this course: How can middle school students identify text structures and work these structures in their own writing? Why do middle school students need to communicate through writing? How can I offer assignments that encourage teachers to think about themselves as researchers of literacy within their own classrooms? In what ways does offering teachers the authoring cycle as a curricular framework (Short, Harste, & Burke, 1996) help them envision new ways to work with oral and written language? How do multiple sign systems offer us different insights into the communication of students?

My reading lists are often quite extensive yet, I believe, helpful in working with ideas for middle school students. Since my students are often practicing teachers, I try to choose professional texts that revolve around the classrooms and stories of teachers. This is why I chose *Seeking Diversity* by Linda Rief (1992) and *Cycles of Meaning* edited by Kathryn Mitchell Pierce and Carol Gilles (1993). Both of these books are firmly grounded in a holistic theory of learning and are centered in real classrooms. These books also contain a number of good examples of students' writing and conversations. My teachers are able to connect with the stories of these teachers, and often draw from their own experiences to extend their meanings of the text. Along with several primary texts, I create a reader of current journal articles that deal with the issues raised in these texts or deal with the issues that my students face in their classrooms here in Atlanta. I particularly like articles that address sociopolitical issues concerning gender, ethnicity, class and sexual orientation. Readings that I often use are written by authors such as Pam Gilbert (1994), Valerie Walkerdine (1991), Georgia Collins (1995), Maxine Greene (1995), Mary Dilg (1995), Myra and David Sadker (1994), Patrick Shannon (1993), Lisa Delpit (1995), Maureen Barbieri (1995), Roger Simon (1992), Donald Arnstine (1995), and Deborah Britzman (1991).

When I construct assignments for my classes, I try to work with the interests of my students. Operating from an inquiry background, I ask my teachers to become teacher–researchers and conduct a mini-study in their own classroom or a different classroom. Their mini-study is focused on a question that they feel passionate about and can be completed within the term. I offer my teachers extensive freedom in their interpretation of this mini-study in order for them to think through the number of ways they could explain their findings. Several of the inquiry questions arising from this course included a gendered perspective on how middle school students choose novels to read, using art as a prewriting strategy, analyzing middle school students' journals in terms of gender, exploring students' responses to Spinelli' (1990) *Maniac Magee*, examining systematic phonics as a way to teach young children to read, and analyzing students' written responses to an abstract math problem. Even though these mini-studies were time-consuming, my teachers found this experience to be very beneficial. Because this is a course that emphasizes how writing and talking influence learning, I also have my teachers write responses to the various readings, and be responsible for conducting the discussions for a particular night's readings. In this way, my teachers get a sense of how to encourage their own students to write and engage in thoughtful conversations.

I believe that my first attempt at teaching this course was successful. Teachers learned more about other teachers' ideas and strategies for working with oral and written communication, engaged in interesting and thought-provoking discussions about literacy and middle school students, and explored and wrote up an issue in-depth. Here is my syllabus for oral and written communication for middle childhood education.

REFERENCES

Arnstine, D. (1995). *Democracy and the arts of schooling*. New York: SUNY.

Barbieri, M. (1995). *Sounds from the heart: Listening to girls listen to girls*. Portsmouth, NH: Heinemann.

Britzman, D. (1991). *Practice makes practice: A critical study of learning to teach*. Albany, NY: SUNY.

Collins, G. (1995). Art education as a negative example of gender-enriching curriculum. In J. Gaskell & J. Willinsky (Eds.), *Gender in/forms curriculum: From enrichment to transformation* (pp. 43–58). New York: Teacher's College Press.

Delpit, L. (1995). *Other people's children*. New York: The New Press.

Dilg, M. (1995). The opening of the American mind: Challenges in the cross-cultural teaching of literature. *English Journal, 84*(3), 18–25.

Gilbert, P., & Taylor, S. (1991). *Fashioning the feminine: Girls, popular culture and schooling*. Sydney: Allen & Unwin Pty Ltd.

Gilbert, P. (1994). 'And they lived happily ever after': Cultural storylines and the construction of gender. In A. H. Dyson & C. Genishi (Eds.), *The need for story: Cultural diversity in classroom and community* (pp. 124–142). Urbana, IL: National Council of Teachers of English.

Graves, D. (1994). *A fresh look at writing*. Portsmouth, NH: Heinemann.

Greene, M. (1995). *Releasing the imagination*. San Francisco: Jossey-Bass Publishers.

Mitchell Pierce, K., & Gilles, C. (1993). *Cycles of meaning: Exploring the potential of talk in learning communities*. Portsmouth, NH: Heinemann.

Murray, D. (1984). *Write to learn*. New York: Holt, Rinehart and Winston.

Rief, L. (1992). *Seeking diversity*. Portsmouth, NH: Heinemann.

Romano, T. (1987). *Clearing the way*. Portsmouth, NH: Heinemann.

Romano, T. (1995). *Writing with passion: Life stories, multiple genres*. Portsmouth, NH: Boynton Cook.

Rosenblatt, L. (1991). Literature—S.O.S.! *Language Arts, 68*, 444–448.

Sadker, D., & Sadker, M. (1994). *Failing at fairness: How our schools cheat girls*. New York: Simon and Schuster.

Shannon, P. (1993). Developing democratic voices. *The Reading Teacher, 47*, 86–95.

Short, K. G., Harste, J. C., & Burke, C. (1996). *Creating classrooms for authors and inquirers*. Portsmouth, NH: Heinemann.

Simon, R. (1992). *Teaching against the grain: Texts for a pedagogy of possibility*. New York: Bergin and Garvey.

Spinelli, J. (1990). *Maniac Magee*. New York: Scholastic.

Walkerdine, V. (1991). *Schoolgirl fictions*. New York: Verso.

Sample Syllabus

Required Textbook/Materials

Seeking Diversity—Linda Rief (1992)
Cycles of Meaning—Mitchell Pierce, Gilles (1993)
Packet of readings; readings on reserve.

Communication

Everyone in this class will need to get an e-mail account (if you do not have one already) as there may be several e-mail assignments throughout the quarter. I will also explain further assignments that are due throughout the course. The best way to reach me is through e-mail as I check my e-mail several times per day.

On Being Successful In This Course

The demands of this course are quite extensive, so it is imperative that you keep up with the readings and the work. In class, writings concerning the readings will be a matter of course, so preparedness to talk about them is essential. The readings are both from academic journals as well as original artifacts from middle school students. Also, keep thinking interdisciplinarily as we know that knowledge domains intersect in synchronicity and naturally.

Course Aims

This course is designed to help you:

1. Gain an insight into understanding of written and oral communication theory, pedagogy, and practice.
2. Demonstrate strategies for effective independent learning in the classroom and beyond.
3. Reflect on own development as a writer, researcher, and communicator.
4. Gain insight into adolescence through written and oral communication theory, pedagogy, and practice.

Class Format

The class will take on this format on most days:

Time Allotted	Class Experiences
1 hour	Work with partners on writing (authoring cyle)
1 hour	Discussion of readings
30 minutes	Break
90 minutes	Demonstrations/Invitations
30 minutes	Reflection

Readings & Assignments

The course syllabus provides a general plan for the course. We may need to alter these assignments. As such, the instructor may ask you at times to complete other assignments that may not appear directly on this syllabus.)

Session 1: New Beginnings, New Connections

Introductions, course description. What are our assumptions about teaching written and oral communication? What is the nature of and what constitutes classroom discourse? Introduction of the authoring cycle. Discussion of early literacy experiences followed by an explanation of literacy biographies. Perusal of professional texts/materials concerning the philosophy, pedagogy, and practice of communication. Discussion of course assignments. Sign up for book presentations.

Session 2: Reading/Writing Connection

Readings:
"Consider Your Roots"; Graves (1994)
"Learning While Writing"; Murray (1984)
"Truth Through Narrative"; "Truth, Risk, and Passion";
Romano (1995)
"Using Writing"; Romano (1987)

Session 3: The Big Picture of Writing

1. Reading Stances—Aesthetic/Efferent
    Readings:
    "Literature—S.O.S.!"; Rosenblatt (1991)
    Two reader stances; The big picture; Big idea #1; Reader/writer transactive processes; Changing dynamics of r/w transaction
2. Text Structures: Hierarchy of Ideas (HOI)
    Readings:
    (Newspaper Articles)
    "No Way Out"

"Family Values"
"Town Struggles to Come to Terms With Dead Teen's Life"
"The Richter Scale"
Hierarchy of ideas; Creating HOI; Blueprint; General/specific; Generalization format; Recommendation

3. Text Structures: Opinion/Reason/Recommendation (ORR)
    Readings:
        (Newspaper articles)
        "Weeds Can Become Flowers"
        "In Praise of Uniforms"
        "Brutality as a Teen Fashion Statement"
        "Classic"—cigarette ad
    Using ORR pattern

4. Text Structures: Problem/Effect/Cause/Solution (PECS)
    Readings:
        (Newspaper Articles)
        "Killer Balloons"
        "Steroids the Rage in High School"
        "Teen Crimes Must Result in Tough Terms"
        "Dealing With Deadly Mix of Teenagers and Alcohol"
        "Code of Silence"
    Have title of professional book chosen today.

Session 4: Enacting Writing in Classrooms

Readings:
Seeking Diversity, Rief (1992) Ch. 2, 3, 6, 7, 8
Literacy Autobiographies Due

Session 5: Markers of Difference

Readings:
Fashioning the Feminine; Gilbert & Taylor, Ch. 2, 5 (1991)
"'And They Lived Happily Ever After'"; Gilbert (1994); "Sometimes I Wish: Figuring Out What Matters Most"; Barbieri, Ch. 2 (1995)
"The Opening of the Mind"; Dilg (1995)
Failing at Fairness: How America's Schools Cheat Girls; Sadker & Sadker (1994)

Session 6: The Importance of Classroom Talk

Readings:
Literature Circles (video)
Written transcripts of students' talk about literature (Ledbetter/Albers—Research in progress)
Cycles of Meaning—Mitchell Pierce & Gilles (1993)—Ch. 1

Session 7: Talk, Community, and Democracy

Readings:
Cycles of Meaning—Mitchell Pierce & Gilles (1993) Ch. 4, 6
Book Presentations (3)

Session 8: Talk, Inquiry, and Evaluation

Readings:
Cycles of Meaning—Mitchell Pierce & Gilles (1993) Ch. 9, 11, 17
Book Presentations (4)

Session 9: Framing the Whole Picture

Presentation of inquiry projects to colleagues.
Inquiry Project Due

Assessment

Final grades will be based on the points earned through completion of the following:

	Grading Scale
Class Participation/Discussion of Weekly Topics:	20
Literacy Autobiography	20
Inquiry Project	40
Professional Book Review/Presentation	20

Guidelines for Grades

A Extraordinarily high achievement; shows unusually complete command of the course content and exceptionally high degree of originality and/or scholarship

B Very good work; above average in performance and comprehension

C Not wholly satisfactory; marginal performance on several aspects of the course

D Unacceptable work; performance or comprehension falls substantially

F Wholly unacceptable; little or no command of the course content

To receive a range of "A" in this course, you must read all assignments and contribute to weekly class discussion; complete all assignments on time; demonstrate thorough understanding of basic concepts presented in the readings; complete all assignments professionally, consciously integrating the concepts of the readings and discussion in your writing as well as outside sources.

To receive a range of "B" in this course, you must read all assignments and contribute to weekly class discussion; complete all assignments on time; demonstrate solid understanding of basic concepts presented in the readings; complete all assignments professionally, often integrating the concepts of the readings and discussion in your writing.

To receive a range of "C" in this course, you read many of the assignments and contribute often in class discussion; complete all assignments on time; demonstrate basic understanding of concepts presented in the readings; complete most assignments professionally, often integrating the concepts of the readings and discussion in your writing.

Description of Activities/Assignments

On Being Professional/Class Participation/Discussion of Weekly Topics.   All work turned in for this course should be of professional level quality and polished (i.e., typed, proofread for clarity and mechanics). As professionals, strive to meet class responsibilities on time; be active in class discussions. All assignments must draw on the main concepts in the readings. You should demonstrate evidence that you understand the authors' main points and should be fluent in discussing these points. When writing papers, use either APA/MLA style. Attendance is required as our demonstrations directly relate to the readings. Your thoughtful contributions are valuable as we strive toward becoming a community of learners. 20 points.

Literacy Autobiography.   To better understand the literacy development of middle school students, our reflection on our own early and present literacy experiences is valuable. In this assignment, you will develop a history of your own literacy learning. You might ask yourself such questions as, "What written and oral language experiences, both in and out of school, do I remember?", "Why do I remember these?", "What constitutes good writing and talk?" On Day 1, we will create several themes together that focus on what is expected from this autobiography. 20 points.

Inquiry Project.   This assignment asks that you decide on an area of interest (within the course topic) that you want to investigate in more depth. You should think about conducting a mini-study in which you analyze original research and write it up as a professional article of about 10 to 15 pages. Throughout this course, we will meet weekly in partners/small groups, work through the authoring cycle as a way to help sort out research questions, share information, talk about data collected and your analysis, and how to write up the research. On Day 1, we will discuss possibilities for research questions. 40 points.

Book Review on a Professional Book.   You are asked to choose a professional book that interests you, read it, critique it, and then present a summary and recommendation of the book to your colleagues. For examples of book reviews, consult any of the various professional literacy journals. 20 points.

12

Teaching of Writing
as Story[1]

David Schaafsma
University of Illinois at Chicago

The "course" described here—which is really a two-course, simultaneously taught, "sequence"—is one that is required within the Secondary (6–12) English Education Master of Arts with certification program at Teachers College, Columbia University. The course has been taught by me and several others over the past several years in various ways. I think we can all say that each of our versions of the course is evolving, and is never taught the same way from year to year, though we all have certain principles we hope to aspire to in our courses. So, the course described here is one instance of its being taught by me, in terms of my own emerging notions about writing and teaching writing.

Several years ago Teaching of Writing/Writing Workshop (TW/WW) had been designed as two separate but related courses, each taught by different teachers, with *The Theory* being taught in Teaching of Writing, and *Practice* in writing being taught—presumably, enacting the theory—in the Writing Workshop course, but over time the strict separation of theory and practice has largely been abandoned, and the two courses have been combined. In other words, in a course that has traditionally been conceived as practice-based, like a writing course—and we have several content-based courses in writing and literature in this program—we always make room for talk for discussions of theoretical issues, and discussions, too, about how one can enact such practices in public school classrooms.

---

[1] This chapter describes a course I taught while on the faculty at Teachers College, Columbia University.

One of the historical sources for this course is the model proposed by the National Writing Project, which encourages teachers of writing to also be writers. In other words, we feel that "prospective" teachers of writing—who in our program are also in-service teachers in both fall and spring semesters—should have the opportunity to read into various theories of teaching writing, but they must also take the opportunity to practice writing themselves, struggle with it as they expect their students to do. Also following the NWP model in principle, this course expects teachers to create demonstrations based on their expertise—in this case, projects based on their own self- or group-chosen inquiry—to be shared with their colleagues.

I also try to model being a reflective practitioner in the course (Gere, Fairbanks, Howes, Roop, & Schaafsma, 1992; Vinz, 1997). I regularly interrupt classroom discussions or activities to open up critique of the decisions I have made as a teacher, or to question the assumptions behind my actions. I write letters to the students on a weekly basis about the previous classes and my perceptions about them, and invite them to reflect on the process of the course's development, as well. I have regular email contact with many of the students through a campus listserve, and keep a kind of running "dialogue" journal with them through my weekly response to their papers. I invite them to teacher research their teaching as I do.

One goal of the course as I see it is to model a workshop setting where assumptions about various approaches to writing can be interrogated. I try to get them to question their own assumptions even as I—as much as I can—question my own assumptions with them. The texts themselves from this past year give some indication of that grappling with assumptions. I often start with some very useful curricular work on workshop issues like Nancie Atwell's (1987) *In the Middle* (which as far as I can tell is still the best description of a workshop based classroom, and one I still strongly support in many respects), and then throughout the course "deconstruct" that narrative of a workshop classroom through explicit (i.e., reviews) and implicit critiques of the Atwell–Calkins–Graves model. We read works such as Patti Stock's (1995) *The Dialogic Curriculum* that takes a more social and cultural community-based approach to literacy, and work by Lisa Delpit, Tim Lensmire, and Linda Brodkey from critical and/or postmodern perspectives to help us question our assumptions about the naturalness of certain workshop/process approaches that may ignore issues of difference.

In this course, I attempt another kind of modeling: I try to enact some kind of balance between my own purposes and theirs; in other words, I negotiate the curriculum (Boomer, et al., 1992) with them to a certain extent, acknowledging that curriculum is never enacted without students, even when you think it is (Stock, 1995). My intention, although making my own political basis for literacy instruction clear, is to help them become the best teachers of literacy they want to be, in keeping with a range of philosophical perspectives. In other words, although I think it is responsible for me to share my perspectives and experiences, I do not think it is ethical to approach students as potential carbon copies of me. I help them develop their own theories of teaching writing and practices consistent with those theories (Gere et al., 1992). I try as much as possible to enact (a college version of) an inquiry-based curriculum, where students have the opportunity to read and write and research on topics of their own choosing. As in other courses I have taught for several years, my tendency is to interrogate theory–practice connections on issues of curricular authority.

One dimension of a recent version of the course that is also a less-negotiated demonstration of my philosophy: This time, I developed the invitations dimension of the course around the theme of storytelling; both Atwell and Stock take up this focus explicitly in their work, and the novels I chose were also consistent with that focus. It was my hope that my story frame in this particular version of the course would demonstrate how a "student-centered" course design—one of the primary intentions of which is to honor student needs/choices—can incorporate certain kinds of "teacher-directed" notions or perspectives. The story theme as a teacher-named frame for inquiry-based work (see Stock, 1995) can be a particularly useful one for allowing for student project ideas—their various stories—to emerge, in my experience. The story frame—a crucial dimension of my theory for teaching writing—leads me to a variety of ideas for practice consistent with my theory, including oral history, writing stories from photographs, writing stories from literature, writing stories about health issues (connected to the Write for Your Life project I have co-directed), writing stories about home, dreams, and social concerns.

The privileging of narrative in this course obviously led me to do less work with other forms and genres, although the syllabus that follows reveals discussions about argumentation and persuasion and other forms prospective teachers are required to teach in school, with essays included by theorists such as Paul Heilker and Stephen Toulmin. We have several courses in our program where students can focus on writing and the teaching of writing, so I feel fortunate not to have to do everything in this one course.

REFERENCES

Atwell, N. (1987). *In the middle: Writing, reading and learning with adolescents.* Portsmouth, NH: Heinemann.

Boomer, G., Lester, N., Onore, C., & Cook, J. (1992). London: Falmer.

Gere, A., Fairbanks, C., Howes, A., Roop, L., & Schaafsma, D. (1992). *Language and reflection: Integrated approach to teaching English.* New York: MacMillan.

Stock, P. L. (1995). *The dialogic curriculum.* Portsmouth, NH: Heinemann.

Vinz, R. (1997). *Composing a teaching life.* Portsmouth, NH: Heinemann.

Sample Syllabus
Teaching of Writing as Story
Secondary English (9–12) Two-course block

Required Texts

Atwell, Nancie. (1987). *In the middle: Writing, reading and learning with adolescents.* Portsmouth, NH: Heinemann.

Stock, Patricia Lambert. (1995). *The dialogic curriculum*. Portsmouth, NH: Heinemann.
     Occasional handouts, selected essays from Lensmire, Brodkey, Delpit, and many others.
     Your own writing and the writing of your peers.
     And two of the following books:
Cisneros, Sandra. (1989). *The house on Mango Street*. New York: Vintage.
Grimsley, Jim. (1994). *Winter birds*. New York: Scribner.
Sapphire. (1996). *Push*. New York: Vintage.
Diaz, Junot. (1996). *Drown*. New York: Riverhead.

Recommended Texts

Lamott, Anne. (1995). *Bird by bird: Some instructions on writing and life*. New York: Doubleday.
Weaver, Constance. (1996). *Grammar in context*. Portsmouth: Heinemann.

Course Description

As prospective English teachers, you already know a great deal about writing, about general issues of teaching and learning, and the teaching of writing in particular. Research seems to indicate that what you know from your own writing and classroom experiences has the greatest influence on the kind of teacher you will become. Many of you already have some pretty strong ideas about what a successful classroom or successful writer should be. Rather than assume you know nothing, and simply attempt to lecture my ideas into your heads, I hope to draw on what you know, and what you have experienced and will experience throughout this semester (in your own classroom teaching/observing experience) in shaping our class activities. One of the ways we can continue to think about the teaching of writing is to write, and talk about that writing, and the process of writing what we have written.

I propose that we begin writing by telling and writing stories, stories about ourselves and others, including your stories of yourselves as writers, students, and teachers, if that makes sense to you. I hope through this sharing we will begin to get to know each other, begin to develop a classroom community, and learn to share knowledge with each other. I believe that both explicitly and implicitly the stories we tell will begin to reveal what we believe and value about the world, and the world of teaching of writing, too. From there, we will begin to read what others have written, and we will begin to share stories from our own experiences in the schools, from our observations, our interactions with students, and our own teaching. The basis of this approach is that we learn from sharing the stories we have about our experiences, and these stories can in part form the basis of learning about teaching.

We intend by fusing these two courses together in this program to suggest the close relationship between writing and the teaching of writing. Or to put it more specifically: We think that teachers of writing should also be writers. By that, I do not mean that one necessarily has to be an excellent writer to be a teacher of writing, but I do think one should be able to do the tasks one asks students to do, and (possibly) reveal that you have struggled and continue to struggle as one who uses writing to make sense of the world. A way I have already suggested we might approach our writing is through the lens of story, stories of ourselves, of others, of our students, of our classrooms. Soon, we will see how various teachers (Atwell, Stock) in a variety of frameworks have worked with the storytelling and story writing to develop their writing (and reading) curricula.

The story framework we will work with here is grounded in theory that would (I hope) gradually be evident, but I will also from time to time (in meta-analytical classtime breaks and letters I write you) reveal how the practice is grounded in theory (or theories). The books I have chosen (with Tony Tendero, who is teaching a similar version of this course) have been carefully considered in terms of our shared beliefs, and over time I think you have a right to know what those beliefs are. I hope that in turn you will be able to explain your own beliefs and practices to your students (and their parents, and your colleagues, and your administration). I believe it is important to say why we do what we do. I believe that teachers reveal through their practice what they believe about the way literacy is best learned and the way knowledge is best constructed by the things they choose to have students do. I think the more we say it and see how what we say matches with what we do, the more we will grow (this some folks call meta-cognition, and I believe it is as important for teachers like you and me as it is for students). I also think it is important for all of us to challenge each other on the assumptions we bring to our teaching, so I hope you will fee comfortable challenging my assumptions—including my assumptions imbedded in this syllabus about the viability of using a story approach to teach writing, for instance—as I challenge yours.

I believe you need the opportunity to write and revise and edit and publish together as writers sometimes work together in workshop fashion in this class, and I also believe you need the opportunity to develop and articulate a theory (*why*) you will teach in particular ways, and then develop strategies (*what* and *how*) consistent with what you believe. Along the way, I promise I will help you discover resources for creating the kind of classroom you believe is right. I will of course have strong opinions in terms of my beliefs about classrooms, and share what I think are great ideas for many students, but I am not about trying to mold you into images of myself.

In other words, I hope this class will not be very typical, reshaping itself to some extent according to your needs, and providing you with resources to help you develop into the teacher you would most like to be. Although I hope it will be obvious that I have thought long and hard about what this course should look like, based on our experiences as writers and teachers of writing, I feel very strongly that we have to negotiate to some extent what will happen during this semester. I will make several assignments in reading and writing; try to do these as you can, but also try to make the course what you need. Let me and your classmates know what issues you would like to address, what work you feel would be most useful. If you do not want to do an assignment, tell me what you would rather do. In this fashion I am trying to model a way of teaching and learning that you might consider, a way that positions the teacher as a resource, yet one that is willing to shift stream to some extent as the situation requires.

My goal in this course is to look more specifically at what it means to be a writer and teacher of writing today: not only the practical concerns of how to run a class, but also ethical and theoretical considerations. No doubt that, as you who are just beginning this program also begin your student teaching, you are more than a little apprehensive about the day-to-day issues of how to run a class, such concerns as turning lesson plans into reality, evaluating and commenting on student papers, or putting forth the kind of person that will inspire your students to learn. My belief is that in order to make sense of any possible practical concerns, you must consider theoretical perspectives, or why you would do what you do. Thus, in this class we will look carefully at theory/practice connections: developing and shaping our beliefs about literacy and language learning, so that our classroom practice will be consistent with what we believe.

Course Requirements

Individual grades on work will not be given during the semester (although I promise lots of feedback on your work, in process and on final products). On the final day of the semester (and also halfway, in "draft" fashion), you will hand in a portfolio of work you have completed during the semester, including a letter evaluating yourself according to criteria you in part, create for and in terms of yourself. Ultimately, I do have to grade each of you during this term, but I invite you to join me in this process.

1. Daily reading and writing assignments
2. Participation in large and small group class discussions. I do not mean you get a higher grade for talking more than anyone else in these discussions. I do believe quiet listening is (sometimes? often, for some of us?) a form of participation. Small group participation may be more comfortable than large group participation for some of you. We can work on defining *participation* together.
3. Regular attendance (I will lower your grade by half a letter grade if you miss more than two evenings (8 hours!), and if you miss twice that many, I will lower your grade accordingly. Although this may seem inconsistent with what I said above about treating you like a professional, it is my goal to create a productive, supportive, learning community, and for that to exist, I think we all have to be here as much as possible. I really take this semester—and particularly this class—seriously, and I strongly encourage you to do the same. If you cannot be in class, please call me and let me know.

4. A few short papers; well, to be honest, you will be writing several papers during this semester, some of them short, and some of them long, three or four of which we will ask you to bring to final, or polished state for your portfolio.

5. A portfolio of your work from the semester, including a collection of writing and a teaching of writing project (could be action research, library research, teaching philosophy, or discuss options with me).

6. A letter evaluating your portfolio and your work in this course.

Schedule (Always Tentative, Flexible, Negotiable, Co-Composed)

Week 1: Telling/Writing Our Own Stories

Class Activities. Introductions: Writing stories about ourselves/Getting to know each other: community-building and sharing our stories/Large and small group and paired discussions about writing and teaching of writing, various theories and practices that we have encountered in our classroom histories, and the relationship between essay and story, reading, and writing.

Invitations for Next Time. Write about yourself as writer/metaphor for teaching writing/Write about how your views of writing and teaching writing relate/Read the first three chapters from Atwell on writing, and make a one-page dialogic notebook response/Open writing topic: Write about what you most want to/need to.

Week 2: Atwell's Writing Classroom Stories

Class Activities. Large group discussion of the first three chapters of Atwell—her theory and practice, reading–writing connections, grammar/"Fishbowl" demonstration of responding to one student's piece/Large group discussion on productive response/Small group discussion of writing and teaching of writing pieces.

Invitations. One-page response to Atwell, chapters 4 to 6/Read one of the novels, 2 to 3 page dialogic notebook response/New or continuing piece, with three copies for peer response.

Week 3: Fall Retreat

In our certification program, we have a 2 to 3 day fall retreat that coincides with the meetings of various classes, including the teaching of writing. It is an opportunity to read, write, and talk about connections across courses that we hope they will continue to discover throughout their year or more with us. There is an important community-building function that is served by this retreat, too, our modeling a principle we hope gets enacted in various ways in prospective teachers' English classrooms. In their evaluations of this program and individual classes, the importance of the retreat for helping us broaden the role of what constitutes teaching and learning cannot be ignored.

One of the activities in which students were involved at the retreat was reading growing up stories; reader-response invitations included our own growing-up stories. There was also writing-on-location about the (beautiful, seaside Madison, CT) retreat site and plenty of other analytical and narrative reading and writing options during the 2-day stay.

Week 4: Stories of the Past: Novels and Memoirs

Class Activities.   Fast-write/Small group novel discussion groups/Large group discussion of issues in writing fiction and memoir/Group share of a couple student pieces/Writing groups.

Invitations.   Memoir and/or fiction piece, possibly in terms of issues raised in the novel you read/Bring photographs/Continuing piece.

Week 5: The Stories Photographs Tell

Class activities.   Discussion of Atwell chapters 4 to 6/Writing from photographs/Fishbowl on responding to texts (a few other ways)/Writing groups.

Invitations.   Early course evaluation/Photo piece/Read Stock, chapter one/Continuing piece.

Week 6: The Stories We Tell About the Stories Other People Tell

Class Activities.   Oral History presentation (based on community-based oral history writing projects in which I have been involved), viewing Marian Mohr's "From Snake Hill to Spring Bank" (video on classroom use of oral history)/Large group discussion of Stock, chapter 1 (which in part focuses on using interviewing as a basis for writing), including discussions of inquiry-based, negotiated, and dialogic curricula, revision/Writing groups/Group share.

Invitations.   Interview, transcribe, and create piece, or reinvent your continuing piece in terms of oral history information/A letter, compare-contrast essay, story, or whatever you wish to the remainder of *The Dialogic Curriculum.*

Week 7: Stock's Writing Classroom Stories

Class Activities. Whole/small group discussion of Stock/Whole group fishbowl discussion response to one or two pieces/Small group discussions of student work/Large group discussions of teaching of writing projects.

Invitations. Proposal for teaching of writing research project/Midterm self-evaluations–portfolio progress report/Read *Our so- called teen years: Stories about teenage pregnancy from the Bronx*, classroom writing project, Jennifer Tendero's "We're Worth Waiting For," and Schaafsma's "Things We Can't Say" about the Write For Your Life project.

Week 8: Stories Students Write For Their Lives: Personal and Social Change in the Bronx

Class Activities. Presentation with Tony Tendero, Jennifer Tendero, some of her students, and myself about a Write For Your Life project site, Authors Workshop, IS 306, the Bronx, including video, discussion of student and teacher essays/Writing prompt.

Invitations. A piece of writing for your life—health and well-being/Bring copies of student work/Propose an individual or group teaching of writing project—action research on teaching, and otherwise/Continuing project/Evaluation–assessment–grading–portfolio assessment pieces to read, including chapters from Weaver on teaching grammar in context.

Week 9: Assessment, Grading and Grammar in Meaningful Contexts

Class Activities. Self-evaluation–portfolio progress report due/Conferences–writing groups/Course–Schaafsma midterm evaluation/Large group discussion on evaluation, including discussion on portfolio criteria.

Invitations. Read Lensmire, Brodkey, and Delpit essays, and *Rethinking Schools* pieces on writing, ethnicity, and culture, essay response to any combination of these pieces/Read essays about essays/Continuing or new piece.

Week 10: Problematizing Process Classroom Stories and Writing Stories

Class Activities. Writing prompt: "Standing Tall" (or any number of others) from *The Sun*/Large group discussion of project-portfolio requirements/Small group discussions of Lensmire, Brodkey, Delpit, *Rethinking Schools*, and essays about essays/Group Share/Writing Groups.

Invitations.

"Standing tall" writing/Revise teaching of writing and writing piece based on semester experience/Read second novel/More essays about essays/Some progress on teaching of writing research project/Continuing or new piece.

Week 11: More of Our Own Stories, and (Back to) the Essay

Class Activities. Georgia Heard "Writing about Home" writing exercise/Small group examination of student essays and large group discussions on creative approaches to essays, and the politics of genre/Small group discussions about new metaphors teaching of writing and writing/Small group share and work on progress on teaching of writing research project/Writing conferences.

Invitations. Heard Home writing exercise/Essay on the teaching of writing or on the subject you have written a story about/Writing projects/Teaching of writing projects.

Week 12: Second Novel Stories/Essays

Class Activities. Second novel discussions/Writing Groups and Conferences

Invitations. Writing projects/Teaching of writing projects/New writing based on response to novel.

Week 13: Dream Stories

Class Activities. Dreams exercise—writing from dreams, fantasies, sharing professional and student dream poems/Writing Groups and Conferences.

Invitations. Work on Teaching of Writing and Writing projects for Portfolios, and Self-evaluations.

Week 14: Last Class

Class Activities. Group share/Portfolios due/Party/Final Schaafsma-course-self evaluations.

III

LITERATURE AND THE TEACHING
OF LITERATURE

13

The Art
of the Picture Book

Kathy G. Short
University of Arizona

Cheri Anderson
Tucson Unified School District

The "Art of the Picture Book" is a graduate course taken by students completing masters' and/or doctoral degrees in the Department of Language, Reading and Culture at the University of Arizona. Within our department, students choose a focus area, one of which is children's literature. The majority of students in the course are full-time teachers and school librarians, but there are also a few full-time graduate students and individuals who want to illustrate children's books.

We developed the course because we believe readers need to interpret both print and pictures to actually *read* a picture book. The illustrations are not an extension of the print that only reinforce the meanings of the words, but are essential for constructing understandings of the story. Although most educators have strong backgrounds in language, many do not understand art as a meaning-making system and so are unable to support students in exploring the role of illustrations in picture books.

We co-teach the course by drawing on Kathy's expertise with children's literature and reader response and Cheri's background as a visual artist and a curriculum specialist working with teachers and children in visual literacy. Because of our previous experiences with language, we knew that students would need to both compose and interpret art. It has become a cliché that students learn to write by reading and to read by writing. We believe that for students to be able to read and interpret pictures, they also have to compose their own illustrations. Interpreting art involves constructing meaning through "reading" illustrations and artwork while composing art involves constructing meaning through authoring a piece of art (Short & Kauffman, in press). If students see themselves as artists and authors, their responses to picture books are more complex because of "insider" knowledge about how to tell stories through illustrations and words. On the other hand, their close examination and interpretation of picture books and art prints provides a repertoire of artistic strategies for their own artwork.

These understandings about art as a meaning-making process are based in semiotic theories of sign systems (Peirce, 1966; Siegel, 1984). A sign system perspective defines literacy as all the ways in which people share and make meaning, including music, art, mathematics, movement, drama, and language. These sign systems are tools for thinking as well as ways to communicate with others. Each sign system has a special contribution to make to human experience and a different potential for creating meaning (Eisner, 1994). Based on these understandings, we redefined "text" to mean any chunk of meaning that has unity and can be shared with others, such as a picture book, piece of art, a dance, a mathematical equation, or a song (Short, 1986). Thus, the course is really more broadly about art as a sign system.

Although schools have focused almost exclusively on language, we believe that all of the sign systems are *basic* processes that should be available to all learners. We do not accept the view that these sign systems are special talents possessed by a few "gifted" people. Although there are differences in our abilities within specific systems, we all possess the potential to use these as natural ways of making and sharing meaning. We do not have to become professional artists in order to use art in our daily lives. Children's and adults' discomfort with some sign systems results from the lack of exposure to, and use of, those systems. We believe that if learners were immersed in all sign systems in the same ways they are surrounded with language throughout the day, they would be able to use these systems in powerful and meaningful ways in their lives (Anderson, Kauffman, & Short, 1997).

These beliefs about sign systems are the basis for our explorations of art as a meaning-making process involving both interpreting and composing. In our university classroom, students studied art as a process, but also had opportunities to use it as a tool for making meaning as they responded to picture books or created pieces of art. Therefore, each class session included working in a studio as well as looking at and discussing picture books. The course changes each time we teach it so the following description is based on the last time we taught it.

Exploring Our Understandings of Picture Books and Art

The course began by exploring several broad questions—What is a picture book? What is art? How do visual images and words work together to create meaning within a picture book? We foregrounded students' own experiences and understandings. To explore "What is a picture book?," we talked about *Where the Wild*

Things Are (Sendak, 1963) and browsed many picture books. Students also engaged in actual art experiences with artists' tools to examine the relationship between print and illustration. Based on these experiences, students worked in small groups to web their definitions of picture books. Only then did they read how scholars in the field defined picture books (Kiefer, 1995). We began the next class by discussing the work of scholars, comparing their work to our previous brainstorming, and adding new understandings to the webs. We wanted to validate students' experiences instead of prioritizing the views of experts but we also wanted to learn from experts. By reversing what typically happens in a university course and reading professional materials *after* students had engaged in experiences on a topic, they brought stronger backgrounds and interest to their reading.

In the next class session, we explored "What is art?" To tap into students' understandings, we asked them to bring an artifact that reflected their definition of art. These were shared in small groups and then used to establish a museum display on students' definitions of art. Students also read *The Monument* (Paulson, 1991), sketched the book's meaning to them, and met to discuss their responses in literature circles.

Studio always included a range of artists' tools and mediums along with open-ended suggestions to support students in further exploring the class focus. In this class session, we set up studio invitations that explored various aspects of the art world, such as sculpture, painting, drawing, weaving, collage, textiles, and photography. These studio invitations included art prints and artifacts as well as materials for students to make their own creations.

These initial classes established the complex relationship we saw between interpreting and composing. Teachers came into the course expecting to look at books and interpret the illustrations. They were not expecting studio and some reacted with fear and trepidation at creating their own artwork, even though we reassured them that our focus was process, not product. We usually began class sessions with interpretation because that was more comfortable for teachers. They browsed picture books that had been organized into different text sets, conceptually related sets of 10 to 15 picture books that highlighted particular aspects of illustrations we were considering in the class session. They also met in literature circles, small groups of 4 to 6 students, to discuss and analyze a particular picture book. Sometimes the entire class would discuss the same book in small groups and then share as a whole group. Other times, students met in literature circles with each group reading a different book. One of our concerns was that students respond personally to the meaning of the books and not simply analyze the technical aspects of illustrations. We wanted them to connect their personal experiences, understandings of the book, and knowledge of illustration.

In each class session, the browsing and literature circles were followed by studio invitations that built from the visual aspects that students had examined in the picture books. During studio time, they could play with a wide range of art materials to explore the same concepts, but through a composing process. Picture books and art prints were always available so that students could move back and forth between composing and interpreting.

We knew that students needed more time to play at composing in a nonthreatening way than what we could provide within the studio in class. They needed to broaden their experiences of using art as a tool for thinking so that they could get inside the thinking processes of illustrators. Sketch journals provided this time, although some students initially were insecure about their ability to use sketching to observe their world. They were asked to make entries outside of class twice a week and then share their entries with someone informally at the beginning of the class, although they could choose not to share. We spent one studio exploring different types of entries students could make in their journals and assuring them that we would not evaluate their entries, only check whether they had made regular entries.

The journal was a place to observe and capture what was happening around them through sketches, webs, and words (Robinson, 1996). The observations came from daily life, their classrooms, readings, professional experiences, studio, and so forth. Some students used the journal to sketch subjects of interest, such as children or flowers. Some used it to explore a particular medium, such as watercolor, or an aspect of art, such as line or color. Others used abstract images to explore emotions. Some reproduced famous works of art or a book illustration. Still others used the journal to plan a particular project, such as quilt blocks, a classroom arrangement, or their own picture book. Some students used it to refine their skills as artists and were deliberate in their entries, yet others used it for free exploration or to relax and unwind.

Examining the Strategies of Illustrators

These initial explorations were followed by several sessions examining the strategies of particular illustrators so that students could see the interplay between strategies and the complexity of illustrators' choices. We defined strategies as the methods used by illustrators to create meaning as they make decisions in their composing. Each illustrator develops a repertoire of methods to draw on in particular circumstances.

In one class session, each literature group closely examined one picture book and talked about the book's meaning and the illustrator's strategies. They then moved to studio where each person reproduced an illustration from that book using the same media as the illustrator. This process was designed to encourage them to go "inside the illustrator's head" and to closely attend to the media and to details such as how color and line create a composition. They had to look much more closely than they had in their literature discussions to see small details that they would normally have missed when only attending to the overall impact of the illustration.

The following week students met in literature circles to examine text sets of particular illustrators. They then went to studio and explored the same medium of that illustrator, but made their own original artwork. We also began reading professional books that introduced technical art vocabulary and concepts (Kiefer, 1995; Stewig, 1995). By this point, students felt a strong need for these concepts and were not overwhelmed by these technical aspects. Their experiences with looking at books and creating their own art had created a strong need to know what experts in the field thought.

Learning About Art

Over the following weeks, we examined art elements, style, technique, and book design. In each case, students engaged in professional reading and then came to class and looked at text sets which highlighted these aspects. For example, when we studied book design, the text sets were sets of 10 to 15 picture books that highlighted unusual formats, formal and informal text placement, types of paper and print, borders, endpapers, front matter, and pop-ups. In studio, students could use a storyboard to compose a story or lay out a book, create a double-paged spread, make multiples images for borders, explore print placement with self-stick notes, make endpapers using a range of mediums, explore different kinds of bookbinding, and assemble their own pop-ups. For technique, we pulled books into sets that each highlighted particular media, such as watercolor or pen and ink and then students explored the same media in studio.

Many students listed the studio invitation that followed the text sets on the art elements of color, shape, line, light and dark, texture, and space as the most powerful. Building on their professional reading (Bang, 1991), students created scary pictures using simple shapes cut from white, red, black, and purple construction paper. These pictures were taken to the center of the room and we gathered around them to talk about which were most effective in their use of the elements to create fear. Because the shapes were not glued down, we moved shapes around on a few pictures as we talked about ways to increase tension. Students then retrieved their pictures and returned to their work tables to discuss tension and make revisions.

The final part of the course focused on students' inquiry projects. Some students took the text set and studio invitations from our class and tried them out with their students. Others created and illustrated their own picture books. During this time, we revisited particular invitations according to student requests in the studio. In our class sessions, we invited local elementary teachers as guest speakers to share their experiences using picture books in their classrooms. We also invited an illustrator to share his illustrating processes and visited a photography museum where we explored the process of aesthetic scanning. The focus of these sessions came out of student requests and reflections and were not determined ahead of time. At our last class session, we returned to *Where the Wild Things Are* (Sendak, 1963) and asked students to examine the book in small groups and then as a whole class. The discussion of this book during our first class had been very brief. During the final class session, we had to cut off their responses after 40 minutes because we had run out of time. Students brought up an incredible range of issues, such as light sources, use of shape to convey scariness, the rhythm of the illustrations, the placement of the print on the page, the size of the pictures related to the fantasy, the use of crosshatching, the passage of time, the changing perspectives, and the use of implied lines. All of these aspects of illustration were considered as they contributed to this story about imagination, fear, and love.

We believe that it was the complex interplay of interpreting and composing that created a powerful environment for learning in this course. When in studio, adults continuously referred to picture books and art prints as they played with art materials. When they discussed books in literature circles, they sketched and webbed their responses. Their experiences as artists became important reference points for interpreting the books they were reading. Through professional readings, illustrator studies, and visits to a photography museum, they gained insights into how other illustrators thought and worked. These insights into others' composing processes informed both their reading and artwork.

An important aspect of this environment was the balance between open-ended contexts where adults could explore interpreting and composing and specific engagements where they learned about art. The sketch journals and studio experiences where they could freely play with art immersed them as artists. These experiences created a need for learning about art through discussions, readings, specific engagements, and strategy lessons. These lessons were demonstrations of what learners *might* think about or do in their work, not models of what they *must* do. Our focus was on providing them with more options, not on imposing a particular procedure or way of thinking. We did not begin the class by teaching lessons about art. We started by having students look at books, talk about interpretations, and create art. Based on these experiences, we thought about the types of engagements and discussions that might support learners in deepening their understandings of art and illustration. We built the curriculum of the course *from* and *with* students.

REFERENCES

Anderson, C., Kauffman, G., & Short, K. G. (1998). Now I think like an artist: Responding to picture books. In J. Evans (Ed.), *What's in the picture? Responding to illustrations in picture books* (pp. 146–165). London: Chapman.

Bang, M. (1991). *Picture this: Perception and composition.* Boston: Little Brown.

Eisner, E. (1994). *Cognition and curriculum reconsidered.* New York: Teachers College Press.

Kiefer, B. (1995). *The potential of picture books: From visual literacy to aesthetic understanding.* Englewood Cliffs, NJ: Merrill.

Paulson, G. (1991). *The monument.* New York: Dell.

Peirce, C. (1966). *Collected papers, 1931–1958.* Cambridge: Harvard University Press.

Robinson, G. (1996). *Sketch-books: Explore and store*. Portsmouth, NH: Heinemann.

Sendak, M. (1963). *Where the wild things are*. New York: Harper.

Short, K. (1986). *Literacy as a collaborative experience*. Unpublished doctoral dissertation, Indiana University.

Short, K., & Kauffman, G. (In press). Exploring sign systems within an inquiry curriculum. In M. Gallego, & S. Hollingsworth (Eds.), *Challenging a single standard: Multiple perspectives on literacy*. New York: Teachers College Press.

Siegel, M. (1984). *Reading as signification*. Unpublished doctoral dissertation. Bloomington, IN: Indiana University.

Stewig, J. W. (1995). *Looking at picture books*. Fort Atkinson, WI: Highsmith.

Sample Syllabus[1]
The Art of the Picture Book

Course Intent

In this course, we will explore visual literacy through the art of the picture book. A picture book conveys its messages through a seamless whole of two sign systems, language and art. The illustrations do not just reflect the action in the text but share in moving the story forward and in conveying and enhancing the meaning of the story. Readers must be able to "read" both the text and illustrations in order to fully engage with the story. Teachers, librarians, and students need to be both visually and verbally literate.

Course participants will read about art, illustration, picture books, and the role of visual literacy in children's lives. They will also participate in experiences using various art media and styles and in literature circles on illustrations and picture books. They will consider the relationship between illustrations and text in picture books and ways to integrate art and picture books into classroom inquiry. Participants will engage in their own inquiries related to illustration and children's picture books.

Our class experiences are based on the following beliefs about learning:

1. Learning is an active process.
2. Learning is a social process of collaborating with others.
3. Learning occurs as we make connections to our own experiences.
4. Choice allows learners to connect to their experiences and feel ownership in their learning.
5. Learning is reflective as well as active.
6. Learning occurs in a multicultural world with many ways of knowing.
7. Learning is a process of inquiry.

---

[1]The following is an abbreviated version of the course syllabus. The complete version of the actual syllabus can be found on the Web site at: http://msit.gsu.edu/handbook.

Course Materials

Barbara Kiefer, *The potential of picture books: From visual literacy to aesthetic understanding*.
   Prentice-Hall, 1995.
Molly Bang, *Picture this: Perception and composition*. Bullfinch, 1991.
   Packet of articles
   A professional book related to your inquiry focus.
   Optional: John Warren Stewig, *Looking at picture books*. Highsmith, 1995.

Course Organization

This course is based on learning as a process of authoring, of creating meaning to
make sense of the world, and of inquiry, asking and exploring questions that are significant to us. To facilitate our authoring and inquiry, we will use the following time
blocks:

4:15–4:30	Whole class meeting, announcements, read aloud
4:30–5:00	Discussion of readings/small group meetings
5:00–6:30	Whole group presentation/demonstration Literature circles/browsing/studio
6:30–6:45	Whole class meeting/reflection

Course Learning Engagements

   1. Professional readings. Find a way of keeping track of your responses so that
you are ready to share your questions and connections during class sessions. Choose
one professional book to read with a small group in the second half of the semester.
   2. *Sketch journal*. This journal is a place to observe what is happening around you
through sketches, words, webs, and so forth. These observations can come from
daily life, nature, experiences in school, readings, professional experiences, class, our
studio, and or elsewhere. Purchase some kind of notebook or journal and art materials that you can easily carry with you. Twice a week make an entry in your sketch
journal. Each week, when you arrive at class, find someone and share one of your entries with that person.
   3. *Children's literature readings*. Devise some type of record-keeping system so
that you are able to keep track of the books you read for later use. This system is for
your use so the format, types of information, and extensiveness of the record is your
decision.
   4. *Inquiry project*. Choose an issue, topic, or question that you want to explore
and learn more about related to illustration, art, picture books, or visual literacy.
The project will involve developing a plan for exploring your focus, engaging in

your inquiry, and sharing the results with others. Your inquiry can be done with a group or partner or individually. We will form small groups to support individuals involved in related inquiries. You will choose a professional book to read and discuss in these groups.

Inquiry projects can take a variety of forms:

a. Classroom or field-based inquiry where you work with children in investigating a question or issue that intrigues you. You might try illustrator studies or classroom experiences that focus on styles of illustration, techniques, artists, elements of art, design, or bookmaking. You might integrate art experiences into a theme unit or inquiry focus or work with children in writing, illustrating, and publishing their own picture books. You might examine children's responses to art work or illustrations in literature circles. These experiences can occur in the classroom, library, school-wide program, or a home setting. Keep track of your "planning to plan" and then what actually occurs through field notes, teaching journals, transcripts, interviews, student artifacts, and such.

b. Theoretical research or a literature review of a question or issue explored primarily through professional readings on topics such as visual literacy, the role of imaging in learning, sign systems, or the history of illustration.

c. Critical analysis of a particular type of children's picture books, such as picture books from a specific country, culture, genre, or topic.

d. Development of a curricular framework or plan for how to organize the integration of illustration and creating meaning using art throughout your curriculum in the classroom, library, or school. This could include gathering resources and information on illustration, illustrators, and/or different aspects of art, organizing them, and creating a "plan of possibilities" for their use in your curriculum. These plans might also involve planning a professional development workshop, course, or set of materials for educators.

e. Learning something new. Choose a topic such as a particular art media that you know little about but are interested in and develop a plan for learning about that topic. Keep a journal about what you are learning and how you are going about that learning.

f. Illustrate your own book. Work on a rough draft of your own children's book, focusing particularly on the illustrations.

g. Your proposal.

As part of your inquiry, keep track of your process of research including all notes, rough drafts, artifacts, etc. Some type of written product will be turned in at the end of the course such as a paper, curriculum notebook, learning log and reflections, or draft of a book. In addition, each project will be shared with other class members. You will also write a self-evaluation of the process and product for your inquiry project.

5. *Class participation*. Participate in class sharing times, literature circles, written responses to class sessions, small group projects, studio time, and curricular invitations. More than one absence from class will affect your grade in the course. Your attendance and active participation in course engagements is highly valued and an essential aspect of the course. Write a self-evaluation of your learning at midterm and at the end of the course.

(For more information regarding the course schedule, a bibliography of professional books for small group discussion, a description of the midterm reflection, inquiry project plan, and the inquiry project and final self evaluations, readers are invited to visit the Web site, http://msit. gsv.edu/handbook.)

14

Children's Literature
in the Curriculum[1]

Lee Galda
The University of Minnesota

"Children's Literature in the Curriculum" at the University of Georgia, is a course designed for master's or doctoral students interested in prekindergarten through grade 8; the enrollment varies but is usually between 20 and 25. Typically, the students range from beginning MEd students with no teaching experience other than student teaching, to teachers with several years of experience working on their MEd, to doctoral candidates more interested in apprenticing as a university instructor than in applying what they learn to the elementary or middle grades classroom. All students in the course should have a working knowledge of children's literature, having had a survey of children's literature course within the past 10 years; some are more knowledgeable than others. Students come from many disciplines—language education, reading, early childhood education, middle school education, social science education, science education, mathematics education, and child study—as well. Those who are in-service teachers arrive in class having taught all day and then commuted for up to 2 hours.

The diversity of interest and experience in the class is at once a strength and a challenge. I have learned to spend the first half of the course creating shared knowledge about the theory and pedagogical principles that support literature-based instruction and the second half listening to students share their own interests and

---

[1]This course was developed and taught while I was on faculty in the Department of Language Education at The University of Georgia.

expertise with each other. The book sharing that begins each session, the two literature study sessions that we do as a class, and the individual projects serve to introduce students to new children's books as well as model some good teaching practices. Demonstrating good teaching practices might be the most important thing that I do in this course. Telling classroom teachers how to teach never works; showing how practice affects their own attitudes, productivity, and process does. Frequently, these demonstrations are followed by commentary, usually initiated by me, on the implications of what I have just done or said and how that might translate into their classroom practices.

As research and practice in literature and instruction continue to develop, the course continues to change. Each time I teach it, I use different texts. This syllabus represents an attempt to combine an emphasis on reader response, always present in the course, and examples of teaching that supports children's responses. Multicultural literature is also a focus that appears in the texts we read, the children's books we read, and the individual projects. After closely considering the Karolides (1997) and the McMahon, et al. (1997), texts as presenting both the theory that supports good instruction and examples of how that instruction might look, we go on to explore issues and ideas in study groups. These typically range from topics such as "literature and special needs students," "multicultural literature and instruction," and "talk that supports literary understanding."

My own teaching is profoundly influenced by the writings of Louise Rosenblatt, James Britton, and Jerome Bruner, as well as the models of thoughtful, and thought-provoking, teaching provided me during graduate school by Bernice Cullinan, John Mayher, and Gordon Pradl. Current scholarship in children's literature, especially in the area of cultural diversity (see, e.g., Rogers & Soter's *Reading Across Cultures*, Teachers College Press, 1997), also influences the way I structure my courses. Thoughtful treatments of complex issues by Rudine Sims Bishop and others continue to stretch my thinking.

Sample Syllabus
EEN 712—Children's Literature in the Curriculum

Goals for the Course

To update your knowledge of current children's literature and the qualities that mark excellent children's literature;

To help you discover how literature reflects our culturally diverse world and appropriate ways to evaluate diverse literature;

To help you understand the process of responding to literature, and how to work with children as they read and respond;

To explore various models of literature-based instruction in elementary and middle grades;

To help you learn how to keep current on children's books and teaching practices through professional journals.

Requirements

1. Attend and participate in class. We will be discussing the ideas presented in the required texts and topics that extend the texts. We will form small study groups and each group will select an additional professional text (or a series of articles in professional journals) to read, discuss, and present to the class. To fully participate in the class, you will need to keep current with your reading and be a contributing member of your group. We will also form response groups to read and respond to the children's literature we select during the first class session.

2. Individual project. 40 points. Using the ideas presented in chapter 11 of *Literature and the Child* and your other readings, design four interrelated units of study in which you and your students explore (a) an aspect of cultural diversity which you then trace through (b) a theme, (c) a genre, and (d) an author or illustrator. Prepare an annotated bibliography, a description of ideas for exploring the books you select, and project ideas for each unit as well as ideas for culminating projects. Be sure to include poetry and nonfiction, when appropriate. We will share these projects with others and take orders for duplication during session 13. Due on session 13.

3. Study group project. 40 points. In addition to the book that you read as a group, read other professional materials related to the particular aspect of literature-based teaching that your study group has decided to investigate. Prepare a paper in which you explore your topic, citing both formal research and informal descriptive studies, and suggest principles for effective teaching practices. Present a brief summary of your research to the class along with a bibliography of readings and a summary of principles for effective practice. Hand these in to me along with one-page summaries of the articles and chapters that you read. Due to me on session 17.

4. Response journal and book talks. 20 points. Keep a journal in which you respond to the trade books you read for class discussion and for your projects. You should bring your journal to class on the evenings that we discuss each book. We'll decide as a group on a theme to explore and select books to read in common and in small response groups. [NOTE: At the beginning of the course, I ask students to write down three themes they are interested in exploring through children's books. I compile their suggestions and we agree on a focus. I then suggest books, and solicit suggestions from students, and we decide on one or two books to read as a class and several books to read in small response groups. Because this is not a general children's literature class and students have expertise in children's literature, no attempt is made to balance books across genres, etc.] You will also need to do book

talks to inform your peers about especially good books. Plan to do at least five over the quarter, either for the whole class or in small groups. Keep track of the book talks you give and include a list of titles and dates of book talks in your journal. Due on the last day of class. [NOTE: When the class is large, as it often is, we split into interest groups for book sharing. Those interested in books for preschoolers share with each other, primary grades with each other, etc. This allows a lot of titles to be shared with interested others in a short amount of time.]

Required Texts

Cullinan & Galda (1998), *Literature And The Child, 4th ed.*;
Karolides (1997) , *Reader Response in Elementary Classrooms*;
McMahon, Raphael, Goatley, & Pardo (1997), *the Book Club Connection*
Selected articles on reserve in the CET.

Recommended Texts for Study Groups:

Lukens (1995), *A Critical Handbook of Children's Literature, 5th ed.*, *A Critical Handbook of Literature for Young Adults*; Short & Pierce (1990), *Talking about books*; Routman (1998), *Transitions*; Peterson & Eeds (1994), *Grand Conversations*; Purves, Rogers, & Soter (1995), *How Porcupines Make Love*; Gambrell & Almasi (1996), *Lively Discussions!*; Rogers & Soter (1997), *Reading Across Cultures*; Harris (1997), *Using Multiethnic Literature in the K–8 Classroom*; Daniels (1994), *Literature Circles: Voice and Choice in the Student Centered Classroom*; Hill, Johnson, & Noe (1995), *Literature Circles and Response*. Plus, other texts suggested by me or discovered by you. See also both the professional resources sections and the articles in professional journals such as *The New Advocate, The Horn Book, Language Arts, The Reading Teacher, Research in The Teaching of English, Journal of Literacy Research, Reading Research Quarterly, Bookbird, Children's Literature Quarterly.*
Children's books will be available later in the quarter at the bookstore.

General Class Schedule for Sessions 1–13

Read aloud and/or booktalks and discussion—20–30 minutes
Discussion of topic/readings for the day—60–90 minutes
Study group meeting—planning and discussion—20–30 minutes
Sessions 16–19 will begin with a book sharing and discussion and then move to study group reports.

Schedule of Topics/Readings

Session 1: Introduction and course planning. Set up study groups. Decide on literature study and select books.

Sessions 2 & 3: Response to literature: Theory and practice. Readings: Cullinan and Galda, Ch. 2; Karolides, Ch. 1; Packet #1.

Session 4: Response-based literature curriculum. Readings: Cullinan & Galda, Ch. 12; Karolides, Ch. 2, 4, 5, 6, 7, 9; Packet #2

Session 5 & 6: The Book Club model. Readings: McMahon et al., Chapters 1–5, 10.

Session 7: Talking about books with children. Readings: Karolides, Ch. 3, 8, 16; Packet #3.

Session 8: Multicultural literature and the canon. Readings: Cullinan & Galda, Chapter 11; Packet #4.

Session 9: Planning a literature curriculum: Selection and censorship. Readings: McMahon, Ch. 11, 12, 13.

Session 10: Planning a literature curriculum: Teaching toward diversity. Readings: Karolides, Ch. 10, 13; McMahon, Ch. 6, 7, 8.

Session 11: Planning a literature curriculum: Thematic instruction, cross-curricular connections. Readings: Karolides, Ch. 11, 12, 14; McMahon, Ch. 14.

Session 12: Balancing a literature curriculum: Individual and group work, the basal and trade books. Readings: Packet #5.

Session 13: Assessment. Readings: McMahon, Ch. 9, 15.

Session 14: Individual project roundtables.

Session 15: Whole class/response group discussions of children's books: Looking for themes, connections, and extensions.

Sessions 16–19: Exploring models of and issues in literature-based instruction: Reports from the study groups.

Session 20: Whole class/response group discussions of children's books: Genre studies and thematic connections.

Material in packets:

#1—Beach, R. (1993). *A teacher's introduction to reader-response theories* (chap. 1). Urbana: NCTE.

Galda, L. (1988). Readers, texts and contexts: A response-based view of literature in the classroom. *The New Advocate, 1*(2), 92–102.

Rosenblatt, L. M. (1982). The literary transaction: Evocation and response. *Theory into Practice, XXI*(4), 268–277.

#2—Galda, L., Cullinan, B. E., & Strickland, D. (1997). *Language, literacy, and the child.* (chap. 4). Ft. Worth: Harcourt Brace.

McGinley, W., Kamberelis, G., Mahoney, T., Madigan, D., Rybicki, V., & Oliver, J. (1997). Re-visioning reading and teaching literature through the lens of narrative theory. In T. Rogers & A. Soter, *Reading across cultures* (pp. 42–68). New York: TCP.

#3—Almasi, J. (1996). A new view of discussion. In L. Gambrell & J. Almasi (Eds.), *Lively Discussions! Fostering engaged reading* (pp. 2–24). Newark, DE: IRA

#4—Bishop, R. S. (1997). Selecting literature for a multicultural curriculum. In V. J. Harris (Ed.), *Using multiethnic literature in the K–8 classroom* (pp. 1–19). Norwood, MA: Christopher Gordon.

Purves, A. C. (1993). Toward a reevaluation of reader response and school literature. *Language Arts, 70,* 348–361.

#5—Rosenblatt, L. M. (1991). Literature-S.O.S.! *Language Arts, 68,* 444–448.

REFERENCES

Cullinan, B. E., & Galda, L. (1998). *Literature and the child (4th ed.).* Fort Worth, TX: Harcourt Brace.

Daniels, H. (1994). *Literature circles: Voice and choice in the student centered classroom.* York, ME: Stenhouse.

Gambrell, L. B., & Almasi, J. F. (1996). *Lively discussions! Fostering engaged reading.* Newark: IRA.

Harris, V. J. (1997). *Using multiethnic literature in the K-8 classroom.* Norwood: Christopher-Gordon.

Hill, B. C., Johnson, N. J., & Noe, K. L. S. (1995). *Literature circles and response.* Norwood: Christopher-Gordon

Karolides, N. (Ed.) (1997). *Reader response in elementary classrooms.* Mahwah, NJ: Lawrence Erlbaum Associates.

Lukens, R. J. (1995). *A critical handbook of children's literature* (5th edition). Reading, MA: Addison-Wesley.

McMahon, S., Raphael, T., Goatley, V., & Pardo, L. (1997). *The book club connection.* New York: Teachers College Press.

Peterson, R., & Eeds, M. (1994). *Grand conversations.* New York: Scholastic.

Purves, A., Rogers, T., & Soter, A. O. (1995). *How porcupines make love III: Readers, texts, cultures in the response-based literature classroom.* White Plains, NY: Longman.

Rogers, T., & Soter, A. O. (1997). *Reading across cultures: Teaching literature in a diverse society.* New York: Teachers College Press.

Routman, R. (1988). *Transitions: From literature to literacy.* Portsmouth, NH: Heinemann.

Short, K. G., & Pierce, K. M. (1990). *Talking about books: Creating literate communities.* Portsmouth, NH: Heinemann.

15

Mediating Multicultural Children's Literature

Patricia E. Enciso
The Ohio State University

My course title, "Mediating Multicultural Children's Literature" implies I am not only concerned with how students and teachers select children's literature, but also how they participate in specific contexts, histories, and dialogues about this literature. In my courses, students read a wide range of multicultural literature, but do so in the service of three interrelated goals: (1) to broaden and deepen our understanding of the varying histories, purposes and range of representations of many people's experiences in multicultural children's literature, (2) to examine and often challenge the dynamic co-construction of cultural assumptions, positions, and interpretations about ourselves and others, and (3) to develop a working knowledge of resources for selecting and talking about literature with children that will facilitate their critical engagement with literature, one another, and society.

I turned to a number of intersecting disciplines to support our study of multicultural literature and cultural mediation in the classroom. These disciplines include children's literature and response to literature, literary theory, sociolinguistics, anthropology, critical theory, cultural studies, and multicultural education. Across these areas, questions emerge pertaining to the production of texts, the critical reception and interpretation of texts, the positioning of texts and readers in particular contexts, and the relationships among texts, readers, and historical and popular constructs of difference, power, access, and legitimacy.

Like many educators who are committed to pedagogies that affirm and extend our understanding of diversity in schooling and society, I often encounter ideological conflicts among students and between myself and students' perceptions of reality. It is important, for the sake of equity in the class and for purposes of opening pathways to new insights and experiences that I facilitate an inclusive, respectful, but not wholly relativistic, or "conflict-free," learning environment. This is the most challenging aspect of teaching this course. From the beginning of the course, I advocate a dialogic relationship with the multiple views and experiences expressed by students, myself, authors, and illustrators. *Dialogism* (Bakhtin, 1981), most simply stated, is the practice of bringing together multiple voices, each emerging from differential relationships of power and status. A dialogic approach sets in motion these different ways of viewing and speaking about oneself and others, to create a dynamic interplay of ideas, tensions, and potential, unimagined, directions for thinking and learning. Dialogism also implies that as ideas are expressed through different images, texts, and experiences, they will be examined in terms of their capacity to engender possibilities, and critiqued in terms of their representations of diversity as a settled, certain, finished narrative. Finally, dialogism seeks a restatement of multiple views in one's own words, through the lens of one's own, limited experiences. Thus, throughout the course, students are encouraged to write, talk, and reflect on their own and others' perceptions, while they also place their perspectives and social status (as imagined or realistic as that might be) in relation to others' meanings and experiences. The dialogic conversations I hope for sometimes fall short, especially when I become frustrated or unnerved by a side remark or persistent resistance to another's perspective. In these moments, my talk and our conversations might become monologic instead of dialogic; that is, we revert to what we think is known, certain, and true. Often, we have to struggle to find our way back to uncertainty and unfamiliarity. I find that I can often turn to remarkable pieces of literature as hopeful spaces for learning and reimagining our relationships with one another, children, art, and society.

THE CONVERSATION BEGINS

I begin the course with authors' and illustrators' perspectives and purposes for writing multicultural literature. My intention is to help students recognize the legacy of under representation and misrepresentation of diverse views and lives in children's literature. What do authors say about their work? For some, multicultural literature is a genre that speaks of the movement from discontent to harmony, often facilitated by the love and understanding of a child. For others, it is the medium through which never-before-told stories find a place in the vast numbers of children's books published annually in the United States. And for others, multicultural literature is a "critical fiction," a story told that disrupts the imaginations and expectations of "North American" readers.

As Claribel Alegría (1991) writes, the literature she and her contemporaries are creating (for adults, in this case) is intended to interrupt long-standing hegemonic views and dialogues so that a more inclusive, just society may be imagined and made:

We Latinos must assume the roles of historians, politicians, journalists, sociologists, and teachers. We must take on the role of educators with respect to *latinidad*, because no one else is doing the job. To do that job effectively, we must celebrate cultural diversity, take pride in *la raza*, in our Spanish language, in our cultural heritage stemming from *la hispanidad*, which has given the world as rich a tapestry of prose, poetry, painting, drama, and music as any other major world culture.... The more we assert our culture and history, the more we insist on representing ourselves, the more difficult it will be for North Americans to ignore the extermination of our peoples. (p. 106)

Alegría describes the range of cultural education that many writers take up as they struggle to represent their experiences for one another, for children, and for "North Americans." For many students, to read this literature and to be situated as "North American" is to experience being "the other," outside another's world, reaching, *hoping* for the familiar. Yet, an aim of multicultural literature is often to disrupt the familiar and to name unspoken norms and assumptions that produce racism, sexism and related oppressions. Thus, in conjunction with our reading of authors' stories and purposes, students and I also work to understand the stories in our own lives that shape our sense of "the familiar." We look for stories that tell us who we are as we relate to others and the world. Through these stories we can begin to name what is familiar and how it includes and excludes what we can and cannot say about ourselves, our relationships, and our experiences. Some of our familiarities are quickly available for telling; for example, "I always had a lot of friends" or "We read the bible every night before bed." Other stories must be "called out" through our reading of multicultural literature. For example, access to timely, skilled medical care is by no means a guaranteed right in this country, though it may be taken for granted as an expectation and right by many of my students. However, after reading *The Circuit* (Jiménez, 1997) or *Uncle Jed's Barbershop* (Mitchell, 1993), students find that in the presence of someone else's story they are able to talk about the precarious health of a family member, or their own health, and the high cost of prescriptions, time and energy required to preserve good health. We begin to see our own privileges, or lack thereof, and talk more honestly about familiarities that may be, in fact, pernicious inequities that are part of the production and institutionalization of discrimination.

These stories, particularly critical fictions, lead us to look outward at society as well as inward at ourselves in society. We no longer read solely for the beauty of language, imagery and narrative form, although literary qualities are always discussed and savored; we read to understand ourselves, the coconstruction of difference in our lives and in society, and to examine why we might commit to read literature that questions habits of complacency or acceptance of the status quo.

Although during the course, students will have read a wide range of contemporary multicultural literature, read literary theory and criticism, and participated in discussions, the question remains, of whether or not they will take up this literature, along with their own stories and mediate these in classrooms. Furthermore, what will they select and how will they mediate it?

By the midway point in the course, students know enough to know that they could get it wrong; they are ever fearful that they might offend or alienate a student or peer by admiring a book that contains inaccuracies or generalities. I need to show them repeatedly that despite their fears and frustrations, born of the endless, futile search for a complete, infallible representation of the other, they *can* stay in the conversation. I need to show them that culture and difference are not finished products wrapped up in a book that they are mediating, but rather cultural representations that are part of an ongoing, dynamic conversation about race and rights in the everyday lives of children and their families in this country. I tend to insist that they stay in the conversation.

IN EVERY COURSE OUR CONVERSATION EVENTUALLY SOUNDS SOMETHING LIKE THIS

Students point out that this is going to be hard. Uhm hmm. There's censorship. Uhm hmm. There are angry parents. Uhm hmm. There are principals who will make you leave the school. Uhm hmm. Maybe a special letter to parents would help, that *warns* them of the planned breach of mainstream history and stereotypical images. Maybe that would work. Hmm. Other ideas? Okay. We'd better stick with *Little House on the Prairie*. No. No. Wait a minute. But even if we read these stories, there will still be racism and oppression. So, why bother?

Okay. Let's see how democracy might work in our favor a bit, here. What are the intellectual freedom policies in your school and state? What are the steps of communication you can follow in negotiating with angry or maybe confused and uncomfortable parents? How can you justify your literature selections with a principal? Right. You don't just go into this enterprise as though the world is waiting for you to save it from itself. That's a bit arrogant really. Parents and principals want to know what kind of education you are giving their children. You need to consider what your curriculum conveys, how it benefits all children and how you will explain inclusions and exclusions in classroom materials and the curriculum.

But what if the kids have a fight that is actually sparked by a book or discussion? And what if a kid says something that is really racist or homophobic? And another thing. Not everyone is like the kids in those books. What if the class gets the idea that all Mexican families are migrants?

You'll be reading more than one book, right? And you'll probably analyze some of the commercials and movies that have historically portrayed Asian, African, Latino and, for that matter, European people as uni-dimensional and homogeneous. Right? (see Banks, 1993) Why would anyone—or a corporation—be interested in promoting such a portrayal? Who gains when someone else is dehumanized? What is the loss to us all when dehumanization and other forms of exclusion are enacted and not interrupted? Can multicultural literature interrupt injustice or discriminatory practices? Can we?

The Conversation Continues

As the course concludes, we read intellectual freedom policies, talk with teachers who regularly use multicultural literature in their teaching, review selection journals and reference books, and view popular cultural images to compare these with contemporary portrayals of, for example, Native American cultures. A culminating assignment for students is to create a "text set" that is based on a far-reaching topic of inquiry such as "How do children today understand and experience immigration?" (see Hartman & Hartman 1993; Short, Harste, & Burke 1996). Students need to write about why their chosen topic and question matters to them and why it might matter to children. As described in the syllabus, the text set must include literature that reflects cross-cultural, cross-genre, and cross-curricular points of view. I encourage students to look for "disruptive" texts; that is, the stories and images that clearly show long-standing stereotypes or that provide counter images to stereotypes or singular points of view. I want students to consider not only how, but why, they will mediate the disruptive books as well as the other books included in their bibliography. Through this assignment, students demonstrate their ability to (1) plan a provocative, engaging inquiry, (2) find well-conceived literature that presents multiple, critical viewpoints with thoughtful attention given to children's lives, interests, and familiarity with the topic, and (3) imagine mediating the stories that the literature and children might bring to the topic.

Finally, I want students to understand that despite their best intentions, they will meet resistance; indeed, they may often be the source of resistance even more than parents or principals (Enciso 1994a; Felman & Laub 1990). They will also find themselves in the middle of conversations that are filled with fears and passion; but they can learn to hear the sense in children's stories as well as the ignorance. And despite the naiveté and sometimes pointed exclusions and slurs their students might express, they can question and direct children toward an examination of the production of racism, sexism, and other oppressions. It is worth it to continue the conversation. They will never know enough about anyone, including themselves; they may offend, embarrass, or alienate someone, but they can learn to retrace their ignorance and offenses and enter conversations that have otherwise been silenced. Through these conversations, they may create the possibility for telling stories about themselves and others that defy the familiar.

REFERENCES

Alegría, C. (1991). Latinidad and the artist. In P. Mariani (Ed.), *Critical fictions: The politics of imaginative writing* (pp. 104–107). Seattle, WA: Bay Press.

Bakhtin, M. M. (1981). *The dialogic imagination: Four essays.* M. Holquist (Ed.) C. Emerson & M. Holquist (Trans.). Austin, TX: University of Texas Press.

Enciso, P. (1994a, December). *Teaching for everyone's strongest self: The selection and use of literature and cultural knowledge by five exemplary 1–6 grade teachers.* Paper presented at the annual meeting of the National Reading conference, San Diego, CA.

Enciso, P. (1994). Cultural identity and response to literature: Running lessons from Maniac Magee. *Language Arts, 71*, 524–533.

Felman, S., & Laub, D. (1992). *Testimony: Crises of witnessing in literature, psychoanalysis, and history.* New York: Routledge.

Hartman, D., & Hartman, J. (1993). Reading across texts: Expanding the role of the reader. *The Reading Teacher, 47*, 202–211.

Jiménez, F. (1997). *The circuit: Stories from the life of a migrant child.* Albuquerque: University of New Mexico Press.

Mitchell, M. K. (1993). *Uncle Jed's barbershop.* Illustrated by J. Ransome. New York: Simon & Schuster.

Short, K., Harste, J., & Burke, C. (1996). *Creating classrooms for authors and inquirers.* Portsmouth, NH: Heinemann.

Sample Syllabus
Mediating Multicultural Children's Literature
Graduate Seminar—Ten weeks; 3-hour class session

This seminar is intended for graduate students and practicing teachers who are interested in reading current multicultural literature and raising questions regarding the theories and practices of selecting and mediating representations of oneself and others in K–8 classrooms.

Major Topics and Questions

(1) Mediation: How does multicultural literature create limitations and possibilities for understanding one's own and others' cultural memberships? How can differences in power and knowledge contribute to teachers' and students' interpretations of multicultural literature? How does popular culture influence our own and children's interpretation of and resistance to multicultural literature? How might the arts create a "third space" through which we can explore conflicting interpretations of ourselves and others?

(2) Selection: What criteria have been used to analyze and critique multicultural literature for children and young adults? How are these criteria related to publishing and teaching multicultural literature?

(3) Politics and policies: What are the politics and policies of publishing houses, schools, and communities regarding the production and inclusion of multicultural literature? How are policies understood and enacted in the specific locations of our teaching and learning?

Assignments

Notecards for each class session: Quotes, ideas, and questions that will be used during our whole group and small group discussions.

Four Stories that Matter Paper: Select four distinct stories that have either been told about you, told by you, or read by you, from your childhood and young adulthood, that reflect your relationship to reading, schooling, family, and society.

Reflective Paper #1:   Consider your commitments and concerns as a cultural mediator as these relate to the literary and transformative qualities in a single selection of multicultural literature.

Reflective Paper #2:   Consider your enthusiasm, resistance, ideas, insights and questions about reading and discussing multicultural literature in the context of this class.

Text Set: A thematic collection of literature that represents and intentionally juxtaposes cross-cultural, cross-genre, popular, mainstream, and transformative perspectives (see Week Eight, article by Banks, 1993). This collection will be written in the form of an annotated bibliography and presented to the whole group. Select approximately 20 books that exemplify the qualities and issues associated with multicultural literature discussed in class. This assignment will also include a "Text Set Rationale" that describes how and why you would use this text set collection with children. Pay particular attention to the ways you would intend to mediate the questions and representations of self and others that this set evokes.

Schedule of Topics and Readings

Week 1

Topic: Understanding ourselves and others in the making and mediation of culture

Discussion Focus: What are our familiar injustices? What stories do authors and illustrators tell? How do these stories arise from different locations of power, status, and experience in U.S. society?

Children's Literature   Selections shared by Dr. Enciso

                                          Meet Danitra Brown (Grimes)

                                          Watsons go to Birmingham–1963 (Curtis)

                                          I hadn't meant to tell you this (Woodson)

                                          The space between our footsteps (Nye)

                                          Barrio: José's neighborhood (Ancona)

Related Reading

(Readings will be read *during class* today)

Alegría, C. (1991). Latinidad and the artist. In P. Mariani (Ed.), *Critical fictions: The politics of imaginative writing* (pp.104–107). Seattle, WA: Bay Press.

Week 2

Topic: The politics of telling stories

Discussion Focus: What does it mean to tell a story to a particular audience? What is the teller's purpose and risk? What is the teacher's role and risk?

Children's Literature

A boy becomes a man at Wounded Knee (Wood)

The Journey: Japanese Americans, racism and renewal (Hamanaka)

Related Reading

Baillie, A. (1995). Pol Pot's reign of terror: Why write about it for children? In S. Lehr (Ed.), *Battling dragons: Issues and controversy in children's literature* (pp. 148–154). Portsmouth, NH: Heinemann.

Hamanaka, S. (1991). Making *The Journey*. In A. Manna & C. S. Brodie (Eds.), *Many faces, many voices: Multicultural literary experiences for youth* (pp. 51–60). Fort Atkinson, WI: Highsmith Press.

Mohr, N. (1992). A journey toward a common ground: The struggle and identity of Hispanics in the U.S.A. In A. Manna & C. S. Brodie (Eds.), *Many faces, many voices: Multicultural literary experiences for youth* (pp. 61–68). Fort Atkinson, WI: Highsmith Press.

Narayan, K. (1993). How native is a "native" anthropologist? *American Anthropologist, 95*, 671–686.

Seale, D. (1991). 1492–1992 from an American Indian perspective. In M. V. Lindgren (Ed.), *The multicolored mirror: Cultural substance in literature for children and young adults* (pp. 101–116). Fort Atkinson, WI: Highsmith Press.

Week 3

Topic: (Mass) producing culture

Discussion Focus: How are differences and forms of discrimination constructed in literature and education as natural relations versus socially produced categories of status and power? How do we interpret ourselves and others through popular cultural representations of difference and discrimination?

Children's Literature   *Maniac Magee* (Spinelli)

Through My Eyes (Bridges)

Related Reading

Enciso, P. (1994). Cultural identity and response to literature: Running lessons from Maniac Magee. *Language Arts, 71*, 524–533.

Taxel, J. (1995). Cultural politics and writing for young people. In S. Lehr (Ed.), *Battling dragons: Issues and controversy in children's literature* (pp. 155–170). Portsmouth, NH: Heinemann.

Sims Bishop, R. (1996). Letter to the editor. *The New Advocate, 9*(2) vii–viii.

Week 4

Topic: Production of our own cultural identities

Discussion Focus: How does multicultural literature create possibilities and limitations for understanding one's own and others' cultural memberships?

Children's Literature   *Friends from the other side* (Anzaldúa)

Dancing backward (Bauer, in Am I Blue?)

Honey, I Love (Greenfield)

Related Reading

Hidalgo, N. (1993). Multicultural teacher introspection. In T. Perry & J. Fraser (Eds.), *Freedom's plow: Teaching in the multicultural classroom* (pp. 99–108). New York: Routledge.

hooks, b. (1991). Narratives of struggle. In P. Mariani (Ed.), *Critical fictions: The politics of imaginative writing* (pp. 53-61). Seattle, WA: Bay Press.

Spears-Bunton, L. (1990). Welcome to my house: African American and European American students' responses to Virginia Hamilton's House of Dies Drear. *Journal of Negro Education, 59,* 566–576.

Week 5

Topic: Selecting multicultural literature: Definitions and issues

Discussion Focus: What criteria do scholars, teachers, and librarians use to select multicultural literature? What criteria are significant in your view? Why?

Children's Literature

This land is my land (Littlechild)

Chita's Christmas (Howard)

Related Reading

Howard, E. (1991). Authentic multicultural literature for children: An author's perspective. In M. V. Lindgren (Ed.), *The multicolored mirror: Cultural substance in literature for children and young adults* (pp. 91–100). Fort Atkinson, WI: Highsmith Press.

Mitchell, A. H. (1992). The magic of imagining: Transaction with young adult fiction and poetry. In A. Manna & C. S. Brodie (Eds.), *Many faces, many voices: Multicultural literary experiences for youth* (pp. 15–28). Fort Atkinson, WI: Highsmith Press.

Sims Bishop, R. (1991). Evaluating books by and about African-Americans. In M. V. Lindgren (Ed.), *The multicolored mirror: Cultural substance in literature for children and young adults* (pp. 31–45). Fort Atkinson, WI: Highsmith Press.

Week 6

Topic: Cultural substance and form in outstanding multicultural children's literature: How are authors and illustrators selecting language and imagery?

Discussion Focus: What do we recognize as strengths in the cultural substance and form of outstanding multicultural literature? Why? How do we mediate the author/illustrator's art?

Children's Literature   *The circuit: Stories from the life of a migrant child* (Jiménez)

Related Reading

Bryan, A. (1993). Deep like rivers. In A. Manna & C. S. Brodie (Eds.), *Many faces, many voices: Multicultural literary experiences for youth* (pp. 113–123). Fort Atkinson, WI: Highsmith Press.

Cooperative Children's Book Center. (1991). Commentaries on cultural authenticity and accuracy in multicultural children's and young adult books. In M. V. Lindgren (Ed.), *The multicolored mirror: Cultural substance in literature for children and young adults* (pp. 159–173). Fort Atkinson, WI: Highsmith Press.

Feelings, T. (1991). Transcending the form. In M. V. Lindgren (Ed.), *The multicolored mirror: Cultural substance in literature for children and young adults* (pp. 45–57). Fort Atkinson, WI: Highsmith Press.

Jiménez, F. (1999). Boston Globe-Horn Book Award Acceptance: The Circuit. *The Horn Book Magazine,* 75(1), 49–52.

Kiefer, B. (1995). The disturbing image in children's picture books: Fearful or fulfilling? In S. Lehr (Ed.), *Battling dragons: Issues and controversy in children's literature* (pp. 51–62). Portsmouth, NH: Heinemann.

Week 7

Topic: Reading through many lives

Discussion Focus: What does multicultural literature become among children? How might children and teachers use artistic forms to mediate their interpretations of multicultural literature?

Children's Literature	*The gold cadillac* (Taylor)
	A chair for my mother (Williams)
	Family pictures/Cuadros de Familias (Garza)

Related Reading

Enciso, P. (1997, October). *Learning to be/read together: A sociocultural analysis of children's art, reading, and relationships.* Paper presented at the National Academy of Education annual meeting, Boulder, CO.

Paley, V. G. (1997). Frederick. In V. Paley (Ed.), *The girl with the brown crayon: How children use stories to shape their lives* (pp. 5–8). Cambridge, MA: Harvard University Press.

Wolf, S., & Enciso, P. (1994). Multiple selves in literary interpretation: Engagement and the language of drama. In C. Kinzer & D. Leu (Eds.), *Multidimensional aspects of literacy research, theory and practice: Forty-Third National Reading Conference Yearbook* (pp. 351–360). Chicago, IL: The National Reading Conference.

Week 8

Topic: Creating a culture for multicultural literature

Discussion Focus: How do we interpret literature and one another in classroom and school contexts where many people hold divergent expectations of and goals for multicultural literature?

Children's Literature

Bring two multicultural literature selections to class that you would like to read and mediate with children or young adults.

Related Reading

Banks, J. (1993). The canon debate, knowledge construction, and multicultural education. *Educational Researcher, 22*(5), 4–14.

Barrera, R. (1992). The cultural gap in literature-based literacy instruction. *Education and Urban Society, 24*(2), 227–243.

González, P. (1993). Reading against the cultural grain. In S. Miller & B. McCaskill (Eds.), *Multicultural literature and literacies: Making space for difference* (pp. 163–178). Albany: SUNY Press.

Lehr, S. (1995). Fourth graders read, write, and talk about freedom. In S. Lehr (Ed.), *Battling dragons: Issues and controversy in children's literature* (pp. 114–140). Portsmouth, NH: Heinemann.

Week 9

Topic: A deeper consideration of censorship

Discussion Focus: How are boundaries made? Why are these boundaries enforced? How are boundaries transformed?

Children's Literature *Places I never meant to be* (Blume)

Related Reading

McClure, A. (1995). Censorship of children's books. In S. Lehr (Ed.), *Battling dragons: Issues and controversy in children's literature* (pp. 3–30). Portsmouth, NH: Heinemann.

Oddi, S. (1995). But will they buy them? In S. Lehr (Ed.), *Battling dragons: Issues and controversy in children's literature* (pp. 249–252). Portsmouth, NH: Heinemann.

Week 10

- In small groups, organized by topic, class participants will present the key literature for and purposes of text sets they have created.

- In small groups, we will analyze our roles as mediators of multicultural literature by creating visual metaphors for our relationships with literature, culture, and classroom life.

- As a whole group, we will analyze our roles as reading educators, listing our goals and strategies for insuring the inclusion of multicultural literature as a medium for engagement in literary experiences and growth for all readers.

Children's Literature

Ancona, G. (1998). *Barrio: José's neighborhood.* New York: Harcourt Brace.

Anzaldúa, G. (1993). *Friends from the other side.* San Francisco, CA: Children's Book Press.

Bauer, M. D. (1996). Dancing backwards. In M.D. Bauer (Ed.), *Am I blue?* New York: ???.

Blume, J. (Ed.). (1999). *Places I never meant to be: Original stories by censored writers.* New York: Simon & Schuster.

Bridges, R. (1999). *Through my eyes.* New York: Scholastic Press.

Curtis, C. P. (1996). *The Watsons go to Birmingham–1963.* New York: Delacorte.

Greenfield, E. (1972) *Honey, I love and other love poems.* New York: Harper & Row.

Grimes, N. (1994). *Meet Danitra Brown.* New York: Lothrup, Lee & Shepard.

Hamanaka, S. (1990). *The journey: Japanese Americans, racism and renewal.* New York: Orchard Books.

Howard, E. F. (1989). *Chita's Christmas.* New York: Bradbury.

Jiménez, F. (1997). *The circuit: Stories from the life of a migrant child.* Albuqurque: University of New Mexico Press.

Littlechild, G. (1993). *This land is my land.* San Francisco, CA: Children's Book Press.

Lomas Garza, C. (1990). *Family pictures/Cuadros de familia.* San Francisco, CA: Children's Book Press.

Nye, N. S. (1998). *The space between our footsteps: Poems and paintings from the Middle East.* New York: Simon & Schuster.

Spinelli, J. (1991). *Maniac Magee.* Boston: Little, Brown.

Taylor, M. (1989). *The friendship/The gold cadillac.* New York: Yearling.

Williams, V. B. (1983). *A chair for my mother.* New York: Greenwillow.

Wood, T., & Wanbli Numpa Afraid of Hawk. (1992). *A boy becomes a man at Wounded Knee.* New York: Walker.

Woodson, J. (1994). *I hadn't meant to tell you this.* New York: Bantam.

Related Readings

Alegría, C. (1991). Latinidad and the artist. In P. Mariani (Ed.), *Critical fictions: The politics of imaginative writing* (pp.104–107). Seattle, WA: Bay Press.

Baillie, A. (1995). Pol Pot's reign of terror: Why write about it for children? In S. Lehr (Ed.), *Battling dragons: Issues and controversy in children's literature* (pp. 148–154). Portsmouth, NH: Heinemann.

Banks, J. (1993). The canon debate, knowledge construction, and multicultural education. *Educational Researcher, 22*(5), 4–14.

Barrera, R. (1992). The cultural gap in literature-based literacy instruction. *Education and Urban Society, 24*(2), 227–243.

Bryan, A. (1993). Deep like rivers. In A. Manna & C. S. Brodie (Eds.), *Many faces, many voices: Multicultural literary experiences for youth* (pp. 113–123). Fort Atkinson, WI: Highsmith Press.

Cooperative Children's Book Center. (1991). Commentaries on cultural authenticity and accuracy in multicultural children's and young adult books. In M. V. Lindgren (Ed.), *The multicolored mirror: Cultural substance in literature for children and young adults* (pp. 159–173). Fort Atkinson, WI: Highsmith Press.

Enciso, P. (1994). Cultural identity and response to literature: Running lessons from Maniac Magee. *Language Arts, 71,* 524–533.

Enciso, P. (1997, October). *Learning to be/read together: A sociocultural analysis of children's art, reading, and relationships.* Paper presented at the National Academy of Education annual meeting, Boulder, CO.

Feelings, T. (1991). Transcending the form. In M. V. Lindgren (Ed.) *The multicolored mirror: Cultural substance in literature for children and young adults* (pp. 45–57). Fort Atkinson, WI: Highsmith Press.

González, P. (1993). Reading against the cultural grain. In S. Miller & B. McCaskill (Eds.), *Multicultural literature and literacies: Making space for difference* (pp. 163–178). Albany: SUNY Press.

Hamanaka, S. (1991). Making the journey. In A. Manna & C. S. Brodie (Eds.), *Many faces, many voices: Multicultural literary experiences for youth* (pp. 51–60). Fort Atkinson, WI: Highsmith Press.

Hidalgo, N. (1993). Multicultural teacher introspection. In T. Perry & J. Fraser (Eds.), *Freedom's plow: Teaching in the multicultural classroom* (pp. 99–108). New York: Routledge.

hooks, b. (1991). Narratives of struggle. In P. Mariani (Ed.), *Critical fictions: The politics of imaginative writing* (pp. 53–61). Seattle, WA: Bay Press.

Howard, E. (1991). Authentic multicultural literature for children: An author's perspective. In M. V. Lindgren (Ed.), *The multicolored mirror: Cultural substance in literature for children and young adults* (pp. 91–100). Fort Atkinson, WI: Highsmith Press.

Jiménez, F. (1999). Boston Globe-Horn Book Award Acceptance: The Circuit. *The Horn Book Magazine, 75*(1), 49–52.

Kiefer, B. (1995). The disturbing image in children's picture books: Fearful or fulfilling? In S. Lehr (Ed.), *Battling dragons: Issues and controversy in children's literature* (pp. 51–62). Portsmouth, NH: Heinemann.

Lehr, S. (1995). Fourth graders read, write, and talk about freedom. In S. Lehr (Ed.), *Battling dragons: Issues and controversy in children's literature* (pp. 114–140). Portsmouth, NH: Heinemann.

McClure, A. (1995). Censorship of children's books. In S. Lehr (Ed.), *Battling dragons: Issues and controversy in children's literature* (pp. 3–30). Portsmouth, NH: Heinemann.

Mitchell, A. H. (1992). The magic of imagining: Transaction with young adult fiction and poetry. In A. Manna & C. S. Brodie (Eds.), *Many faces, many voices: Multicultural literary experiences for youth* (pp. 15–28). Fort Atkinson, WI: Highsmith Press.

Mohr, N. (1992). A journey toward a common ground: The struggle and identity of Hispanics in the U.S.A. In A. Manna & C. S. Brodie (Eds.), *Many faces, many voices: Multicultural literary experiences for youth* (pp. 61–68). Fort Atkinson, WI: Highsmith Press.

Narayan, K. (1993). How native is a "native" anthropologist? *American Anthropologist, 95*, 671–686.

Oddi, S. (1995). But will they buy them? In S. Lehr (Ed.), *Battling dragons: Issues and controversy in children's literature* (pp. 249–252). Portsmouth, NH: Heinemann.

Paley, V. G. (1997). Frederick. In V. Paley, *The girl with the brown crayon: How children use stories to shape their lives* (pp. 5–8). Cambridge, MA: Harvard University Press.

Seale, D. (1991). 1492–1992 from an American Indian perspective. In M. V. Lindgren (Ed.), *The multicolored mirror: Cultural substance in literature for children and young adults* (pp. 101–116). Fort Atkinson, WI: Highsmith Press.

Sims Bishop, R. (1991). Evaluating books by and about African-Americans. In M. V. Lindgren (Ed.), *The multicolored mirror: Cultural substance in literature for children and young adults* (pp. 31–45). Fort Atkinson, WI: Highsmith Press.

Sims Bishop, R. (1996). Letter to the editor. *The New Advocate, 9*(2), vii–viii.

Spears-Bunton, L. (1990). Welcome to my house: African American and European American students' responses to Virginia Hamilton's House of Dies Drear. *Journal of Negro Education, 59,* 566–576.

Taxel, J. (1995). Cultural politics and writing for young people. In S. Lehr (Ed.), *Battling dragons: Issues and controversy in children's literature* (pp. 155–170). Portsmouth, NH: Heinemann.

Wolf, S., & Enciso, P. (1994). Multiple selves in literary interpretation: Engagement and the language of drama. In C. Kinzer & D. Leu (Eds.), *Multidimensional aspects of literacy research, theory and practice: Forty-Third National Reading Conference Yearbook* (pp. 351–360). Chicago, IL: The National Reading Conference.

16

Teaching Multicultural Literature:
Struggling With Aesthetic, Educational, Political, and Cultural Change[1]

Violet J. Harris
University of Illinois

The individuals who influence my teaching promulgate provocative and intellectually intriguing ideas about literature, culture, and society. Among them are Henry Louis Gates, Jr. (1992), Toni Morrison (1992), Virginia Hamilton (1986), bell hooks (1984), and to a lesser extent, but only because I read fewer of their works, Albert Murray (1970) and Stanley Crouch (1998). That the conservative views of Crouch and Murray are intellectually attractive is a surprise. Each of these individuals argues for the central role of African American, Black, or Negro culture(s) in the creation of an American identity, certainly a radical notion. Rudine Sims Bishop's work, especially *Shadow and Substance* (1982), exerts considerable influence on the course and my evaluation of multicultural literature.

I do not wish to leave the impression that the ideas which shaped my courses derive solely from Black intellectuals; ideas, not the gender, race, or ethnicity of the creator are what matter. My conscious selection of these and other intellectuals of color stems from a deliberate stance against what I label the "politics of citation." By this I mean, the refusal to cite people of color. I also cite Gates, Murray, Crouch, Arnold Rampersad, bell hooks, and others because their work is excellent, insightful, and deserves consideration by those of us who teach courses in children's and young adult literature.

---

[1] Rather than include one sample syllabus, I have chosen to incorporate excepts from my syllabi from across the years.

Many tenets emanating partly from the work of the aforementioned individuals influence the children's literature courses I teach for undergraduate and graduate students. These emerged over the past 12 years and I evaluate them continuously. More than likely, I will retain a few throughout my teaching career, others will disappear. Some may reappear in a few years or decades. For now, these ideas are dominant.

First, literature is an individual artistic endeavor shaped by numerous sociocultural, historic, economic, and political factors. A literary work ceases to be the private property of its creator when published and made available for sale or reading. Certainly, the author maintains copyright privileges but the work is subject to criticism, accolades, close scrutiny, or benign neglect when made available to the public, however one defines that entity.

Second, literature is an important part of life but it is not essential. A few authors, however, disagree with this stance and write about literature saving their lives. For example, Chris Lynch, author of young adult novels such as *Mick* (1996) suggested the life-saving function of writing in a presentation during the 1995 NCTE ALAN workshop in San Diego. In a similar fashion, Jacqueline Woodson, whose ground-breaking novels *I Hadn't Meant to Tell You This* (1994) and *From the Notebooks of Melanin Sun* (1995) address the fluidity of identity and friendship, assumed a similar stance at the same conference. Writing enabled her to tell the world that she mattered and that her life was important.

Third, literature serves many functions but the aesthetic intent remains primary. This is not to suggest, however, that other functions, for example, educative, political, moralistic, or nationalistic, are not important. Rather, the success or failure of the work is partly determined by its structure and the author's ability to manipulate language and imagery.

Fourth, readers should have an opportunity to share their initial responses to texts unencumbered by my personal beliefs, attitudes, or ideologies. Creating a space for difference also entails providing a forum for differences in opinions. Theorists such as Louise Rosenblatt (1995) and Wolfgang Iser (1978) served as catalysts for this stance. Often, this becomes difficult when some students "deracialize" a text such as *The Watsons Go To Birmingham—1963* (Curtis, 1996) with comments that only tangentially touch on the bombing of the four Black girls attending Sunday School. My initial impulse is to force attention on these matters that some students perceive of as enforcing political correctness or engendering guilt.

Lastly, my role is to help students understand the literature and its role as a literary product and its position in relation to social, historical, political, or other issues. Whether one can discuss literature labeled *multicultural* solely on the basis of literary merit remains debatable. Texts such as *A Critical Handbook of Children's Literature* (Lukens, 1995), *Mother Was a Lady* (Kelly, 1974), *The Pleasures of Children's Literature* (Nodelman, 1997), *Children's Literature and Critical Theory* (May, 1995), *The Child as Critic* (Sloan, 1984), standard handbooks such as *Children's Literature in the Elemen-*

tary Program (Huck, et. al 1997), and journals—*Children's Literature Association Quarterly, Children and Education, HornBook Magazine, Journal of Children's Literature, The Lion and the Unicorn,* and *The New Advocate* keep my attention focused on literary merit of a work and, in some instances, the extraliterary ones as well.

Living up to the tenets outlined here becomes quite difficult under some circumstances. The balancing act involves not reducing literature to some form of propaganda. Instead, my goal is to guide students to an understanding of important issues suggested by the literature, the authors, the community of readers, and the publishers.

These struggles with aesthetic, educational, political, and cultural ideas and changes play out in the multicultural children's literature course I teach. The course was first offered during 1991, 4 years after I arrived at the University of Illinois. I note this context because, then, the U of I was notable, among many other reasons, because it housed the Center for the Study of Reading. The course, C & I 399ML was offered under an "omnibus course number" because trial offerings were needed in order to demonstrate demand for the course. Since then, the course has been offered at least once a year and has undergone some significant reincarnations. Those beginnings and subsequent changes are examined next.

IN THE BEGINNING … FOCUSING ON RACE AND ETHNICITY

The first syllabus developed in 1990 was relatively simple. The tone and philosophical perspectives were suggested by the following quotation excerpted from a column written by Rudine Sims Bishop in the now defunct journal devoted to children's literature, *Perspectives.*

> Books are sometimes windows, offering views of worlds that may be real imagined, familiar, or strange. These windows are also sliding glass doors, and readers have only to walk through in imagination to become part of whatever world has been created or recreated by the author. When lighting conditions are just right, however, a window can also be a mirror. Literature transforms human experience and reflects it back to us, and in that reflection we can see our own lives and experiences as part of the larger human experience. Reading then, becomes a means of self affirmation, and readers can seek their mirrors in books. (Bishop, 1990, ix–xi)

By highlighting this quotation, I hoped that students would come to agree that literature labeled *multicultural* served aims comparable to all literature. Further, multicultural literature could elicit the same types of responses from its readers.

The reading list consisted of 37 texts—fiction, nonfiction, and poetry, and 14 articles. I wanted to cover most genres, works by major authors, award winners, texts that contained innovative structures or controversial content, and works that were literary or artistic exemplars. Given the uncertainty about the course's future existence, I sought to cover as much as possible. Then and now, the amount of reading was too much. Six requirements and assignments were listed on the syllabus: completion of assigned readings, participation in class discussions, weekly journals, midterm and final examinations, a research paper (if taken for one unit of credit), and occasional viewing of films. Literature about African Americans, Asian Americans/ Pacific Islanders, Latinos/as, Native Americans, Jewish Americans, and Appalachian Whites comprised the reading list. Topics focused on issues such as the depiction of the groups prior to 1970, the advent of culturally conscious literature (Bishop, 1982), historical information, the interrogation of myths and stereotypes, the literary and artistic merit of the works, and their use with children.

My conceptions of multiculturalism at the time determined the literature of the groups included in the course. For me, race was and remains one of the most significant aspects of difference in this country and in many others as well. The status and exclusion of literature about people of color prompted me to focus on their literary depiction. Jewish Americans and Southern Whites were included because their depictions were limited, in varying degrees, as well. Other elements of differences, although important, were not a central focus. So, if disability was a factor, it was discussed in relation to a particular racial or ethnic group. In class discussions, I noted that conceptions of multiculturalism included race, ethnicity, gender, class, language, age, disability, sexual orientation, and other interrelated and intersecting identities. Later, two books I edited contained explications for the sole emphasis on people of color (Harris, 1992, 1997). This perspective generated opposition (Shannon, 1994 [see responses by Harris and Sims Bishop in the same issue]). Criticism centered on the perceived exclusion of Whites from conceptions of multiculturalism and assumed omission of issues of power, culture, and privilege.

My experiences suggested that race, as lived in the United States, remains one of the great, impolite topics. It is far more comfortable to talk about people of color within an international context rather than the domestic situation. Further, my past experiences suggested that discussions revolving around gender often centered primarily on White women.

One aim of the course was to read and discuss many texts and determine the multivaried meanings of what it meant to a person of color in a particular place during a specific time. Additionally, I attempted to place these meanings and experiences at the center of a children's literature course and not in the margins. Implicit in this position was the understanding that power, hegemonic or otherwise, societal transformation (conservative, radical, and everything in between), social relationships, and privilege would all be given due consideration through the filter of race. Consider one text I taught during the first course, *Paul Robeson: The Life and Times of a Free Black Man* (Hamilton, 1974). The title precludes any discussion not inclusive of critical commentary about the status of Black men, the artist as political radical, the social meanings of an intelligent, educated, articulate, and handsome man revered by many women of all races during a time when lynching was nearly a weekly affair, and the deliberate attempts of government representatives to silence radical political views.

An excerpt from the first syllabus provides a glimpse at the bare bones nature of the course. The topics, assignments, and texts devoted to Hispanic-American literature were fairly typical.

October 16

Depiction Before 1960

Culturally Conscious Literature

"Children's Literature on Puerto Rican Themes—Parts I & II"

"Paternalism and Assimilation in Books About Hispanics—Parts I & II"

Meltzer, M., *The Hispanic Americans*

Henry Cisneros

October 23

"Latino Writers in the American Market"

Felita

The House on Mango Street

Soto, G., *Baseball in April*

Class discussions progressed, as I recall, without overt signs of tension during the initial weeks of the course. The graduate students, mainly female and White, politely discussed the text and ideas. I was ill-prepared for their comments about some of the aforementioned books and a "poem" and cartoon titled "Injun Summer" (McCutcheon, 1907).

Each fall, from 1912–1992 , the *Chicago Tribune* published "Injun Summer " (McCutcheon, 1907) to herald the advent of fall. I shared the poem with students as an example of the kind of text which promoted stereotypes, perpetuated harmful images, and illustrated the power of one group to shape the image of another. Further, I indicted the poem and the *Chicago Tribune* as examples of racism and how it becomes institutionalized via cultural products and processes.

Some students were angered by my characterization of the poem. As I recollect, they viewed the poem as part of wonderful, nostalgic memories connected to their lives and their interactions with family members. They enjoyed the poem, did not regard its intent as racist, and argued that some characterizations were unsupported. Also, they wanted it known that they were not racists because they enjoyed the poem. Their reactions parallel those voiced by people who enjoy *The Five Chinese Brothers* (Bishop & Wiese, 1938), *The Story of Little Black Sambo* (Bannerman, 1899), and *Ten Little Rabbits* (Grossman, 1991). Neither the students nor I were willing to change our views. More than likely, an opportunity for critical discussion and enlightenment, on both sides, was missed.

Our reactions forever colored the manner in which I taught the course in subsequent years. Unfettered discussions were desired but concern about the intense anger directed against some authors and the attitudes about "Injun Summer" prompted serious self-reflection about the choice of texts, journal articles, groups, and the order in which the literature was read. I changed the syllabus in terms of the number of books read, structure of the course, and the discussion format.

Literary merit, status of the writer or artist, thematic issues, and historic or contemporary importance remained central elements in my book selection. In a like manner, my views about the political, cultural, and social aspects of texts remained a cornerstone of the course. Now, however, my discussion questions, the provision of background information, especially historical, and constant comparisons and attempts to create empathy or some level of identification among the students with characters, themes, or contexts became more important. The syllabus created for the fall 1992 semester reflects these changes.

CHANGES IN STRUCTURE

Two excerpts from W. E. B. Du Bois's *Souls of Black Folk* (1903, 1965) anchored this syllabus; they are two of his more frequently cited comments. The quotations posit ideas about "double consciousness," "the warring of two souls, " and the problem of the color-line, all of which predate the current postmodernist or postcolonial emphasis on the "fluidity of identity." Here, I seemed to be moving to the view that non-Whites possessed multiple identities, shared some experiences, differed in many ways, and occasionally wrote literature with parallel themes.

Course purposes included: reading and discussing literature by and about people of color, developing critical evaluative skills, identifying major issues, literary and extraliterary, and discovering ways of using the literature in elementary schools. I dropped the journal requirement, retained the midterm and final exams and research paper. I also added a new requirement: Now, each student had to guide the discussion of at least one text. My intent was to allow students to decide on the issues most germane to them; however, I reserved the right to add additional information, offer alternative interpretations, and pose questions. Moreover, two texts, *Teaching Multicultural Literature in Grades K–8* (Harris, 1992) and *A Critical Handbook of Children's Literature* (Lukens, 1995) were added, along with journal articles and literature. Two entries from the syllabus suggest the change in direction.

August 31

Introduction

Reading Biography

Overview of Children's Literature and Philosophical Perspectives

Assignment: Read Harris volume and the first half of Lukens.

- Questions for consideration: What are your conceptions of children, children's literature, and memories of reading literature as a child? What constitutes a classic? Should we continue to view certain books as permanent entries in canons? What are the roles of classics in a children's literature curriculum? How do we evaluate children's literature?

September 7

No class—Federal Holiday

Assignment: Read second half of Lukens.

September 14

Reader Response

Stereotypes

Multiculturalism

Assignment: Read Now Is Your Time! And An Indian Winter

- Questions for consideration: How do you respond to books? What situations elicit positive responses? What factors influence the manner in which you respond to literature? What images, attitudes, and beliefs to do you possess about people of various ethnic backgrounds? What books did you read as a child that included people of various ethnic backgrounds? What evaluation criteria do we use to judge this literature?

The questions for consideration reflected my attempts to elicit a different kind of discussion, one that remained candid but also one that moved toward critical inquiry. The first month or so was spent acquiring historical knowledge. Many of the students possessed minimal knowledge about the histories of people of different races beyond traditional "great men and great women." Furthermore, the texts about each group were linked on the basis on genre, historic period, and/or thematic content.

An additional change was the adoption of literature circles and discussion groups as the prevailing in-class discussion format. However, students were given the freedom to organize the discussions they led in the manner most suitable to them. As I recall, the small group discussions were much richer in content and enthusiasm when compared with the whole class discussion format of the first class. On the whole, I viewed this course as more successful than the first.

From the beginning, I tinkered with the course's content, objectives, structures, requirements, and texts. I do not envision a time when I am completely satisfied with any of the aforementioned. As I engage in the process of critical self-reflection, the need to expand my perspectives becomes increasingly important. Consider the latest syllabus (1997) that differs markedly from the first. The quotations from Du Bois remain with these comments added.

Many individuals who are members of the groups placed under the rubric of multiculturalism—Asian Pacific Islanders, Latinos, Native Americans, gays and lesbians, language minorities, people with disabilities, the elderly, and so forth—write about similar and different psychological, political, and socio-cultural issues. Other ideas have gained currency as well as such notions of the "Other," post-colonial narratives, marginalization, silencing, "pc," victimization, and various and sundry ideological views. Some may wonder what any of this has to do with children's literature. Should aesthetic concerns remain dominant or do the aforementioned "extra-literary" issues have a role? These and other issues are pondered in the course; however, the literary merit of the work is an essential component of the discussions.

Two professional texts were required: *Sharing Multiethnic Literature in Grades K–8* (Harris, 1997) and *Research and Professional Resources in Children's Literature* (Short, 1995). Three excerpts from the syllabus suggest the dramatic changes.

1/22   Introduction

Assignment: Select, read, and critique (2 pgs.) an article in support of multiculturalism by an author such as James Banks, Ron Takaki, Carl Grant, and one article written by an individual who presents an oppositional view such as Dinesh D'Souza, Lynn Cheney, Arthur Schleslinger, Jr., or any other individuals who have acquired media or academic prominence. Questions for consideration: What is multiculturalism? What are the major tenets? Can one consider it a progressive movement? Will it result in the destruction of a unifying identity among "Americans?" Is there any merit to the argument that multiculturalism is a liberal stop-gap measure that prevents needed social reconstruction/reformation? How do proponents of other ideological movements such as feminism, womanism, Afro-centrism, and Neo-Marxism view multiculturalism? Is multicultural literature relevant, needed or beneficial?

2/6   Developing Historical Knowledge: "The Others"

Anthologies

Assignment: Select two books from one of the following series: 18 Pine Street, Willie Pearl, the Baby-Sitters Club (books featuring Claudia or Jessie), Pony Pals, Ziggy and the Black Dinosaurs, Addy of the American Girls, Magic Attic, or other series featuring people of color or any other groups featured under the rubric of multiculturalism. Skim the books in preparation for discussion. Questions for consideration: What accounts for the phenomenal appeal of series fiction among children? Some earlier series, Nancy Drew, the Bobbsey Twins, and Raggedy Ann and Andy, for example, contained stereotypes. Many of today's series include some ethnic or racial diversity. Do these new series raise the literary standards of series fiction or continue well-established traditions such as gendered identities, consumerism, and conservatism?

4/1   Fantasy

Assignment: Read Annie on My Mind and From the Notebooks of Melanin Sun. Questions for consideration: Two of the most censored books in children's literature are Heather Has Two Mommies and Uncle Tim's Roommate. Many people oppose the inclusion of literature featuring gays and lesbians. What are some of the reasons for opposition and support? What is the most appropriate age at which to introduce the literature? Do the authors challenge stereotypes of gays and lesbians? Is there a gay and lesbian aesthetic apparent in these works? How would you share the books with students?

The differences among the syllabi are astounding. To a great extent, they reflect the ways in which my definition of multiculturalism is organic and in a state of constant fluctuation. Now, for example, religion has become more salient for me as an aspect of children's literature. Some of the picture books on this topic I shared with students included *Magid Fasts for Ramadan* (Matthews, 1996), *Glorious Impossible* (L'engle, 1990), and *Celebration Song* (Berry, 1994). A central question for me remains whether or not the seemingly progressive changes will continue or will I turn to a more conservative stance?

REFERENCES

Crouch, S. (1998). *Always in pursuit: Fresh American perspectives, 1995–97*. New York: Pantheon Books.

Du Bois, W. E. B. (1903, 1965). *The Souls of Black folk*. New York: Fawcett Books.

Gates, H. (1992). *Loose canons*. New York: Oxford University Press.

Hamilton, V. (1986). On being a Black writer in America. *The Lion and the Unicorn, 10*, 15–17.

Harris, V. J. (Ed.). (1992). *Teaching multicultural literature in grades K–8*. Norwood, MA: Christopher-Gordon.

Harris, V. J. (Ed.). (1997). *Sharing multiethnic literature in grades K–8*. Norwood, MA: Christopher-Gordon.

hooks, b. (1984). *Feminist theory: From margin to center*. Boston, MA: South End Press.

Huck, C., Hickman, J., Hepler, & Kiefer, B. (1997). *Children's literature in the elementary school* (6th ed.). Madison, WI: Brown & Benchmark..

Iser, W. (1978). *The act of reading: A theory of aesthetic response*. Baltimore, MD: Johns Hopkins University Press.

Kelly, R. G. (1974). *Mother was a lady*. Westport, CT: Greenwood Press.

Lukens, R. (1995). *A critical handbook of children's literature* (5th ed.). New York: HarperCollins.

May, J. (1995). *Children's literature and critical theory*. New York: Oxford University Press.

Morrison, T. (1992). *Playing in the dark*. Cambridge, MA: Harvard University Press.

Murray, A. (1970). *The omni-Americans: New perspectives on Black experiences and American culture*. New York: Dutton.

Nodelman, P. (1996). *The pleasures of children's literature*. White Plains, NY: Longman.

Rosenblatt, L. (1995). *Literature as exploration* (5th ed.). New York: Modern Language Association.

Shannon, P. (1994). I am the canon. *The Journal of Children's Literature, 20*(1), 1–5.

Short, K. (Ed.). (1994). *Research and professional resources in children's literature*. Newark, DE: International Reading Association.

Sims, R. (1982). *Shadow and substance*. Urbana, IL: National Council of Teachers of English.

Sloan, G. (1984). *The child as critic* (2nd ed.). New York: Teachers College Press.

Williams, R. (1983). *Culture and society*. New York: Columbia University Press.

Children's Books Cited

Bannerman, H. (1899, 1943). *The story of Little Black Sambo*. New York: HarperCollins.

Berry, J. (1994). *Celebration song*. New York: Simon & Schuster.

Bishop, C., & Wiese, K. (1938). *The five Chinese brothers*. New York: Coward-McCann.

Curtis, C. (1995). *The Watsons go to Birmingham–1963*. New York: Delacorte.

Grossman, V. (1991). *Ten little rabbits*. San Francisco: Chronicle Books.

Hamilton, V. (1974). *Paul Robeson: The life and times of a free black man*. New York: Harper & Row.

L'engle, M. (1990). *Glorious impossible*. New York: Simon & Schuster.

Lynch, C. (1996). *Mick*. New York: HarperCollins.

Matthews, M. (1996). *Magid fasts for Ramadan*. New York: Clarion Books.

McCuthcheon, R. (1907). *Injun Summer*. Chicago: Chicago Tribune.

Woodson, J. (1994). *I hadn't meant to tell you this*. New York: Delacorte.

Woodson, J. (1995). *From the notebooks of Melanin Sun*. New York: Blue Sky Press.

17

Adolescent Literature
and the Teaching of Literature

Robert E. Probst
Georgia State University

Adolescent Literature is intended primarily for middle and secondary school language arts and English teachers, although it occasionally also draws elementary school teachers who are interested in directing their older students toward slightly more sophisticated reading. Its title suggests that it is about the books for young adults, but it is also, perhaps primarily, about the ways in which those books might be read and then addressed in class.

Rosenblatt (1995) argues that literature is a transaction, one in which the reader and the text come together to create a unique event that is the poem (or story, novel, play, film, or any other literary genre). If you accept that vision, then designing any literature course becomes a more complicated matter than simply arranging the texts. The readers, too, have to be, if not arranged, at least taken into consideration. Who they are is inevitably going to shape what they make of the texts they encounter. This course, originally conceived as an introduction to that body of literature especially suitable for young adults, thus rapidly and necessarily evolved to include within its focus not the texts alone, but also the ways in which we might read and react to them. In order to examine the role adolescent literature might play in the schools, it seemed essential to read not only such novelists as Cormier and Crutcher, but also theorists like Rosenblatt and Iser (1978, 1974). The course has thus come to consist of at least two strands, one examining the nature of literary experience, and the other focusing on the literature for adolescents.

We are sometimes virtually unaware of what we are doing as we read a work of literature. We pass our eyes over the page and something mysterious happens. When we come to the end of the story, or the novel, we may be able to say something about what it made us feel, or whether we enjoyed it, but many readers, perhaps most, seem either to lose or to have no language for describing the complex events that have transpired while they were immersed in the text. They will quite likely have recalled events in their own lives at some point in the story, have been reminded of people they knew, have had fleeting thoughts of other texts they have read or movies they have seen, have felt some nameless uneasiness or satisfaction with happenings, have formulated judgments about characters, have begun, at least, to articulate questions and thoughts about the writer, the characters, the tale. But much of that is lost. It flashes by and evaporates like a dream. Part of the course, then, is devoted to making the students aware of what happens, of what they do, as they read.

Rosenblatt's (1995) *Literature as Exploration* has usually been the central text for the part of the course examining literary experience. It offers a vision of reading that respects both the text and the reader, arguing that neglect of either element can only distort our understanding of what happens between reader and book. Rosenblatt's conception of literary experience, humane and democratic as it is, usually finds a receptive audience among teachers, although there are many who have difficulty envisioning its application in the classroom, and others who resist the notion that there is not one right, best, most accurate reading to which they might lead their students. The former find some assistance in the other articles and books that attempt to draw inferences from her theories for the schools. The latter are occasionally persuaded to value more highly the unique readings of their diverse students by an examination of their own reading processes. Both may be helped by the experiments and demonstrations of literature teaching that take up about a third of the class time.

The reflection on the process of reading has been encouraged, in small part, by asking students to write reflectively on their own history as readers. These assignments are short pieces, requiring little more than 15 or 30 minutes, and are discussed during the first part of each class session. A more important assignment is the task of analyzing their own processes of reading as they work through a novel they have chosen. Early in the course they are asked to choose a text they would like to read for their own entertainment. With luck, there will be some who have titles in mind and others who are willing to go along with someone else's recommendation, so that we find the class in groups of about three to five, each group reading a book they have chosen. They agree on a schedule for their reading and then meet each week during class. They are asked to spend part of their time together just talking about the book in whatever way suits them. (If possible, I ask them to tape these conversations and transcribe the tapes to assist in the analysis.) Then they are to spend some time talking about the talk, trying to figure out what they had been doing as they read, how they were influenced by the others in the group, what aspects of the reading and the conversation they found pleasant and productive, or painful and useless, and anything else they are able to observe about the nature of literary experience. Ultimately, they are asked to consider the implications of their observations for the teaching of literature in the schools.

As they are reading their own novels, studying Rosenblatt and related works, and participating in or conducting demonstrations of teaching approaches, they are also asked to read as much adolescent literature as they can. Some of this they read in small groups that change in composition each week. Several rotation plans have been devised, for classes from 12 to 36 students. The plans establish different groups of roughly four students for each of 8 weeks, and requires each student to be in charge of the group twice. His responsibility for those two nights is to assign the text to be read, choosing young adult works likely to be easily available to others in the class, to conduct the discussion, to report back to the full class afterwards, and perhaps to write up the small group's deliberations for a course notebook, if we choose to do that during the quarter. These groups meet during the dinner break necessary in our long evening classes, enabling us to use time that would otherwise be lost.

If all works well during the quarter, now semester, students in the course will broaden their acquaintance with adolescent literature and refine their understanding of what happens when reader and text come together.

Adolescent Literature and the Teaching of Literature
Sample Course Description

Memorandum

> To: Students in "Adolescent Literature"
>
> From: Bob Probst
>
> Re: Tentative plans for the course.

Objectives

The course will be divided between two points of interest—literary theory and instruction, and the literature for adolescents. We will try to examine the principles that might govern instruction in literature, perhaps experimenting with some of the practices they suggest, and we will try to acquaint ourselves with some of the literature appropriate for the students in middle and secondary schools. Although some of the work may be practical, leading to resources immediately useful in the schools, much will be theoretical and philosophical, on the assumption that a clearer conception of the nature of the reader's interaction with the literary work will lead ultimately to better teaching.

Resources

The texts, assigned and suggested, reflect the two major issues for the course. The first and most important book is Louise Rosenblatt's, *Literature As Exploration*, (5th ed.). Although it was written in the 1930s it is very much contemporary and remains the single most important book ever written on the teaching of literature. Critical theory has only recently begun to catch up to it.

Rosenblatt is the most valuable reading on the teaching of literature, but there are other texts that may be occasionally useful. *Readers, Texts, Teachers*, Corcoran and Evans (1987), is a good collection of essays, and Donelson and Nilsen's *Literature for Today's Young Adults*, 5th ed., (1996) which focuses on the body of literature that has been found to be especially provocative for secondary school students. Its approach is basically historical, and it contains an excellent collection of bibliographies, which should be useful to you in identifying works of adolescent literature to read during the quarter. You might also consider *Teaching Literature in the Secondary School*, Beach and Marshall (1991) *Response and Analysis*, Probst (1988), and *Reading and Response*, Hayhoe and Parker, editors (1990).

I'll recommend readings for each session. The books you will have, of course, and the articles are almost all from the journals of the National Council of Teachers of English, which are readily available. Please read as much as you can, respond to the items in a journal or a log, and come with issues, problems, concerns, ideas to discuss. Much of the first part of class will usually be devoted to undirected discussion of the reading in small groups.

Read as much adolescent literature as possible during the quarter. Although I prefer a broad definition of adolescent literature, we might want to restrict ourselves to that literature written especially for adolescents and that literature found to be popular with adolescents. For recent titles, *English Journal* (especially the "Books for Young Adults" section), *The ALAN Review*, and the various library journals will be helpful.

Readings in Critical Theory and Methodology

You may also wish to read beyond the suggested text in literary theory and research. Rosenblatt is excellent, but in the past two decades a great many others have addressed the issues she raised initially. A bibliography will be available within a week or two. In it, scattered among many works on literary theory, are several texts that deal primarily with methods of literature instruction, research in the teaching of literature, and literature for adolescents. [Readers of this resource book may turn to the Web site for a list of recommended readings.] Although I have not ordered any of these for the course, you may wish to read one or two of the methods texts early in the quarter if you feel the need to refresh your background in literature instruction. A knowledge of the sort of material they cover will be assumed.

Take a look at the journals, too, especially *Research in the Teaching of English, College English, The ALAN Review, The Advocate*, and the *English Journal* (some of the most useful issues of *English Journal* are February, September, and November 1974, February 1975, February and March 1977, February 1978 and 1979, December 1979, November 1984, January 1988, and March 1994). You might also glance at *New*

Literary History, *Genre, Criticism, Critical Inquiry, Diacritics, PMLA,* and *Reader: Essays in Reader-Oriented Theory, Criticism, and Pedagogy.*

Structure of the Course

Literature and Its Teaching

As I envision the course, there will be several strands running concurrently. The first will deal with questions about the nature of literary experience and about the teaching of literature. This will draw heavily on Rosenblatt, other suggested readings, and whatever reading you may undertake from the bibliographies in the texts, and from the one I will distribute later in the quarter. We will share the responsibility for the discussions, so do not hesitate to lead us into more profitable areas if the questions I, and others in the class, raise are not satisfactory to you.

I will invite each of you to prepare and teach in this class one lesson that exemplifies the principles and practices you consider appropriate for the secondary school literature class. We will try to work out a suitable schedule.

The Analysis of Literary Experience

I suspect that we are largely unaware of what we do when we read. Like breathing, we just do it, without giving it much thought. If, however, we are to think productively about the process, we have to become conscious of the act and reflect on what we do and how we do it. Toward that end, I want to devote part of the course to a close look at our own literary experience. Briefly outlined, here is what I hope we will do:

1. By week 2, select, in groups no larger than 4, a novel that no one in the group has read previously. It may be current or classic, but it must be new to all in the group, and preferably to all in the class. It should be of a size that will permit you to read it comfortably in about 4 to 6 weeks.
2. By week 3, read the first several chapters (agree within the group on a suitable chunk). On that evening, part of the class (45 minutes?) will be devoted to conversation within the groups about the text. At first, this will be unstructured and free-flowing, but if in later weeks you want to experiment with various structures, we can do so. The talk will be taped, so that following class, one member of the group can transcribe it for the following week. That responsibility will be rotated through the group. The transcriber will get a disk copy of the tape to me in time for me to prepare formatted text for the group to analyze.
3. During the meeting of week 4, the groups will again spend part of the class time in conversation about the next section of the book. We will distribute the transcripts of the previous week's talk at this time, and during the fol-

lowing week we will read on in the novel, and we will analyze the transcripts.

4. During the meeting of week 5, we will again discuss the book, but we will also spend part of the time reading, analyzing, and discussing transcripts from the previous week's conversation. We will repeat this pattern during the following weeks.

Over the final weeks of the course, we will write a brief paper in which we consider the analysis of our own literary experiences in the light of theory and of our teaching. These papers should take into account our own private readings of the text, the conversations within the group, the literary theory we have been reading, the implications for teaching.

Writing Exercises

During the quarter, there may be occasional or regular requests to write brief statements on topics I suggest. These papers will be closely related to the reading and discussion, and will, I hope, encourage the clarifying and crystallizing of thought about the substance of the course. None of them will be a major burden—they are intended to elicit the sort of writing that you might naturally do if you were stimulated by the reading to reflect on paper. They will constitute something like a directed journal, and I will be interested in knowing, as the quarter progresses, whether or not the writing helps you think about the work of the course.

The Adolescent Literature

Another major strand of the course will focus on the adolescent literature. For this part of the course we'll divide into groups of about three or four according to a schedule you will receive. One person in each group will be responsible for assigning the book to be read during the days before the group will meet, and then, when the group convenes, he will be responsible for conducting the discussion, and, if time permits, summarizing the discussion for the class.

During the first several weeks, I may suggest a pattern for the discussion groups to follow for at least a part of period. During the last weeks of the course, after we are immersed in the theories Rosenblatt and others develop, the leaders may be asked to design plans of their own to organize the discussions. These plans should represent an effort to tie the theories of instruction directly to the specific literary work. The talk should deal with interpretations of the work, its place in a literature curriculum, anticipated student response to the work, possible strategies for teaching, and anything else the group considers interesting or useful.

Cultural Diversity in the Literature Program

It is during this strand of the course that we will best be able to address the issue of cultural diversity in the curriculum. As you select titles, please be alert to that factor and try to help me ensure that the titles we chose represent the widest possible range of ethnic, religious, regional, and cultural identities. We would like to have as many perspectives on the human condition represented as possible. A frequent complaint about the typical literature curriculum is that it is too centered on the European tradition; we will try to monitor the selections we make to help us broaden our perspective.

Each student will select the book and conduct the discussion twice during the quarter. For one of the two books you choose—it doesn't matter which one—you'll be asked to prepare a fairly detailed teaching plan, to be reproduced for the class.

Individual Work

This strand of the course will be devoted to group or individual work that you choose to pursue. The only specification for this work is that it be related to literature instruction. If possible, we will identify those whose interests are similar and encourage them to trade ideas, resources, and suggestions as work proceeds. If some decide to work as a more formally constituted group, perhaps dividing work on one topic into suitable subtopics, then we may try to allot some time each week for that group to meet during class hours.

As examples of the sort of project suitable for this segment of the course consider the following:

1. Designing a unit in which the techniques of improvisation or creative dramatics are applied to instruction in literature.
2. Developing a set of criteria for a literature curriculum and using it to analyze either one of the curricula of local schools or that suggested by a literature textbook series.
3. Studying the implications of the recent work in communication theory for instruction in literature.
4. Studying the reading interests of students in local schools.
5. Studying the problems of correlating instruction in reading with instruction in literature.
6. Testing the efficacy of several different styles of questioning.
7. Devising a classification system for literary works that identifies the conflicts, situations, or problems that may characterize works. See Carlsen's *Books and the Teenage Reader* (1980) and Burke's *The Philosophy of Literary Form* (1957).
8. Designing a scheme for assessing a student's growth in literary sophistication over a school year.
9. Designing and conducting case studies of the reading process.

10. Studying the implications of the research on values for instruction in literature.
11. Devising strategies for dealing with censorship or backtobasics or other idiocies that afflict the teaching of literature.
12. Devising a complete plan for a literature course suitable in an elective program.
13. Developing a rationale for the literature program, 7–12 or K–12, explaining how instruction will vary from year to year.
14. Developing a rationale for eliciting imaginative writing—literature—from students.
15. Demonstrating techniques for teaching certain literary concepts or genre.
16. Analyzing and criticizing the works of an author of books for adolescents.
17. Analyzing a set of works, 10 to 20, of adolescent literature that constitute some sort of group.
18. Taping, transcribing, and analyzing a series of lessons emphasizing (1) eliciting and exploring personal response, (2) clarifying and refining ideas and perceptions within the class, (3) reading and discussing two or more related works.
19. Critically analyzing one or more of the major works of literary theory.
20. Writing an adolescent novel, or part of one, or a short story or two.
21. Compiling and assessing a collection of computer-based instructional packages useful in literature instruction.

These are simply suggestions—you are not restricted to this list. I would prefer that you identify topics you think significant and work on them. There is also a great deal of latitude in form. The results of your work might be a research paper in the traditional mold, an experimental study, or something else that you devise.

Keep in mind that we will want to share the results of our labors with the rest of the class. I'll allot some time near the end of the quarter for that purpose. As you work on the project, anticipate the obligation to present it and plan for it.

Schedule

The evening's schedule for most sessions, though always subject to change, will be something like the following:

4:40–4:45	Opening remarks.
4:45–6:00	Full-group discussion/lecture/experiment. Consideration of special issues, work on individual projects.
6:00–7:15	Dinner and discussion of adolescent novels, in small groups.
7:15–7:45	Discussion of adolescent novels, in full group.
7:45–8:50	Discussion of assigned readings—texts and articles—probably in small groups.

8:50–9:20   Planning, wrap-up.

The class schedule that follows is at best a rough prediction. You'll receive more detailed reading suggestions each week, and we will adjust the schedule as seems appropriate.

Class 1—Introductions, organization of the course.

Class 2—"The nature of response." The reader and the literary text.

Class 3—"The nature of response." Writing in response to literature.

Class 4—"The Community of Readers." The reader and other readers.

Class 5—"The Range of Discourse." Genre and the literature for adolescents.

Class 6—"The Literature for Adolescents." Censorship. Writing from and about literature.

Presentations of individual or group projects will probably begin today.

Class 7—"The Literature Curriculum."

Class 8—"The Problems of Assessment."

Class 9—"Theory and Research in the Teaching of Literature."

Class 10—Final reports, wrap-up.

Procedures

Although you are not required to do so, I would appreciate it if you would tell me about your plans for the project fairly early in the quarter, and of course, I'll discuss it and any other work you are doing whenever you wish during the quarter. Ideally, we would talk early in the quarter, as ideas are taking shape, again midquarter during or shortly after drafting the paper, and then again after the work is polished. I realize that schedules are full and so these conferences are not mandatory, but they are the only way that I can offer any assistance.

I hope to give papers a careful reading early in the quarter. Obviously, at that point they will be drafts—I would not expect to see finished products—but I would hope that they would be legible. The rationale for reading unfinished drafts is that there is no other way for me to offer any advice or assistance likely to affect our work during the quarter. Suggestions offered at the end of the quarter are too easily ignored, and so the reading of the final draft will be simply evaluative. Any comments I have to make will be brief, although, of course, we'll be able to discuss any aspects of the paper you wish to consider in the final conference.

A brief word about grading.... Unless you prefer an alternative, the grades will represent my judgment of the quality of work, taking into consideration the contributions to the deliberations of the class, the annotations, the paper (undoubtedly the single most significant item), and any exams that may be offered. If you are uneasy with that scheme, I will be happy to work out another arrangement with you either as individuals or as a group. It might be something as simple as a weighting system for the various aspects of the work, or as complicated as a contract arrangement. If you are interested in an alternative, let me know by about the second week of the course so that we can negotiate it.

Evaluation is, of course, different from grading, and I will be happy to meet with you to evaluate work whenever you wish. I will rely on you to let me know how things are going.

REFEENCES

Beach, R., & Marshall, J. (1991). *Teaching literature in the secondary school.* New York: Harcourt Brace Jovanovich.

Burke, K. (1957). *The philosophy of literary form.* New York: Vintage Books.

Carlsen, G. R. (1980). *Books and the teenage reader: A guide for teachers, librarians and parents* (2nd ed.). New York: Harper & Row.

Corcoran, B., & Evans, E. (1987). *Readers, texts, teachers.* Upper Montclair, NJ: Boynton/Cook.

Donelson, K. L., & Nilsen, A. P., (1996). *Literature for today's young adults.* (5th. ed.) Glenview, IL: Scott Foresman.

Hayhoe, M., & Parker, S. (Eds.). (1990). *Reading and response.* Milton Keynes, England: Open University Press.

Iser, W. (1974). *The implied reader: Patterns of communication in prose fiction from Bunyan to Beckett.* Baltimore: Johns Hopkins University Press.

Iser, W. (1978). *The act of reading: A theory of aesthetic response.* Baltimore: Johns Hopkins University Press.

Probst, R. E. (1988). *Response and analysis: Teaching literature in junior and senior high school.* Portsmouth, NH: Boynton/Cook- Heinemann.

Rosenblatt, L. M. (1995). *Literature as exploration* (5th ed.). New York: Modern Language Association.

Rosenblatt, L. M. (1978). *The reader, the text, the poem: The transactional theory of the literary work.* Carbondale, IL: Southern Illinois University Press.

IV

EMERGENT LITERACY

18

Literacy Development in the Early Years:
Helping Children Read and Write

Lesley Mandel Morrow
Rutgers University

Literacy Development in the Early Years is a course designed for students seeking initial certification, teachers working toward a master's degree in early childhood education or as a reading specialist, and administrators. The students in the course are often diverse in educational and professional experience, from the novice who is entering the field of teaching in pursuit of an initial certification to doctoral students who are supervisors, principals, and so on. Because the participants in the course have diverse backgrounds, there is differentiation of assignments. The more sophisticated students will spend more time on the more scholarly work, such as the research project and be exempt from some practical assignments such as creating an integrated language arts unit if they choose.

The purpose of the course is to review recent research and theory concerning early literacy development. In doing so, we also study learning theorists particularly associated with early childhood. We study the different areas of literacy development specifically oral language, writing, and reading. We discuss theory and research first, and then translate that into practical strategies, materials, preparation of the environment to match teaching strategies, and assessment concerns.

From a personal perspective, the course was developed based on my experience as a student in a teacher education program at Syracuse University. A wonderful professor motivated my enthusiasm for teaching and opened my mind to infinite number of ideas for making classrooms wonderful joyful places for children to learn. My experience as a classroom teacher in the early childhood grades has had an influence on the course development. I still show slides of my classrooms and work samples I kept from children I taught. Then, I had my own child and watched and helped with her early literacy development. This added a new dimension and insight for my teaching. I do plan the course carefully, fully cognizant of the fact that if I am a teacher educator preparing teachers to not only know their content, but to know about methodology that keeps individuals engaged, motivated, and interested in learning, that my classes must be engaging, motivating, and interesting. I try to be a model for their teaching.

The course emphasizes integrating literacy development throughout the school day as an integral part of all content areas. There is an effort to reflect on the current issues in early literacy today, specifically: Balancing constructivist approaches to early literacy and more explicit transmission models for skill development, early intervention programs, teaching skills in a developmentally appropriate setting, dealing with standards, and attending to individual needs of the struggling and advanced reader through guided reading instruction in small groups and providing productive independent work for student functioning independent of the teacher.

Although the basic course remains the same because theories have not changed dramatically, when new issues arise the emphasis in a given semester will change.

There is a field component to the course that is mandatory for students seeking initial teacher certification. For all students there are a series of experiences they must participate in with a young child, such as collecting and analyzing a language sample, an analysis of a story retelling or doing a running record on a selection read.

The class is run with many types of experiences for the students. We have lectures, whole group discussions, and group projects that are done both in and out of class. We use a great deal of modeling of strategies, materials are shared throughout the semester, with teachers bringing in projects done by their students. They share assessment materials from their districts as well.

Students are asked to bring specific materials to class almost on a weekly basis that coincide with the discussion at hand. These could include genres of children's literature, a typed transcribed story retelling, or a writing sample. These real materials enrich the class. I also have several videos, slide presentations, and audio tapes for different topics studied. These are not commercially purchased materials; they are videos, photos, and audio tapes that I create as I visit classrooms in which I do research. This keeps me current, in the classroom, and in touch with real life at school.

One difficult task in teaching the course is the diverse backgrounds of the students enrolled. I have students with no teaching experience seeking initial certification in early childhood/elementary education. I have master's level students who are experienced teachers, and I have doctoral level students who are in supervisory positions and may teach at the college level themselves. Differentiating instruction to meet their needs is a challenge.

The other difficult part of teaching the course is the lack of time to deal with all of the topics in an in-depth manner and to determine which topics to spend the most time with. It seems the more we know about a particular area, the more difficult it becomes to teach. I often try to give too much to my students and in doing so tend to overwhelm them particularly in the beginning of the course. I have to remember that more is not necessarily better. However, it seems that in the end my strength is my weakness and my weakness is my strength. I tend to do a great deal at a quick pace. Early in the course as I mentioned, students seem overwhelmed, at the end of the course most say it was worth it and when I ask what should I change or delete and most say nothing. When I meet students who are teaching years after they have had my class, they will often remind me of how overwhelmed they felt, but that after the course they would reflect and keep my materials and to this day have use for everything we studied and refer back to the reading materials and notes regularly.

Sample Syllabus
Early Literacy Development

Objectives for the Course

1. Review recent research and theory concerning early literacy development.
2. Study the areas of literacy development specifically oral language, writing, and reading. Strategies for classroom practice, generated by the theory and research, will be studied.
3. There will be an emphasis on integrating literacy development throughout the school day and as an integral part of all content areas.
4. Critical issues in literacy today will be addressed when and as they do arise.
5. The student will be asked to participate in and demonstrate ability in scholarly assignments and practical application as well.

Required Texts

Morrow, L. M. (2001). *Literacy development in the early years: Helping children read and write* (4th ed.). Boston: Allyn & Bacon.

McInyre, E., & Pressley, M. (1996). *Balanced instruction: Strategies and skills in whole language.* Norwood, MA: Christopher-Gordon.

Morrow, L. M. (1997). *The literacy center.* Stenhouse Publishers.

Cunningham, P. (1995). *Phonics they use: Words for reading and writing* (3rd ed.). New York: HarperCollins.

A book of handouts and pertinent articles are provided to supplement readings.

Topics

1. *Foundations of Early Literacy*
   a. perspectives concerning Early Literacy
   b. learning theories effecting practice
   c. the integrated–interdisciplinary language arts curriculum

    d. a balanced perspective in early literacy instruction (constructivist approaches and explicit instruction models)

2. *Research Methods in Early Literacy*
    a. qualitative and quantitative designs
    b. teacher as researcher

3. *Family and Literacy Development*
    a. Family literacy—Programs that focus on the child, the parent, Intergenerational Programs

4. *Language and Literacy Development*
    a. theories of language acquisition
    b. developmental stages
    c. objectives, strategies and materials for learning
    d. assessment strategies
    e. integrating oral language into the curriculum: The language experience approach, whole language
    f. children with special language needs (ESL, non standard English, communication, disorders)

5. *Writing and Early Literacy Development*
    a. theories of writing acquisition
    b. developmental stages
    c. objectives strategies and materials for learning
    d. assessment strategies
    e. integrating writing into the total curriculum
    f. addressing children with special needs in writing development

6. *Children's Literature and Literacy Development*
    a. objectives for using literature
    b. genres of children's literature, authors, and illustrators
    c. strategies and materials: Promoting voluntary interest in reading and writing
    d. integrating the use of literature in the total curriculum
    e. cooperative and collaborative learning
    f. children's literature and special needs

7. *Developing Comprehension: Construction and Reconstruction of Meaning Related to Books*
    a. objectives, strategies, and materials
    b. portfolio assessment
    c. integration into the total curriculum
    d. addressing children with special needs in comprehension

8. *Developing Knowledge of Print: Phonics, phonemic awareness, context clues, sight, and so forth*
    a. objectives, strategies and materials

    b. integration into the total curriculum

    c. addressing children with special needs knowledge about print

  9. *Organizing and Managing the Literacy Development Environment*

    a. preparing rich literacy physical classroom environments

    b. integrating literacy into the total curriculum through thematic units in art, play, music, science, math, and social studies

    c. organizing strategies for instruction in a language arts block (Guided Reading Instruction, whole class, small group, individualized and collaborative learning)

    d. attending to children with special needs: Intervention pullout an inclusion programs

    e. fostering change in literacy programs

    f. technology in the early childhood literacy program

 10. *Assessment Issues*

    a. standardized measures

    b. portfolio assessment

Requirements

In-Class Requirements

1. Please participate in class discussions and bring materials when requested for demonstrations and displays. This is a major part of the course work. No credit for participation is given if absent.

2. For students who are in the Master's Certification Program you need to have a formal field experience with seven visits, three hours each. Others who wish a field experience may have one. Everyone will need access to a child between the ages of 2 through 7 to carry out field assignments. This can be done with a relative, a friend's child, one that you visit in a school setting, or your own child. We will be collecting language samples, writing samples, and you will be asked to try literacy strategies with the children. Keep a portfolio of performance samples of your work with the child during the course.

Out-of-Class Requirements

1. Students are expected to read all assigned readings and participate in related discussions in class.

2. Select a literacy skill. Select a piece of children's literature from which you can teach that skill. Select a storytelling method to tell the story to children and teach the skill. Develop a lesson plan; include the title of the book, author, and publisher. This material is for a center where children will use it after you have modeled its use. It should reinforce the skill. *If you use resources, cite references and describe one or two theo-*

ries utilized. You will select a date and present the story in class. If you can, copy your lesson plan for the entire class.

3. There will be a take-home test. It will deal with readings and class work. The test will focus on what has been emphasized in class.

Due Date:_____

6.a. Conduct a piece of research dealing with young children's literacy learning. The project should include some data collection and analysis. It could also be an in-depth review of literature with some observations about the topic. A format for the project will be outlined. If you cannot find a population of children I will be able to help.

6b. Early in the semester submit a one-page abstract outlining your project. Select and read a research article from a professional journal, that deals with your topic and attach the article to your Abstract. Suggested journals for your article are: *Reading Teacher, Reading Research Quarterly, Journal of Literacy Research, Reading Research and Instruction, Elementary School Journal, Journal of Educational Research, Child Development, The National Reading Conference Yearbook, Language Arts, Young Children, Early Childhood Research Quarterly*, and so on.

Due Date for Abstract _____ Due Date for Paper_____

6c. Group Project: Prepare an integrated language arts unit based on a topic in social studies or science utilizing many pieces of children's literature. Follow the format distributed.

Due Date _____

7. In the course of the semester be sure to talk with me on a one-to-one basis. This can occur in class, in my office, elsewhere. This does not require an appointment.

8. Visit our course Web site to chat about readings and current issues.

Recommendations

1. Please hand assignments in on time; grades will be lowered for each class day they are late.
2. All work must be done on a word processor.
3. Attendance is important. Grades are affected after two absences.
4. Materials to bring to class are important and count in your grade.
5. Join a professional organization (NAEYC, IRA, NJEA, etc.).
6. Subscribe to a professional journal.
7. Subscribe to a teacher magazine.
8. Attend cultural events regularly.
9. Read novels, newspapers, and magazines regularly.
10. Attend professional conferences dealing with literacy. Rutgers Reading And Writing Conference is the 3rd week in March.
11. Ask questions at any time. I am happy to help you with your work.

Grading

A+ 97–100	A 94–96	A– 90–93
B+ 87–89	B 84–86	B– 80–83
C+ 77–79	C 74–76	C– 70–73
D+ 67–69	D 64–66	D– 60–63

Below 60 = F

1. Storytelling:

2. Research Project:

3. Test:

4. Class Participation:

a. Discussion, b. Materials brought for class, c. Group unit project, d. Attendance, e. Web site chats

In-Class and Field Assignments

At least 2 weeks' notice will be given for the following:

1. Sign up to bring a snack to class once during the semester. The snack should have a theme and teach a literacy skill.
2. Make a bound book based on the directions found in the Morrow text in the chapter dealing with writing.
3. Once during the semester bring something for our bulletin board such as a news article, a happy event, a notice, a work sample from a child, and so forth.
4. In groups, choose a theme for a science or social studies unit. Each group member selects one or two items, one literacy skill and one content area. Display a material in class relating to the theme, the content area, and that teaches a literacy skill. Choose from: Science, Social Studies, Art, Math, Music, Dramatic Play, Writing, Comprehension, Children's Literature, Word Analysis Skills (Phonics sight words), Oral language, Listening.
5. Bring five samples of children's literature to class representing different genres. Select one book that can help teach a specific word recognition skill and a specific comprehension skill.
6. Select a child to do activities listed and collect the work in a portfolio to review at the end of the semester:
   a. Tape record a language sample. Evaluate the child's development on age descriptions in the Morrow text, Chapter 4. Fill out the checklist for their language development found on p. 117, and segment the language into t-units as discussed on pp. 117–119 noting syntactic ele-

ments used. To prompt language samples: Ask the child about pets, school, trips taken, favorite TV shows, brothers, sisters.

b. Read a story to a child. Tape record them retelling the story. Transcribe and evaluate it (refer to pp. 214–216 in the Morrow text). Use form on p. 216 to evaluate the sample.

c. Collect a writing sample and evaluate using the checklist in Morrow on p. 292 including the Mechanics of Writing section. Write NA when an item does not apply. Give the child an 8.5x11 white paper and thick black marker. Write the child's name and age in the left hand corner of the page. Ask the child to draw a picture for what has been written.

d. Carry out a *Guided Reading Lesson* with your child and keep a running Record of their reading behavior with the form provided. (You can tape record this if you wish). If the child is not reading conventionally, use the Independent Story Reenactment summary form.

e. Complete the form Guidelines for promoting early Literacy At Home with the parent for the child you have selected to study. Pose the questions to find out if the parent has or does these things and help them to plan to do a few.

19

Research and Theory
for Constructivist Leadership
in Early Childhood Education

Mona W. Matthews
Georgia State University

An essential premise of constructivism is knowledge is constructed by the individual and interpreted from the perspective of the individual's experience and cultural history. Furthermore, learning is stimulated by shared inquiry and self-reflection and is enhanced by meaningful collaboration (Fosnot, 1996). Consequently, classroom environments guided by constructivist perspectives of learning differ in significant ways from environments modeled after traditional transmission views of learning. Students assume more ownership for their learning; teachers are considered facilitators, and the classroom is a community in which students collaborate and share their learning with others. Teachers are members of this community and by reflecting on their own teaching behavior and the behavior of their students, they alter their teaching responses. Moreover, learning is fluid, not fixed; teaching is adaptive, not prescribed; and as a result, classrooms are more responsive to the children and the teachers in them (Lambert, 1995).

These principles are familiar to us in the literacy field, for many have written and researched about what literacy learning looks like for children when designed and implemented from a constructivist perspective (e.g., Morrow, 1997). Currently, I am challenged to use these principles to guide my work with adult college learners. These learners are enrolled in an Educational Specialist (EdS) degree program guided by constructivist principles. All participants have a master's degree and at least 3 years of teaching experience. The EdS program is guided by academic and program givens (i.e., requirements that cannot be changed). Additionally, the content that is covered and the requirements that must be met are not organized around traditional 10-week quarter courses but rather extend throughout the 15-month length of the program. Two university faculty guide the students through the program. In addition to the program directors, there are other faculty who work with the students; I am one of these faculty. My responsibility is to guide the students as they plan and implement their action research projects.

The syllabus included here is not a traditional syllabus. Rather than outlining future class experiences, this syllabus documents our ongoing work and describes strategies we identified as a group to ensure that the course goals are met. Furthermore, because the course is guided by constructivism, how we go about our work is as important as the content we cover. Consequently, we have dual and equal goals to satisfy. One is to strengthen our understanding of the tools and language of action research, and the second is to organize the course experiences around constructivist principles.

Working in a program guided by constructivist principles has its challenges and rewards. Because the students participate in deciding how the program is run, time is spent processing these decisions. A major challenge, therefore, is to balance the time spent on process issues (e.g., deciding how to organize class time) with the time needed to build our background about course content. One strategy that helps maintain this balance is to indicate on the day's agenda an approximate time needed for each class experience. Then, at the beginning of class, a timekeeper is appointed to inform us if we exceed the allotted time. More time can be spent on the experience but we stop and decide if this is what we want to do.

Another challenge is to meet the needs of the 24 individuals in the class. I pull heavily from my literacy background to assist me in meeting the needs of these 24 individuals. For example, we use a "Status of the Class" sheet to track progress on our individual action research projects, and book talks are used to select course readings. In addition, time is set aside during each class for "Meeting Individual Needs." During this time, the students choose among several options that include but are not limited to reading, writing, working with their peers, conferencing with me, or going to the library. However, the most effective way I have found to identify the needs of the individuals is to ask them. Because I am limited in the numbers of students with whom I can personally interact, a planning group composed of six students are my extra "eyes and ears" in the class. This group meets with the students after the day's events but during the scheduled class time to debrief the class and to gather suggestions for future agenda items. Then, the group meets with me, and by the time this meeting is concluded, there is a draft of the agenda for the next class.

Although the agendas do not appear to be much different from the ones I have used in previous traditional college courses, they differ significantly from the others in that they are created in concert with the students. More significantly, because the agenda describes how we choose to organize our time, it reflects the values of our class (learning together, working on individual interests, and sharing the planning of our future work).

Undoubtably, the most challenging aspect of working in a program guided by constructivist principles is to first recognize and then alter elements of my teaching that have their origins in a traditional transmission instructional model. Many of these elements are in conflict with constructivist teaching, and, as I came to discover, are tenacious and resistant to change. In fact their presence remained hidden from me, until I stopped to reflect on the critical events I analyzed for my own action research project (Matthews, 1999). The insights I gained from a personal inquiry reinforced the importance of participating in my own action research project. Not only did I gain significant insights into my practice, but I experienced personally the difference between viewing reflection as a mere "… replay of a series of events … [and viewing] reflection … [as a] rich source of … professional growth" (Killion & Todnem, 1991, p. 14).

Whereas, the challenges of working within the program stimulate my understanding and growth as a constructivist teacher, the rewards from the work reinforce my commitment to constructivist learning. The most rewarding aspect is the personal connection I make with the students; a connection, I believe, that has its basis in collaborative work. Tharp and Gallimore (1988) talk about the value of joint work and how through joint activity individuals come to know and understand each other. Our classes are designed to encourage collaboration. We spend time discussing our work with each other. We spend time defining critical elements of the work, for example, identifying characteristics of good action research, and we spend time deciding which topics we will explore in class. However, as the faculty guide, I believe it is incumbent upon me to use my understanding of the course content to structure class activities and my experience in ways that enhance the students' professional growth.

Another rewarding aspect is that the students and I share responsibility for creating and guiding course experiences. This responsibility empowers the students. They become comfortable with asking for what they believe will help them accomplish their personal goals and with stating when course directions or experiences are not meeting their needs. Moreover, their empowerment empowers me, for I become comfortable with asking for their assistance. For example, because they have a history of working together that extends beyond our class time, they have developed strategies that enable them to handle more efficiently situations that require the group to reach consensus on program directions. When an activity or issue arises that needs agreement from the group, I ask the students to take over. Then, in a figurative way, I sit "outside" the circle and observe the collaborative work that proceeds before me. Without exception, the result is more effective and appropriate than any I could have proposed.

Perhaps the appeal for me of constructivism resides in my work as a literacy educator. The cornerstone of this work is to assist others to gain understanding of written and spoken language. Current theories of literacy development describe how this understanding of language is impacted by the individual's experience and cultural history (Ruddell & Unrau, 1994). Hence, literacy and constructivism share a common theoretical base. Moreover, my work in programs guided by constructivist principles has raised the bar on my expectations when I teach. Before, I was satisfied if students left my courses with knowledge of content I deemed important; now I want them mentally engaged with the content. This is more likely to occur, I believe, if they can situate their learning within questions that are personally significant and if they can share their inquiry with others.

REFERENCES

Fosnot, C.T. (Ed.). (1996). Constructivism: A psychological theory of learning. In C. T. Fosnot (Ed.), *Constructivism: Theory, perspectives, and practice.* (pp. 8–33). New York: Teachers College Press.

Killion, J. P., & Todnem, G. R. (1991). A process for personal theory building. *Educational Leadership, 48*(6), 14–16.

Lambert, L. (1995). Constructing school change. In L. Lambert, D. Walker, D. Zimmerman, J. Cooper, M. L. Lambert, M. Gardner, & P. J. Fordslack, (Eds.), *The constructivist leader* (pp. 52–82). New York: Teachers College Press.

Matthews, M. W. (1999). Yours, mine, and ours: How 24 teachers and one teacher educator collaborated to make their work meaningful. *Journal of Professional Studies, 7*(1), 42–151.

Morrow, L. M. (1997). *The literacy center: Contexts for reading and writing.* York, ME: Stenhouse.

Ruddell, R. B., & Unrau, N. J. (1994). Reading as a meaning–construction process: The reader, the text, and the teacher. In R. B. Ruddell, M. R. Ruddell, & H. Singer (Eds.), *Theoretical models and processes of reading* (4th ed., pp. 996–1056). Newark, DE: International Reading Association.

Tharp, R. G., & Gallimore, R. (1988). *Rousing minds to life: Teaching, learning, and schooling in social contexts.* Cambridge, England: Cambridge University Press.

Sample Syllabus
Research and Theory for Constructivist Leadership
in Early Childhood Ece 892: In-Process Course Record

ECE 892 is included in the Education Specialist (EdS) program to provide each of us with opportunities to participate in and learn how to use action research to address educational questions and as a catalyst for professional growth. Action research, which derives its vitality from shared inquiry, self-reflection, and collaboration, is compatible with the philosophy of this EdS program. It is hoped that the experiences in this course not only stimulate our professional growth during this year but also will be useful to each of us as our work extends beyond the year.

This document provides an ongoing record of the wonderings, experiences, and information that inform and stimulate our work as we enhance our understanding of action research. Because we are co-creators of this work, your feedback on my recollections and perceptions of this work is essential. Review this document and let me know if you see inaccuracies or misconceptions in this record.

Course Readings

To increase our knowledge of the tools and language of action research, we will read related chapters, books, and articles. The class bibliographer will record the materials read for this course.

Course Goals

ECE 892 is part of the requirements of the Georgia State University's Department of Early Childhood Education's EdS degree program. This EdS program is based on the principles that learning is a constructivist process that builds on the knowledge and experiences of the learners and that ultimately individuals must construct their own knowledge. Therefore, the learners are involved in planning and implementing the course experiences. These experiences are planned around academic and program givens (i.e., requirements that cannot be altered) and the interests and needs of the students. Hence, the integrity and rigor of an EdS program are maintained while the unique and individual interests of the learners are at the forefront when course experiences are planned. Consequently, the course objectives are organized around two parallel and equivalent goals:

1. To ensure that the integrity of the constructivist process is maintained as the students participate in course experiences.
2. To ensure that the participants increase their understanding and knowledge of the language and tools of action research.

Course Givens

Each participant will design and implement a classroom/school-based action research project. The results of the project will be shared with the group and will be part of the student's end-of-program capstone.

Experiences and Strategies for Achieving Course Goals

Goal 1

The course is designed to ensure that the integrity of the constructivist process is maintained as the program participants increase their understanding and knowledge of the language and tools of action research. The following strategies are included to ensure that this goal is met:

1. A survey is used to identify the needs and interests of the students.
2. A student liaison group meets after each class with the students to debrief that day's class and to identify future agenda items. The liaison group then meets with Mona to discuss the information gathered from their meeting

with the students. This information guides the development of future course experiences.

3. Two students represent the group at the EdS faculty meetings.
4. A few minutes are spent at the beginning of each class to clarify the day's journey. This time is spent: addressing logistical issues related to the program, reviewing the day's agenda, and, if needed, prioritizing agenda items.
5. Mona is involved in her own action research project.
6. When Mona creates course materials, they are considered drafts and input from the students is solicited.
7. A "Status of the Class" sheet is used so the program participants are aware of the status of each person's action research project.
8. Mona distributes a schedule of days and times she is available to meet with individual and small groups of students.
9. Students facilitate and lead some of the class experiences.

Goal 2

The course is designed to ensure that the participants increase their understanding and knowledge of the language and tools of action research. The following strategies are included to ensure that this goal is met:

1. A syllabus documents the work of the program participants.
2. Charts are placed in the classroom so that Mona and the students can record the language of action research, tools of action research, and characteristics of good action research.
3. There is a course resource box. A variety of information is included in the resource box. This includes, but is not limited to, information related to specific components of action research, resource checkout list, and notes from previous classes.
4. A timekeeper is selected at the beginning of each class to ensure that there is a balance between the process and content components of the course. The timekeeper keeps track of the time and checks with the group to see if it wants to continue with the current discussion or move to the next topic.
5. The program participants are creating an assessment process guide. This guide will identify the characteristics of a "good" action research project and will be used by the participants to assess their work.

Class Schedule

(To illustrate to the reader how this course evolves, next I have included the record of the dates and content of whole group meetings for one rendition of this course.)

2-20-97

Topic: Getting Acquainted With Each Other and the Content

Readings: Readings from Cochran-Smith & Lytle, 1993

Issues Identified for Future Meetings:

What kind of research is action research?

What does school/classroom based action research look like?

3-31-97

Topic: Identifying Individual Needs and Interest

Issues Identified for Future Meetings:

How can we support each other's work?

4-28-97

Topic: Choice Night: Students Meet With Individual EdS Faculty to Discuss Program Issues.

Issues Identified for Future Meetings:

How can students be involved in planning course experiences?

How will the action research project be evaluated?

What are the requirements for the action research project?

6-2-97

Topics: Clarifying Our Journey

Framing Our Work: Content Framework and Process Framework

Readings: Action Research Examples: Cunningham, Hall, & Defee, 1991; Gallas, 1992; Keffer, Carr, Lanier, Mattison, Wood, & Stanulis, 1996

Action Research Process: Fischer, 1996; Odell, 1987

Issues Identified for Future Meetings:

What are the components of the action research process?

Where are relevant books, journals, resources located in the library?

What books will we read?

How will our action research projects be evaluated?

6-24-97

Topics: Presenting and Discussing a Concept Map of the Action Research Process

Selecting Books to Read

Touring the GSU Library

Readings: Books Selected: Teachers Doing Research: Practical Possibilities
Burnaford, Fischer, & Hobson, 1996
Teachers are Researchers: Reflection and Action
Patterson, Santa, Short, & Smith, 1993

Issues Identified for Future Meetings:

       How is quantitative data analyzed?

       Can we spend time with Mona in small groups to discuss action research projects?

       How can we ensure that our action research projects will be planned and completed within the parameters of the program and school calendars?

7-14-97

Topics: Presenting an Insider's Perspective of Action Research

       (Speaker: Cathy Mathis, Taylor Elementary School,

       Gwinnett County School System)

       Identifying Characteristics of "Good" Action Research

Readings: Burnaford, Fischer, & Hobson, 1996

       Patterson, Santa, Short, & Smith, 1993

Issues Identified for Future Meetings:

       What are the characteristics of pieces published in professional journals?

       Mona's input on the "Characteristics of Good Action Research" list generated in class is due 7-30-97

9-24-97

Topics: Conferencing With Mona: Observing the Process

       Finalizing "Characteristics of Good Action Research" (Product Characteristics and Process Characteristics)

       Deciding Where We Go From Here

       Deciding How Mona Can Support Our Work Between Now and the Last Class

Readings: Burnaford, Fischer, & Hobson, 1996

       Patterson, Santa, Short, & Smith, 1993

Issues Identified for Future Meetings:

       More time to meet with each other during class

       More access to Mona

       What is meant by "unpacking" our research questions?

9-29-97

Topics: Unpacking our Research Questions: What is Meant by the Terms We Use?

       Enriching our "Class Pot": Book and Chapter Talks Related to Data Collection

       Reflecting on Our Small Group Sessions: What is Helpful and How Can We Make These Sessions More Effective?

Readings: Hitchcock & Hughes, 1995; Patton, 1990; Stringer, 1996

Issues Identified for Future meetings:

       How is quantitative data analyzed?

10-13-97

Topic: Analyzing Quantitative Data: An Overview

             Guest Speaker: Martin Wesche

Issues Identified For Final Class:

             How do we move from data collection to data analysis to the write-up of our action research projects?

12-3-97

Topics: Moving From Data Collection to Data Analysis to Write-up

             Small Group Discussion of Student-Selected Examples of Action Research

             Analyzing Qualitative Data

Readings: Student-selected readings that illustrate ways to analyze, interpret, and present action research

January - March, 1998

             The students will complete their capstones. Mona will be available to read drafts of the action research components of the capstones.

BIBLIOGRAPHY

Burnaford, G., Fischer, J., & Hobson, D. (Eds.). (1996). *Teachers doing research: Practical possibilities.* Mahwah, NJ: Lawrence Erlbaum Associates.

Cochran-Smith, M., & Lytle, S. L. (1993). *Inside outside: Teacher research and knowledge.* New York: Teachers College Press. Cunningham, P. M., Hall, D. P., & Defee, M. (1991). Nonability-grouped, multilevel instruction: A year in a first-grade classroom. *The Reading Teacher, 44,* 566–571.

Fischer, F. C. (1996). Open to ideas: Developing a framework for your research. In G. Burnaford, J. Fischer, & D. Hobson (Eds.), *Teachers doing research: Practical possibilities* (pp. 33–50). Mahwah, NJ: Lawrence Erlbaum Associates.

Gallas, K. (1992). When the children take the chair: A study of sharing time in a primary classroom. *Language Arts, 69,* 172–182.

Hitchcock, G., & Hughes, D. (1995). *Research and the teacher: A qualitative introduction to school-based research* (2nd ed.). New York: Rutledge.

Keffer, A., Carr, S., Lanier, B. R., Mattison, L., Wood, D., & Stanulis, R. N. (1996). Teacher researchers discover magic in forming an adult writing workshop. *Language Arts, 73,* 113–121.

Odell, L. (1987). Planning classroom research. In D. Goswami, & P. R. Stillman (Eds.), *Reclaiming the classroom: Teacher research as an agency for change* (pp. 128–160). Portsmouth, NH: Boynton/Cook Publishers.

Patterson, L., Santa, C. M., Short, K. G., & Smith, K. (Eds.), (1993). *Teachers are researchers: Reflection and action.* Newark, DE: International Reading Association.

Patton, M. Q. (1990). *Qualitative evaluation and research methods* (2nd ed.). Newbury Park, CA: Sage.

Stringer, E. T. (1996). *Action research: A handbook for practitioners.* Thousand Oaks, CA: Sage.

20

Initial Encounters With Print:
Beginnings of Reading and Writing

David B. Yaden, Jr.
Angela Chavez
Camille Cubillas
University of Southern California

One insight that I think I have gained about my own teaching particularly over the past 6 years is that students' experiences in my courses are seldom what I had planned, even though I try to construct relatively detailed syllabi about expectations, assignments, evaluations, and so forth. For this reason, when I contemplated describing my emergent literacy course for other teacher-educators who might use this resource book as an aid to their own teaching, I was concerned that I would only write from one point of view and, therefore, not allow a more accurate picture of the intellectual and emotional effort on the part of both myself and the students that seems to be required in order to have a useful learning experience in this course.

Therefore, for the purpose of opening up an introspective discourse about the teaching of this course, my co-authors, former students in the course, and I have framed the rest of the discussion loosely around the format of a play dialogue (see MacGillivray, Tse, & McQuillen, 1995) wherein the four "acts" represent major shifts in the conversation around (a) issues in course design, (b) actual topics discussed, (c) tensions felt by both instructor and student, and (d) highlights as experienced by each one of us. We hope that the readers' experience in examining the delivery of this course is as informative as was the writing of this chapter to its authors.

ACT I—ISSUES IN COURSE DESIGN

Scene I: Expectations

David: I want students in this course to gain both empirical and theoretical knowledge of emergent literacy as well as practical skills to apply such knowledge. For a doctoral seminar, my expectation is that the time in class should be spent in theoretical and critical discussion with a lively exchange of ideas gained from reading and examination of these ideas based on working with a real child in a real context. Did any of these things happen?

Camille: To answer your question, yes. In addition to substantially refining my theoretical knowledge base, I was able to critically examine in-depth two of my course expectations by means of lectures, assigned readings and stirring group discussions. These expectations included (a) understanding how a young child learns about literacy both individually and collaboratively and (b) the outcomes of early literacy acquisition interventions in the context of fostering and supporting a child's eagerness to learn about reading and writing. Because I am the mother of two preschool-aged children as well as an emergent literacy project director, I was extremely excited about the opportunity afforded to us to engage in task assessment activities. I was remarkably struck by your confidence with this class urging us to prescribe a plan for each child participant's ongoing literacy growth. Choosing my 4-year-old daughter as my emergent participant was truly a rewarding experience for both of us. The reward was certainly worth the effort.

Scene 2: Course Format

Angela: I looked forward to attending each session because, even though the actual setup of the course seemed routine, the conversation that resulted from each meeting was stimulating and unpredictable. A balance of formal and informal instructional methods was maintained during the class sessions. We had an opportunity to converse with our classmates, in small groups, about the assigned readings. Yet, it was when we disclosed information about the emergent reader with whom we each worked that we sparked enthusiasm and created that "lively exchange" that you mentioned earlier, David. Although your weekly lectures had a formal exterior, we were always free to interject comments and ask questions throughout. Your way of arranging the class resulted in many insightful conversations.

Camille: Throughout the entire semester, I think we all appreciated the blended theoretical and practical application presentations of *where* children learn about literacy; *what* children learn (i.e., the components learned); *how* children learn (i.e., a developmental sequence) and *how* adults model instruction. I appreciated the course arrangement because I was able to observe myself as I began to progressively advance and broaden my knowledge foundations, while at the same time, witness the parallel advancement of my emergent participant. Many creative ideas pertaining to early literacy acquisition were generated when I engaged with my child participant.

Angela: I appreciated the fact that we had a choice in how to respond to the weekly reading assignments. The reflective responses allowed me to set my own agenda with the required readings; I could react, agree, argue, or inquire. We took our responses further when we verbally shared them during our small group discussions. I cannot express how valuable the opportunity was to exchange reactions, to listen to my classmates' perspectives, and to share my own point of view.

Scene 3: Text Selection

David: It is always a struggle, every time I teach the course, deciding what types of texts to use. My rationale this past semester was to choose texts that I thought complemented one another in terms of theory, practice, and critical analyses of both. I sensed, though, that some texts were much more well received than others.

Angela: You're right on target about that! I, personally, favored the *Literacy's Beginnings* text by McGee and Richgels (1996). It provided a general overview of various emergent literacy theories and presented the information in a practical format. After reading each chapter, I easily employed their ideas with the early literacy learners in my own classroom.

ACT II—MAJOR IDEAS AND APPROACHES THAT HAVE INFLUENCED THE COURSE

Scene I: Major Theorists

David: I spent a great deal of time in the course explaining the developmental movement of literacy as I understand it. The works of Piaget, Vygotsky, and emergent literacy theorists such as Goodman, Sulzby, Ferreiro, Dyson, Wells, and Holdaway, are heavily drawn on. Increasingly, I also see the connection between the aspects of oral culture and children's literacy learning, hence, the readings from Eric Havelock, Goody and Watt, and others like Egan, Ong, and Olson who have followed up on those ideas. Did these connect for people?

Camille: Although I knew enough about most of these theorists, I think David could have spent more time and detail distinctively discussing and shaping the developmental sequence framework—the general to the more specific and how it relates to the developmental issues surrounding early literacy acquisition. I wish we could have extensively examined ideas such as "Scaffolding" and "The Zone of Proximal Development," which are definitely developmental across the board. Then, more specifically, smoothly transitioning and shifting the focus to include discussions examining Dyson, Yaden, Sulzby, and Ferrerio and Teberosky because they lean more toward the development of reading and writing.

Scene 2: Assessment Rationale

Camille: Although the assessment tasks were easily administered, I would have appreciated the distribution of the Architectonics of Emergent Literacy handout—where, what, and how of emergent literacy—to have occurred during the first or second class meeting. This handout (see Fig. 20.1) was extremely useful for me in many ways. When I think of defining and attaching meaning to this handout, I immediately think of it as the premier "Emergent Literacy Reference Aid." What it boils down to is this handout served as the course's "foundations" blueprint. I used this handout while I was reading the assigned texts and articles. I used this handout as I was analyzing my task assessment results and when I was formulating the theoretical interpretation segment of my final project. Essentially, for me this handout became the "fact sheet" of emergent literacy.

Angela: I agree. That outline became my "Emergent Literacy Quick Reference Guide" because I referred to it frequently throughout the term and especially consulted it when constructing my final project. It is a guide that I still employ in my literacy work. It is a valuable summary of emergent literacy research and ideas.

Camille: In fact, I found the Early Literacy Perspectives chart—the chart distributed at the third class meeting—comparing different emergent literacy viewpoints (see Crawford, 1995) somewhat confusing. I found it confusing because the chart did not provide a crystal-clear explanation of how the components of emergent literacy flowed from theory in terms of their development, aspects of appearance, and ability to be assessed. Although we did discuss the theorists and their respective bodies of work as cited in this chart, I shake my head as I realize we did not examine the components of this chart with the amount of depth and understanding that I would have liked to have had taken place.

David: I agree with you. In thinking about it now, I feel like approaching assessment from one or two theories, even one, and working it all the way through to application is better than comparing several on a more surface level.

Angela: Emergent literacy is a vast and growing area. It's a toss-up; is it better to learn a little about many researchers in the field or to learn a great deal about a few?

ACT III—TENSIONS

Scene I: Shared Tensions

David: I know that two of the tensions I felt in the course had to do with my role in small group activity and the tendencies of the graphics (i.e., one form of reading re-

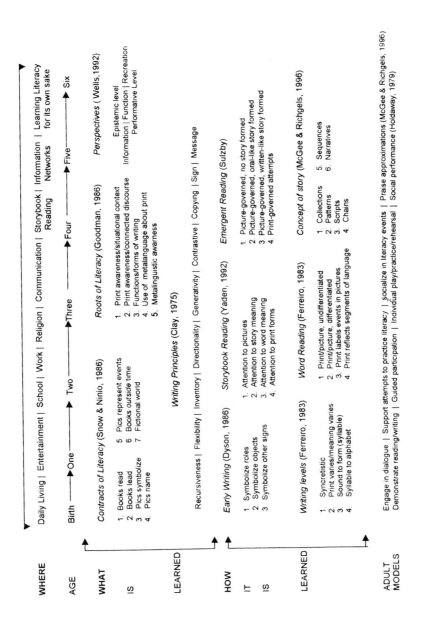

FIG. 20.1. The architectonics of emergent literacy.

sponse), I felt, to be simplistic. I was really frustrated that my revolving presence in the small groups seemed to stifle conversation.

Camille: Funny you cite these two tensions as your individual tensions. I felt the same tensions. Case in point, the graphic reader responses. At first, you encouraged but did not clearly define the criteria for submitting graphic reading responses. Halfway through the semester, we hit a wall! Personally, I could sense your discomfort, irritation, and disappointment with our submissions. You stated there was too much drawing and not enough cohesion between the drawings and the assigned readings. I find it odd that you initially claimed to desire the interpretations to include—"what struck you the reader as important or problematic." Well, it seems to me that the entire experience became problematic for the professor. The next time you present the course, I suggest you do the following: Have the students submit a written explanation along with each graphic representation.

Scene 2: What's Really Important To Read?

Angela: My tension of the course revolved around the content of the readings. Although I could understand the purpose of providing different voices through text, I often felt the urge to ask, "What is important here? What should I focus on?" Most weeks we received copies of articles to read for the following meeting, in addition to the already assigned chapters. That was when I began to see the need to prioritize the readings. It would have been helpful to classify certain readings as crucial (required) and others as beneficial (supplementary).

Camille: I think the way to resolve this dilemma is to provide an extended reading list citing authors and researchers. What graphically comes to mind, is a webbing of sorts which explains key points, theorists and models representing the hub and the affiliated theorists and models representing the expansive associated reading routes. Had a reading list been available, that would have been a coveted amenity! Again, it is just a suggestion.

David: Ugh … I'm afraid I'm not too much help here. I think everything is important to read, even though we only have one semester! But you're right—its overwhelming. I need to do something about it. Reading lists, pointing out primary, ancillary readings—these are good ideas.

Scene 3: The Difficulty Of Interpreting Data

Angela: I'd like to make a suggestion for use with future classes as well. With respect to interpreting data, it may have been helpful to our class if samples of data, resulting from the administration of the emergent literacy tasks, were presented. My idea is that student groups could analyze the outcomes of the assessments and apply particular literacy models. I believe this group effort would instill a sense of confidence in those students who are hesitant about applying literacy models on their own.

David: Actually, you all did a fine job of analyzing and interpreting the data, although I sensed that you struggled while doing it on your own. I must say, I expected students to share more of their individual experiences during the small groups for additional feedback. What I hear you saying, however, is that a general session analyzing common data would be helpful from time to time.

Angela and Camille: Yes!

ACT IV—COURSE HIGHLIGHTS AND CONCLUSIONS

Scene I: Highlights

Angela: A highlight of the course that vividly remains with me, David, is the way your genuine enthusiasm for, and plethora of knowledge in literacy was apparent through your weekly lectures. Your presentations did more than merely provide me with information about Emergent Literacy. You enlightened me, motivated me, and encouraged me to internalize the information and apply it to my work in literacy.

One particular lecture, the "Psychology of Poetic Performance" is what you called it, is especially memorable. You spoke ardently, as if you were an actor on a stage, telling us how (the idea of) story came about. Your performance broadened my literacy schema and made a powerful impact on me.

Camille: Yes, that was a good one. As I drove home, I thought to myself, "In 15 years from now, will I be able to passionately package my expertise with as much cognitive artfulness as David did this evening?" But of course, emergent literacy is woven into every aspect of my life. Thanks for the lecture, David.

David: One of the highlights for me was finding a group of people with whom I shared an intellectual affinity. Hearing people talk about their projects outside of class, having late night conversations about emergent literacy over the phone, by e-mail—this is really satisfying. The fact that I have found collaborators to do research and write with from that class is one of the true benefits of academic life.

Scene 2: Conclusions

David: So, what did you walk away with?

Camille: As you can see, I am smiling as I think about answering this question. I feel a certain degree of personal empowerment. I am capable of translating my emergent literacy knowledge into practical application albeit with my children or other children whom I am fortunate enough to serve. One of the most important insights articulated as a result of my experience in this course is my ability to confidently and open-mindedly entertain others' emergent literacy perspectives without feeling the need to recalibrate my emergent literacy stance every time I listen to someone else share their thoughts.

Angela: Empowerment is a good word to describe the accomplishment of this course. I, too, have that feeling as I apply these early learning models to my students' literacy abilities. I know I have grasped the ideas presented through this course because, in addition to being able to speak about them, I can extend those ideas and formulate my own thoughts on literacy development.

David: Interestingly, after this conversation, I feel some sense of sadness that although the next class will benefit from the changes we have talked about, you and your classmates will not be the recipients of that change.

REFERENCES

Crawford, P. A. (1995). Early literacy: Emerging perspectives. *Journal of Research in Childhood Education, 10*(1), 71–84.

MacGillivray, L., Tse, L., & McQuillan, J. (1995). Second language and literacy teachers considering literature circles: A play. *Journal of Adolescent and Adult Literacy, 39,* 36–44.

Sample Syllabus

Catalogue Description

Prerequisite: Doctoral standing. Theoretical, empirical, pedagogical issues of initial literacy learning; parallels between oral and written language development; effects of culture and home environment; developmental patterns and strategies.

Expanded Course Description:

This course examines the development and conceptual foundations of literacy growth in young children from the viewpoints of sociohistorical, constructivist, and critical perspectives. Topics examined in the course include formal and informal assessment techniques of early literacy knowledge, the influence of home, family, and peers on young children's perspectives on reading and writing, the relationship between drawing and writing, the characteristics of developmental stages in reading, writing, and invented spelling, the efficacy of storybook reading as well as issues of gender, class, and the politics of classroom instruction. Students will conduct an emergent literacy assessment of a preschool, kindergarten, or first-grade child and interpret the findings within a developmental framework.

Course Goals

1. Students will become familiar with theory-based, longitudinal research in emergent reading and writing, including issues of research design, analysis and interpretation of findings.
2. Students will learn to administer informal assessment techniques to measure the growth and development of knowledge in print awareness, early writing, invented spelling, storybook reenactments, and metacognitive perspectives.
3. Students will become familiar with the major tenets of theories within which early literacy acquisition is viewed, including cognitive–developmental, sociohistorical, constructivist, feminist, and critical literacy.
4. Students will have opportunities to discuss, react to, and critically evaluate the current literature pertaining to the early acquisition of literacy knowledge.
5. Students will suggest a plan for the ongoing literacy growth of a young child based on current theory integrated with their own project findings and analysis.

Course Texts: Required

Clay, M. M. (1991). *Becoming literate*. Portsmouth, NH: Heinemann.
McGee, L. M., & Richgels, D. (1996). *Literacy's beginnings*. Boston: Allyn & Bacon.
Yaden, D. B., & Templeton, S. (1986). *Metalinguistic awareness and beginning literacy*. Portsmouth, NH: Heinemann.
Chukovsky, K. (1968). *From two to five*. Berkeley, CA: University of California Press.
Clay, M. M. (1987). *Writing begins at home*. Portsmouth, NH: Heinemann.
Newman, J. M. (1984). *The craft of children's writing*. Portsmouth, NH: Heinemann.

Course Evaluation

1. *Administration of Emergent Literacy Assessment (25%) and Final Project (25%)*. 25% of the grade will be based on the summed letter grades for the various tasks to be completed, handed in on the specified dates (see course schedule) with a preliminary discussion of findings. The final project will be worth 25% and include a description and interpretation of findings, and a suggested plan for future growth.
2. *Reflective Reading Responses (25%)*. For each class session, you are to respond to one of the assigned readings of each session by either a graphic organizer (i.e., a flowchart, diagram, figure—not an outline) or a half-page, single spaced statement of what struck you as important or problematic. At least

four of the responses must be graphic organizers. Bring enough copies of your response for distribution to each class member.

3. *Class Participation (25%)*. Full credit for this portion of the grade will be comprised of the following:

a. Attendance at all sessions.

b. Completion of three, one-page summaries of recent articles dealing with issues, research, or classroom applications relevant to emergent literacy. Bring enough copies of your reactions for distribution to each class member. Be prepared to give a brief 5 to 10 minute presentation.

c. Participation in class and small group discussion.

ACKNOWLEDGMENTS

The report described herein was supported in part under the Educational Research and Development Centers Program, PR/Award Number R305R70004, as administered by the Office of Educational Research and Improvement, U.S. Department of Education. However, the contents of the described report do not necessarily represent the positions or policies of the National Institute on Student Achievement, Curriculum, and Assessment or the National Institute on Early Childhood Development, or the U.S. Department of Education, and you should not assume endorsement by the Federal government.

V

CONTENT AREA LITERACY

21

Reading for Secondary Teachers

Carol V. Lloyd
University of Nebraska at Omaha

The title of this course, "Reading for Secondary Teachers,"[1] might lead one to think that the purpose of the course is to teach preservice secondary teachers how to become better readers. On the other hand, the course description in the undergraduate catalog sounds as if the course will show preservice teachers strategies to use when they give their future students reading assignments from textbooks. Although these future teachers *do* learn strategies they can apply to their learning and ways to use textbooks in their future classrooms, the purpose currently stated on the course syllabus takes a different focus.

> *Purpose of the Course*: The general purpose of this course is to introduce students to some of the theories of literacy processes and to show their relationships to content-area learning and literacy in secondary schools. In preparation for their roles as orchestrators of the learning environment, preservice teachers will learn ways to assess students, materials, and tasks; prescribe appropriate instruction; learn about instructional strategies to implement; and evaluate students' learning within the context of understanding and learning from

---

[1]The title of this course was changed to "Applying Reading and Writing in Secondary Schools" subsequent to the writing of this chapter. This change resulted from student input.

content-area texts.[2] Individual differences of secondary students, including background, interest, ability, culture, and ethnicity will be considered. A practicum experience in the schools will provide a meaningful context in which to explore ideas from class.

This course is required of all preservice teachers who will receive an endorsement in grades 7–12 in any subject area. Students take the course during their junior or senior year. During any semester, the endorsement areas of the class usually represent the range of courses in any middle or senior high school. Thus, we begin the semester with people who are going to teach physical education; art; music; foreign language; business; English/language arts; and the various maths, sciences, and social sciences wondering why they have to take a course about reading.

My philosophy that guides the way I approach this course emanates from three related experiences: being a K–12 student, being a student in a preservice course about reading in content-area classrooms, and being a secondary science teacher. As a K–12 student, I often saw school as tedious and irrelevant. Fortunately, I always remained curious and excited about learning. I believed that my teachers *could* have promoted some of that curiosity and excitement I found outside of school. (See Lloyd, 1998, for a discussion of this issue.) My only education professor[3] who provided useful ideas was the one who taught a required course in reading in the content areas. When I taught science in both junior and senior high schools, I actually used the ideas I had learned from that content reading course. And, because I did not want my students to be as disinterested as I had been in school, I also tried to pay attention to my students' needs and interests.

My overarching framework for this class is that student learning, rather than curriculum, should be the primary goal of K–12 education. I tell my preservice teachers that though the class is entitled "Reading for Secondary Teachers," we focus on ways to facilitate their students' learning. This class differs from other methods courses in their program in that we pay special attention to ways in which the texts students read and write can help them learn. However, many of the classroom practices we study can be used without text. I also tell them that I will show them ways to use texts that account for the continuum of reading abilities that will most likely be represented in their classes. Learning is the umbrella; reading and writing are two important tools to facilitate that learning.

There are several obstacles related to this class that I strive to overcome. The first is overcoming preservice teachers' displeasure and occasional resentment at having to take this course. Most believe that they should put their energies into learning more about their content area than about pedagogy. And, many wonder if this class

---

[2]The terms *orchestrator of the learning environment, assessment, prescription, implementation,* and *evaluation* are required to be in all course descriptions; they reflect the college's knowledge base statement as mandated by NCATE.

[3]Dr. Malcolm Wilson was my professor for this course at California Polytechnic State University at San Luis Obispo.

will be redundant to a required general methods course ("The Art and Science of Teaching") in secondary education.

A second obstacle is overcoming preservice teachers' image of an academic subject classroom as a place in which the teacher and textbook embody and impart all important knowledge as students soak up the ideas to pass the course. A student's failure reflects his or her lack of trying or ability. The preservice teachers I work with have seen few, if any, models of the teaching practices I propose. Although I model most of the practices I suggest they consider in their teaching, *my* content is about ways to use reading and writing to enhance learning; *their* content will be about new ideas related to subjects such as algebra, government, or chemistry.

A third obstacle is overcoming the image of physical education, art, and music classrooms as places in which text is seldom needed to help students learn. These future teachers have rarely, if ever, seen textbooks in those classes. Thus, they believe that there is little possibility of relevant reading. And, they have infrequently observed writing in these classes that require more than filling in blanks or choosing a multiple-choice response.

A fourth obstacle is overcoming the belief that a teacher's major purpose is to teach curriculum. One of my major tasks becomes, therefore, showing my preservice teachers that their responsibility is to help their students learn ideas in their content areas. To accomplish this, they must address different interests, background knowledge, reading abilities, language proficiencies, and learning needs of their students.

I have always been concerned with preservice teachers' abilities to relate the ideas from the university to their subsequent teaching. It is extremely difficult to construct knowledge in an environment (the college classroom) that does not require that knowledge. (See Richardson, 1996, for a discussion of the roles, limitations, and possibilities of teacher education programs in preservice education.) Although I could require the preservice teachers in my classes to enact sample lessons while their classmates role-play secondary students, it is impossible to provide them with an authentic duplication of a middle or high school classroom at the university. To overcome this obstacle, several years ago I added a practicum component to this class. Because the preservice teachers in my classes do not receive additional credits for this experience, the practicum is a brief 3 weeks. During this time, they observe two classes and teach four, implementing the strategies learned in class.

Sample Syllabus
Reading for Secondary Teachers

My syllabus consists of a list of topics with readings, a list of assignments, and a grading scale. For the purpose of this chapter, I decided that it would be more informative to elaborate on those topics, list the assignments with their topics, and explain why I chose those topics and their related assignments. I did not include the textbook assignments because I tend to skip around in a textbook, selecting those chapters or parts of chapters that best relate to the topics. For several years, I used the most current edition of *Content Area Reading* by Vacca and Vacca. I have recently replaced that book with *Content Area Literacy: An Integrated Approach* by Readence, Bean, and Baldwin (1998). In addition, anyone taking my class purchases a packet of handouts I have prepared, and reads several published materials that are kept on reserve in the library. They are also required to read articles in current professional journals that focus on reading or writing in secondary classrooms; and find, read, and write an annotation of a trade book that could be used with secondary students in their endorsement areas.

Technology is integrated into this course as well. For example, I show preservice teachers a HyperCard stack developed by a high school geography student in response to an assignment. These future teachers converse with each other about their practicum experiences over a discussion board (a function of Blackboard Course Info™ software). And, I incorporate many of their assignments onto a Web site I developed for this class. (See http://www.unomaha.edu/~clloyd.)

TABLE 21.1

Sample Outline, Activities, and Rationale

Topic	Description	Some Assignments and Classroom Activities	Rationale
1. Literacy and content area learning	Consideration of what it means to be literate in their subject area Recollections of content area teachers; relationships between teaching and learning Discussions of secondary teachers' responsibilities to students' literacy development	View and discuss video Teachers (Russo, 1984) "Write a letter to a content teacher ..." "Real World Reading" Begin portfolio	I want preservice teachers to begin thinking about: • the natural connections between learning content and reading and writing in their fields. • their responsibilities to their students learning how to read and write about science, art, math, etc. • the teaching models they have seen that they might like to emulate and those they should not reproduce. • the multiple sources of texts that relate to their content areas
2. Teaching for learning: Possibilities	Current frameworks or standards for all content areas focus on in-depth learning and thinking rather than lists of facts Importance and relevancy of ideas to understanding content must be considered in lesson planning (authenticity)	Preservice teachers read one of the following articles: "On teaching for understanding: A conversation with Howard Gardner" (Brandt, 1993) or "Five standards of authentic instruction" (Newman & Wehlage, 1993). Preservice teachers begin working on assignment: "Developing a Unit of Study"	• I want preservice teachers to think about the content they want students to learn and their related assignments while always considering whether or not it is important for their students to learn those ideas. • Thinking about ideas (concepts) that they believe are important for students to learn helps them develop lessons that address important issues rather than lists of facts.

(Continues)

TABLE 21.1 (Continued)

Topic	Description	Some Assignments and Classroom Activities	Rationale
3. Learning theories and content area learning	Introduction to the complexities of comprehending Overview of the reading process as explained by contrasting theories [transmission (Freire's banking model), behaviorist/bottom-up, interactive (schema theory), metacognition, transaction] Applications of theories and research on content area literacy instruction	Look at examples of texts that are easy to decode but difficult to comprehend to consider role of background knowledge in comprehension Read text with "x's" replaced for some letters to learn about redundancy and relationships between cuing systems	• Preservice teachers are more likely to understand the relationship of background knowledge to comprehension through experiences. • Preservice teachers begin to see that they can affect their students' comprehension; sending students to get remedial instruction may not be the best solution for struggling readers.
4. Background knowledge: Assessing, activating, and building	Development of rationale for engaging students in strategies before beginning formal instruction Multiple examples of strategies that assess, activate, and build background Relationship of strategies to theories	(Classroom activities are designed to give preservice teachers direct experiences with a strategy and to address an issue.) In groups, preservice teachers develop a graphic organizer about "Being a First Year Teacher" Class participates in PReP about a current topic In groups, preservice teachers develop an anticipation guide for Robert Frost's "The Road Not Taken" Preservice teachers read a current newspaper article about a local issue in education and develop "Student-Generated Questions" Preservice teachers participate in a K-W-L about whole language, then read one of multiple articles about whole language (secondary school focus) In content groups, preservice teachers develop a specific prereading strategy	• The introductory strategies are so important since they address students' motivation and background. • These strategies can address the varying reading abilities of students. • I focus on how many of these strategies help teachers develop classrooms that are open-ended, encouraging students to develop their ideas and interests. • We spend a lot of time on this topic; many of the strategies can be used during units or as culminating activities.

| 5. Discussion, questioning, and classroom contexts | Various purposes of questioning and resulting classroom contexts
I-R-E/recitation and classroom contexts
Characteristics of discussions, ways to facilitate
Impact of these participation structures and learning | Preservice teachers find strategies already studied in class that promote discussion (e.g., anticipation guides, graphic organizers developed in groups)
Preservice teachers develop a discussion web related to one of the concepts identified for their "Unit of Study" assignment | • Teachers often erroneously label recitations as discussions.
• The classroom interactions are usually based on textbook readings.
• I want preservice teachers to see the relationships between the use of texts, discussions, and student learning. |
| 6. (More) Comprehension instruction | Overview of the complexities of reading comprehension
Impact of social context on comprehension
Relationships between learners' characteristics and comprehension
Mention of text factors (in-depth look in subsequent topic)
Importance of political influences over curriculum
Tasks effects on comprehension processes
Reading strategies that facilitate comprehension not yet discussed | Preservice teachers brainstorm ideas related to the various factors that affect comprehension
Class looks at different ways to ask questions that encourage responses along an efferent–aesthetic continuum
Participate in Directed Reading–Thinking Activity
Participate in "Role Playing and Simulations"
Read lyrics while listening to pop music containing ideas that can be related to content area units; discuss how music can be used; get ideas for more songs | • As we consider more classroom practices related to reading, I emphasize the complexities of comprehension. Hopefully, this helps preservice teachers see that they can change texts, contexts, tasks, etc., to have positive effects on students' learning.
• Though all previously studied classroom practices have had comprehension as their goal, many of these practices focus on student participation, motivation, engagement, and availability of multiple texts. |

(Continues)

TABLE 21.1 (Continued)

Topic	Description	Some Assignments and Classroom Activities	Rationale
7. Writing to facilitate learning	Writing can promote learning. Writing helps people think about ideas. Writing in content areas is not extra; it's directly related to helping students learn. Technology is a tool that can encourage nonlinear writing, motivation, and learning.	Contrast typical writing assignment with open-ended writing assignment in terms of student learning Preservice teachers read sample learning logs from algebra and chemistry classes Presentation of HyperCard™ Stack developed by high school student for geography assignment; discussion about process required and probable learning. Preservice teachers develop list of "Writing Project Ideas" appropriate for their subject areas Consider strategies with writing components and purposes ("Writing Strategies' Purposes") Participate in "Reaction Log" based on current newspaper article related to education	• With the exception of English teachers, most secondary teachers have a limited notion of writing. • Preservice teachers look at and participate in many writing practices that they come to see as interesting, do-able, and enhancing learning. • By having preservice teachers come up with a lot of the writing activities they could use, they tend to see them as possibilities.

| 8. Vocabulary development and teaching strategies | Teaching vocabulary is not separate from teaching content. Vocabulary is a label for the concepts students need to learn. All the strategies studied so far address vocabulary, as it is embedded in all forms of discourse. Vocabulary/concepts are best learned when those labels are integrated with prior knowledge, are used meaningfully, are repeated, and help develop in-depth knowledge. | Preservice teachers are introduced to hypotheses explaining relationship between vocabulary knowledge and reading comprehension. Preservice teachers look at several examples of graphic organizers, including Venn diagrams, semantic feature analyses, concept maps, Frayer models, etc. Preservice teachers read one of several references from content-area methods books or literacy journals that describes a vocabulary strategy. Preservice teachers select one strategy, and teach others in the class some related words from their content area using that strategy. | • I want preservice teachers to see these strategies as integral to their classroom teaching. I emphasize how they are not extras, but part of effective teaching.
 • Preservice teachers develop a vocabulary list from their "Unit of Study" for their strategy example to make the assignment more useful. |
| 9. Study strategies | Relationships between meta-cognition and studying Use of strategies discussed in studying Other strategies specific to studying | Demonstration of note-taking strategies (2 column notes) Reference to importance and relevancy of ideas to learning and studying Class finds strategies discussed that are effective for independent studying. | • I often begin the semester with some examples of study strategies. Preservice teachers typically report that they have never been taught study strategies, and their intentions to use the strategies in their current coursework. |

(Continues)

TABLE 21.1 (Continued)

Topic	Description	Some Assignments and Classroom Activities	Rationale
10. Textbooks: A critical assessment	There are multiple factors related to texts that affect how understandable they are. There is no simple relationship between students' standardized test scores and the books they can comprehend. Textbooks should be only one source of information; multiple texts should be available for student learning. Local and national political agendas often determine textbook content and their allowed presence in classrooms.	The class brainstorms factors that affect the understandability of textbooks. Preservice teachers evaluate the textbook used in their practicum experience using the Fry Readability Graph and "General Textbook Readability Checklist" (found in Vacca & Vacca, 1996). Discuss limits of readability formulas. Look at examples of difficult text with low readability levels. I present information about the political factors that determine textbook content.	• I want preservice teachers to understand the limitations of textbooks in terms of perspectives and information. They often assume that all the important information students need to know should be found in this one book. • I want preservice teachers to think of themselves as decision-makers about text selection. Though they may not be able to select the textbook they use, they should be able to look at it critically and find other texts that will add to their students' learning.
11. Making connections across disciplines	Though courses in secondary schools are often taught as isolated knowledge domains, they are actually broader. Interdisciplinary units and courses promote in-depth learning.	Examples are provided of local teachers who have developed interdisciplinary units and classes. As a class, we brainstorm ways in which many content areas can be involved in a unit about a current issue. Preservice teachers work in interdisciplinary groups and develop a general description of a "Unit Across Disciplines" that relates all of their content areas.	• Preservice teachers expect to use numbers only in math and some science classes, and to write only in English classes. Reading and writing in all classes can enhance their learning. • The concepts students learn in various subjects were developed in the real world in relationship to other ideas, events, and circumstances. Learning these relationships helps students better understand the ideas and makes the content more interesting.

12. Assessing and evaluating students in content classes	Effective assessment should be ongoing. All interactions with students provide opportunities for assessment and evaluation. What teachers count towards grades tells students what is important. Learning opportunities discussed in this course throughout the semester provide much data about students.	Preservice teachers review strategies learned, developing list of assessment opportunities. View video *Redesigning assessment: Portfolios* (ASCD, 1992) and discuss ways in which portfolios could be implemented in their content areas. Brief review of standardized testing and their limited use to content area teachers.	• Though there are many traditional ways of assessing students' abilities to comprehend textbooks (e.g., cloze, content reading inventory), they do not consider the variety of instructional practices that impact students' comprehension. • Though I address assessment and evaluation in a separate unit, I have integrated these issues throughout the course as we consider various practices.
13. Students with special needs	Classrooms will usually be composed of students representing a range of reading abilities, knowledge, and language proficiency. Most of the practices explored, including providing multiple texts, give students opportunities to develop their understandings.	"Considering Students' Needs" assignment. Discussion focusing on how the practices we have examined can address the multiple needs of diverse students.	• Teachers need to consider all students in their teaching. • The students who know a lot and are good readers still need to learn more. • Students who typically struggle must be given opportunities to use appropriate texts to learn content.

REFERENCES

Association for Supervision and Curriculum Development (ASCD.) (1992). *Redesigning assessment: Portfolios* [Video]. Alexandria, VA: ASCD.

Brandt, R. (1993). On teaching for understanding: A conversation with Howard Gardner. *Educational Leadership, 50*(7), 4–7.

Lloyd, C. V. (1998). Engaging students at the top (without leaving the rest behind). *Journal of Adolescent and Adult Literacy, 42*, 184–191.

Newmann, F. M., & Wehlage, G. G. (1993). Five standards of authentic assessment. *Educational Leadership, 50*(7), 8–12.

Readence, J. E., Bean, T. W., & Baldwin, R. S. (1998). *Content area literacy: An integrated approach* (6th ed.). Dubuque, IA: Kendall/Hunt.

Richardson, V. (1996). Teacher education: Research, policy, and practice. In D. J. Leu, C. K. Kinzer, & K. A. Hinchman (Eds.), *Literacies for the 21st century: Research and practice.* Forty-fifth yearbook of the National Reading Conference (pp. 47–58). Chicago, IL: National Reading Conference.

Russo, A. (Producer). (1984). *Teachers* [Video]. MGM/UA Home Video, Inc.

Vacca, R. T., & Vacca, J. A. L., (1996). *Content area reading* (5th ed.). New York: HarperCollins.

22

Secondary Content Area Reading

Victoria Gentry Ridgeway
Clemson University

Before my career in the field of reading education, I taught science at the middle and high school level. Trained as a biology teacher, over the span of 20 years, I taught everything from life science to physics. In 1974, I was teaching physical and life sciences at a junior high school in Orlando, Florida. Against my will, I went to a "reading meeting" with the intention of grading, surreptitiously, a few papers to avoid wasting an entire afternoon. Joy Monahan challenged me to try a few of the suggested strategies and to let her know the results. I fully intended to show her that I knew more about teaching science than she did. After all, I taught hands-on science courses in which no reading was necessary. My students, I thought, could not read the text. What good would reading strategies do them? I taught my advanced classes "normally" and tried two of her suggestions with my basic science classes. I then gave both groups the same test. To my great surprise, the basic science class average was higher than that of the advanced class. The students in my basic classes had actually read the assignments and had done their homework. Their behavior had improved.

At the time that Joy Monahan introduced me to content area reading strategies, Harold Herber was the consultant for the Orange County, Florida, Reading in the Content Areas project. The ideas in Herber's content reading text together with my initial experiments with content reading strategies changed my teaching and my life. Eventually, my interests and experiences led me to complete my doctoral work with Donna Alvermann at the University of Georgia. Because I come

213

to the field of reading from science, my approach to content reading is more focused on comprehension of expository text than on narrative text. Content area teachers feel that their respective subject area is more important than other disciplines. I understand that mind-set and know that they would not be good math, science, or history teachers if they did not feel that way. I also know that literacy strategies are powerful tools to help students acquire knowledge of a discipline that goes beyond mere facts.

Secondary Content Area Reading is a required course for all undergraduate secondary education majors at Clemson University. Programs that lead to certification include the content areas of English; Foreign Language [Spanish, French, German]; Mathematics; Science, including biology, physics, chemistry, and earth science; and Social Studies, including history/geography, political science, and psychology/sociology. Approximately 10% of the students are classified as nontraditional. That is, they hold a degree in a content area and are returning to take courses required for certification.

For the past several years, the content reading course has been taken concurrently with the content area methods courses in English, foreign language, mathematics, social studies, and science. A 30-hour field component is required of all students and is shared by both the methods courses. The field component involves observing, tutoring, grading papers, teaching one or more lessons, and assisting the teacher in labs and other activities. Students typically take their methods courses during the semester immediately preceding their student teaching. Prior to this, students have taken introductory courses in the history of education, educational psychology, and adolescent development.

In addition to the specific goals listed on the syllabus, I have several overall goals for this course. First, I want content reading students to see the connection between concepts studied in my class and those studied in their content specific methods classes. To that end, I encourage students to submit work completed in other courses as artifacts for appropriate objectives of the portfolio assignment. In the rationale paper, which is required for each objective assessed by the portfolio, students explicate the connection between their artifacts and the objective. The portfolio serves as a bridge between the content reading course and other education courses.

Second, I want them to become reflective practitioners. The Learning Log requirement connected with the field component directly addresses this general goal. I model reflective practice by posting my professional journal on a class electronic bulletin board. In my weekly entries, I reflect on what happened in class, what I might do differently next time, and think through plans for the next class. All students are welcome to respond to my journal entries. Several times during the semester I conduct analysis sessions in which students reread and analyze their own learning log entries. Students note the content focus of their entries [topics such as preteaching, or student–teacher interaction]. At the end of the internship experience, students select a theme of interest and write a reflective paper based on their learning log entries.

A third goal for this course is related to the use of instructional technology. Several projects require students to become proficient with specific software packages and with the use of the Internet. The Conversations in the Round project involves conversations with students at other universities. Students may choose the instructional technology venue through which to conduct their conversations: a Listserv, a Discussion Board, or via instant messaging through the use of Chat Room software. The dialogue journal with me involves the use of the Collaborative Learning Environment (CLE) maintained by the Division of Computing and Information Technology.

Finally, the ultimate goal for me is to model the instructional principles I advocate. To that end, I build choice into the assessments, model strategies described in their text, and conduct "postmortem," on my modeling. A "postmortem" is an activity in which they critique my adaptation of the strategy I model for them. These postmortem sessions serve a dual purpose: they help me become a better teacher, and they provide content reading students with an opportunity to think like a teacher.

As I approach the content reading course each semester, I struggle with a balance between teaching specific strategies, a theory base from which students might invent their own strategies, and examining the contexts in which my students will be teaching. The tension inherent between being prescriptive and being more conceptually oriented is difficult to resolve. On the one hand, preservice teachers lack classroom experience that might facilitate their ability to generalize characteristics of strategies from specific illustrations. They need to see specific content reading strategies in action. On the other hand, I do not want them to leave my class thinking they must adopt the strategies exactly as they have been modeled or described, rather than adapt them. Thorough content area knowledge in addition to conceptual understanding of content reading strategies are required for a teacher to be able to adapt content reading strategies to complement the content, the learning context, and the students.

The course assignments are the vehicle through which I try and mediate this tension. There are two categories of assignments: alternative and required. Students choose from the alternative assignments to acquire 100 points of credit. All students must complete the required assignments: a literacy autobiography, the portfolio and the Learning Log. In the following sections, these assignments are described and the grading rubrics for alternative assignments are provided. These rubrics change each semester, based on feedback from students and my own self-evaluation of them. The current syllabus in which projects are described and rubrics for required assignments are provided may be viewed on the Web site accompanying this book, or on my university Web site: http://people.clemson.edu/~rvictor.

Alternative Assignments

1. Conversations in the Round (100 points).   Participate in conversations with content area reading students from other universities as part of a Listserv, Discussion Board, or Chat Room. Conversations will be focused on readings taken from current educational literature. All readings will be posted on the Collaborative Learning Environment (CLE) for easy access and will be held on reserve in the main library. Listserves are set up and maintained by the Division of Computing and Information Technology at Clemson University. The Discussion Board is maintained by the Clemson University Center of Excellence for Instructional Technology Training and may be accessed through their Web site at the following URL: http://itcenter.clemson.edu/forum/contentreading. Chat Room software is available free from the following Web site: http://thePalace.com. Download the software or plan to conduct your conversation from a computer in one of Clemson University' computing labs. Times for Chat Room discussions will be negotiate among Chat Room participants early in the semester. A reflective paper based on your participation in the project, which must be word-processed or typed, is required. Your reflective paper should include elements listed in the assessment rubric.

Assessment Rubic: Each element is rated on a 1–5 scale, each rating is multiplied by the elements's weight, and the results are summed for a total out of 100 points.

Responses (3): Minimum number of timely and consistent responses;

Response content (8): Processing of article content; synthesis of information from articles, course, conversations, and text;

Reflective paper (7): Processing of article content addressed, major understandings gained as a result of project; syntheses of information from articles, class, and conversations; suggested changes in project;

Quality of writing (2): Well-written, well organized, and mechanically and grammatically correct.

2. Dialog Journal (100 points).   Participate in a dialog journal with the professor. Respond to each electronic reflective journal entry posted on the CLE Discussion Board. Responses should reflect thoughtful consideration of class activities and discussions from the standpoint of a student and from the view of a teacher. Keep hard copies of your responses to the professor's journal and submit them with your reflective paper. At the end of the semester, analyze your responses and write a two to three page reflective paper of your experience based on this analysis. Your reflective paper should include elements listed in the assessment rubric.

Assessment Rubric: Each element is rated on a 1–5 scale, each rating is multiplied by the elements' weight, and the results are summed for a total out of 100 points.

Weekly class responses (3): Minimum number of timely and consistent responses (one per week); responses were of sufficient length;

Response content (8): Processing course content; analysis of class evident; synthesis of information from class, internship, experience, readings, and text; assertions are supported with evidence; suggestions for class are offered;

Reflective paper (7): Processing of course content addressed; major understandings gained as a result of project; synthesis of information; suggested changes in project;

Quality of writing (2): Well-written, well organized, and mechanically and grammatically correct.

3. Mini-ethnography (100 points).   Focus on one element of interest from your field experience (content presentation, assessment, classroom management, use of text, student culture, school culture, etc.), and write a mini-ethnography examining the issue. You must include a minimum of three (3) data sources: focused observation, interview, document analysis. It may be useful to think of a mini-ethnography as a feature article in the Sunday paper. You may choose to tell a story, ask questions, take alternative perspectives, or critique the status quo. Submit a proposal to the professor no later than midterm. Final draft of the mini-ethnographies will be published in a class ethnography collection. This assignment must be typewritten or word-processed.

Assessment Rubric: Each element is rated on a 1–5 scale, each rating is multiplied by the element's weight, and the results are summed for a total out of 100 points.

Focus (4): Element of interest clearly defined and explicated, rationale for choice of issue explicated, importance of topic noted, topic explored in sufficient depth;

Data (6): Minimum number and type of data sources, data sources clearly delineated, data sources related to element of interest, choice of data sources explicated;

Development of ideas (8): Ideas developed logically, information from data sources integrated, assertions are supported by data;

Quality of writing (2): Well-written, well organized, and mechanically and grammatically correct.

4. Microteaching: (50 points).   Demonstrate a specific content reading strategy for the class using content drawn from your area of specialization. You should have a peer critique your lesson plans prior to meeting with the professor one week before your microteaching. After your microteaching experience, write a self-evaluation of the lesson and submit the peer critique, typed or word-processed lesson plans, and self-evaluation to the professor one class period after the microteaching.

Assessment Rubric: Each element is rated on a 1–5 scale, each rating is multiplied by the element's weight, and the results are summed for a total of 50 points.

Microteaching: (4): Teacher is prepared; strategy is appropriate to content; students are actively involved in the lesson; literacy is integrated with content instruction; teaching procedures are appropriate;

Lesson Plans: (2): Procedures are logical and clearly described; peer critique included;

Paper: (4): Peer critique of lesson is addressed; self-evaluation is analytic; conditional information related to the strategy is addressed; strategy advantages and disadvantages is addressed; well written and organized.

5. Annotated bibliography: (50 points).

Trade books can be used in any content area to enrich and extend instruction as well as to provide instructional material at a variety of reading levels. Prepare a typed annotated bibliography of 20 expository or narrative trade books in your content area. Generate a set of criteria, with a minimum of four elements, with which to evaluate the books on your bibliography. Students with a concentration in Language Arts should prepare an annotated bibliography of books with a multicultural perspective. Students with a concentration in Modern Languages are to focus on the culture and history of people whose native language you teach. Other possibilities include children's books written in the target language. Consult your text for further information and examples of annotations.

Assessment Rubric: Each element is rated on a 1–5 scale, each rating is multiplied by the element's weight, and the results are summed for a total of 50 points.

Criteria (2): Are explained in an introduction to the bibliography and are used to evaluate the books reviewed;

Annotations (6): Summarizes story line or focus of book, includes an evaluation using the criteria developed; provides information about instructional use of book, includes necessary cautions about subject matter or language;

Quality of writing (2): Citations are complete and in APA editorial style; annotations are well written, grammatically and mechanically correct.

6. Synthesis Paper (50 points).

Using information gleaned from class experiments and discussions, text readings, interviews with teachers and/or students, and assigned outside readings, write a paper addressing the topic: Factors Involved in the Learning Process: How Students Learn. The paper must be typed, double-spaced, 3 to 4 pages in length. Include citations indicating where information originated, and a reference list at the end of the paper.

Assessment Rubric: Each element is rated on a 1 to 5 scale, each rating is multiplied by the element's weight, and the results are summed for a total of 50 points.

Content (6): Factors that influence learning identified and explicated; rationale provided for choices of factors; assertions are supported with evidence; information synthesized from data sources;

Data (2): A variety of data sources used, rationale for choice of data source explicated, data sources are appropriate;

Quality of writing (2): Well written, grammatically and mechanically correct, citations and references in APA (4th edition).

7. Article summaries: (25 points).   Read, summarize, and critique three (3) articles from professional journals that deal with literacy in your content area: reading, writing, speaking, listening. The summary should be typed or word-processed. Summaries are due on the same date and will be evaluated as a whole. This project may be repeated, using three different articles.

Assessment Rubric: Each element is rated on a 1 to 5 scale, each rating is multiplied by the element's weight, and the results are summed for a total of 25 points.

Summaries (4): Present major points succinctly, include intertextual references (connections among the articles) as well as connections between articles and course text; assertions in critiques are supported;

Quality of writing (1): Well written, grammatically and mechanically correct, citations and references in APA (4th edition).

8. Text analysis: (25 points).   Analyze a secondary (high school or junior high) text in your major field, using the guide found in your text, p. 86, or one you devise. College texts are not acceptable for this assignment. Provide a complete reference for the text, in APA editorial style. Write a summary report that includes an in-depth analysis of strengths and weaknesses, and information about the readability level as determined by one of the methods discussed in class or found in your text (pp. 83–84). This assignment must be typed or word-processed.

Assessment Rubric: Each element is rated on a 1–5 scale, each rating is multiplied by the element's weight, and the results are summed for a total of 25 points.

Analysis content (4): All areas addressed: content, format, utility, style, and readability; specific examples from the text used to illustrate and support assertions;

Quality of writing (1): Well-written, grammatically and mechanically correct, citations and references in APA (4th edition).

Required Assignments

1. Reflective paper (20 points).   Reflect on your own literacy development. Include evidence of early and present literacy development. You may wish to submit artifacts in support of your assertions. Appropriate artifacts include anecdotal notes; samples of student work; lists of favorite authors, books, or genres; lists of ways you use reading and writing in everyday life. This paper must be typed or word-processed, double-spaced, and should not exceed three pages.

2. PORTFOLIO (100 Points).   The purpose of the student portfolio is for you to demonstrate your learning in this class. It may become the basis for a professional portfolio that you maintain throughout your teaching career.
Portfolio Contents: For each portfolio evaluation, you are to provide evidence of any type you wish to demonstrate that you have achieved the course objectives for that evaluation.

Gather, collect and organize your artifacts for each objective. Artifacts may include entries in the Learning Log, lesson plans, notes from class, notes from observations, strategy descriptions, student work, microteaching materials, etc. Artifacts do not have to be from this class, but they must relate to this class. Organize the materials you are submitting; make sure that everything is labeled.

Write an explanation/rationale for your choices of artifacts that includes the following elements and submit the rationale with your portfolio. Be sure to provide explanation and rationale for EACH DESIGNATED OBJECTIVE.

Your rationale paper should include the following elements: (a) What you chose to submit; (b) Why you chose it; (c) How your artifacts connect the literacy objective and content learning in your content area; (d) Provide evidence of your knowledge of the concept(s) assessed by the objective.

The following specific objectives will be assessed through the student portfolio:

- Show that you can apply informal assessment approaches to evaluate students' literacy development in your subject area. Appropriate evidence for this objective might include a close exercise that you have developed, a list of fast- or free-write prompts together with an assessment plan, or a fast-write activity that has been completed by students and analyzed by you.
- Show that you can use specific instructional strategies to prepare students to read a content assignment. Appropriate evidence for this objective might include a prereading strategy description that has been critiqued by a peer and/or your cooperating teacher; or lesson plans from microteaching or your field experience.
- Show that you can guide reading to learn in your content area. Appropriate evidence for this objective might include a reading guide (analogical, text-structure, or graphic organizer) developed for a specific piece of text, and critiqued by a peer and/or your cooperating teacher.
- Show that you can use informal writing strategies to promote refection on reading/learning. Appropriate evidence for this objective might include an informal writing strategy description that has been critiqued by a peer and/or your cooperating teacher. Alternatively, student papers produced as a result of an informal writing activity may be submitted.
- Show that you can reinforce conceptual growth through vocabulary reinforcement on the interpretive level. Appropriate evidence for this objective might include a vocabulary reinforcement exercise on the interpretive level developed for a specific concept(s), and critiqued by a peer and/or your cooperating teacher.
- Show how you can adjust instruction or instructional materials in your classroom to accommodate differential student learning that results from cultural, language or achievement variation. Appropriate evidence for this objective might include original lesson plans and alternative lesson plans

that address student differences. A strategy description that is flexible enough to be used in a variety of specified ways with different student populations would also be appropriate.

- Show that you can design instructional activities that promote growth in research skills. Evidence for this objective can best be provided through a plan for extension activities that involve research on the part of students. The activity descriptions should include procedures for introducing the research, guiding students in their work, and evaluation/assessment criteria.
- Show that you can integrate the use of authentic text (literature, primary source text, etc.) into your content instruction. Evidence for this objective may involve other objectives. Strategies, research activities, and/or lesson plans developed for primary text, magazine articles, videos, and so forth may be submitted for this objective.

3. Learning Log {LL} (100 points).   The Learning Log is intended to provide a record of your observation and participation in the internship experience as well as an opportunity for your to develop reflective habits with respect to teaching and learning. Each entry should be made in response to a field experience session/visit and should be labeled with the following information: (a) date; (b) time—beginning to end; and (c) location. The easiest way to keep the Learning Log is to write your observations and/or reactions during the field visit or immediately after. Record observations of teaching methods, management methods, use of literacy in the classroom, student involvement and/or behavior. Do not simply list what students did or what you did during the class period. Be sure to include your response to the lesson, students, teacher's methods, and so forth.

Keep your Learning Log in ink on loose-leaf paper in a secure folder or three-ring notebook. Begin each entry on a new page. At specified times during the semester, you will conduct an in-class content analysis of your entries. During these in-class sessions, you may wish to add ethnographic memos, with Post-A-Notes. This process will be modeled for you. At the conclusion of the internship experience, choose one or two significant categories of entries that emerged from your content analysis of the Learning Log. Write an introduction to your Learning Log that provides a description and delineation of the significant categories selected as well as a rationale for your choice of significant categories. At the front of your Learning Log, prior to the Introduction, include a summary sheet detailing your visits, times, and providing the total time spent in your field experience. A list of significant categories would also prove helpful. The Learning Log is most appropriately kept in longhand, but may be kept electronically.

CONCLUSION

Working with undergraduates who have little to no experience teaching is a challenge I enjoy and try to meet in several ways. I provide students with alternative assignment choices that enable students to tailor their work to suit their needs and interests. I allow students to choose portfolio objectives that seem best suited to their content area and their developing teaching style. I share my professional journal with my students to model reflective "thinking like a teacher." Finally, I provide an apprenticeship experience that is the basis for class discussions and activities to ground theory in the "real world" of the classroom. Teaching this course is always a joy, because I know how my secondary preservice teachers feel—I was once in their shoes.

23

Content Area Literacy

Thomas W. Bean
University of Nevada, Las Vegas

Content Area Literacy (ICG 732) is a 3-credit graduate course typically offered once or twice each year for Reading/Literacy Education master's degree candidates in Curriculum and Instruction. In order to earn their MEd, they must complete a minimum of 36 semester hours of study. The MEd involves a 9-credit hour core of three semester hours in research, three semester hours in foundations (historical, philosophical, ethical, psychological, or sociological disciplines), and three semester hours in curriculum and instruction. The remaining 27 credits center on literacy courses. MEd students take a comprehensive examination or complete a professional paper as their culminating activity.

The Students

I taught 16 students in a recent offering of the course. All of these in-service teachers taught in the elementary grades (1st through 5th). One student served as an elementary librarian. Forty percent of the teachers had 4th grade classrooms. Thus, although not typical of the students found in undergraduate secondary preservice content area reading classes, these in-service teachers were directly involved in teaching elementary students content area text material and concepts in science, mathematics, social studies, and language arts. They were very enthusiastic about teaching strategies introduced in the course. They wrestled vicariously with their own ethnic and personal identity clarification issues through the two multicultural young adult novels we read and discussed (i.e., Soto, 1991; Velasquez, 1994). This project was part of a qualitative case study on students' literature response patterns (Mallette, Bean, & Readence, 1998).

My syllabus evolves each semester but there is an enduring emphasis on illuminating content area concepts through literature and discussion. For example, the novel *California Blue* (Klass, 1994) offers a powerful model of illustrating science and social science concepts and their interrelationship with the ethical issues of personal decision-making as a member of a community and responsible citizen (see Bean, Kile, & Readence, 1996). I used this novel recently in the course with very good results in terms of vibrant discussion of environmental and citizenship issues.

I try to bring a number of experiences into the course from a cooperative high school research project aimed at understanding students' literary discussions (Bean, Valerio, Money-Senior, & White, 1999). Content literacy graduate students taking the course have an opportunity to be electronic mail keypals with a group of juniors at the Advanced Technology Academy High School in Las Vegas as both groups read and discuss Amy Tan's (1991) *The Kitchen God's Wife*. The Advanced Technology Academy is a magnet school with an emphasis on computers and other technology. Every classroom is equipped with more than enough computers for each student and a substantial amount of learning takes place using this medium. For example, in English, students read novels and write about their reading. They engage in peer editing via computer.

In a recent research project at the school (Bean et. al., 1999), ninth-grade students read and discussed the novel *Heartbeat, drumbeat* (Hernandez, 1992). As one of their major writing assignments, we asked them to develop a research paper exploring the degree to which the novel displayed cultural authenticity concerning Navajo and Hispanic cultures. Students used the Indian Center, libraries, guest speakers, and the Internet to gather sources. They learned how to construct a research paper and how to reference these diverse sources of information.

Another newer element in my syllabus involves greater use of Web sites to gather material for science, social studies, mathematics, English, and so on. Our department has a particularly strong technology emphasis with a number of doctoral students who strive to involve faculty in the integration of technology and teaching (e.g., Falba, Strudler, Bean, Dixon, Markos, McKinney, & Zehm, 1999).

Key Issues

One of the major issues I have had to come to terms with since moving from Hawaii to Nevada is the absence of an undergraduate secondary preservice requirement in content area literacy for majors in core fields outside English. Our undergraduate version of the graduate class profiled in this chapter is only required for English majors, not future teachers from other content fields. The graduate class at least encompasses a greater range of content fields but I do want to lobby for a broadening of the undergraduate content literacy course to reflect standards adopted in most states.

Another issue I wrestle with is my commitment to integrating literature in content fields. I suppose I approach this as a kind of crusade where I bring into the class stacks of novels in addition to those we read and discuss. As a result, we may not cover as much content ground in the course but the depth of thinking and discussion seems worth the trade-off.

The philosophy in our text is one of practicing what we preach and I do try to model modes of teaching I think might make content concepts more friendly and understandable. The elementary in-service teachers taking the course are an enthusiastic group and they experiment with many of the ideas, strategies, and recommendations in our book.

I also have to be careful in teaching this class that I do not develop a false sense of security about content literacy. The literature discussion research project in the high school setting helps keep an edge on my thinking about what is possible and what is realistic. Working with doctoral students and middle and secondary teachers challenges my assumptions and thinking about content literacy.

In the section that follows, I want to offer a brief tour of the general content of the course, looking at selected class meetings in more detail. Readers can turn to the Web site accompanying this book for a glimpse of a recent rendition of my syllabus for this course.

THE SYLLABUS AND CLASS

Content Area Literacy

I usually follow the chapter structure of our book (Readence, Bean, & Baldwin, 1998) in my syllabus design. The newest edition of the book features a CD-ROM companion reader loaded with articles by colleagues in content literacy from around the country, as well as content text chapters, novels, and other supplemental material. Thus, during our second class meeting we go the lab and run an orientation on how to use the CD material.

I augment the activities in the text and CD with countless others that I have collected over the years. I sometimes get a brainstorm while jogging, taking a shower, windsurfing at the lake or some other inconvenient spot. These often occur a day or less before class. I then set about creating a prototype version of a new activity with related props, overheads, and so on. The ReWrite strategy (Bean 1997/2000) published in *Reading Online* International Reading Association's electronic journal developed initially in this fashion a few years ago. My students also bring in a wealth of great ideas, activities, and strategies. Nine colleagues in literacy in our department and an ongoing focus group in literacy with teachers in the Clark County School District also enriches my teaching.

The course is probably best considered using the first and second halves as demarcation points. Although there is much more overlap in content than appears using these category labels, they help show the early focus on foundation building and the later focus on strategy application.

The First Half of the Course

The first half of the course centers on developing essential epistemological knowledge about what content area literacy entails as well as a consideration of sociocultural and attitudinal dimensions Bean, 2000). In addition, we consider a strong position statement on adolescent literacy developed by the International Reading Association's Adolescent Literacy Commission (Moore, Bean, Bindyshaw, & Rycik, 1999).

During our first class meeting, I go over the materials we will be using. I introduce an initial assignment asking students to create a literacy autobiography charting their early and later literacy experiences. I often read a quote from Samuel G. Freedman's (1990) compelling account of an urban high school English teacher, Jessica who learns so much about her students through this assignment. Freedman (1990, p. 45) said:

> Jessica will proceed into her survey of American literature, only after she begins to know who she is teaching. She has memorized names and faces, but characters remain indistinct. In the course of writing an autobiography, each one will gradually turn, like a Polaroid photograph, from a dull brown emulsion to a focused and fully colored portrait.

The essential difference in my autobiography assignment is the audience. I ask students to write for a peer audience and we share our autobiographies in the second class meeting.

In addition to quotes from various trade books, I also use a fair number of cartoons in my course for each of the topics. This holds true for the autobiography assignment. I collect cartoons from a variety of sources and keep them in a large envelope for whatever topic I am preparing.

During this first class introduction to content area literacy, I ask students to read a very technical one-page article for kayak and canoe enthusiasts on how to read river currents in a fast moving river. They meet in small groups to brainstorm strategies they used to comprehend the article. This sets the stage for an overview of prior knowledge and its role in helping students develop power over difficult text material through careful foreshadowing of reading assignments.

In subsequent class meetings, we share autobiographies, complete a paired sociocultural interview on pages 28 and 29 of our text (Readence, Bean, & Baldwin, 1998), and do simulations that expand students' understanding of the content area reading process (chap. 3 of our text). Students conduct a text evaluation, read and share an article from the *Journal of Adolescent and Adult Literacy* or *Reading Online*, and engage in literature circle discussion of a young adult novel. The emphasis in this assignment is on figuring out ways to integrate tradebook literature and content texts. We also explore formal and informal assessment with an emphasis on portfolios and performance assessment. I usually demonstrate performance assessment with an anticipation–reaction guide activity on the topic of "ramen" or Japanese noodles. One of my former students, Darlene Okada, taught in Japan for a year and created a kinetic anticipation–reaction guide activity where students move to the right or left side of the room if they agree or disagree with a statement. This account of ramen eating departs from our western view of table decorum and challenges students' thinking. For example, the anticipation–reaction guide statement: "The emperor of Japan eats ramen very carefully and quietly" seems, on the surface, to be one we would want to agree with. However, students then read an account of ramen eating called "Stand up and slurp if you must" (Okada, 1994) that gives a view of this practice that typically differs from students' initial assumptions or misconceptions.

Much of my teaching is hands-on and activity-based. I can still recall a teaching interview years ago where I was asked to describe my philosophy of teaching and I said, "activity-based." This undoubtedly reflects the early influence of my two cooperating teachers during student teaching in the early 1970s. Pieper and Lois Toyama were great models of how to take challenging material in English literature and reading classes and, through creative tactics, make this material accessible to a variety of students. Their classrooms used centers before centers were popular. They used task grouping and small group conferencing with the teacher as a means of personalizing large high school classes. At that time, Hilo High was the only high school on the east side of the Big Island and it was very overcrowed at 3000 or more students.

We also spend some time reconsidering unit and lesson planning with a look at concept-oriented reading instruction. Much of this material I gathered while serving as a visiting scholar at the National Reading Research Center at the University of Georgia and University of Maryland (Guthrie, Alao, & Rinehart, 1997). We also read and discuss the first of many vignettes or mini-cases starting on p. 80 of our book.

Most importantly, we look at attitudes and interests in reading by surveying books and other materials students in class are currently reading. We look at the crucial interaction of reading attitude and achievement and I introduce engagement theory, again from the National Reading Research Center work. We begin reading and discussing Amy Tan's novel, *The Kitchen God's Wife*.

The Second Half of the Course

That takes us to the second half of the course with a focus on teaching strategies in vocabulary, comprehension, writing, and studying. I have an endless array of demonstration lessons for graphic organizers, KWL, Polar Opposites, and so on. The real danger here is not pitching out the old material and bringing in new material. I get attached to some of the older text props and eventually have to force myself to remove them from the course. The other danger is in inundating students with too many strategies, resulting in a grab bag of tricks impression. In order not to do this and put the learning emphasis on my students, we develop text guide material to microteach concepts from a variety of content areas. We also analyze and discuss the various chapter vignettes which helps make day-to-day teaching issues more transparent. Because most of my students are experienced teachers, much of what they do automatically in teaching concepts needs to be revisited from a more analytical perspective. This part of the course encourages a critical look at lesson design and delivery, particularly in content areas where students may get lost and become disengaged.

I rarely complete the content provided in our text, opting instead for depth over coverage. It takes time to read and discuss the text and two novels. In addition, we use Web sites as a content resource and interact with other students and teachers via e-mail.

Students select a midterm and final project option to complete from among those listed in the syllabus or others they can propose. Thus, the last few class meetings are devoted to demonstrating these student-generated products in class. This is an exciting time because these experienced teachers have a chance to tap the wealth of teaching ideas their colleagues bring to class. My students often come from diverse sections of Las Vegas spanning the north, northwest, southeast, and sometimes rural areas of our county. Our evening graduate classes bridge these geographic distances and technology allows my students into the world of the Advanced Technology Academy High School as well.

REFERENCES

Bean, T. W. (2000). Music in the content areas. In M. McLauglin & M. Vogt (Eds.), *Creativity and innovation in the content areas: A resource for middle and high school teachers* (pp. 91–103). Norwood, MA: Christopher-Gordon.

Bean, T. W. (2000). Reading in the content areas: Social constructivist dimensions. In M. Kamil, P. D. Pearson, R. Barr & P. Mosenthal (Eds.), *Handbook of reading research: Volume III* (pp. 631–644). Mahwah, NJ: Lawrence Erlbaum Associates.

Bean, T. W. (1998). Teacher literacy histories and adolescent voices: Changing content area classrooms. In D. Alvermann, D. Moore, S. Phelps & D. Waff (Eds.), *Toward reconceptualizing adolescent literacy* (pp. 149–170). Mahwah, NJ: Lawrence Erlbaum Associates.

Bean, T. W. (1997, May). ReWrite: A music strategy for exploring content area concepts. *Reading Online*. Electronic journal of the International Reading Association (http: //www.readingonline.org).

Bean, T. W., Kile, R. S., & Readence, J. E. (1996). Teaching citizenship with trade books in high school social studies. *Social Education, 60,* 227–230.

Bean, T. W., Valerio, P. C., Money-Senior, H., & White, F. (1998). Secondary English students' engagement in reading and writing about a multicultural young adult novel. *The Journal of Educational Research, 93,* 32–37.

Falba, C. J., Strudler, N., Bean, T. W., Dixon, J. K., Markos, P., McKinney, M., & Zehm, S. J. (1999). Choreographing change one step at a time: Reflections on integrating technology in teacher education. *Action in Teacher Education, 21,* 61–75.

Freedman, S. G. (1990). *Small victories.* San Francisco: Harper & Row.

Guthrie, J. T., Alao, S., & Rinehart, J. M. (1997). Engagement in reading for young adolescents. *Journal of Adolescent & Adult Literacy, 40,* 438–446.

Hernandez, I. B. (1992). *Heartbeat, drumbeat.* Houston, TX: Arte Publico Press.

Klass, D. (1994). *California blue.* New York: Scholastic.

Mallette, M., Bean, T. W., & Readence, J. E. (1998). Using Banks' typology in the discussion of young adult multiethnic literature: A multicase study. *Journal of Research and Development in Education, 31,* 1–12.

Moore, D. W., Bean, T. W., Birdyshaw, D., & Rycik, J. A. (1999). Adolescent literacy: A political statement. *Journal of Adolescent & Adult Literacy, 43,* 97–112.

Okada. D. (1994). *Stand up and slurp if you must.* Hilo, HI: Unpublished paper.

Readence, J. E., Bean, T. W., & Baldwin, R. S. (1998). *Content area literacy: An integrated approach* (6th ed.). Dubuque, IA: Kendall/Hunt.

Soto, G. (1991). *Taking sides.* San Diego, CA: Harcourt Brace.

Tan, A. (1991). *The kitchen God's wife.* New York: Putnam.

Velasquez, G. (1994). *Juanita fights the school board.* Houston, TX: Arte Publico Press.

VI

LITERACY ASSESSMENT
AND INSTRUCTION

24

Assessment and Instruction in Literacy Courses and a Tutoring Practicum

Penny A. Freppon
University of Cincinnati

This course is the first in a sequence of three required graduate courses for students seeking a master's or a doctorate in literacy. The three courses also fulfill part of the requirement for a reading specialists endorsement that attaches to a current teaching license. I have included in this chapter a summary of the first course and its syllabus and some discussion of essential features of the next two courses. The three courses are taken consecutively and all students tutor one child as they take these courses. This practicum component consists of twice-weekly, 1-hour tutoring sessions in the Literacy Center, which is located on campus.

The practicum (or clinical) component will undergo revision in the next few years because the state-approved endorsement will focus on early childhood, middle childhood, and adolescence rather than K–12. Other changes being considered are including TESL (teaching English as a second language) graduate students who would tutor non-native speaking children and adults. In addition, I mention these changes to emphasize that the program is in the process of change and that the course and tutoring component described in this chapter are changing also. However, this chapter provides a basic description that I hope may be useful to others.

I teach these courses, supervise the graduate students' tutoring, and carry out the administrative work needed to operate the Literacy Center. The program and coursework I describe stands on the shoulders of several colleagues at my university and elsewhere (Purcell-Gates, 1996) who were instrumental in conceiving this Literacy Center and its philosophy. The work described here is also supported by the writing and thinking of other literacy researchers and teacher educators some of

233

whom are referenced below. Learning and teaching theory (Bransford, 1979; Feuerstein, Rand, & Hoffman 1979; Schone, 1983; Vygotsky, 1978; Wood, Bruner, & Ross, 1976) provide a foundation throughout.

This three-course sequence is in a Literacy Program that is part of a Division of Teacher Education. Each course and successive practicum experience builds on the preceding courses and addresses both the principles and procedures of assessing and teaching children with literacy difficulties, and the development of the literacy professionals/ teacher researcher. The majority of graduate students with whom I work are teachers currently practicing in schools. Other students have teaching backgrounds but have not taught for some time; a few have been certified or licensed in art or music. Some doctoral students come from diverse backgrounds. Students enroll in the literacy sequence to improve their knowledge and skills, complete a graduate degree, and sometimes to gain the expertise needed to reenter the job market. At times, students from other Colleges take the sequence, for example, graduate students in Communication Disorders in the College of Arts and Science.

Because this course is embedded in a year-long sequence of study and tutoring practicum, I have grappled with providing enough structure to help students feel comfortable; but not so much that it limits their opportunities for reflection, problem solving, and ownership. The course reflects my "teacher development" philosophy which is based on whole language and constructivist theory (Goswami & Stillman, 1987; Rich, 1985) and teacher research (Allen, Michalove, & Schockley, 1993; Cochran-Smith & Lytle 1993; Gitlin, Bringhurst, Burns, Cooley, Myers, Price, Russell, & Tiess, 1992). I work on teacher development and empowerment issues somewhat differently each term depending on the needs and strengths of my students.

The course challenges students' and the instructor's juggling skills because it is so integrated with the tutoring practicum. Tutoring by its very nature is intense and even experienced and highly effective teachers encounter some initial frustration. It takes time to adjust to teaching just one child, closely tracking that child's responses, and integrating tutoring experiences and the course assignments. A school classroom observation and interview with the child's teacher, parent conferences and use of parents' written responses, conversations about the child with peers and the instructor all coalesce in this course (see syllabus). Various sources of information help graduate students understand how children's literacy may vary across the contexts of school, home, and the Literacy Center. Moreover, close observations in the Center help students see how children differ according to: (a) the assessment or instruction experienced, (b) their personal stance toward literacy, (c) home and school background, and (d) their unique evolving understands about reading and writing. Center observations combined with formal and informal assessments help show the children's unique needs, interests, and strengths. The course structure also supports a developmental perspective for all the participants, children and tutors. The course functions as a seminar that is research-based and highly practical. Among its goals are supporting students that engage in reflection and cope with the uncertainty of teaching and its relational and interpersonal nature. (Dudley-Marling, 1997; Hargreaves, 1994; Hargreaves & Tucker, 1991).

The more obvious course goals are to provide learning opportunities in which students acquire strategies for assessment and instruction that is in tune with children's learning. In addition, students need to understand that children's ability to "take from" instruction varies in pace and personal preference even though they may need similar literacy skills and concepts. For example, it is typical for struggling readers to have "off days" in which they may not engage well or make immediate progress. One-on-one tutoring highlights these factors. Thus, another goal is learning to see this as part of the process of teaching and learning rather than respond to it with teacher frustration or anxiety. Children who have experienced failure in school need affective skills and strategies as well as reading and writing skills. For example, these children are often passive, or they engage in avoidance behaviors. Such children much need support to become true learners who proactively take on the tasks of literacy (Gaskins, 1998).

Another goal is for graduate students to see that they can rely on themselves to organizing and implementing good literacy instruction without new commercial programs. They learn to use children's literature and existing materials well. Above all, I want students to gain confidence, be open to risk-taking in their own learning, and to see themselves as developing professionals. Acquiring this kind of "teacher stance" or disposition is a key issue, and its achievement varies. The small talk and peer interactions in the Literacy Center and class discussions are as helpful for teacher growth as the assignments and my feedback. My observations on this issue and the previous goals are supported in research on teacher learning and teaching excellence (Ayers & Schubert 1994; Duffy, 1990).

Conversations and questions occur throughout the week in the Center. At weekly class meetings, the students discuss the readings, their tutoring observations and questions, and their connections to what is happening in the course and what they are experiencing in their own classrooms. Graduate students describe the problems they encounter and share their own and the children's successes. They also practice and interact with various assessments and instructional techniques, and discuss children's literature. Essentially, students engage in a year of ethnographic-based action research as they learn more about literacy assessment, instruction, and themselves as teachers.

The Next Two Courses in the Literacy Sequence

The subsequent courses require different resources but continue to use several core texts (see the syllabus). Graduate students' self-selected readings expands in the second and their courses. Tutors' and children's collaboration and some family literacy interactions begin in the Winter quarter and continue until June. The assignments of Case Reports, Self-Evaluation, Session Reports, Dynamic Assessments, and Instructional Techniques continue in the next two courses. However, I weight the session reports and the self-evaluations more heavily in each successive quarter. Specific assessments and teaching are required, for example, assessment of children's writing and spelling using rubrics and developmental benchmarks, and teaching children based on these assessments. A goal is learning the "assessment language and thinking" typically used in schools and in our program and to base tutoring practice on research-informed decisions. This helps graduate students compare and contrast: (a) the concepts and theory that undergird assessments, (b) to distinguish between empirical data and teacher interpretations based on observations, (c) and to learn from both as a teacher–researcher. As the year proceeds, students use their growing expertise to select and create more of their own assessments.

Instruction itself becomes embedded in assessment; it is ongoing and changing. Graduate students make instructional decisions and draw specifically on the course readings. I provide input as necessary, and I require students to identify specific instructional techniques that they see as helpful in their work. For example, they "structure a program" of moving the child into more challenging reading, building word knowledge and comprehension, and improving spelling. These techniques and the children's own self-assessment is part of this program. Tutors and children decide on how self-assessment will take place and how they will display and share progress in the Center. This work contributes to the quality of session and case reports and is highly beneficial to children's learning.

Included next are some closing comments on session and case reports, graduate students' self-evaluations, and the dynamic assessment assignments.

Session reports are about one page each. They have required mini-sections that: (a) describe the assessment and instruction that took place, (b) elaborate on the tutor's interpretation of the child's responses, and (c) express reflection on their own teaching and what they are planning to do next. I provide written and oral feedback weekly that identifies good tutoring, makes suggestions, and I intervene as needed. Case Reports average about 20 pages. I give written and oral feedback on the first draft and also conference with some students to clarify work that needs to be done on the second draft. Processing this assignment is fairly complex and it varies with the students' needs, effort, and growth. However, it is helpful for the students—and it provides the means to produce a document that goes beyond a course assignment. This document must also be appropriate for the child's permanent Literacy Center record, and for parents, physicians, psychologists, or school personnel.

In addition to reflecting through writing in class seminars and writing twice-weekly session reports, graduate students write a self-evaluation at the end of each quarter. Students describe their views on their own progress, bring up questions or issues about their learning, and discuss what they want to work on in the future and the support they need. As with the other student work, self-evaluations generally improve with time; however, I find that some students do not easily identify their own strengths. It was because of this that I began to require self-evaluations, and it brings me to a final issue with which I constantly grapple. Some students need a great deal of support in understanding and trusting their growing expertise; and this realization is essential to their learning. Once students begin to explicitly describe what they are able to do well, they also identify more readily the things they need to improve. In short, I find this assignment is very helpful and that it addresses a general problem I see in teacher education. Some of our students are passive learners. These students tend to be those who also tolerate ambiguity poorly in themselves and in their teaching. They want *answers* to teaching dilemmas rather than strategies and techniques to improve the process. I "watch like a hawk" for constructive ways of supporting such students.

Throughout my work with graduate students, I identify and support their own recognition of "critical incidents" (Tripp, 1993) in their tutoring and in their own classrooms. Critical incidents are events in which the teacher documents and reflects on data to gain insights into how an event relates to deeper interpretations. Developing professional judgment is critical to successful teaching (King & Kitchener, 1994), and critical incidents, self-evaluation, and dynamic assessment are all helpful.

Dynamic assessment (Brown & French, 1979; Delclos, Burns, & Kulewicz, 1987; Feuerstein, Rand, & Hoffman, 1979; Johnston, 1992) is not new. However, its use in clinical course work may not be common. Briefly, such assessments are transactions in which the tutor takes the child back through part of a test or other assessment that has recently taken place (either immediately or very soon after). For example, this may be a reading miscue analysis (see Goodman & Marek, 1996 and retrospective miscue analysis) or a normed test of reading comprehension. The goal of this activity is to complete the session with the child feeling more successful and with the tutor having gained new insights into the child's abilities and problems. Conducting dynamic assessments helps bring testing and teaching together—students actually experience how assessment and instruction inform each other in one process. In a dynamic assessment, the tutor assists the child through explicit scaffolding in order to ensure success (e.g., use reading strategies). They usually discuss what "went wrong," how the child understands more now, and teacher and child engage in some practice. Essentially, dynamic assessment is a well-structured learning opportunity. The tutor has the advantage of a very focused event on which to reflect; and the procedure is very helpful for the children—it is especially nice following a testing situation. Dynamic assessments enrich the data base that graduate students use to complete their assignments and can truly help them see the child in a new light.

In conclusion, I want to note that after teaching this sequence for sometime and finding my handouts ever increasing, I developed a "Literacy Center Guidelines" packet to supplement the syllabus. This packet provides structure and is the very first reading assignment; it is used as a reference throughout the year-long sequence. The guide is specific to our program and includes models of major assignments, instructional and assessment materials, procedural suggestions, theoretical statements, a guide for family conferences, and so on. A summary of the syllabus follows the reference section.

REFERENCES

Allen, J., Michalove, B., & Shockley, B. (1993). *Engaging children.* Portsmouth, NH: Heinemann.

Ayers, W. C., & Schubert, W. H. (1994). Teacher lore: Learning about teaching from teachers. In T. Shanahan (Ed.), *Teachers thinking, teachers knowledge: Reflections on literacy and language education* (pp. 105–130). Urbana, IL: National Council of Teachers of English.

Bransford, J. D. (1979). *Human cognition, learning, understanding, and remembering.* Belmont, CA: Wadsworth.

Brown, A. L., & French, L. (1979). The zone of proximal development: Implications for intelligence testing in the year 2000. *Intelligence, 3,* 255–273.

Cochran-Smith, M., & Lytle, S. L. (1993). *Inside/outside: Teacher research and knowledge.* New York: Teachers College Press.

Delclos, V. R., Burns, M. S., & Kulewicz, S. J. (1987). Effects of dynamic assessment on teachers' expectations of handicapped children. *American Educational Research Journal, 24,* 325–336.

Dudley-Marling, C. (1997). *Living with uncertainty: The messy reality of classroom practice.* Portsmouth, NH: Heinemann.

Duffy, G. (1990). What counts in teacher education? Dilemmas in educating empowered teachers. In J. Zutell & S. McCormick (Eds.), *Learner factors/teacher factors: Issues in literacy research and instruction.* Fortieth yearbook of the National Reading Conference (pp. 1–18). Chicago, IL: National Reading Conference.

Feuerstein, R., Rand, Y., & Hoffman, M. (1979). *The dynamic assessment of retarded performers: The learning potential assessment device: Theory, instruments, and techniques.* Baltimore, MD: University Park Press.

Gaskins, I. W. (1998). There is more to teaching at risk and delayed readers than good reading instruction. *The Reading Teacher, 51,* 534–547.

Gitlin, A., Bringhurst, K., Burns, M., Cooley, V., Myers, B., Price, K., Russell, R., & Tiess, P. (1992). *Teachers' voices for school change: An introduction to educative research.* New York: Teachers College Press.

Goodman, Y. M., & Marek, A., M. (1996). *Retrospective miscue analysis.* Katonah, NY: Richard C. Owen.

Goswami, D., & Stillman, P. R. (1987). *Reclaiming the classroom.* Portsmouth, NH: Boynton/Cook.

Hargreaves, A. (1994, April). *Development and desire: A postmodern perspective.* Paper presented at the annual meeting of the American Education Research Association, New Orleans, LA. (ERIC Document Reproduction Service No. ED 372 057)

Hargreaves, A., & Tucker, E. (1991). Teaching and guilt: Exploring the feelings of teaching. *Teaching and Teacher Education, 7,* 491–505.

Johnston, P. (1992). *Constructive evaluation of literate activity.* New York: Longman.

King, P. M., & Kitchener, K. S. (1994). *Developing reflective judgment.* San Francisco, CA: Jossey-Bass.

Purcell-Gates, V. (1996, December). *Apprenticeship at the Harvard Literacy Lab.* Paper presented at the meeting of the National Reading Conference, Charleston, SC.

Rich, S. J. (1985). Restoring power to teachers: The impact of "whole language." *Language Arts, 62,* 717–724.

Schone, D. A. (1983). *The reflective practitioner.* New York: Basic.

Tripp, D. (1993). *Critical incidents in teaching : Developing professional judgements.* New York: Routledge.

Vygotsky, L. S. (1978). *Mind in society.* Cambridge MA: Harvard University Press.

Wood, D., Bruner, J. S., & Ross, G. (1976). The role of tutoring in problem solving. *Journal of Child Psychology and Psychiatry, 17,* 89–100.

Sample Syllabus
Literacy I

Required Texts for the First Course:[1]

Bear, D. R., Invernizzi, M., Templeton, S., & Johnston, F. (1996). *Words their way.* Columbus, Ohio: Merrill.

Lipson, M. Y., & Wixson, K. K. (1996) *Assessment and instruction of reading disability.* New York: HarperCollins.

Rhodes, L. K., & Dudley-Marling, C. (1996). *Readers and writers with a difference.* Portsmouth, NH: Heinemann.

Goodman, Y., Watson, D., & Burke, C. (1987). *Reading miscue inventory.* New York: Richard C. Owen.

Approximately 35 articles are updated quarterly and kept on reserve in the library. These materials are available for self-selected reading assignments.

General Course Description for the Literacy Sequence:

The course addresses the principles and techniques of diagnosis and remediation of literacy difficulties and the development of the literacy professional. A practicum experience is combined with course work. These tutoring experiences provide individual and collaborative procedures and materials for teaching and learning. Many course objectives are met in tutoring activities and experiences as well as the class discussions and assignments. The more specific objectives noted are central to the entire sequence of courses and help fulfill the practice-based objectives. These objectives provide students opportunities to:

- Become skilled diagnosticians of children with reading/writing problems through learning about a variety of diagnostic procedures, tests and child-centered observations.
- Become familiar with effective ways to help children learn to read and write through observations of and diagnosis of reading/writing problems.
- Learn about current issues and trends in diagnosis and remediation of reading/writing problems.
- Learn how to synthesize data (both formal and informal) and present findings to parents and educators.

Assignments and Content:

1. Weekly readings and class assignments.

---

[1]The first three texts are used in all three courses in the sequence.

2. Attendance and participation in all classes.

3. Observe, instruct, and assess a child in the Literacy Center. *This will involve two, 1-hour sessions per week.*

4. Carry out a school visit to observe the child and collect data.

5. Completion of Session Report forms for every tutoring session.

6. Complete a diagnostic work-up on this child or children that will be written up in a Case Study Report form and presented to parents during prearranged conferences (held during finals week each quarter).

7. Selected students will write and orally present an instructional technique report.

Evaluation:

Grades for this quarter will be based on the following:

1.	First Draft of the Case Report	25%
2.	Final Draft of the Case Report	25%
3.	RMI & Dynamic Assessment (included in case report)	20%
4.	Completion and Quality of Session Reports	15%
5.	Self-evaluation	5%
6.	*Technique report:	10%

*In the next two course of this three-course sequence, the value of the completion and quality of session reports and self-evaluation assignments (numbers 4 & 5) increases.

Case Report:

Each of you will observe, instruct, and diagnose a child enrolled at the Literacy Center. As part of your diagnosis and instruction, you are required to administer and engage in the following:

1. One Reading Miscue Inventory & Dynamic Assessment. See the Dynamic Assessment guideline in the Center Guidelines reading packet. (Any other information such as reading/writing interview or other assessment is left to the discretion of the graduate student). We will discuss both these assessments in class and you will practice the RMI coding and analysis procedures in class.

2. Begin instruction immediately and document it in your session reports. See the model for session reports in the Center Guidelines reading packet. As you learn about your child's needs and strengths use the instructional technique(s) we discuss in class and in your readings to get tutoring started.

Diagnosis at the Center also includes the following for which you are responsible:

1. Parent contact information (see the Center files also)
2. Classroom teacher contact and questionnaire
3. School records
4. Classroom observation of your child engaged in literacy activities
5. Any pertinent medical and/or psychological evaluations and information
6. Observations and impressions from working with the child in the Literacy Center (session reports, instruction and assessments)

All the information from the above sources is to be synthesized. See the Center Guidelines reading packet for explicit examples, and model case reports in the Center files. This information is written up in a Case Report and is presented to parents at the end of the quarter. Remember that your observations from working with the child are the foundation of your report. Recommendations for future instruction should be specific and must clearly draw on the readings and class discussions (cite and describe appropriate instructional techniques and their rationale). The Case Report is presented to the parents at a formal conference in the Literacy Center. Turn in your notes or brief parent conference summary (½ to 1 page) following this meeting.

Case Report Guidelines

1. Case Reports are to be typed double-spaced, and follow the format illustrated in the model Case Reports.
2. Case Report writing is objective, non-accusatory, and sufficiently detailed with observational or assessment date to support conclusions you draw. *The Session Reports you write after each tutoring session become the major data source for writing your Case Report.*
3. Case Reports contain as little jargon as possible so that parents, classroom teachers, and school administrators can use them for the benefit of the student. Write so that the reader can "see" the child. Use actual examples of student talk, written work, and actions. Parents often request a copy of your Case Report.
4. All information about the child is to be handled *in the most careful language.* Interesting but non-pertinent information is to be omitted. This is a professional document.

Instructional Technique Reports Guidelines

Choose an instructional technique to try with your child in the Center. Choose a technique which appears to address an identified need. Use any chapter or article assigned. Try the technique with your child, note his/her response(s) and write a five- (or fewer) page report on this experience. Include the following sections: (1) evidence of need for chosen technique, or rationale; (2) description of technique and its source; (3) description of what happened (what your child did, what you did, etc.); (4) reflection on the experience/technique, for example, why you think it went the way it did with your child, ideas for future instruction, your reflection (Feel free to use language such as "what I wish I had done," or "this did not work well, but ...," it is often in this kind of reflection that very good insights are gained.) An appendix with samples of student work, or lesson format is usually helpful.

25

The Analysis and Correction
of Reading Disabilities

Steven A. Stahl
University of Georgia

Historically, there have been two basic approaches to teaching children with reading problems. One could "fix the child" by remediating underlying reading processes. The title of this course goes back to a time when the medical model predominated, as reflected by the words analysis, correction and disabilities. We do not take this approach, although it is still a strong component of learning disabilities and school psychology. I would change the title, but that would involve paperwork and committees. The other approach is to determine what a child's *abilities* are in various aspects of reading. Instruction can be targeted to teach the child what he or she does not know, in order to enable the child to progress in reading. In this approach, the purpose of assessment is to decide what level to work on and what aspects of reading to target, rather than to decide why the child failed to learn to read. This is an approach typical of reading clinics and the approach we take in this course.

This course syllabus covers a class in the assessment and instruction of children with reading problems. The course covers the basic topics of such a course, assessment, especially informal assessment, and instruction, again especially instruction appropriate for children with reading problems. Students[1] also work with children in the University of Georgia Reading Clinic. I took over this course about 8 years ago. Originally, this course was largely a lecture and instruction class, preparing students for work in the practicum that follows. I changed the class to have children

---

[1]For clarity, *students* refers to university students; *children* refers to children being tutored.

come as soon as possible. My philosophy has been that students learn to work with children with reading problems by working with them, and that learning about assessment and instruction is more meaningful to my graduate student tutors if they have to apply that learning to a real child. As I discuss later, our tutoring has been highly successful for the children we serve.

The University of Georgia Reading Clinic was founded in 1951 by Ira Aaron. It is one of the oldest continually operating university-based reading clinics in the country. We have a variety of rooms to work in, including four rooms with one-way glass and microphones. We have a small library with a collection of instructional materials. This collection largely consists of children's books, but we do have a number of kits, high-interest vocabulary books, and a computer.

We do things differently than were done 47 years ago, but maintain a focus on traditional areas of reading instruction for children with reading problems—word recognition, comprehension, and study strategies.

An Instructional Model

The model we work from is based on Stahl, Kuhn, and Pickle's (in press) adaptation of Gough and Tunmer's (1986) "Simple View" of reading. We use this model for both targeted assessment and instruction. Gough and Tunmer view reading comprehension as the product of Decoding (or the ability to recognize written words) and Comprehension (or the ability to understand the language in which the text is written). In Gough and Tunmer's view, a person who can understand language but not decode would not be able to comprehend a text, nor would a person who could decode but not understand the language.

Stahl et al. (in press) have added a third component to encompass the aspects of meta-cognitive control of the reading process enables children to read differently for different purposes. They suggest that these components—called Automatic Word Recognition, Language Comprehension, and Strategic Knowledge in their model—can each be broken down into subcomponents.

To be a fluent reader, one must recognize words automatically, use context to confirm ongoing meaning, recognize a corpus of words by sight, know strategies of how to decode basic words, and understand that words are made of phonemes. These can be thought of as a developmental continuum of sorts, at least in that a child who reads fluently can be supposed to have an adequate knowledge of decoding, or a child who decodes words well can be assumed to have adequate phonological awareness. We assess automatic word recognition through the oral reading subtest of an informal reading inventory. We do not withhold the reading of connected text until a child has reached some milestone; on the contrary, as discussed later, children are supported in their reading of connected text regardless of their knowledge.

We are interested in three components of language comprehension, because these are the components in which children with reading problems have been found to have difficulties. We assess children's knowledge of vocabulary, because vocabulary is a strong predictor of their success in reading comprehension (Stahl, 1998). We also are interested in children's knowledge of text structure, especially story structure. This is mainly assessed informally, through retellings, but is more important in instruction. We also include background knowledge in the model, but background knowledge varies from selection to selection. We assess and instruct in relation to reading specific passages, but not as a general trait.

We also see Strategic Knowledge as moving from global concepts of print (such as directionality and concept of "word"), to a more general understanding that print carries meaning, to specific purposes that one might have for reading (studying, recreational reading, etc.). We assess early stages of print concept with the Concepts about Print test (Clay, 1995) and later stages through interviews.

Instruction

Tutoring is also based on this model. We attempt to meet the meets of children, through instructional targeted to their instructional needs. There are some basic principles, however, which guide our work. First is the 50% rule. At least 50% of the time must be spent reading or working with connected text. When I started working in reading clinics 15 years ago, it was difficult to get students to let children read. Instead, the zeitgeist was to do skills instruction. I remember watching a student spend 45 minutes teaching a child how to look words up in the dictionary, all without using a dictionary. Instead, we had a collection of worksheets dealing with alphabetization, guidewords, and so on. Currently, the pendulum has shifted so that we have to remind students to teach some skills. Gambrell, Wilson, and Gantt (1981) found that children spent an average of under 10 minutes per day reading connected text; poor readers spent under 5 minutes. I believe that our success lies in increasing the amount of reading that children do.

Second, we try to scaffold children's performance at reading more and more complex texts, and consciously try to push the child to work at the upper end of his or her "zone of proximal development (ZPD)." The notion of ZPD comes from Vygotsky (1978), who suggests that rather than a single fixed ability, children really have a range of ability from what they can do independently to what they can do with strong support. We try to have children work at the upper ends of their abilities and find benefits in terms of motivation and achievement (see Stahl, 1998).

Third, although we do teach skills, both comprehension and phonics skills, we do not "beat the child over the head" with them. I assume that other teachers have covered these skills and that children with reading problems need practice in integrating the use of skills and strategies into the reading of connected text. We do not have a "Reading Clinic approach" to teaching comprehension, decoding, or fluency, but instead try to acquaint our students with as many approaches as we can cover. I assume that, for every approach to teaching some aspect of reading, there is a child who would benefit from that approach, and that a good teacher of children with reading problems should know as many approaches as possible.

The course appears fairly successful, with both graduate students and children. We not only get a healthy enrollment of students from our Reading master's program, but also from School Psychology and Special Education. As for the children, both winter and summer for the past five years, at least 80% of all children have made 1 year's progress on an informal reading inventory in 20 hours of tutoring. As a result we currently have a waiting list of 90 to 100 students for 30 or so slots with nothing but word-of-mouth.

REFERENCES

Clay, M. M. (1993). *An observation survey of early literacy achievement.* Portsmouth, NH: Heinemann.

Gambrell, L. B., Wilson, R. M., & Gantt, W. N. (1981). Classroom observations of task-attending behaviors of good and poor readers. *Journal of Educational Research, 74,* 400–404.

Stahl, S. A. (1988). Teaching children with reading problems to decode: Phonics and "not-phonics" instruction. *Reading and Writing Quarterly, 14,* 165–188.

Stahl, S. A., Kuhn, M., & Pickle, J. M. (1999). An educational model of assessment and targeted instruction for children with reading problems. In D. Everson & P. Mosenthal (Eds.), *Advances in Reading Language Research, 6,* 249–272. Greenwich, CT: JAI.

Sample Syllabus
The Analysis and Correction of Reading Disabilities
Graduate Reading Course

This is a first course in the assessment and instruction of children with reading difficulties. It is intended for a beginning graduate student. No previous experience with children with reading problems is assumed. By the end of the course, students are expected to have a diagnostic model that will help them understand why children develop reading difficulties, and to use that model to understand children's difficulties in reading. They will also be able to administer informal reading inventories and other measures of reading skill. They will also be aware of various techniques that have been found useful for teaching children with reading problems from the prereading stage through secondary school.

Texts

Wixson, K. K., & Lipson, M. Y. (1991). *Assessment and instruction of reading disability.* New York: HarperCollins.

Leslie, L., & Caldwell, J. (1995). *Qualitative reading inventory—II.* New York: HarperCollins.

Tierney, R. J., Readence, J., & Dishner, E. (1995). *Reading strategies and practices* (3rd. Ed.). Boston: Allyn & Bacon.

Clay, M. M. (1993). *An observation survey of early literacy achievement*. Portsmouth, NH: Heinemann. (Includes *Stones*)

Course Requirements

1. Students will work with one child the last 7 weeks of the course. For this child, they will (a) complete an informal reading assessment, and write a report based on that assessment, (b) develop a program based on that assessment, (c) provide individual tutoring based on that program, and (d) develop a portfolio demonstrating the child's progress.
2. There will be a single examination covering the course material. The examination will be based on some basic course concepts (such as test and measurement concepts, basic knowledge of remedial techniques). A study guide will be provided prior to the exam.

Calendar[2]

January

8	Elvis Presley's birthday Introduction, Models of Reading Readings: Wixson, Chapter 1, 2
9	Richard M. Nixon's birthday (No class, Nixon or us.)
13	Assessment of Reading Disability, Informal Reading Inventories. Readings: Wixson, Chapter 3, 5, QRI (entire)
15	Martin Luther King's Birthday (We do have class, but you can dream). Miscue analysis and interpretation of Informal Reading Inventories Reading: Shearer & Homan, Chapter 6
19	We-are-going-to-pretend-it's-MLK's-birthday (No School)
20	Assessment of emergent reading, strategic knowledge, and language Readings: Clay Book
22	Getting Ready for Children to begin Assessment
	Children Begin
27	Emergent Literacy Assessment (2) Readings: Wixson, Chapter 4, 6 Assessment
29	Complete Assessment Interpretation of Standardized Tests Readings: Shearer & Homan, Chapter 4

---

[2]Dates are from Winter Quarter, January–March, 1998.

February

3   Begin Tutoring
     Beginning reading (word recognition, phonics, and so on)
     Readings: Wixson, Chapter 12, Tierney, Unit 1, other readings
     to be assigned

5   Tutoring
     Case Study

     Diagnostic Report Due (First Draft)

10   Tutoring
     Emergent Literacy
     Readings: Wixson, Chapter 4, Tierney, Unit 10, others to be assigned

12   Tutoring
     Case Study

15   Susan B. Anthony Day

16   President's Day

17   Tutoring
     Comprehension Instruction 1
     Readings: Wixson Chapter 14, Tierney, Units 2, Shearer & Homan,
     Chapter 7

19   Tutoring
     Case Study

22   George Washington's Birthday

24   Tutoring
     Comprehension Instruction 2
     Readings to be Arranged

26   Tutoring
     Case Study

March

3   Tutoring
     Reading Recovery
     Readings: Pinnell, G. S., Fried, M. D., & Estice, R. M. (1990).
     Reading Recovery: Learning how to make a difference. The Reading Teacher, 43,
     282–295.

5   Tutoring
     Case Study

10   Assessment
     Vocabulary instruction
     Readings: Wixson, Chapter 13, Tierney, Unit 6

12   Assessment
     Post-assessment, Wrap up, Party

17   **Examination**

Other Matters:

1. In all dealings with the public schools and parents, students are to conduct themselves as professionals and proper representatives of the University of Georgia. This means professional dress and demeanor are required when you are working with children in the clinic.

2. During tutoring, promptness is expected. You are required to be ready to tutor at 4:30. If you cannot tutor, please call Terri (the clinic secretary) at 542-7866 as soon as possible. One of us will have to substitute for you. Please get plans to us (or call one of us) before the session begins. A doctor's note is required for a missed tutoring session. If your child misses a session you are still required to be here. On those days you may observe other tutoring or substitute.

3. Confidentiality must be respected. No information about children you are working with may be discussed with *anyone* other than the instructor or fellow students. This means not with your spouse, significant other, the bus driver, or anyone.

4. Hours of Instructional Materials Center, second floor Aderhold, are: (M-Th) 8–8, (F) 8–5. This collection contains children's literature, basal readers, and some additional material that we will use for tutoring. Other materials can be found in 306 and in the Tests room as part of the 302 suite. You may gain access to the 302 collection any time the clinic is not in use by School Psychology personnel (see door for schedule). Ask one of us to let you in.

5. We follow the course calendar. I do not make assignments every week, but instead assume that you will have read the material and be able to discuss it. We may shift lecture day from Tuesday, as on syllabus, to Thursday if class prefers. Class will not be canceled or shortened for personal reasons, such as on St. Valentine's Day.

26

Learner-Centered Assessments
for Preservice Classroom Teachers

Robert J. Tierney
University of British Columbia

with Lora Lawson and Elizabeth Murray
Wittenburg University
University of Wisconsin–Milwaukee

For many years, I have been interested in helping teachers develop classroom assessment systems that help teachers teach and students learn. My first opportunity to teach such a course arose in conjunction with a request from faculty involved in the Master's of Education program that prepares preservice teachers. The faculty were concerned that the courses that had been offered in the past had emphasized technical aspects of testing rather than meeting the needs of preservice teachers as they were learning to meet the needs of students and address classroom management issues.

Offering courses dealing with classroom-based or learner-centered assessments may require swimming against some strong political currents, especially in a College of Education that historically has subscribed to traditional views of assessment. In my own institution, those faculty who traditionally teach assessment courses have been reluctant to engage in the kinds of hands-on engagement and shift in orientation that those of us invested in preservice teacher preparation deem essential. Even our literacy program tends to maintain a tradition of clinically oriented diagnosis and remediation courses.[1]

---

[1] The faculty who approached me were keen to capitalize on my ongoing working relationships with teachers tied to exploring the portfolio process and other learner-centered assessment possibilities. The faculty who had taught the course seemed to be dismissive of the very thing preservice teachers needed and wanted—learner-centered and classroom-based assessment techniques. Furthermore, it seemed problematic

One of my primary goals throughout the course is to use the development of a classroom assessment system to interweave the various class activities, field-based experiences, readings, and assignments. As I introduce the students to a range of specific assessment practices, the overall goal of the class is to generate and critique an assessment system where these separate practices are interfaced within what I term as a *classroom-based assessment system*. A classroom-based assessment system is intended to meet initial and ongoing assessment needs of teachers, students, and parents. It is an assessment system that is intended to incorporate a range of assessment practices from various sources to meet the needs of students. In such a system, teachers assess themselves (review their literacy gains through different lens, set goals, and plan activities).

Learner-centeredness is a major focus of the assessment system. Students are expected to be involved in assessing themselves—keeping track of their own progress as they maintain portfolios and other ways to track their progress. In a host of ways, the teacher's task is to help the students manage the assessment system rather than have the teacher assume an inordinate amount of the responsibility for such.

You will notice many of the materials developed for the course have been integrated into a Web site and is dependent on e-mail. These include: the course outline, an updated course calendar, access to a glossary, selected materials, hints drawn from e-mail exchanges or class follow up and direct access to selected references. To circumvent copyright issues, a preponderance of the readings (especially those available on the web for downloading) are my own (including published articles as well as pieces that may never be disseminated beyond the class).

The class itself is a combination of exploration, discussion, exploration, show and tell as we encourage students to address assessment issues and explore possibilities in their classroom. The class itself is intended to be a kiva for discussion, presentation, problem-solving, and invention. The course extends to working with the mentor teachers who support the students in partnership with the faculty as well as to other methods classes that the students are taking. As I have suggested, the key to the course is the commitment to having them develop a classroom assessment sys-

---

to simply have these faculty add material on certain techniques. It is as if to teach such a course, you need someone who should aspire to be the following: a constructivist who looks more for thick descriptive, verifiability, emergent possibilities; a ethicist and learner-centered educator who is concerned for how students and parents are positioned as partners in decision making and learning how to assess themselves; a pragmatist who wants an assessment system that is manageable and seamless with classroom operations, yet useful as a teaching tool befitting my ongoing curriculum and everchanging curriculum development; and a professional teacher educator interested in the ongoing professional development of teachers. Indeed, those responsible for the preservice program suggested that to teach such a course, you need individuals who have had first-hand experience exploring learner-centered assessments and are aware of the epistemological tenets and ethics that undergird such courses. Perhaps the psychometrician, without a background in qualitative methodology or an interest in sociopolitical nature of education, may not have the qualifications to teach such a course—indeed, may have a bias that clouds their judgment and ability to entertain the possibilities that such practices and viewpoint demand.

tem. Reading assignments are intended to orient them, address their issues and serve as a resource. In addition, selected faculty and school personnel join in the discussion. For example, the Director of Assessment for Columbus City Schools participates in the class offering a district- and state-level perspective. Slides and videotapes of K–8 teachers' assessment activities are presented. Faculty from various disciplines are also accessed. An interview of one of the science educators on our faculty is included as an example.

Unfortunately, I am required to grade the students. As you can imagine, this is a struggle as I find the grade can take over the course and denigrate what students have done. Although not addressing all of my concerns around grading, I think I do some things that seem to alleviate the tension that arises between grading and providing support for individual development, effort, process, progressive improvement, and self-determination in learning.

I view my role in the class as an expert consultant and partner in helping preservice teachers develop professionally. In this role, I am constantly advising and providing feedback to the students. Together we establish joint expectations for their efforts that include their exploration of issues through their readings as well as their try-out of selected strategies and an emerging proposal of a classroom assessment system. Toward the end of the quarter, they are expected to share in concrete terms their process/journey through the readings and the elements of their classroom assessment system with self-critique and ongoing goals specified. A few weeks prior to our deadline for submission, the students present drafts of these assessment systems for feedback. The critique and ongoing goals are considered as integral. I am not interested in bells and whistles so much as having an opportunity to follow their journey and what they explored so that I can offer feedback. What I receive is often a mix of rough notes, post-its, photographs, and various analyses and self-critique in the form of margin notes to me and others. At the end of the quarter, I respond to each student with an extended letter that details what I perceive to be accomplishments and areas to pursue further. I do indicate an overall grade tied to my judgment of the individual professional engagement in an ongoing exploration of the issues and projects. To encourage an ongoing conversation, I ask for feedback on my views and will arrange for an incomplete if the student and I differ on the grade. In some cases, I employ the use of the incomplete as a means to have time for the student to resubmit or do further explorations of the issues.

As you examine the syllabus, it should be stressed that the course involves students exploring assessment from multiple perspectives—in terms of assessments' relationship to school and society, the ethics of assessment, social justice and assessment, ways of knowing, school reform and assessment as well as specific assessment practices. Students enrolled in such a course need to interrogate their own notions of assessment. Indeed, in exploring these issues, it is not uncommon to discover that both preservice and practicing teachers have a history of acquiescing to traditional assessment beliefs and practices that have not been challenged. Many accept assessment as needing to have certain technical attributes that may be antithetical to constructivist tenets. They might accept an ethic of pursuing assessment that is objective and detached versus learner-centered, subjective and supportive. Most educators need to be encouraged to rethink testing by examining the extent to which testing is judicious and supportive of students and whether or not it supports teaching and learning. I stress we need to assess our assessments in terms of standards that fit with our views of teaching, learning, advocacy, empowerment, and ways of knowing. In so doing, I encourage them to rethink reliability as verifiable and more interpretative, to redefine generalizability in terms of issues of transferability, to question notions of standardization and objectivity and to scrutinize the ethics of assessment. I stress that I see classroom assessment as involving a shift from a priori to emergent and from approach that redefines the relationship of assessor to assessee from evaluator to advocate and coach. (See Tierney & Clark, 1998 and Tierney, 1998 for a more extended discussion of these perspectives).

It is noteworthy that our preservice teacher preparation program has continued to pursue an orientation to assessment that primarily addresses classroom-based assessment needs. For those concerned that we may have displaced technical issues related to standardized testing and state mandates, I would stress that we do address such but they are embedded within the course rather than superordinate as they once were.

In some ways, courses dealing with classroom-based, learner-centered literacy assessment seem more the exception than the rule. Indeed, more traditional assessment courses or clinical approaches to literacy assessment appear to be the incumbent and, as a result, teachers are often ill-prepared to engage in assessment practices that are learner-centered or can be managed in a classroom in a manner that complements rather than disrupts curriculum. It is as if preservice teacher preparation programs have had a tendency to focus on courses that approach assessment as if teachers have the luxury of working as a clinician with their students or default to an approach to assessment that reveres standardized testing. Preservice teachers are not the only group shortchanged. In my own institution, there are limited opportunities for advanced graduate study of classroom-based assessment and the constructivist tenets and sociopolitical considerations that undergird them.

The curriculum that we will share is one involving preservice teachers who are simultaneously doing an internship in classrooms. The internship ensure that the students have an opportunity to consider the relevance of the issues under consideration as well as try and refine their own repertoire of assessment strategies with the support of ourselves and their teacher mentor as well as fellow students. I cannot understate the power of being able to explore with the students assessment issues and practices in a range of settings. It is one thing to embrace the tenets of assessment that are espoused, it is another to develop practices that are workable and can exist when one's assessment history and the reverence with which schools often have for traditional practices, including grading practices.

In sharing with you one of my syllabi, I would stress that my approach to teaching such courses has been as collaborative as my research exploring learner-centered assessments. The team includes: students taking the course for credit as part of the team; my colleagues teaching other courses—hopefully, in tandem with some of the issues and practices of both courses; graduate student colleagues who problem-solve, plan and monitor how things are going; and teachers who serve as mentors and as consultants/resource personnel for ourselves. Two of the colleagues who contributed to the course, Lora Lawson and Elizabeth Murray, have been listed as co-authors here.

REFERENCES

Tierney, R. J., & Clark, C. (1998). Portfolios: Assumptions, tensions, and possibilities. *Quarterly, 33*(4), 474–486.

Tierney, R. J. (1998). Negotiating leaner-based literacy assessments: Some guiding principles. *The Reading Teacher, 51*(5), 374–391.

Sample Syllabus
Classroom Assessment

Why Are We Here?

To develop your own learner-based assessment system for your classroom

To explore assessment's ongoing relationship to teaching and learning in your classroom

To expand your variety of lenses and approaches in observing and assessing students in a range of classroom situations

How Do We Do That?

Observe. Watch how and what others (teachers, parents, professionals, experts, self-directed learners) assess. Study their ways of and goals in assessing.

Broaden your frame. Help yourself to see learning as something that happens over time, with affective, cognitive, social, and political elements.

Look through different lenses. View assessment variably across situations, including formal and informal settings, over extended periods.

Help students assess themselves.

Continually assess your own assessment and decision-making.

What Resources Have We Got?

Yourself

Your students

Web site for course outline, articles, ongoing notes, slides, and so on

E-mail

Journal

Listserv

Critical friends

Mentors

Class meetings, every Wednesday, 2:30–4:00

What Do We Hand In?

Classroom assessment system.   The bulk of your energy will go toward creating your own classroom assessment system. This is not a one-time assignment, rather a project that will originate from and inform your classroom practice. It will grow as you grow, with the ultimate goal being an assessment frame that you can take to use as a beginning place in your own classroom next year (when you all get hired, of course).

Share a video clip of an assessment "incident" from your class.   From   a longer segment of videotape, choose a 2-3 minute assessment-centered segment to share with your colleagues in class. Here are some ideas of potentially rich sharings.

Unit start-up

Student wrestling with a problem

Spontaneous conference

Teaching intended to assess and advance learning

Using journals

Planned conference

Crash and burn: DISASTER

These are only a few categorical ideas. Keep in mind that this is an opportunity for feedback, not show-and-tell of your finest hour. Bring in a clip you're proud of or bring in a clip you're frustrated with or bring in a clip you're stumped by. Whatever your connection to the clip, make certain it reflects some aspect of assessment on which you're working.

Any Helpful Hints?

Of course ... but they will only amount to hints until they are brought into action in your practice.

Brainstorm all the assessment practices already in place in your classroom.

Recall assessment practices you've tried out as part of your course work (e.g., miscue analysis, running record, anecdotal records, etc.) and assessment practices you've observed in visiting other classrooms, talking with colleagues and mentors, reading, and so forth.

Think of assessment as being multifaceted and complex, but always approximate.

Imagine assessment as having many layers.

  a) Time: immediate, short-term, interim, long-term
  b) Perspectives: teacher, students, parents, resource support, administration, community, and so forth
  c) Purposes: gauge teaching and learning, inform planning and teaching, record progress, activate prior knowledge, check status, and so on
  d) Foci: individual, small group, whole group, grade level

Try stuff; experiment. Trust yourself.

Look for ways to have the kids gain self-assessment tools.

Try to make links between assessment and goals/objectives/planning.

What Happens When?

Week 1:

Introduction and Expectations

The Web site

The nature of a classroom assessment system; Goals, principles, elements

Week 2:

Due: Detail elements of the classroom assessment system associated with their field experience—periodic assessment

Introduction to ways to get to know your students—initial assessment—review of records, prior portfolios, roaming the known, interview, artifacts of reading and writing behaviors

Week 3:

Due: Tryout ways to get to know your students

Ongoing monitoring teaching and learning

Record keeping, logs, portfolios, running records, retellings, think-alouds.

Understanding retellings, miscues

Introduction to portfolios

Week 4:

Due: Develop a draft of portfolio unit plans

Grades, peer assessment, conferencing, and rubrics

Week 5:

Due: Video clip as described earlier

Class discussion around video clips

Helping students assess themselves—developing a criteria, looking at evidence, claims and goal setting

Week 6:

Developing more formal classroom assessment, introduction to standardized tests—norm referenced, criterion-referenced, and performance-based

Assessments as genre

Week 7:

State mandated tests; high-stakes assessment and developing legally defensible assessments

School level assessment reform

Week 8:

Case studies of students with special needs

Week 9:

Reports, records, analyses, teacher—student—parent conferences

Week 10:

Due: Classroom Assessment Systems. Class discussion around assessment systems. Be prepared to give a brief overview of a few highlights on your "journey" to this particular assessment system. What were major turning points or deciding factors? What are its strengths? How do you anticipate your system will accommodate further growth and change?

On the Accompanying Web site

Readers are encouraged to visit the website accompanying this book to view materials such as a glossary of literacy terms, an extensive list of related readings, sample assignments, and notes used on the course Web site.

VII

LANGUAGE AND LITERACY
IN A DIVERSE SOCIETY

27

Reading:
Community Literacy

Jim Hoffman
Rachel Salas
Beth Patterson
The University of Texas at Austin

BACKGROUND

The community literacy course is a new one for our elementary teacher education program at The University of Texas at Austin (UT). We have never seen a course like this described in other programs, nor have we ever seen a textbook designed for such a course. In making these statements, we are being honest about our ignorance, not making claims for something new and revolutionary. We are certain that courses like this exist elsewhere. As we continue to work in this area, we hope to make contact with those who work in these programs in the hope of future collaboration.

The community literacy class emerged as a part of the development of a new undergraduate reading specialization program at UT. This specialization is optional for our students and requires an additional field-experience semester (i.e., a total of three semesters, rather than just two), and additional reading courses. The additional hours in reading include: a literacy acquisition course that deals with basic psychological, social, and cultural dimensions of reading and writing; a development and assessment course that focuses on tools for examining reading acquisition; and the community literacy course. During the specialization semester, the students are enrolled in all three courses. They spend 2 days a week tutoring a child in an elementary school that serves a low-income, Hispanic community in Austin. This tutoring experience is coordinated with the lectures, demonstrations, readings, and conversations in the literacy acquisition and development and assessment courses.

As part of the community literacy course, the students are required to serve as a volunteer instructor in one of the many adult literacy and family literacy programs that are offered in the east Austin community. We have made contacts with the various programs who need tutors, but it is up to the individual students to make the actual arrangements for training and scheduling of involvement. Preservice teachers were involved in tutoring adults from the local community in English as a Second Language (ESL), assisting them in acquiring their high school diplomas through a Graduate Equivalence Degree (GED), learning computer skills, and improving their English reading and conversation skills. All preservice teachers volunteer a minimum of 40 hours of service to the specific adult literacy program they have selected. Additionally, the students must complete a project in which they investigate some aspect of literacy in the east Austin community. These projects can be done individually, in pairs or in small groups. The ideas for projects and methods of conducting the research are selected and designed by the students. Past projects have involved researching GED programs in the prison system, looking at student motivation in an ESL program, investigating book clubs in an innercity setting, and a variety of other interesting topics. Students discuss and share their projects with the class near the end of the semester.

As we thought about and discussed the possibilities for such a course, and how it might fit into the ongoing teacher education program at UT, we were most interested in having these prospective teachers begin to see literacy and learning to read from a different perspective than inside the walls of a classroom or a school. We wanted them to see literacy as it is meaningful in the community—in particular, a community where poverty, language, and cultural diversity are an integral part of the setting. We wanted to provide them with a different view, perspective, and experience other than the stereotypes and myths of parents (who don't care), neighborhoods (where literacy is not used), and institutions (that are just wasting taxpayers' money). We wanted them to see schools that serve communities of poverty from the outside in rather than the inside out—or not at all. We want to insure that when they move ahead in their careers as teachers, they will see communities and families as resources rather than as obstacles, and that they would view cultural and language as assets rather than deficits.

To the degree there are theoretical roots for this course, they derive from the philosophy and writing of Paulo Freire (1991). We believe that prospective teachers will benefit from working with the adults and children in their community to read their world with them. Prospective teachers need to understand how texts operate within these communities—as barriers and as doors to new opportunities. Shirley Brice Heath's work has also influenced our thinking. We hope our students can become good ethnographers and anthropologists—learning to observe carefully and infer critically regarding communication within communities. Luis Moll, and the entire funds of knowledge construct has also been influential on our thinking and planning for this course. We must learn to look for how the cultural capital that exists within all communities can be accessed and used in supportive ways. We consider the work of Kathryn Au as important in our thinking about the possible ways in which culture and learning might help us better understand effective instructional practices. And finally, we find that the work and writing of Lisa Delpit (1986) challenges us to think carefully about cultural assumptions imbedded in innovative practices.

We have worked through two cohorts of students with this course, with a third group getting ready to start. It is hard not to talk about the excitement that comes with participation in this course. We read and talk, and sometimes even argue a lot during this course. We connect with our personal roots and our current experiences working in the community. There is a great deal of passion and insight. The personal commitments and investment for most students goes far beyond anything demanded on the course syllabus. The students become articulate about literacy and the personal meanings of literacy in a community of economic poverty. The research projects are of graduate level quality in their focus, content, and expression. Perhaps the comment we hear most often from students in this course is: Why aren't all students who plan to teach enrolled in a program like this? Why isn't everyone required to read these articles and talk about them?

We are learning as we go with this course and practicum experience. We cull our required readings list based on student responses and add new ones all of the time. We are expanding our network of volunteer organizations in the community. The opportunities range from work in preschool, family literacy programs to working directly in the prison system. We have yet to followup in any systematic way with our graduates to evaluate the impact of this experience on their long-term development. We intend to do so. The one point of impact that we can document is the number of students who request to be placed in a low-income school for the two semesters of their professional development year (i.e., observation and student teaching). Over half of the students now request such a placement, whereas in the past, without the community literacy experience, it would have been only a handful. We believe that our students, who are mostly from White, middle-class backgrounds, are coming to embrace the challenge of learning to teach in a world that is vastly different from their own school experience. Our short-term goal is to help them be successful in this learning environment at the preservice level. Our long-term goal is to motivate these students to seek out and teach effectively in schools that serve economically disadvantaged and culturally diverse communities.

REFERENCES

Au, K. H. (1998). Social constructivism and the school literacy learning of students of diverse backgrounds. *Journal of Literacy Research, 30*(2), 297–319.

Au, K. H. (1993). *Literacy instruction in multicultural settings.* New York: Harcourt Brace.

Bruner, J. S. (1994). Life as narrative. In A. H. Dyson & C. Genishi (Eds.), *The need for story* (pp. 28–37). Urbana, IL: National Council of Teachers of English.

Ceprano, M. A. (1995). Strategies and practices of individuals who tutor adult illiterates voluntarily. *Journal of Adolescent and Adult Literacy, 39,* 56–64.

Crawford, R. (1996). Examining the literacy perceptions of non-reading parents. *Journal of the Texas State Reading Association, 3,* 5–26.

Delpit, L. (1986). Skills and other dilemmas of a progressive black educator. *Harvard Educational Review, 56,* 379–385.

Dyson, A. H., & Genishi, C. (1994). *The need for story: Cultural diversity in classroom and community.* Urbana, IL: National Council of Teachers of English.

Edwards, P. (1989). Supporting lower SES mothers' attempts to provide scaffolding for book reading. In J. B. Allen & J. M. Mason (Eds.), *Risk makers, risk takers, risk breakers: Reducing the risk for young literacy learners* (pp. 222–250). Portsmouth, NH: Heinemann.

Elish-Piper, L. (1996). Literacy and their lives: Four low-income families enrolled in a summer family literacy program. *Journal of Adolescent and Adult Literacy, 40,* 256–268.

Fallon, D. (1995). Making dialogue dialectic: A dialogic approach to adult literacy instruction. *Journal of Adolescent and Adult Literacy, 39,* 138–147.

Friere, P. (1991) The importance of the act of reading. In B. M. Power & R. Hubbard (Eds.), *Literacy in process* (pp. 21–26). Portsmouth, NH: Heinemann.

Gonzalez, N. E., Moll, L. C., Tenery, M. F., Rivera, A., Rendon, P., Gonzales, R., & Amanti, C. (1995). Funds of knowledge for teaching in Latino households. *Urban Education, 29*(4), 443–470.

Heath, S. B. (1994). Stories as ways of acting together. In A. H. Dyson & C. Genishi (Eds.), *The need for story* (pp. 206–220). Urbana, IL: National Council of Teachers of English.

Heller, C. E. (1994). Writing as a foundation for transformative community in the tenderloin. In A. H. Dyson & C. Genishi (Eds.), *The need for story* (pp. 221–236). Urbana, IL: National Council of Teachers of English.

Hirsch, E. D., Jr. (1987). *Cultural literacy: What every American needs to know.* Boston: Houghton Mifflin.

Invernizzi, M., Juel, C., & Rosemary, C. A. (1996, 1997). A community volunteer tutorial that works. *The Reading Teacher, 50,* 304–311.

Kozol, J. (1985). *Illiterate America.* Garden City, NY: Anchor Press/Doubleday.

Lazar, A. M., & Weisberg, R. (1996). Inviting parents' perspectives: Building home–school partnerships to support children who struggle with literacy. *The Reading Teacher, 50,* 228–237.

McConnell, B. (1989). Education as a cultural process. In J. B. Allen & J. M. Mason (Eds.), *Risk makers, risk takers, risk breakers: Reducing the risk for young literacy learners* (pp. 201–221). Portsmouth, NH: Heinemann.

Moll, L. C., Amanti, C., Neff, D., & Gonzalez, N. E. (1992). Funds of knowledge for teaching: Using a qualitative approach to connect homes and classrooms. *Theory into Practice, 31*(2), 132–141.

Philliber, W. W., Spillman, R. E., & King, R. E. (1996). Consequences of family literacy for adults and children: Some preliminary findings. *Journal of Adolescent and Adult Literacy, 39,* 558–565.

Purcell-Gates, V. (1996). Stories, coupons, and the TV Guide: Relationships between home literacy experiences and emergent literacy knowledge. *Reading Research Quarterly, 31,* 406–428.

Scribner, S. (1984). Literacy in three metaphors. *American Journal of Education, 93,* 6–21.

Sears, S., Carpenter, C., & Burstein, N. (1994). Meaningful reading instruction for learners with special needs. *The Reading Teacher, 47,* 632–638.

Shannon, P. (1996). Literacy and educational policy. *Journal of Literacy Research, 28,* 429–449.

Smith, M.C. (1996). Differences in adults' reading practices and literacy proficiencies. *Reading Research Quarterly, 31,* 196–219.

Taylor, D., & Strickland, D. (1989). Learning from families. In J. B. Allen & J. M. Mason (Eds.), *Risk makers, risk takers, risk breakers: Reducing the risk for young literacy learners* (pp. 251–277). Portsmouth, NH: Heinemann.

Course Syllabus
Reading: Community Literacy

Course Overview

This course is focused on literacy as it is situated in a particular community. We will explore the challenges and opportunities associated with literacy in this community. The community is low-income and minority. Many of the adults in this community speak English as a second language. We will read in the professional literature and discuss current issues in literacy from a broader societal perspective as well.

Students enrolled in this course will become involved in literacy support within this community. Students will commit at least 4 hours of work (minimum) per week in support services. Students may select from a variety of programs to fulfill this requirement for participation.

The course is designed for students who aspire to teach in the elementary grades. Our major goal is to provide students with a perspective on literacy that reaches beyond the traditional walls of the classroom or the school. By building these connections and understandings, we hope to more effectively assume the role of classroom teacher.

Course Requirements

1. Read course materials (articles, chapters, etc.) as they are assigned.

Accountability: Turn in 3 x 5 cards with summary responses to each of the reading assignments. These responses must be turned in on the day that the readings are to have been completed. These responses will count a total of 42 points toward your final grade. Two articles will be assigned for each class session. You are expected to read and be prepared to discuss both. You are expected to read and respond to one of the two (your choice) and be prepared to take the lead in discussions. Reports on the other articles may be completed for extra credit.

2. Actively contribute to literacy support with a minimum of 4 hours of service work per week.

Accountability: Keep a log of time spent and activity focus. Use this log as a journal for planning and reflection. Reflect on your learning.

Provide a status report on your work once during the semester.

Turn in a schedule to us describing your plans for work during the semester in the field. Keep it updated. We would like to observe and work with you.

You will be assigned a faculty advisor for the semester (one of the course instructors). Arrange for individual meetings with your faculty advisor to discuss your work. Four meetings are required (one in January, February, March, and April). The meeting in January will be a small group meeting that includes all of the students working with that faculty advisor. The remaining meetings may be individual or group. Meetings will last approximately 20 to 30 minutes.

At the end of the semester, you will be required to turn in your log as well as a summary report that is typed and no longer than three pages. The summary should focus on (a) what you feel you were able to accomplish through your efforts, and (b) what you learned this semester that is important to you as a person and as a future teacher. Your journal and report will count a maximum total of 50 points toward your final grade.

3. Explore the literacy in a low-income community.

Accountability: This is a requirement that will tap your creativity. Learn about some aspect of literacy in the community and share (in a creative way) what you have learned. You can work in small groups or alone in completing this assignment. You can work with your faculty advisor's group or in other clusters. By the third week of class, you should submit a brief project proposal describing what you plan to do and who will be working with you on your project. 25 points possible. Points are awarded based on: Content (Is the information/perspective important and new to us?); Effort invested in the gathering of data (How much time and effort did you put into data collection?); and Presentation of findings (How creative and innovative were you in sharing your learning?).

4. Attend and participate actively in course discussions.

Accountability: Attend class. You must attend at least one-half of the 14 class seminars. If you fail to attend seven sessions, you will suffer a loss of all points in this area. Frequent tardies will have the same result. Twenty-five points possible. Don't forget you are still required to complete the readings assignment regardless of your attendance at seminars.

Reading Summary Reports

Reading summary reports should be approximately two-page, word-processed documents.

Front:

ID: Author, Title, Date of your response, and Your Name

Summary: List the three most important ideas you got from this reading. Paraphrase or quote.

Connections: Does this article connect in any ways to: Course lecture content? Your field experience? Other readings in this course? Other readings elsewhere? Your prior knowledge? Describe and explain the connection.

Back: (or the second page of your word processed paper)

Puzzles: What puzzles you about this article? What didn't you understand? What questions does it raise in your mind?

Rating: On a scale of 1–5 (with 1 the most positive and 5 the least),
               how would you rate this article in terms of its
               value to you in learning about assessment?

Comments: (Optional) additional comments you would like to make.

Scoring Rubric for Summary Reports:

3   Three important ideas identified, perhaps even additional ones.
       Responses use both paraphrasing and direct quotes from the author.
       At least two different connections are described.
       At least two important questions are identified that are germane to the topic.

2   Less than three ideas are identified, or some of the ideas are minor.
       Responses are simple restatements of propositions from the text.
       Connections are limited to one source or type. Connections have limited application
       or importance.
       The questions have either obvious answers or are unanswerable.

1   Important ideas are not identified.
       Descriptions of ideas are severely limited and superficial.
       Connections are trivial.
       The questions are unrelated to the content and/or insignificant to the course focus.

0   Assignment not turned in or response not following format guidelines.

Grades

Total number of points possible divided into the points earned.

90–100%	A
80–89%	B
70–79%	C
60–69%	D
Below 60%	F

Class Sessions

A typical class session, once we are in the routine of the semester, will include the
following:

1.   Discussion of assigned reading(s) for the day.

2.   Individual reports of involvement (5 to 10 minutes). You must report at least once during
       the semester. You will sign-up for your time to present. You can give additional status
       reports along the way.

3.   The last three class sessions follow the same schedule for readings. In addition, we will be
       sharing project reports. You will sign-up for a time to present.

Sample Meeting Schedule

1.	Course Orientation and Introductions	Jan. 16th
2.	Field visit to complete orientation: The Austin Learning Academy Even Start Family Literacy Program, Oak Springs Elementary School (a map and directions to the school will be provided).	Jan. 17th 12:30–3:30
3.	Reading Assignment Due: 1 & 2 Assigned Reading 3 & 4	Jan. 23

Turn in your work schedule. Arrange for your first conference with your faculty advisor.

4.	Reading Assignment Due: 3 & 4 Assigned Reading 5 & 6	Jan. 30
5.	Reading Assignment Due: 5 & 6 Assigned Reading 7 & 8	Feb. 6
6.	Reading Assignment Due: 7 & 8 Assigned Reading 9 & 10	Feb. 13

Be sure to arrange for your second conference with your faculty advisor.

7.	Reading Assignment Due: 9 & 10 Assigned Reading 11 & 12	Feb. 20
8.	Reading Assignment Due: 11 & 12 Assigned Reading 13 & 14	Feb. 27
9.	Reading Assignment Due: 13 & 14 Assigned Reading 15 & 16	March 6
10.	Reading Assignment Due: 15 & 16 Assigned Reading 17 & 18	March 20

Don't forget your March meeting with your faculty advisor!

11.	Reading Assignment Due: 17 & 18 Assigned Reading 19 & 20	March 27
12.	Reading Assignment Due: 19 & 20 Assigned Reading 21 & 22	April 3
13.	Reading Assignment Due: 21 & 22 Assigned Reading 23 & 24	April 10
14.	Reading Assignment Due: 23 & 24 Assigned Reading 25&26	April 17

Final meeting with your faculty advisor! You need to schedule it.

15.	Reading Assignment Due: 25 & 26. Assigned Reading 27 & 28	April 24

Project Reports by:

16.	Reading Assignment Due: 27 & 28	May 1

Project Reports by:

28

Language and Learning

James Marshall
University of Iowa

In my first year of graduate school I took a course from Arthur Applebee entitled "Language and Mental Development." It was my introduction to the work of Michael Halliday, Lev Vygotsky, James Britton, Douglas Barnes, and Gordon Wells, and the reading and thinking it encouraged did more to shape the future direction of my work than any other course I took. When I began teaching at The University of Iowa, I was given the opportunity to develop a comparable course, one that would examine some of the literature on language development, language in school, and the relationships between language and culture. The Iowa course was targeted for undergraduate and master's students, instead of doctoral students, but the themes and some of the readings would be similar to those in Applebee's course, and I was glad for the opportunity to introduce a number of theoretically powerful ideas to students preparing to teach.

After a year or so of teaching the course, I had dinner with Arthur, told him about the course, and told him that I had changed the name from "Language and Mental Development" to "Language and Learning," both as a way of honoring James Britton's formative influence (Britton's book, *Language and Learning* (1970) was central to my thinking) and to distinguish my from Applebee's. Arthur smiled and told me he had taken a course called "Language and Learning" from James Britton when he was a first-year student at The University of London. He had changed the name to "Language and Mental Development" as a way of distinguishing his course from Britton's. The course, then, is now in at least its third generation (my own doctoral students tell me they have developed comparable courses as new faculty members)—a sign, I think, of James Britton's continuing presence in our field and of the way the theoretical framework he helped shape has continued to influence our research and our teaching.

Although it maintains a family resemblance to the course I took with Applebee in 1981, the Language and Learning course that I am teaching this semester (and that I have taught every year since 1987) is in several ways substantially different. On the one hand, the course is still targeted to those preparing to teach in public schools, rather than to doctoral students, and so I usually push discussion in the direction of practice and can seldom assume an interest in the logistics of research. On the other hand, the field of literacy education is now even more fully informed by a sociocultural framework than it was 15 years ago (Vygotksy's and Bahktin's influence are now more deeply felt). So, the readings have changed, and the discussions about those readings have moved in new directions.

Yet, discussion remains both the primary teaching strategy in the course and one of its anchoring themes. Because the course is for students preparing to teach (it is required for three separate certification programs), it seems important that the teaching in the course enact its subject. The course, in other words, should not simply be about the value of interpretive dialogue or the power of self-reflection in teaching; it should create an environment where such dialogue and such self-reflection become possible. The discussions are driven, then, by questions with multiple possible answers, each answer to be examined for the theoretical and political assumptions it makes about teachers, learners, and schools. Because the course is about language, we spend a fair amount of time examining the language we use to describe events in school and out. What is the effect, for instance, of describing college-bound students as *higher* ability, and those who are probably not going to college as *lower*? What kinds of language are allowed between the bells in a typical school, and what kinds of language are allowed in the hallways and parking lots outside of class? Why these patterns? What assumptions are implicit in them?

The writing for the course is comparably open-ended, although the assignments themselves are quite specific. The two large projects ask students to tape record at least 20 minutes of oral language, to transcribe it, and to analyze its turn-taking patterns and internal structures. The first of these asks students to study the language of a young child between the ages of 2 and 5 in conversation with an adult, usually a parent. The second asks them to examine some version of "instructional language"—a large or small group discussion, a writing conference, even a lecture—and again, to study its features. When and how do people talk when teaching is taking place? How are these patterns different from those in the first project.

In addition to these moderately large, moderately formal projects, students are asked to complete about seven shorter piece—we call them *one-pagers*—on topics related to the discussions we have been having in any particular week. A step above course journals in terms of formality, but a step below completely finished work, the one-pagers (always typed, always no more than a page) are an opportunity for students to articulate hypotheses, make connections between the reading and their own experience, or struggle with ideas that may be unfamiliar. They are usually due on Fridays (the class meets three times a week) and usually provide the occasion for small group discussions preceding a large group discussion of the issue they have written about. Topics include writing a response to a 5-year-old child who asks how people learn to speak, writing a description of the literacy environment in which they themselves grew up (comparable to the descriptions in Heath's [1983] *Ways with Words*), conducting a close reading of one page in a popular magazine for adolescent girls when we are reading Finders's (1997) *Just Girls*, or writing a dictionary definition for the word *multiculturalism* and then reflecting on why they defined it as they did.

All of these written materials become part of the students' developing course portfolio. I respond to individual pieces as they are turned in, but I do not grade the pieces individually—this, for at least three reasons. First, the course is taken almost exclusively by students in the teacher education program—a program with quite rigorous standards of admission (including a requirement that students have at least a B average in their major, three letters of recommendation, and a reasonably compelling statement of purpose). These are, in other words, strong, committed, and seasoned students, and I should not, in fact will not, play the role of Robocop with them. So, I tell them the first day that because of their already strong record in school, they should assume that they are receiving an A or a B in this class and to stop thinking about it. If in my view they ever slip beneath that level of performance, I will tell them right away. Perhaps not surprisingly, my students do exceptionally strong work without the pressure of a grade—perhaps because the grade is not present as an issue. They take chances, speak their minds, ask questions, and admit uncertainties on particular assignments; and sometimes, in their shorter work, state clearly that they were distracted or not engaged by the question. The A/B guarantee grants a measure of freedom, then, but it is a freedom that they have already purchased with their evident commitments and the quality of their earlier work.

My second reason for not grading individual assignments is that such a practice would leave unexamined and unproblematized one of the central themes of the course—that is, the relationship between oral and written discourse in school. Why, I ask students early on, is writing so thoroughly privileged in our evaluations of students? Why doesn't talk count?. Why, for instance, is it OK for a student to say, "I'm shy, and I don't speak very well, so and I won't be talking in class" but it's not OK for her to say, "I can't really write very well, so I won't be turning in any papers." In Language and Learning, talk counts, and I do not grade individual pieces of writing because I want to leave room for the talk to make a difference in the final grade.

And finally, I do not grade individual pieces of writing because it keeps me from seeing the writing clearly. It keeps me from listening to what students are trying to say and pushes me toward measurements that are finally irrelevant to the enterprise of learning. I want to be in conversation with my students, and I cannot do that if I am consistently interrupting that conversation with an observation about how well they are doing. Only when the conversation is more or less over can I step back and make an assessment of how it proceeded, what it added up to, did it finally make sense. That is when I offer the grade.

But even here, I try to straddle the border between writing and talk. My hand-writing is terrible—no, worse than that—and carrying a laptop so that I can type responses is often more than I can manage. I have begun asking students to turn in an audiotape with their longer projects and again with their portfolio at the end of the course. They hear me think and talk through their work—commenting, making connections, asking questions, as well as offering a final, more general assessment of how things went. I am able to deliver more response per student than I could if I were writing. More importantly, I can deliver a different kind of response—one that is, quite literally, in my own voice, that registers surprise and pleasure and confusion, and that can explain the evaluation more thoroughly than my writing could. The logistics are sometimes awkward. We all have to be careful not to lose the tapes, and students need to be certain that they are cued properly when they are turned in. But the rewards are fairly substantial, and the lessons about discourse and its powers that the class addresses are reinscribed and reinforced by the process.

The reading for the course moves generally through three somewhat overlapping phases: the transition from home to school (Heath, 1983; Purcell-Gates, 1995), the conventions of language in school (Barnes, 1992; Finders, 1997; Paley, 1979), and the transition from school into the world (Rodriguez, 1982; Rose, 1989). We do not so much discuss the readings as use them as background for the issues they raise: how does the culture children bring with them to school affect what they are likely to learn? how does adolescent popular culture help shape students' expectations of schooling? what are the relationships between the conventions of school language and the kinds of learning that can take place there? Readings are always present to frame the discussions, but the discussions are issue-driven and may move beyond the boundaries of particular texts. As a way of establishing the exploratory agenda for the course, we actually begin with essays by E. D. Hirsch (1987) and William Bennett (1987) in order to establish alternative "voices" that can be called upon when consensus seems too easy. Because most of the readings for the course assume a constructivist, liberal, progressive position, Hirsch and Bennett (and later, Delpit, 1995) help establish oppositional arguments that can be used when students seem sure that they have found an answer. (What would Hirsch say about your position? How would you answer him? Would he be convinced?) The idea is always to keep the conversation going, to undermine easy certainties, to push students in the direction of doubt and self-examination. The course, when it works, is a place where students can practice thinking like teachers—not practice, as James Britton once put it, in the sense of getting ready to do something. It is practice in the sense of practicing a craft—the way doctors practice medicine or attorneys practice law. These students will do practice teaching soon after they have completed my course. Teaching, as Dewey argued long ago, is not just doing—it is thinking about doing. And the course Language and Learning is one attempt to get that thinking started.

REFERENCES

Barnes, D. (1992). *From communication to curriculum.* Portsmouth, NH: Heinemann.

Bennett. W. (1987). *Moral literacy.* An address to the 29th annual convention of the California Association of Teachers of English, San Diego, CA.

Britton, J. (1970). *Language and learning.* New York: Penguin.

Delpit, L. (1995). *Other people's children.* New York: The New Press.

Finders, M. (1997). *Just girls: Hidden literacies and life in junior high.* New York: Teachers College Press.

Heath, S. B. (1983). *Ways with words.* New York: Cambridge University Press.

Hirsch, E. D. (1987). *Cultural literacy.* Boston: Houghton Mifflin.

Paley, V. (1979). *White teacher.* Cambridge, MA: Harvard University Press.

Purcell-Gates, V. (1995). *Other people's words.* Cambridge, MA: Harvard University Press.

Rodriquez, R. (1982). *Hunger of memory.* New York: Bantam.

Rose, M. (1989). *Lives on the boundary.* New York: Penguin.

Sample Syllabus
Language and Learning

Language is the primary means by which we represent the world to ourselves and ourselves to the world. This course will explore the social and cultural nature of language development and its relationship to learning, both in school and out.

Required Texts

Barnes. D. (1992). *From communication to curriculum.* Portsmouth, NH: Heinemann.

Bennett, W. (1987). *Moral literacy.* An address to the 29th annual convention of the California Association of Teachers of English, San Diego, CA.

Delpit, L. (1995). *Other people's children.* New York: The New Press.

Finders, M. (1997). *Just girls: Hidden literacies and life in junior high.* New York: Teachers College Press.

Heath, S. B. (1983). *Ways with words.* New York: Cambridge University Press

Hirsch, E. D. (1987). *Cultural literacy.* Boston: Houghton Mifflin.

Paley, V. (1979). *White teacher.* Cambridge, MA: Harvard University Press.

Purcell-Gates, V. (1995). *Other people's words.* Cambridge, MA: Harvard University Press.

Rodriguez, R. (1982). *Hunger of memory.* New York: Bantam.

Rose, M. (1989). *Lives on the boundary.* New York: Penguin.

Course Requirements

1. Attendance and active participation. This is a discussion course and your contributions to our ongoing conversations will be a very important part of the class.

2. One-page, almost-weekly responses to the issues and texts we will be exploring. These should be typed and either double-spaced or single-spaced, depending on how much you have to say. These will be due most Fridays, and will usually be the

basis for small group discussions. There will be seven to eight of these one-pagers, and you will be turning in all of them in as part of your course portfolio.

3. Two research assignments: The first will ask you to record and study the language of a young child between the ages of 2 and 6; the second will ask you to record and examine some language in a classroom setting.

4. A take-home final that will ask you to address all of the major readings.

5. A panel presentation that will review a selected book for the whole class. On the day of your presentation, your group will provide a one- or two-page handout giving a brief overview of the book's content and your sense of its value.

Grading Policy

I will not be grading individual pieces of writing as you complete them. I will read and respond to your work and then return it to you. At the end of the semester, I will ask you to submit a portfolio of all of your written work for the course—including your one-pagers, your research reports, your final exam, and a self-assessment that reflects on your work for the course. I will assign your grade after a review of all of your written work and a consideration of your contributions to our discussions.

Assignments for Language and Learning

Assignment 1: Observing a Young Language Learner

For this assignment, I would like you to report on at least one observation of a child between the ages of 2 to 5 (about 20 minutes in length) in conversation with an adult. You will be focusing primarily on the child's use of language, but you will also be observing how language is situated in social context. Identify a context you are especially interested in observing—home, school, day-care center, preschool, etc. You will need to audiotape the session, so *be sure to get parental permission.*

In your notes, provide information about the date, time, setting, participants, nature of materials, and compile a running record of the child's behavior. Keep in mind that the child's words will be recorded on tape; the main function of your notes is to allow you to situate those words in the context of gesture, expression, and action. Remember that your main goal in your notes is simply to be observant, but do write down enough so that you can make rich sense of your audiotape.

After you have recorded the child, transcribe the whole tape, laying out the speaker turns on the page as you might the script for a play. If you cannot make out exactly what is being said, use x's to show the elision. If the child or adult speaks in a language other than English, please provide a translation.

In your paper, I would like you to turn in your transcription and to report your reflections on the child's behavior.

What to turn in
1. Your complete transcript in readable form.
2. A brief research write-up that should include:
    a) A designation for your child, e.g., initials, pseudonym.
    b) Child's age (years; months) the day of the recording.
    c) Child's exposure to languages other than English.
    d) Whether the child is an only child or has siblings; whether he or she is at home all day, in playgroup, day care center, and so forth.
    e) The time of day you recorded—and a brief comment on how alert or active and cooperative the was
    f) A brief description of the setting in which you recorded and the kinds of activities the child was involved in during your visit (i.e., a summary of your contextual notes).
    g) An analysis of what was special or interesting about the child's use of language.

Think about how long her turns were when she held the floor, what she spoke about, what special words or verbal constructions she used, whether she ever took control of the topic of conversation, what encouraged her to talk more and what caused her to talk less.

Things you might do, ask, or think about in your analysis:

- Compare the length of turns of the child and adult
- Notice who controls the topic of conversation and how the topic changes
- Note the structural similarities and differences between the child and the adult sentences
- Notice the use of egocentric speech (talking to oneself) on the part of the child
- Notice how the adult language changes because of something child says or does.

On the due date, I would like you to share your observations with a small group of classmates. Bring in a one- or two-page summary of your reflections, and perhaps a sample from the transcript, and be ready to talk about them. The paper you turn in will probably be three to five pages long, not counting the transcript. Be sure to see me if you have any questions.

Assignment 2: Observing Language in the Classroom

For this next assignment, I would like you to begin to think a bit more about linguistic interactions in classroom settings. Here are several data-collection options:

1. Audiotape yourself in two different situations: in an instructional interaction in a classroom, and in an informal interaction with family or friends.

2. Audiotape a small-group instructional interaction in any classroom but this one.
3. Audiotape a portion of a whole-class discussion (but not in this class).
4. Audiotape a brief writing conference (or a portion of a longer one) involving a student writer and a writing teacher or tutor.

You have many other options as well—what we are basically looking for are interesting, provocative bits of classroom language. See me if you'd like to talk through some alternate possibilities.

In preparation for writing your paper, transcribe around 20 minutes' worth of audiotaped talk. Again, I would like you to reflect on these interactions in light of our recent readings. In writing your paper, consider at least some of the following questions:

* What sorts of patterns seem to be recurring here?
* Who initiates most often, and towards what purpose?
* What sorts of questions are asked?
* Who does most of the talking?
* To what extent is this interaction collaborative?
* What seems problematic or successful, and why?
* What does all this suggest about how you will run your own classroom?

One-Pagers

1. Write a response to a 5-year-old child who asks, "How do people learn to talk?"
2. Pick one item for Hirsch's list of about 6,000 and say why it should not be on the list. Pick one item not on the list and say why it should be.
3. Describe the literacy environment of the home in which you grew up.
4. Do a close reading of one page in a magazine intended for adolescent girls (e.g., *YM*, *Sassy*, *Teen*, *Sugar*).
5. Write a description of the ways you used reading and writing outside of school settings when you were an adolescent.
6. Define multiculturalism.
7. How could the teacher education program at Iowa do a better job of preparing students to teach in diverse settings?

29

Creating a Common Project in the Study of Diversity

Michael W. Smith
Rutgers University

I designed "Language in Education I: Stories of Language Learners and Teachers" to encourage preservice and in-service teachers to grapple with questions of diversity and what diversity might mean for how they teach and for how their students learn. More specifically, in the course students read stories of language learners and teachers and write and share their literacy autobiographies. This reading, writing, and sharing is designed to provide data they can use to answer what I think is a fundamental question for teachers to ask: Are there themes that cut across stories or do attempts to generalize across stories (or some meaningful subset of stories) always hurt those who are generalized about by minimizing the unique experience of an individual? I want students to scrutinize both the assumptions of literacy learning and teaching with which they enter the course and the categories of students that they tend to think with.

For example, students might ask, on the one hand, whether it is fair to base their notion of what makes reading and/or writing meaningful for their students on what has made reading and/or writing meaningful for them.

On the other hand, they might ask the extent to which their students' race, class, gender, age, track, ethnicity, language background, and religion, (the list goes on) affects what the students value and how they learn. In their final paper for the course, some students offer generalizations they have come to during the course (e.g., "Writing becomes meaningful to writers to the extent that it strengthens their affiliation to or status in social groups that matter to them"). Others write how they have come to question generalizations that they had made or that are prevalent in education either about all students (e.g., " I had always thought that the emphasis on reading and writing in students' homes was an absolutely crucial factor in their success, but a close look at the stories that we read illustrates just how harmful that assumption can be") or about an identifiable group of students (e.g., "In my teaching, I have always behaved as though gender matters. I think now that I may have been making a questionable generalization that could be hurtful to the boys in my classes").

Because I detail the thinking that went into developing the content of the course in the syllabus itself, in this brief introduction I'd like to highlight two pedagogical principles that inform the activities of the course. The first is my vision of what counts as democratic education, a vision very much influenced by John Dewey. Dewey (1916/1944) believed that "A democracy is more than a form of government; it is primarily a mode of associated living, of conjoint communicated experience" (p. 87). This belief seems to me to place significant demands on teacher educators, for if we treat it seriously we cannot simply say that our courses are designed to prepare students to teach democratically once they are out of our courses. Rather, it means that we must enact democracy in those courses by engaging students in meaningful associated living. As Dewey explains, "It is not of course a question of whether education should prepare for the future. If education is growth, it must progressively realize present possibilities, and thus make individuals better fitted to cope with later requirements" (p. 56). In this course I try to enact democracy by creating a context where students work together on a common project in which differences are resources. If my students were all of the same race, class, gender, generation, ethnic group, and so on, it would be much harder for them to think about the extent to which generalizations across or within groups are justified. What I try to do is create assignments in which my students not only recognize the differences among them but also have to use those differences to do their work. When differences become resources, I believe they are valued. (See Rabinowitz & Smith, 1998, for a more complete discussion of this point.)

The second pedagogical principle relates to the nature of the authority that readers and writers draw on when they do their work. Goldblatt (1995) has persuaded me that authority is vested in institutions and for students to be authorized their reading and writing must be sanctioned by an institution that matters in schools. The institution whose authority students are asked to draw on, it seems to me, is the authority of the discipline. However, for many students, Language in Education I: Stories of Language of Learners and Teachers is the first course they take in their graduate studies. As a consequence, they do not feel authorized by the discipline of education. What I try to do, therefore, is create a context in which the class itself can authorize students. I do this by engaging them in ever widening circles of association. Students begin each class in their dialogue journal groups. The work that they do in those groups seems to me to give them the expectation that what they write and say has value and will be attended to. They carry that authority into their book clubs where, I hope, they are vested with still more authority. By the time they write their papers, they write as a valued member of the class and they can draw on that authority when they do their work.

The discussions, the papers students have written, and their evaluations all suggest that my students have enjoyed and profited from the course. However, I am aware that the design of the course clashes at least in part with the expectations of some students. The narratives we read resist an easy extrapolation into practice and some students find that frustrating, especially those students who are beginning graduate study in order to enhance their teaching. The paper assignment is more open-ended than some students are used to, and this sometimes also causes frustration as students seek to identify what I am hoping they will write and I will not tell them. The clash of expectations could lead to students' dismissing the course or to their feeling excluded by the students who do not seem to share their frustrations. I try to address this potential concern from the first meeting of the class by articulating it and by explaining why I think that the central question of the course and the habits of mind the course seeks to develop through examining that question are crucial for effective practice. Yet, I am also aware that those frustrations are grounded in wanting to be a good student and teacher (goals I, of course, admire) as well as in years of experience in schools (which might include previous classes with me in which I played a more central role.)

Sample Syllabus
Language in Education I:
Stories of Language Learners and Teachers

Course Description

In this course you will be reading the stories of language learners and teachers and you will be writing your own story in order to ask what I think is a crucial question: Are there themes that cut across stories or do attempts to generalize across stories (or some meaningful subset of stories) always hurt those who are generalized about by minimizing the unique experience of an individual?

Why stories? In his book *Eating on the Street* (1993), David Schaafsma argues that stories are central to the enterprise of teaching. In the first place, narratives are, in Barbara Hardy's words "a primary act of mind" (quoted in Schaafsma, 1993, p. 33). Moreover, according to Schaafsma, teachers use stories to construct themselves, their students, and the curriculum they teach. One reason that Schaafsma celebrates stories is what he sees as their potential for representing contrary voices and multiple perspectives. Others (cf. Flood, et al., 1994) see stories not as a way to represent differences but rather as a way to help teachers see similarities among different cultures.

Why consider our own stories? Research in teacher cognition and teacher education (cf. Kagan, 1992) suggests that the primary story that teachers think with is their own. That's only natural, but it does raise some important concerns. In the first place, in the words of Susan Florio-Ruane and Julie deTar (1994), "Our teaching force is culturally isolated" (p. 13) from the students it serves. In addition, they note that teachers and prospective teachers may not have fully articulated their experience as learners and the impact that their cultural background has had on those experiences, so they cannot critically examine the relevance of that experience to their teaching. Why read the stories of others? Reading stories allows a kind of living through the experience of others that non-narrative texts do not (cf. Rabinowitz & Smith, 1998). Living through the experience of others should help us clarify the stakes of the game. That is, it should help us consider both the potential benefits and the potential costs of the kinds of stories we choose to tell.

Readings

Anzaldua, G. (1987). *Borderlands/La frontera: The new Mestiza.* San Francisco: Aunt Lute books.
Brandt, D. (1992). Selected interviews. Unpublished raw data.
Gilbert, L. (Director). (1983). *Educating Rita.* [Film.] New York: RCA/Columbia.
Heath, S. (1983). *Ways with words: Language, life and work in communities and classrooms.* Cambridge: Cambridge University Press.
Paley, V. (1979/1989). *White teacher.* Cambridge, MA: Harvard University Press.
Rodriguez, R. (1982). *Hunger of memory: The education of Richard Rodriguez.* New York: Bantam.
Rose, M. (1989). *Lives on the boundary.* New York: Free Press.

Course Requirements

1. I expect that everyone will come to class prepared to contribute. Involvement in class will count for 20% of your grade. Your grade may be lowered if you miss more than one class. I may fail you if you miss three or more classes.

2. Each week you must write a commentary on the reading that you've done. The commentary can include any of your reactions to the reading. I expect that the commentaries will be approximately one to two double-spaced pages long. At the beginning of every class, you will be exchanging your commentaries with a partner who will be writing a response to what you have written as you write a response to what your partner has written. I will be collecting the journals from time to time and responding to them. I will grade the journals on the basis of their thoughtfulness and the effort that went into them. The journals will be worth 20% of your grade.

3. Write a brief (five pages or so) literacy autobiography in which you tell the story of how you learned to speak, read, and/or write they way you do. You can develop a single incident or several of them. You can focus on what happened in school,

out of school, or both. Your literacy autobiography will be due on Session 6. The literacy autobiography will be worth 10% of your grade.

4. Do an in-depth interview with someone who is different from you in some important way in that person's literacy history. You will be presenting your interview to a group of colleagues on Session 9. You should have prepared an executive summary of the entire interview and a transcription of at least 15 consecutive minutes of it. On the basis of your group's interviews and the reading we have done in class, write a paper (I am thinking of 12-15 pages or so) in which you discuss whether there are themes that cut across stories. You should include your interview with your paper. The papers will be due on December 4. We'll be talking much more about them as the semester progresses. This paper will be worth 50% of your grade.

5. Select a reading for one of your book group meetings.

Schedule

Session 1	An introduction to the course and to each other. Writing our metaphors for literacy teaching. Kids writing their lives: Stories from inner-city Detroit.
Assignment:	Read Heath, pp. 1–189.
Session 2	Language and communities, a discussion of Roadville and Tracton.
Assignment:	Read Heath, pp. 190–369.
Session 3	Language and communities: Instructional implications.
Assignment:	Read Paley.
Session 4	Confronting race and its implications in one elementary classroom.
Assignment:	Read Rose.
Session 5	Literacy education for those on the boundary.
Assignment:	Write literacy autobiography.
Session 6	Sharing autobiographies.
Assignment:	Read selected interviews.
Session 7	Discuss interviews Talking about technique.
Assignment:	Read book group stories.
Session 8	Book Group I.
Assignment:	Do interview and prepare transcript.
Session 9	Sharing interviews. Thinking about aspects of literacy learning that are shared and those that are unique.
Assignment:	Read Rodriguez.

Session 10	Considering the cost of learning a new language.
Assignment:	Read Anzaldua (both the prose and the poetry).
Session 11	Thinking about life on the borderlands.
Assignment:	Read book group stories.
Session 12	Book Group II
Assignment:	Work on papers.
Session 13	Watch *Educating Rita*. What does it mean to sing a better song?
Papers due.	
Assignment:	Journal entry on pedagogical implications of the readings and discussions.
Session 14	Reflections on teaching.
Evaluating the course.	

REFERENCES

Dewey, J. (1916/1944). *Democracy and education*. New York: Free Press.

Florio-Ruane, S., & deTar, J. (1995). Conflict and consensus in teacher candidates' discussion of ethnic autobiography. *English Education, 27*, 11–39.

Flood, J., Lapp, D., Alvarez, D., Romero, A., Ranck-Buhr, W., Moore, J., Jones, M. A., Kabildis, C., & Lundgren, L. (1994). *Teacher book clubs: A study of teachers' and student teachers' participation in contemporary multicultural fiction literature discussion groups*. (Reading Research Report No. 22). National Reading Research Center.

Goldblatt, E. (1995). *Round my way: Authority and double-consciousness in three urban high school writers*. Pittsburgh: University of Pittsburgh Press.

Kagan, D. (1992). Professional growth among preservice and beginning teachers. *Review of Educational Research, 62*, 129–170.

Rabinowitz, P. J., & Smith, M. W. (1998). *Authorizing readers: Resistance and respect in the teaching of literature*. New York: Teachers College Press.

Schaafsma, D. (1993). *Eating on the street: Teaching literacy in a multicultural society*. Pittsburgh: University of Pittsburgh Press.

30

Methods and Materials
for the Bilingual–English
as a Second Language Teacher

Ruth A. Hough
Georgia State University

The impact of English learners on language and literacy in metropolitan schools came clearly to me in an unforgettable moment in the early 1980s during a field observation of a preservice teacher in the reading/language arts methods block. As she was teaching at the "front" of a classroom in an open space school, the principal brought to the teacher stationed at the side of the space a new student with the words "I don't think she speaks any English." There were moments of silence with all the players in this unfolding classroom mini-drama frozen in a tableau of uncertainty with wavering smiles and wide eyes. The possibilities and challenges of that moment colored my teaching for mainstream classroom teachers the rest of that quarter, and when I had an opportunity to team teach the Methods and Materials for the Bilingual/English as a Second Language Teacher course with my colleague, Scott Enright, I knew I had found another "academic hat" I wanted to wear. Scott's love of oral language, both personally and as a focus of his academic scholarship, was legendary.

Although that made it difficult to get a word in edgewise while team teaching with him, the imprint of his curiosity and sensitivity to the effects of context remain in the oral language portions of the course I share in this book, particularly in the assignment now called an oral scaffold. When students in the course take on the senior partner role in a dialogue with their English-learning junior partner, they recognize the importance of factors he identified: relevance of topic and the collaboration of senior and junior partner roles that can lead to authentic construction and expression of meaning. Scott's voice is also evident in the focus on collaboration, purposeful learning built on prior knowledge, variety, and scaffolding in integrated thematic units as a context for integrated content and language instruction (Enright & McCloskey, 1988). In terms of other influences on my design and teaching of this course, teachers and English learners in all kinds of school settings and environments as well as the work of researchers in content-based language instruction (Chamot & O'Malley, 1986; Hudelson, 1989; Samway, Whang, & Pippitt, 1995) have guided the integration of language, literacy, and content.

This graduate level methods course is one of a three-course set that qualifies teachers for the Georgia K–12 English to Speakers of Other Languages (ESOL) endorsement that can be added to existing teaching certification at any grade or degree level. The ESOL label (rather than ESL or bilingual) reflects the demographic and political reality of language learning in this state. Given the diversity of experiences of immigrant and refugee students in state-funded ESOL programs, English may be the most recent of several languages added to the native language. Politically, there is a reluctance to label English as a second language to avoid any implication that English is anything other than the primary mode of communication. In many ways, the methods course serves as the practical culmination and application of applied linguistics, second language acquisition, cultural issues, and assessment concepts considered in the other two endorsement courses. However, since enrolling in this course last is recommended but not required, some students take it before the other foundation courses.

MAJOR IDEAS AND APPROACHES

Because this is the one methods course students take for the K–12 ESOL endorsement, it addresses general instructional issues important to all ESOL students, with particular attention to the possibilities for language and literacy development within the multilingual and multicultural contexts of many Georgia schools. Issues related to instructional environments, organization, and strategies must cover the entire span of public school grades or be adaptable to various age, grade, or proficiency levels. Given the local patterns of immigration and refugee resettlement, teachers can anticipate working with students of similar ages with widely divergent levels of language proficiency and academic experience, including adolescents with interrupted or low schooling due to economic or political stresses. Linguistic diversity among their students is an expectation for these teachers; some schools in the metro Atlanta area report students from 50 different home languages. The largest proportion of students qualifying for ESOL services are native Spanish speakers; however, this group has only recently become a majority, and the students come from many different regions and countries, adding to the native language variation.

As a result of the multilingual (rather than bilingual) character of the student population and the political climate in the state, the focus of the course is primarily on English-as-a-Second- Language strategies rather than bilingual education. The tensions between general-specific, breadth-depth, and theoretical-practical are addressed through course structure, assignments, and activities intended to acknowledge and celebrate diversity in many forms rather than regard it as problematic. For example, there are opportunities to survey different models and approaches to providing services to language minority students, as well as focus on specific strategies that fit particular combinations of school system structures, grade level, language and content proficiency, and learner characteristics.

Consideration of diversity issues begins with the many different types of literacy professionals who enroll in this course for a variety of purposes, leading to both positive possibilities and challenges in its planning and execution. A section of the course may include students with a variety of "day jobs" that span a wide range of public and private school settings: reading specialists, elementary teachers in schools with increasing linguistic and cultural diversity in student population, middle and high school teachers with English learners in their content-area classes, media specialists, speech therapists, teachers for hospitalized students, and "retired" teachers who instruct part-time in churches and other community agencies. There are also likely to be some "career-switchers," who are currently working in or recently have left a noneducational field such as business or the military, and are now pursuing a teaching career as a full- or part-time graduate student. Some intend to switch teaching fields or student groups, often because they feel that ESOL students are highly motivated and would be satisfying to teach.

The range of intended uses for the credit and content of the course also varies, including qualification for the ESOL endorsement that could lead to assignment as an ESOL teacher full- or part-time in a single school or on an itinerant basis, enhanced teaching skills in mainstream classes with multicultural student groups that include a number of English learners, teaching assignments overseas, tutoring, or teaching in after-school or community service programs for children or adults. Although all the students qualify to take the course for graduate credit, their educational and teaching backgrounds also span a wide range. They may represent different certification levels (initial or advanced), graduate programs (MA, MEd, EdS, PhD), major teaching fields (Early Childhood, Middle Grades, Secondary, Language and Literacy, Applied Linguistics), number of years and grade levels (K–12) of teaching experience, and places taught (international, United States, Georgia, urban–suburban–rural settings).

ISSUES AND TENSIONS

A dominant issue in developing this course has been the conflict between general/specific and theoretical/practical topic selection to match the needs and interests of a broad range of university students intending to work with an equally broad spectrum of students. Although the focus of the course is on public school levels, there are many differences across grade levels in content, developmental patterns, interests, materials, school/society expectations, and types of school organization at the elementary, middle school, and high school levels. Teaching situations also vary by the native languages of students, and school system configurations for serving ESOL students that include neighborhood schools, cluster schools, itinerant teachers, and newcomer centers. The politics as well as the practice of literacy education with language minority students can also be a strident issue, especially in schools or school systems undergoing rapid demographic changes. In this course, broad issues are addressed explicitly very early in the term as an introduction to more specific classroom-based instruction, and then again at the end as tying together of programmatic concerns. These "big ideas" are likely to include topics such as language philosophy, theoretical approaches, politics of inclusion, language and literacy as empowerment, language/cultural identity, and implications of grouping and testing for equity, high school graduation, and special services placement. The options for the first assignment are intended to help students develop awareness of the global perspectives of the field that influence ongoing instructional beliefs and practices at the classroom level.

The "what do I do tomorrow to help these students succeed" pragmatic concerns are the focus of the middle part of the course. Teaching strategies that are adaptable across grades and language proficiency levels are a priority; students are expected to pilot the types of language scaffolding that might be used with classroom groups with an individual English learner. Throughout the course there are opportunities for students to work in grade level groups to apply demonstrated strategies to materials appropriate to their students' probable language and literacy proficiencies and schooling backgrounds. Integration of content and developmental emphases culminates in the major group project for the course, a thematic unit designed to facilitate content-based language and literacy development for a focus group of English learners.

REFERENCES

Chamot, A. U., & O'Malley, J. M. (1992). *The CALLA handbook: Implementing the cognitive academic language learning approach.* Reading, MA: Addison-Wesley.

Enright, D. S., & McCloskey, M. L. (1988). *Integrating English: Developing English language and literacy in the multilingual classroom.* Reading, MA: Addison-Wesley.

Faltis, C. (1997). *Joinfostering: Adapting teaching for the multilingual classroom.* Englewood Cliffs, NJ: Prentice-Hall.

Hudelson, S. (1989). *Write on: Children writing in ESL.* Englewood Cliffs, NJ: Prentice-Hall.

Samway, K. D., Whang, G., & Pippitt, M. (1995). *Buddy reading: Cross-age tutoring in a multicultural school.* Portsmouth, NH: Heinemann.

Sample Syllabus
Methods and Materials for the Bilingual–English as a Second Language Teacher

Catalog Course Description

This course familiarizes students with current second language classroom research and methods and materials, emphasizing adaptations of methods and materials to a specific classroom setting.

Required Textbooks

Genesee, F. (Ed.). (1994). *Educating second language children: The whole child, the whole curriculum, the whole community.* Cambridge, England: Cambridge University Press.

Peregoy, S. F., & Boyle, O. F. (1997). *Reading, writing and learning in ESL: A resource book for K–12 teachers* (2nd ed.). New York: Longman.

Course Objectives

Students in this course will be expected to:

1. Apply recent child–adult second language acquisition theory to curriculum development and instructional strategies;
2. Design curriculum and learning activities that provide English learners with quality instruction that combines content and the language processes of listening, speaking, reading, and writing;
3. Become familiar with and apply various techniques for organizing and implementing learning environments to optimize participation and instruction for English learners;
4. Develop strategies for integrating school, neighborhood, and home resources in curriculum for English learners.

Course Topics

Programs for English Language Learners: Linking Schools, Homes, & Communities

Physical & Social Environments: Planning for Participation

Developing Oral Language Scaffolds & Activities

Emergent Literacy: Making Meaning with Print

Process Writing with English Learners: Communicating with Print

Classroom-Based Assessment: Cycling with Instruction

Literacy: Comprehending and Responding to Print

Literacy: Understanding Content Area Instruction

Organizing for Inclusion: Meeting Special Needs

Putting It All Together

Course Assignments

Program/Issues Analysis Options

A. Current Issues.   Read at least three recent articles from professional journals that contain substantive information or opinion related to a current issue or controversy that impacts the education of English learners. Two of the references may be selected from substantive resources (or a combination of brief ones) from the Internet or from professional development activities attended during the semester with the prior approval of the professor. Write a four- to five-page (double-spaced) paper based on the content of these resources, including the following: (1) citations for your resources using APA style;)2) a summary of the important ideas (or sides of the controversy) presented in the articles; (3) analysis of the impact you believe that these ideas might have on the instruction and/or services provided to English learners in Georgia; and (4) potential applications of these ideas for your own teaching with English learners in the future. Be prepared to share key points of your analysis in class on the due date.

B. All-English Teachers' Questionnaire.   Administer the All-English Teachers' Questionnaire (Faltis, 1997) to four to five teachers representing at least two different schools and several different grade levels. [As appropriate given teachers' experience with ESOL students, you may also ask questions such as the following to gain a sense of the classroom participation patterns that may impact ESOL students: (a) How do you handle turn-taking in your classroom? Are there certain times when you allow students to speak at the same time? (b) How are learning topics selected? Are there times when students choose topics? (c) Are students sometimes allowed to talk among themselves to work on tasks? (d) What opportunities are there for students to write for real audiences, such as children in other grades or settings, peers, the teacher as a trusted adult, other adults?] Write a four- to five-page (double-spaced) paper, including the following: (1) a summary of responses to the questionnaire items; (2) analysis of patterns in the responses; and (3) your hypotheses as to possible effects of these teacher views on the experiences provided to English learners. Be prepared to share key points of your analysis in class on the due date.

C. ESOL Class Observation.   Observe and describe an ESOL pullout class, or a sheltered content-area class at the middle school or high school level. Observe the class at least twice for no less than 30 minutes each time, noting the types of interactions that occur among students, teacher(s), assistants, and materials. Also note how students are physically arranged, whether student materials are displayed on the walls, and whether native language is used by teacher or students for teaching and/or communication, and how these factors affect language learning. Talk with several of the students and ask them about their likes and dislikes, their hobbies, and their families. Find out (from students and/or the teacher) whether and how their interests are used as topics for learning in their classrooms. Write a four- to five-page (double-spaced) paper, including the following: (1) a summary of the results of your observations and questioning; and (2) your hypotheses as to possible effects of physical and social environments on the experiences provided to English learners. Be prepared to share key points of your analysis in class on the due date.

Oral Language Scaffolds

Conduct and tape record a scaffolded oral language dialogue with one or two English language learners either inside or outside a school setting. Plan the dialogue either individually or in a small group so that you and your English-learner partner(s) can talk about some activity while you are actively engaged in it. Your English learner may be of any age or native language background and the topic of the dialogue may be flexible as long as it is authentic. An authentic topic is one that is meaningful to the English learner and already part of his/her experience rather than something that is contrived specifically for this assignment. Be sure that you have appropriate consent to tape record the dialogue.

Plan.   Before you begin, submit a two-sentence assignment plan to the professor for approval. Describe the learner(s), topic, and any materials you plan to use during your dialogue.

Process.   Carry out the planned dialogue using recommended scaffolding strategies as appropriate. Listen to the taped dialogue to identify the strategies used by both senior and junior partners in the dialogue and the effects on construction and communication of meaning.

Product.   Based on the taped dialogue and input/response strategies provided in class, write a four- to six-page analysis of the English learner's oral language and supporting scaffolding components you provided. Review the language used in the dialogue from both the perspective of the senior conversation partner (you) and the junior conversation partner (English learner). You are not required to submit a complete transcript of the dialogue, but should include in your analysis excerpts from the dialogue that illustrate the generalizations you make. Summarize by critiquing the dialogue as a whole, including any missed opportunities to support, expand, or extend language or meaning.

Evaluation.   Evaluation of the report will be based on the depth and thoughtfulness of the critique rather than on the quality of the dialogue itself. Although it is always helpful to find willing learners who act and react as you the teacher expect, 20/20 hindsight will also be rewarded in this assignment. Reflective analysis of both "positive" (showing progress) and "negative" (unexpected or seemingly unproductive) interaction patterns can demonstrate your understanding of effective uses of scaffolding strategies with oral language.

Integrated Curriculum Unit

The integrated curriculum unit developed as a group project should be designed to offer language-enriched content instruction for English learners in a selected grade-level range. The unit should include at least 10 activities organized around one content theme. The unit must include the following components: (a) outline of the unit activities; (b) instructional objectives appropriate to selected grade levels for language and content area(s); (c) learning center with at least three activities designed to be completed by students without direct teacher guidance either individually or in small groups; (d) home-school ties, with at least one activity that links home and school experiences; (e) school-community ties, with at least one activity that links school and community experiences; (f) language-content ties, with at least four other activities that link language and literacy processes to instruction in the selected content areas; (g) bibliography, with citations in APA style, of the key sources you used to develop concepts and activities in the unit.

Activity plans should include sections identifying objectives, materials, group size, procedures, and evaluation recommendations. Each unit group will prepare one final copy of the unit submitted on behalf of the entire group. In addition, for the last class meeting each unit group will prepare (1) a 15- to 20-minute oral presentation on their unit; and (2) copies of their unit outline (plus any other materials they would like to share) for distribution to all class members during their presentation.

The final unit will be evaluated as a whole using these criteria: (a) clarity of presentation of ideas that will engage students in developmentally appropriate activities that have meaningful purposes; (b) variety of activities, materials, teaching strategies, and opportunities for interaction that will promote student interest; and (c) integration of the following types: content and language instruction; thinking and the four language processes of reading, writing, speaking, and listening; students and peers or other classroom, family, or community resources in collaborative efforts or groupings; students' previous experience (linguistic, social, and/or cultural) and new learning in these areas.

VIII

LITERACY AND TECHNOLOGY

31

Computer-Based Instruction
in Reading Education

Linda D. Labbo
David R. Reinking
The University of Georgia

Computer-Based Instruction in Reading Education, ERD711, was first developed
at UGA in the early 1980s by George Mason, who designed the course to focus on
the use of software in reading instruction in K–12 classrooms. When we arrived at
UGA with interests in computers and literacy, we subsequently taught or co-taught
the course. For example, David's interest in digital texts on conceptions of literacy
and literacy instruction has led to a shift in the course's emphasis and focus over the
last decade. More recently, Linda adapted the course to reflect trends in software development, current innovations in computer technology, relevant developments in
literacy learning theories and instructional practices, and contemporary research
conducted by UGA faculty and others in the field. It is important to note that in the
midst of the sweeping changes in technology and education that have occurred since
the mid-1980s, we have also continued to adhere to George Mason's original vision
of offering a practical, hands-on approach to a survey of current software with an
emphasis on immediate classroom reading instructional applications.

The following graduate level catalog entry describes the overall intent of the
course for the 10 to 20 masters, specialist, and doctoral level students from a variety
of departments including, Reading, Language Education, Elementary Education,
Educational Psychology, Early Childhood Education, and Instructional Technology,
who take the course:

Examines the computer's role in classroom instruction, learning, and educational research as these topics relate to literacy. Software of potential value to the teaching of reading and writing will be critically examined. Students will use and evaluate a variety of software and will develop plans to implement computer-based instructional activities focusing on reading and writing.

There is also a note in the syllabus about the connection between this course and a related course taught by David, Topics in Computer-Based Reading and Writing (see chapter this volume). This related course attracts graduate level students who are interested in delving into underlying theories of technology related literacy development, unique characteristics of electronic digital text, and the implications of technology for literacy related research.

The course goals include fostering basic competencies in using computers to run literacy-related software, acquainting students with the range of computer applications related to literacy, providing students with a conceptual and pedagogical basis for considering the use of computers in literacy instruction, and exposing students to current issues related to the use of computers for instruction in general and literacy in particular. Students also examine critically a variety of literacy-related software and consider technological developments that have potential to affect reading and writing instruction in the future. One of the primary goals is to enable students to develop workable plans for implementing computer-based instructional activities that focus on reading and writing. And ultimately, we hope to enable students to conceptualize the range of literacy learning computer-related opportunities that are appropriate across the elementary grade levels into middle school.

A major challenge we faced in designing the course is to select and provide a current and appropriate range of software. Our department has made a commitment to ordering literacy/reading related software through educational catalogs several times a year. It is interesting to note that many software programs originally ordered over a decade and a half ago are for all practical purposes outdated because the computers required to run the programs are obsolete and not widely available. Software collected for the course include the following categories that correspond to some of the topics discussed in class: Early literacy applications including reading skills, reading and writing activities, and interactive stories; middle-grade applications including reading and writing across the curriculum; upper-grade and secondary applications including reading and writing hypertexts. Of course, today we also spend considerable time helping students think about how they might integrate the use of the internet and email into their instruction aimed at enhancing reading and writing across the curriculum.

We provide at least four different types of opportunities for students to develop the ability to critically analyze reading/literacy related software. First, many class sessions begin with an instructor demonstration of a software program. This demonstration may consist of several segments including (a) how to initiate and run the program; (b) how to navigate through the program; (c) how to use the program for a whole-class lesson; (d) how to determine potential grade school level student literacy learning opportunities; and (e) how to design an individual lesson plan related to the software. Second, about one third of the class meeting time is devoted to hands-on explorations of additional software in a College of Education computer lab. During this time students analyze the software in terms of factors such as its pedagogical value (e.g., its consistency with accepted principles of literacy instruction, its potential for enhancing or positively transforming instruction), its technological soundness (e.g., freedom from glitches in its operation), its ease of use (e.g., easily navigable), flexibility for instructional purposes (e.g., its capability to be adapted to different students or contexts of use), and so forth . Third, students may also critically analzye software and present a demonstration of that software to the class. For example, some masters or specialists level students who are currently teaching will sometimes opt to analyze software that is available in their school district or on their school campus. Fourth, we require students to complete a special course project. David has required each class member to participate in a small group project to develop an instructional unit or coordinated series of instructional activities that entail using computer technologies to enhance in some way their students' reading and writing. Linda has used a variety of activities for the course project that include writing a traditional research paper, conducting an action research project conducted in a classroom, developing a unit that includes the use of the computer, or conducting an annotated bibliography of software that may be used by teachers at their school. Students are also encouraged to conduct unique course projects that allow them to explore a variety of computer-related areas of interest. For example, some classroom teachers have created hypertext programs specifically designed to allow their students to explore children's literature in a digital, interactive format.

A challenge we have faced is providing a collection of relevant course readings. In the past, readings for the course have consisted of a core of readings supplemented with practitioner-related articles from professional literacy and educational technology journals. Because hardware and software and their availability in classrooms changes so rapidly, publications about the use of technology in classrooms quickly become dated. Thus, we face the challenge of keeping readings current and relevant. Most recently, course readings have consisted mainly of chapters in a book that we co-edited with Michael McKenna and Ronald Kieffer in conjunction with a conference funded by the National Reading Research Center. Selected chapters from the text, *Handbook of Literacy and Technology: Transformations in a Post-Typographic World* (1998) are read and discussed in class. Students are also required to locate, read, and present a contemporary professional article or Web site related to course topics.

Sample Syllabus
Computer-Based Instruction in Reading Education

Text:

Reinking, D., McKenna, M. C., Labbo, L. D., & Kieffer, R. D. (1998). *Handbook of literacy and technology: Transformations in a Post-Typographic World*. Mahwah, NJ: Lawrence Erlbaum Associates.

Class Format:

Approximately
1/3 lecture and discussion
1/3 demonstration and presentation
1/3 hands-on experience with hardware and software

Course Requirements and Evaluation:

Minimum requirements (successful completion of the 9 requirements will result in a B for the course; completion of 8 of the requirements will result in a C; poor quality of work may result in a D or below)

1. Regular attendance (Class activities are central to the goals of this course and are difficult to make up outside of class. More than one absence may negatively affect your course grade).
2. Active participation in class activities and completed course contract.
3. Read and be prepared to discuss assigned readings in class.
4. Submit and discuss in class 3 two-page (double-spaced size 12 font) reactions to self-selected articles or chapters related to technology and literacy. Papers should focus on reacting to the readings and not summarizing their content. These must be submitted by (date listed here).
5. Sign-up to present one self-selected course reading as an oral report to the class. Highlight the relationship between the article or chapter selected and the focus of the course (as detailed in the course description).
6. Sign-up to present on assigned course reading as an oral report to the class. Prepare a handout to help guide the discussion and to highlight key points.
7. Submit all written material as the output of computer-based input such as a word processing program, data base program, graphics program, and so forth. Spelling and grammar checks are recommended. Reactions to readings may be submitted via e-mail.
8. Complete 3 written reviews of individual computer programs or courseware packages that can be used for reading and/or writing instruction (see accompanying review form).

9. Participate actively as a member of a group assigned to develop and present to the class a plan for implementing a computer-based instructional activity.

- Students who wish to pursue an A for the course must complete all of the requirements listed above. In addition, one of the following individual projects must be successfully completed to receive an A for the course.

1. Write a conventional focused research paper on a topic related to technology and literacy. The length of the paper should be 10–20 double spaced pages with a minimum of 8 references excluding ERIC documents. Given the topic, a majority of the references should have been published within the previous 5 years. The paper must follow the 3rd or 4th edition of the Publications Manual of the American Psychological Association.

2. Conduct and write up an action research project related to technology and literacy. An action research project involves identifying a specific question which one them investigates through systematic data collection such as observations, interviews, anecdotal records, instructional products, analysis of audio/video tapes, and so forth. The project might take the form of a case study of a child's use of a particular type of literacy software. The data collection should be sustained over at least 8 to 10 computer-related observations and should include multiple data sources. You do not have to be highly trained in qualitative research methods to satisfactorily complete an action research project for this course. Guidance from the instructor will be available for those who wish to pursue this option.

3. Write an article related to technology and literacy for submission to a particular scholarly or practitioner journal. The instructor will consult with anyone interested in pursing this option, and they must deem the manuscript ready for submission by the end of the summer quarter. State professional journals for teachers such as the Georgia Journal of Reading are perfectly acceptable.

4. We welcome other proposals of ideas that might be negotiated as alternatives to those outlined here. For example, a student could create a hypertext or hypermedia product related to technology and literacy. Alternatively, a detailed written specification and description of a computer-based product might be developed without actually creating it. A detailed book review or an extremely detailed annotated bibliography of software and readings might also be possible.

Linda's most recent course contract follows.

Labbo   ERD 711   Contract Due by:

Name (please print):   Date: Signature:

Check one

I plan to fulfill the minimum requirements (1 through 9) for a potential B.

I plan to fulfill the full requirements (1 through 10) for a potential A.

1. Regular attendance

2. Active participation

3. Read and discuss readings

4. 3 reactions to self-selected articles or chapters related to technology and literacy.

5. Present one self-selected course reading as an oral report to the class.

6. Present one assigned course reading as an oral report to the class.

7. Submit all written material as the output of a word processing program, data base program, or graphics program.

8. 2 reviews and 1 review/presentation of literacy-related computer programs.

9. As a member of a group, develop and present to the class a plan for implementing a computer-based instructional activity.

****

10. Please check one of the following projects and write a brief title/description in the space provided:

A. Research paper

B. Action research project

C. Write an article

D. An alternative project—Title/Description:

ERD 711 Tentative Schedule   (*Chap = chapter pages from the course text)

Date   COURSE OVERVIEW

• Select and Sign-up for Assigned Course Reading, Discuss Contracts and Projects

Date   LITERACY ACQUISITION

• Preschoolers and Computers in the Classroom, Socio-dramatic Play Center

• Labbo, L. D., & Ash, G. (1998). What is the role of computer-related technology in early literacy? In S. Neuman & K. Roskos (Eds.), *Children achieving: Best practices in early literacy* (pp. 180–197). Newark, De: International Reading Association.

• Haughland, S. W. (1992). The effect of computer software on preschool children's developmental gains. *Journal of Computing in Childhood Education, 3*, 15–29.

Date   EMERGING LITERACY

• Turn In Course Contract

• Labbo, L. D. (1995). "Incorporating the computer into the classroom: A kindergarten case study." Instructional resource video, the *National Reading Research Center Grant*, Athens, GA: University of Georgia.

• Labbo, L. D., & Kuhn, M. *Chapter: Electronic Symbol Making: Young Children's Computer-Related Emerging Concepts About Literacy, pp. 79–91.

Date   BEGINNING READERS

• McKenna, M. R. *Chapter: Electronic texts and the transformations of beginning reading, pp. 45–59.

• Jones, I. (1994). The effect of a word processor on the written composition of second-grade pupils. *Computers in the schools, 11*(2), 43–54.

Date   WRITING TO READ

• Labbo, L. D., Phillips, M., & Murray, B. (1995–1996). "Writing to Read": From inheritance to innovation and invitation. *The Reading Teacher, 49*(4), 314–321.

Date   LITERACY PORTFOLIOS

• Kieffer, R. D., Hale, M., & Templeton, A. *Chapter: Electronic literacy portfolios: Technology transformations in a First-Grade classroom, pp. 45–163.

Date   FEATURES OF TECHNOLOGY AND CLASSROOMS

• Miller, L., & Olson, J. *Chapter: Literacy research oriented towards features of technology and classrooms, pp. 343–360.

Date   TRANSFORMING SCHOOLS THROUGH SYSTEMATIC
                                  CHANGE

• Fawcett, G., & Snyder, S. *Chapter: Transforming schools through systemic change: New work, new knowledge, new technology, pp. 115–127.

Date   MIDPOINT OF SESSION: STRUGGLING READERS

• Anderson-Inman, L., & Horney, M. *Chapter: Transforming text for at-risk readers, pp. 15–43.

• Olson, R. K., Wise, B., Ring, J., & Johnson, M. (1997). Computer-based remedial training in phoneme awareness and phonological decoding: Effects on the post-training development of word recognition. *Scientific Studies in Reading, 1*, 235–253.

Date   THE ROLE OF TECHNOLOGY IN THE READING
                                  CLINIC

• McKenna, M., Reinking D., & Labbo, L. D. (1999). "The role of technology in thereading clinic: Its Past and Potential." In D. Evensen & P. Mosenthal (Eds.), Reconsidering the role of the reading clinic in a new age of literacy. Stanford, CT: JAI.

Date   THE INTERNET IN THE CLASSROOM

• Garner, R., & Gillingham, M. *Chapter: The internet in the classroom: Is it the end of transmission-oriented pedagogy?, pp. 221–231.

• Peters, J. M. (1996). Paired keyboards as a tool of Internet exploration of 3rd grade students. *Journal of Educational Computing Research, 14*, 229–242.

Date	STUDENT AUTHORED HYPERMEDIA

• Myers, J., Hammett, R., & McKillop, M. *Chapter: Opportunities for critical literacy and pedagogy in student-authored hypermedia, pp. 63–78.

Date	E-MAIL EXCHANGES AND CURRICULAR ISSUES

• Field, S. L., Labbo, L. D., & Lu, C. (1996). Real people and real places: A powerful social studies exchange through technology. *Social Studies and the Young Learner, 9*(2), 16–23.

Date	COMPUTER-MEDIATED COMMUNICATION

• Beach, R., & Lundell, D. *Chapter: Early adolescents' use of computer-mediated communication in writing and reading, pp. 93–112.

Date	TELECOMMUNICATIONS IN THE CLASSROOM

• Neilsen, L. *Chapter: Coding the light: Rethinking generational authority in a rural high school telecommuications project, pp. 129–143.

Date	PRESERVICE TEACHER TRAINING & MULTIMEDIA

• Kinzer, C., & Risko, V. *Chapter: Multimedia and enhanced learning: Transforming preservice education, pp. 185–202.

Date	MULTICULTURAL ISSUES & TECHNOLOGY

• Technology as enfranchisement and cultural development. *Chapter: Crisscrossing symbol systems, paradigm shifts, and socio-cultural considerations, pp. 253–268.

Presentation of Group Projects

Date	Last Day of Class/Sharing of Individual Projects

32

Topics in Computer-Based
Reading and Writing

David Reinking
University of Georgia

In the Department of Reading Education at the University of Georgia, each faculty member is encouraged to develop an elective graduate course that most closely reflects his or her professional interests and expertise related to literacy. *Topics in Computer-Based Reading and Writing*, the course that I describe here and that I proposed and first taught in 1991, was my response to that customary encouragement. It reflects my primary professional interest in technology, particularly computer technology and digital texts, and how it is effecting changes in our conceptions and use of literacy.

The course compliments another older Departmental course offering related to literacy and technology: *Computer-Based Instruction in Reading Education* (see Labbo & Reinking, this volume). That course was developed in the early 1980s by George Mason, perhaps the most widely known scholar interested in computers and reading during most of the 1980s. When I arrived at UGA in 1985 as an assistant professor, George graciously shared the teaching of alternative sections of the course with me because of my own interests in technology. Reflecting George's primary interests, the course focused on the use of software in the teaching and promotion of reading in K–12 classrooms. After George's retirement in 1990, I continued to teach the course with that focus. More recently, my colleague, Linda Labbo, who is quickly emerging as a recognized scholar in technology and early literacy, and I have team taught a section of the course, and as of this writing Linda has taught it once on her own. I also wish to acknowledge the influence of her research and theoretical perspectives on my teaching of the "Topics" course I focus on here.

Although I have always enjoyed teaching the established course focusing on classroom applications of technology, it did not really allow for a full consideration of the larger issues in which I was also interested. For example, exactly what is the relation between technology and literacy? Are there fundamentally unique characteristics of electronic, digital texts? If so, what are they and how do these characteristics compare to conventional printed texts? What are the implications for literacy theory and research, broadly speaking? Is it possible that computer-based reading and writing may change in some fundamental sense how we conceptualize literacy? May it change what we teach under the head of literacy instruction and how think about teaching it? These are more basic, abstract, forward thinking questions more directly related to theory and research than to day-to-day considerations of using computers in classrooms. *Topics in ComputerBased Reading and Writing*, the course I proposed in 1991 and describe here, allows me and my students to explore such questions.

The course, like many upper-level electives in our Department, is usually taught one quarter (soon to be semester) every other year. A typical section has 10 to 20 students, approximately half who are in a master's or specialist program and half who are in a doctoral program. The students typically come from programs in Reading, Language Education, Instructional Technology, and Elementary Education, not coincidentally because these are the departments to which I send announcements about the course in the quarter before it will be offered. Typically, several of the students have previously taken the older course focusing on classroom applications. Some of the master's in Reading Education have chosen a specialization in the area of technology and literacy, and some of the doctoral students plan dissertations in this area.

There are several challenges I face in planning and implementing this course, and I will highlight a few here. A practical problem has been making students and their advisors aware of the distinction between the course and the established, related technology course. Invariably some students show up the first day of class expecting a hands-on computer course where they will have an opportunity to explore software they might use in their elementary school classrooms. So, the syllabus tries to make this distinction clear. Interestingly, in all but one case, after I go through the syllabus and explain the focus of the course, students who enrolled with the wrong expectations stay instead of dropping the course. This trend and the lively discussions that are typical during the course itself suggest to me that the content is inherently interesting, and relevant, to even more practice-oriented students.

Another problem has been focusing on the concept of hypertext in the course. Hypertext is a useful focal point for the course content because it raises a number of critical questions and issues. For example, the Bolter book (1991) that is required reading for the course focuses on hypertext to raise larger issues. Additionally, all students are required to learn to use Storyspace, a utility software program that enables them to create hypertext documents to complete other course requirements.

However, despite my pointed explanations that hypertext is only an example, many students see the course as promoting hypertexts over printed texts. Some enjoy being involved in a new form of reading and writing, but others seem distracted by a need to defend printed texts as superior, a position that is reinforced by some glitches and difficulties in using Storyspace. I also require students to become involved in small group discussions over email, which has been problematic for some of them.

Perhaps the greatest challenge though is the inherent difficulty in coming to terms with rapidly changing technologies for reading and writing and their increasing use in an ever widening circle of daily events. But, that is not just a problem that must be dealt with in creating the syllabus, it is the justification for the course itself.

Sample Syllabus
Topics in ComputerBased Reading
and Writing

Course Description

Catalog description. Research and theory related to computerbased written discourse. Compares electronic and printed texts, addressing implications for reading and writing texts, for developing literacy, and for conducting research.

Further description and disclaimer. This course focuses on the consequences of the increasing shift from printed to electronic forms of reading and writing. That is, how is literacy changing when we depend increasingly on electronic forms of reading and writing, and what are the implications of the move away from printed materials? The course is designed to address such questions broadly from various perspectives. Classroom instruction, specifically instruction aimed at enhancing literacy, is a dimension of this focus. However, this course is not designed to familiarize teachers with available technology and commercial software that can be used for instruction. Students whose primary interests are related to discovering uses for the computer in teaching reading or writing should consider enrolling in the course ERD 711, Computer-Based Instruction in Reading Education. Occasionally, software will be demonstrated in this course and students will have an opportunity to use computers, but these occasions are aimed at providing examples that lay the ground work for discussing issues and clarifying concepts. That said, it is likely that teachers who take this course will develop a different perspective on the role that technology may play in instruction, which may be quite useful in guiding their use of computers in the classroom.

Required and Supplemental Readings

Required reading

Bolter, J. D. (1991). *Writing space: The computer, hypertexts, and the history of writing.* Hillsdale, NJ: Lawrence Erlbaum Associates.

Supplemental readings:

Supplemental readings are required to receive an *A* or *B* in this course. An annotated bibliography of suggested supplemental printed and electronic readings will be distributed during the first class. [Available to readers at the Web site accompanying this text.]

Computer software:

Bolter, J. D., Joyce, M., Smith, J. B., & Bernstein, M. (1993). *Storyspace.* [Computer program]. Cambridge, MA: Eastgate Systems.

Class Format

Class meetings will typically include the following activities: (a) small and whole group discussion of the weekly required reading in the Bolter text, (b) lecture/presentation/discussion on relevant topics selected by the instructor, (c) demonstration of computer application(s) related to activity *a* or *b*, and (d) independent time for computer work and/or consultations with instructor.

Course Requirements, Grading, and Evaluation

General requirements and conditions:

1. Provide full reference citations in APA style whenever possible.
2. Written work may be submitted via email.
3. No work for the present quarter's grade will be accepted after the date of the final exam.
4. Work submitted to satisfy requirements will be considered acceptable or unacceptable. Unacceptable work may be resubmitted for credit subject to item 3.
5. The instructor will offer to write a letter of recommendation/commendation for students who achieve a grade of *A* and whose performance in the course is especially meritorious.
6. The instructor will not assign a grade of incomplete) Under extraordinary circumstances where the instructor approves completion of some require-

ments after the completion of the course, a lower grade will be assigned and changed when the requirement has been successfully met.

(*Note.* Some course requirements outlined in the following sections are negotiable on an individual basis. That is, students who wish to propose comparable activities relevant to this course are encouraged to discuss their ideas individually with the instructor.)

Minimum requirements (successful completion of which will result in a *C* for the course):

1. Regular attendance and active participation in class activities. (Given that this class meets only once a week, no more than one class may be missed without affecting the final grade for the course.)
2. Weekly participation in an email discussion of the assigned reading in the Bolter text. The class will be divided into small groups for that purpose. Members of the group will take turns jump-starting the email discussion each week. Each week, the assigned reading in Bolter must be read no later than the Monday morning of the week it is due. Small group email discussions will occur from Monday through Thursday of each week culminating in a class discussion. In class, the leaders of each email discussion group will rotate to another small group to summarize the discussion of their respective groups.
3. Submit a two- to three-page, typed reaction to class discussion and activities each week. Written reactions to one class period are due by the subsequent class period. Reactions may be submitted to the instructor via email.

Requirements for a *B*:

1. Satisfy items 1 and 2 under minimum requirements. Completion of item 3 in the minimum requirements is not necessary for those seeking a *B*.
2. Write a two- to three-page reaction to 10 supplemental readings (from at least 5 different sources). At least half of the reactions must be submitted by the fifth class meeting. Supplemental readings not on the suggested list distributed in class or mentioned by the instructor are acceptable but must be approved in advance.
3. Complete *one* of the following:
   a. a take-home final consisting of short answer and essay questions related to the content of this course. *OR*
   b. write a 10- to 20-page paper speculating on the nature of literacy in 20 years.

Requirements for an *A*:

1. Satisfy items 1 and 2 under minimum requirements. Completion of item 3 in the minimum requirements is not necessary for those seeking an *A*.

2. Create a hypertext comprised of one's own prose and existing texts (e.g., the required text, supplemental readings, etc.). The hypertext may also be expanded to include audio and visual elements (thus becoming a hypermedia application) for those who have, or who are inclined to develop, the expertise to do so. To complete this task, students must learn to use *Storyspace*, a word processing program designed to create hypertexts, or they must use some other application that allows them to create a hypertext document. The *Storyspace* application is available for the Macintosh and MS DOS platforms, although the MS DOS version has proved to be far inferior and more frustrating than the Mac version. The goal of the final hypertext document is to reflect the student's engagement with the issues central to this course (as described in the previous section entitled "Course Description" at the levels of learning that Bloom has described as analysis and synthesis.

3. Keep a log describing progress in the developing the hypertext and reflecting on the process of creating it. (Parts of the log may find its way into the hypertext, too.)

4. Complete an electronic take-home final. That task will require that students elaborate on a hypertext dealing with the content of the course and developed by the instructor. In other words, students will add texts and links that merge with the instructor's hypertext perhaps using existing texts from the students' own hypertexts. It is anticipated that the richer and more extensive the effort to complete requirement Number two, the easier this task will be.

(*Note:* Students will be asked to declare the grade they are seeking no later than the third class meeting. After that time students may later opt for a lower grade but not for a higher grade.)

Tentative Class Schedule, Topics, and Assigned Readings

Class 1	Course introduction, introduction to hypertext, demonstration of *Storyspace*
Class 2	Transformations of text, theoretical perspectives and issues, are we moving to a posttypographic era? What does that mean? Historical perspectives?
Class 3	Must declare grade sought for course, transformations of reading and writing, what are the implications of new forms of reading and writing?
Class 4	Transformations of literacy in classrooms and schools, what are the implications of digital reading and writing on the way classrooms and schools deal with literacy?
Class 5	Transformations of teaching and learning, what are the implications of digital reading and writing on the conduct of teaching and learning in classrooms?
Class 6	Transformations of society, what are the implications of an increased use of digital reading and writing on societal issues such as copyright, intellectual property and plagiarism?

Class 7   Transformations of mind, what are the cognitive effects of literacy and how might they change in a posttypographic world?

Class 8   Transformations of literacy research, how might electronic texts effect changes in the agenda of literacy researchers?

Class 9   Summary, reflections, and the future of literacy in a posttypographic era

Class 10   Jay Bolter visits class to respond to your questions and comments

Class 11   Final and all written work due

IX

INQUIRIES INTO LITERACY, THEORY, AND CLASSROOM PRACTICE

33

Action Research
in Educational Settings:
A Graduate Course in Practitioner Research

Leslie Patterson
University of Houston

I usually have a general idea about where I think learners need to go, and 15 years ago, I did not have any trouble taking them there: "All together now, walk this way!" Since then, I have begun listening to the individuals with a bit more care, and I soon found that my teaching practices had to change. After many years of teaching/learning, I now describe my approach as social constructivism. Teaching from that stance, I value each student's individual learning journey, but I also work to see that each group of students becomes a dynamic learning community, with shared goals and lively discussion. My primary challenge is to negotiate the emerging tensions between this individual and group learning. This is particularly true in the course included here—Action Research in Educational Settings.

At times, I have found ways to invite each learner to take charge, to find the right questions, to embark on particular and individualistic quests, yet to find common concerns and discoveries that held the learning community together. Those have been exciting semesters. Students' energy and the synergy that emerges from their conversations makes for powerful learning. At other times, we have worked to generate common questions and a group quest. Those have also been exciting semesters, and challenging. With either approach (and with various combinations), I always face choices between what everyone "needs" and what each individual "needs." These tensions are intensified by the institutional culture and inevitable constraints on time and resources. For me, the essence of teaching/learning is to negotiate those tensions so that everyone benefits.

These tensions make syllabi-building a complex process. Typically, students come to me expecting the syllabus to explain what my expectations and standards are and what the course "content" will be. It takes on a contractual significance: "If you complete these assignments and learn this content, you will receive an A." Increasingly, that has become an uncomfortable way to begin a course. According to social constructivist approaches, the syllabus is not a contract, but an invitation to inquiry: "Here are some flexible boundaries to help us begin asking questions, but what is it that you want to learn? How can I help you?"

I value this open-endedness, and I see my role, not as the source of all knowledge and rigor, but as a resource, guide, cheerleader, listener, editor, facilitator, mentor, and fellow learner. Of course, I have to make both big and small decisions week by week to make that happen, and I usually invite students to help me make those decisions. I use the syllabus as a tool—a way to set boundaries—to get this collaborative process started.

Learning communities cannot self-organize without boundaries. Without boundaries, in the form of common readings, concerns, questions, routines, goals, or tasks, individual learners will remain isolated and will move randomly through a frustrating semester. Boundaries for learning communities must be flexible and permeable, but without boundaries, self-organization will not happen. Learning communities cannot form in a vacuum.

I use the syllabus to provide these initial boundaries, but the syllabus is just the invitation—a springboard to the rest of the semester. Week by week, we add reading lists, timelines, evaluation criteria, descriptions of tasks, procedures, written dialogues, and other documentation of our ongoing inquiries. Sometimes I generate these, but more often they are generated by groups of learners. E-mail and a web presence have helped support this communication during some semesters, but I have found that some groups of learners have resisted electronic communication and seem to work better through more familiar channels.

In the syllabus on Action Research included in this volume, collaborative inquiry is both the content and the process of the course. This course has been offered to advanced Master's and Doctoral candidates, to extend their work in a range of research contexts. It is similar to a teacher research course in that we explore a range of epistemologies which are seldom included in traditional graduate research courses. It is different from a teacher research course in that it includes a focus on inquiry at the school and institutional levels, as well as classroom inquiry. Each semester, students and I struggle to find a balance between what we need to learn together about research frameworks and methodologies and what individual learners need as they proceed with their separate action research studies. That means that we take time to debrief about our own learning in the course. Identifying patterns and principles within our learning can be a catalyst for insights into the research process, as well as insights into the researchers' individual projects.

With such a syllabus, each semester will be different because each group of learners is different, and because I am different each semester I lead this course. The syllabus included here is merely a snapshot during one semester in one course. A whole scrapbook of these snapshots (or a multimedia presentation) would provide a richer and more complete view of my teaching/learning.

I deeply appreciate colleagues and mentors who have helped me, both in person and in print, on this learning journey. My mother and three sisters built my first learning community, and they continue to be a major source of stimulation. John Stansell and Bess Osburn first showed me how a university professor–mentor can work with and for students. As for those colleagues whose published work has been significant, I can mention only a few. Jerry Harste, Virginia Woodward, and Carolyn Burke (1984) were among the first researchers who challenged my formalist/positivist notions of literacy, learning, and research. Shirley Brice Heath (1983) pushed my traditional ideas about the teacher's role in language learning. Ken Goodman and his colleagues (Goodman et. al., 1987; Goodman, Y., 1978, 1989; Goodman, Watson, & Burke, 1987) first suggested how theoretical notions can change the way I think about learning and literacy. Paulo Freire (1985; 1987) and bell hooks (1994) first invited me to connect personal and instructional issues to culture and politics. Donald Murray (1982), Donald Graves (1983) and many others asked and answered important questions about writing instruction. Glenda Eoyang (1997) and Murray Gell-Mann (1984) have helped me understand how chaos science and complex adaptive systems can teach us how to participate in learning communities. Finally, my most important mentors are the teacher researchers I have had the opportunity to work with because they have shown me how teaching/learning approaches work in the lives of children and young adults (Patterson, Santa, Short, & Smith, 1993; Donoahue, VanTassell, & Patterson, 1996).

Each semester begins with this theoretical and research base and ends with new questions. Those questions become the core of my thinking as I build the syllabus for the next group of learners. As an invitation to join a learning community, the syllabus has become my most useful tool, a tool to help me negotiate the tensions between individual and group learning and a tool to help a new learning community come to life each semester.

REFERENCES

Donoahue, M. A., Van Tassell, M., & L. Patterson, (Eds.). (1996). *Teachers are researchers: Talk, texts, and inquiry.* Newark, DE: International Reading Association.

Freire, P. (1985). *The politics of education: Culture power and liberation.* Massachusetts: Bergin & Garvey.

Freire, P. (1987). *Literacy: Reading the word and the world.* New York: Bergin & Garvey.

Eoyang, G. H. (1997). *Coping with chaos: Seven simple tools.* Cheyenne, WY: Lagumo.

Gell-Mann, M. (1994). *The quark and the jaguar: Adventures in the simple and the complex.* New York: Freeman.

Goodman, K., Smith, E., Meredith, R, & Goodman, Y. (1987). *Language and thinking in school* (3rd ed.). Katonah, NY: Richard C. Owen.

Goodman, Y. (1978). Kidwatching: An alternative to testing. *National Elementary Principal, 57,* 41–45.

Goodman, Y. (1989). Roots of the whole-language movement. *Elementary School Journal, 90,* 113–127.

Goodman, Y., Watson, D., & Burke, C. (1987). *Reading miscue inventory: Alternative procedures.* Katonah, NY: Richard C. Owen.

Graves, D. (1983). *Writing: Teachers and children at work.* Portsmouth, NH: Heinemann.

Harste, J., Woodward, V., & Burke, C. (1984). *Language stories and literacy lessons.* Portsmouth, NH: Heinemann.

Heath, S. (1983). *Ways with words: Language, life, and work in communities and classrooms.* Cambridge, MA: Harvard University Press.

hooks, b. (1994). *Teaching to transgress: Education as the practice of freedom.* New York: Routledge.

Murray, D. (1982). *Learning by teaching: Selected articles on writing and teaching.* Portsmouth, NH: Boynton/Cook.

Patterson, L., Santa, C., Short, K., & Smith, K. (1993). *Teachers are researchers: Reflection and action.* Newark, DE: IRA.

Sample Syllabus
Action Research in Educational Settings

Dear Researchers,

I believe that inquiry drives learning, for kids and adults—within and outside schools. For that reason, we will build this course around a set of CORE QUESTIONS. I've listed some of those questions below, but you will also have other questions that emerge as the semester goes on. By the end of the semester, you will have developed answers to all these questions. Your answers will be based on your personal experience, your reading in this and other courses, field work, and class discussions. Of course, these questions will remain relevant throughout your life as a teacher and researcher, as you continue refining and expanding your answers. The content of this course is not a set of skills to master, but a very exciting landscape to explore. The assignments listed below are designed to help us find landmarks on this landscape, to find answers to the Core Questions. Your own questions and inquiries are, however, the heart of your professional development. The most important things you'll leave this course with are ... more questions—more specific, more focused, and more important questions.

Yours in action,

Leslie Patterson

Core Questions

⇒ What philosophical assumptions frame collaborative action research in educational settings?

⇒ What tools and processes are important to action researchers?

⇒ What can we learn from published accounts of action research?

⇒ How is action research similar to and different from other kinds of educational research?

⇒ What can we learn from doing action research—gathering and analyzing observational and interview data and developing reports of the research in progress?

⇒ How do critical perspectives influence the decisions of action researchers?

Core Texts

Hubbard, R., & Powers, B. (1993). *The art of classroom inquiry.* Portsmouth, NH: Heinemann.

Kuhn, T. S. (1996). *The structure of scientific revolutions.* Chicago: University of Chicago Press.

Patterson, L., Santa, C., Short, K., & Smith, K. (1993). *Teachers are researchers: Reflection and action.* Newark, DE: IRA.

Spradley, J. P. (1980). *The ethnographic interview.* New York: Holt, Rinehart, Winston.

Spradley, J. P. (1980). *Participant observation.* New York: Holt, Rinehart, Winston.

Stringer, E. (1997). *Community based ethnography.* Mahwah, NJ: Lawrence Erlbaum Associates.

Stringer, E. (1999). *Action research: A handbook for practitioners.* Thousand Oaks, CA: Sage.

Course Work

Here is a brief sketch of our work together in this course. We will fill in the details together.

Class Project

Together, we will maintain a Web site for the use of educators who want to learn more about action research. (http//:www.uh.edu/lpatters/link/)

Individual Project

Each of us will move forward on an action research project. Because each of us is at a different point in the conceptualization of a project or in an ongoing project, evaluation of this component will be based on an individualized contract.

Researcher's Journal

This is your own reflective journal recording your observations and reflections about the course experiences. You will bring it to class as a resource during our discussions.

Readings and Participation in Seminars

Together, we will schedule reading assignments and decide on topics for seminar discussions. Summary/critiques, etc. will go into the Web site. Here is a tentative list of topics:

⇒ What is action research?

⇒ What are the philosophical foundations of various stances in educational research? Do we need philosophical foundations?

⇒ What are guidelines for participant observation? For interviewing?

⇒ What are guidelines and suggestions for teacher research?

⇒ What are the potentials and pitfalls for educational action researchers?

⇒ What is community-based ethnographic research? How is it useful to educators?

Action Research:
Questions to Get the Process Started

When teaching itself is an ongoing inquiry process, it is sometimes a bit difficult to know where to begin your action research "project." Here are some questions that can serve as "toeholds" for you as you begin your journey.

I. Problem-Framing
   • Who are you as a teacher/learner?
   • What do you want to learn about? Or ... What in your practice do you want to change?
   • Why is this an important focus for research?
   • What is your situation, your research context?

II. Focusing and Designing the "Study"
   • What are the ultimate purposes of this inquiry?
   • Who is the intended audience?
   • What are your preliminary research questions to guide the work?
   • What kinds of data will address your questions?
   • How will you gather that data?
   • How will you invite your participants or informants to collaborate?

III. Gathering and Analyzing the Data
   • How are you going to document your observations and reflections?
   • How do you expect to analyze the data?
   • How are you going to assure credibility?

IV. Writing Up and Presenting Your Findings and Conclusions
   • How will you address the expectations of your audience?
   • How will you display your findings?

34

Creating Curricular Invitations:
Reading, Writing, and Inquiry

Christine H. Leland
Jerome C. Harste
Indiana University

Think of the luxury of spending a whole day, from 8 to 5, thinking about reading. You could call it "Reading Day" and begin by writing about your earliest reading memories, hear what others have to say by reading and discussing professional articles, watch videotapes of exemplary classroom practices, plan mini-inquiries based on questions that are raised, experience the power of moving to art as a way of comprehending and interpreting text, study the miscues of a single reader to understand the reading process, and reflect on these experiences and what they mean for your teaching in a daily reflective journal. You would be exhausted, of course, but what a marvelous day. Very different from the Cha-Cha-Cha Curriculum most of us live!

Now imagine "Writing Day," "Sign System Day," "Inquiry Day," and "Evaluation Day." This is summer in the city, Indiana style, and one of several 1-week intensive workshops available to local teachers.

This particular workshop was designed to invite practicing teachers to explore "education-as-inquiry." Specifically, we wanted teachers to see education as inquiry as a philosophical stance that could permeate the curriculum and to assist them in making connections between inquiry and their individual classroom literacy programs. Inherent in our definitions of both inquiry and literacy is the belief that knowing and learning are semiotic processes involving language, art, music, drama, mathematics, and any of a number of ways that humans have created to make and share meaning. Like subject matter disciplines, around which much traditional curriculum has been organized, the sign systems provide different perspectives on knowing.

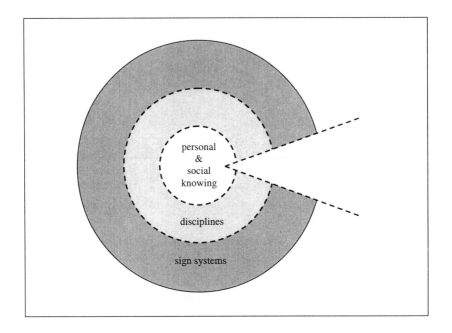

FIG. 34.1.   Education for democracy.

Rather than continuing to organize curriculum around the disciplines, we want teachers to think about organizing curriculum around the personal and social inquiry questions of learners. This does not eliminate the disciplines from curriculum, but it does relegate them to a different status. Rather than being the center of curriculum, the disciplines and the sign systems are seen as perspectives that learners might use to explore inquiry questions they care about. Figure 34.1, "Education for Democracy" (Short, Harste, with Burke, 1996) shows the theoretical foundation for this course. At the center of the circle, personal and social knowing form the core for curriculum. The disciplines and sign systems become curriculum tools that inquirers use in pursuing their interests. Inquiry, shown here as a wedge, cuts through the disciplines and the sign systems and connects directly to personal and social knowing at the core. Figure 34.2 ("Curriculum as Inquiry") is our current rendition of the inquiry cycle. It begins with personal involvement and highlights what we see as key underlying processes in inquiry—observation, collaboration, reflection, tension, and repositioning.

We think it is important that teachers have the experience of living an inquiry-based, multiple ways of knowing curriculum, if only through this 1-week intensive workshop initially. Inquiry is more than reading about things in books;

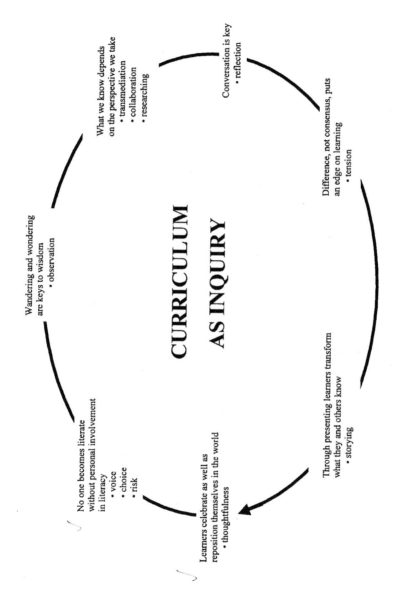

FIG. 34.2 Curriculum as inquiry.

Wandering and wondering
are keys to wisdom
• observation

What we know depends
on the perspective we take
• transmediation
• collaboration
• researching

Conversation is key
• reflection

Difference, not consensus, puts
an edge on learning
• tension

**CURRICULUM
AS INQUIRY**

Through presenting learners transform
what they and others know
• storying

No one becomes literate
without personal involvement
in literacy
• voice
• choice
• risk

Learners celebrate as well as
reposition themselves in the world
• thoughtfulness

inquirers need to be involved in creating knowledge, not just looking it up. To this end, our workshop emphasizes the doing. Participants explore their own questions, engage in the process of transmediation (moving from making meaning in one sign system to making meaning in another), and try out a number of strategies that support classroom inquiry.

The course is framed around the kind of conversations that we want our students to join. For "Reading Day," our framing questions were: What does it mean to see reading as a process of inquiry? How do you organize curriculum to support a reading-as-inquiry perspective? Where does a reading-as-inquiry perspective get us that other perspectives do not? Each day is organized by strands, which were meant to roughly parallel key processes within the inquiry cycle (see Fig. 34.2). For example on "Reading Day," we had strands on Composing (which involved exploring your voice, current stance, and beliefs through writing), Making Connections (reading and discussing professional literature), Seminar (hearing from teachers and other educators who are currently thinking through and studying this area), Research (planning and conducting mini-inquiry projects that we can do tomorrow or next year in our classrooms), Multiple Sign Systems (using art, music, math, process drama, and other sign systems to gain a new perspective on a topic of inquiry), Demonstration (taking a deeper look at the topic using methodologies that the field has found insightful), Reflexivity (purposefully testing our evolving personal theories of literacy and literacy learning by focusing on tension), and New Curricular Directions (repositioning ourselves by developing and field testing new curricular engagements and invitations). Our one-page course syllabus shows how strands remained constant across the 5 days of our workshop (see sample syllabus at end of chapter).

The Composing Strand.   With the exception of the first day when we begin with a seminar strand, which consists of an overview of the syllabus and an introduction to the conceptual models that underlie the course (Figs. 34.1 & 34.2), we begin each day by finding our own voice through writing. On reading day, we explore our earliest memories of learning to read and talk about what this experience means. On writing day, we draft a family story and talk about the importance of using personal experience as a point of departure in writing. On sign system day, we share who we are through our strongest sign system (art, music, drama, language, movement, or mathematics) as well as demonstrate our weakest system. Inevitably this leads to discussions of why we have the strengths and weaknesses we do as well as what it might mean to see the goal of a good language arts program as developing and expanding our human potential to mean. On inquiry day, we write about our best learning experiences, in or out of school. On evaluation day, we share our best piece of writing during the week and talk about what makes it special.

The Making Connections Strand.   One of the objectives of our workshop is to connect teachers to the profession by inviting them to join current conversations. We want teachers to feel like they are at the cutting edge of theory. To this end, we select professional literature that addresses current issues in the field. During the first 2 years that we offered this workshop, we asked students to purchase *Mind Matters* (Kirby & Kuykendall, 1991) to read as a common text. We like this book because it encourages readers to take different perspectives and because it contains lots of what the authors call "Explorations" for readers to experiment with on their own and then bring back to share with the group. Some of the chapters in this book include "Thinking Like an Inventor," "Thinking Like an Anthropologist," and "Thinking Like an Artist." During these first 2 years, we included a second professional reading session each day so that participants would have an opportunity to read and discuss selected journal articles and book chapters. Last summer we used the first two chapters of *Mind Matters* as a common reading for "Sign Systems Day" but substituted in its place four articles for the other days. Three of these were issues of *School Talk,* a new publication of the National Council of Teachers of English. Each eight-page issue of *School Talk* addresses a single topic and is designed with classroom teachers in mind. The issues we selected were *Why Talk About Phonics?* (Routman & Butler, 1995), *Invented Spelling: What It Is and What It Isn't* (Routman & Butler, 1996), and *So You Want to Use Portfolios: Perspectives, Possibilities, and Pitfalls* (Routman & Butler, 1997). Another new choice you might also wish to consider is *The Teaching of Reading Strategies* (Maxim & Five, 1997). For "Inquiry Day," we selected an article by Kathy Short which appeared in *Learning* entitled "Inquiring into Inquiry" (1997). We read each of these articles in class using the "Say Something Strategy" (Harste, Short, with Burke, 1988) in which participants pair up and say something after natural breaking points in the article. We used the last 15 minutes of this strand to hold a whole class discussion with various participants taking responsibility for orchestrating this event.

The Seminar Strand. This strand was designed to take advantage of the experiences and expertise within the group. We gave the first seminar which, as mentioned, was a conceptual overview of the course and an introduction to our current thinking about "education as inquiry." Although we invited local teacher researchers to talk about what they were exploring in their classrooms in the name of inquiry-based instruction, often participants in each of the workshops we offered had things they wished to share. One local teacher talked about how she was using process drama to help students in her classroom comprehend and interpret novels. Another teacher shared how she organized literature circles in her classroom. On other occasions we have had teachers share a professional book they found helpful or lead a discussion about a student they found problematic. Often we bring in guests such as local writers or colleagues from the university who have expertise in special education, multicultural education, or some area of the language arts.

The Research Strand. As the intent of this strand is to support teachers in using their classrooms as sites of inquiry, we use the week to walk teachers through a mini-inquiry of their own. We begin on Monday by making a mini-inquiry journal using the book making procedures outlined in *Creating Classrooms for Authors and Inquirers* (Short, Harste, with Burke, 1996) and by identifying and sharing a talent that we have, be that Japanese floral arrangements, cake decorating, French hair braiding, or you name it. Given the array of talents displayed, participants are asked to select one thing they would like to learn to do. On Tuesday they find something to read about their topic and record initial thoughts and notes in their mini inquiry journal. On Wednesday they conduct interviews and one half of the class has a hands-on experience relating to their topic of study. Interview notes and notes taken during the hands-on experience are recorded in mini-inquiry journals as well. On Thursday the other half of the class repeats the process. On Friday participants demonstrate their new talents and walk us through their mini-inquiry journals, describing what they see as highlights of learning and insights into curriculum. While these presentations are going on, participants conduct a second inquiry searching for what they see as commonalities as well as tensions between and among the experiences shared. Throughout this strand, we talk about the importance of 24-hour inquiries and how variations of this strategy might be used with students in their classroom as well as how they, themselves, can use this strategy to follow up on professional readings and questions they have about teaching.

The Multiple Sign Systems Strand.   Often this strand focuses on responding to children's literature and involves an activity. Over the years we have begun this strand in any number of ways, sometimes by simply reading a children's book and asking participants to respond by noting one observation, one surprise, one connection, and one question in a literature response log we have created (see Short, Harste, with Burke, 1996 for alternative ideas). One of our favorite engagements is what we call "The Molly Bang Strategy" (Short, Harste, & Burke, 1996). This strategy is based on the book *Picture This* (Bang, 1991) and features Molly Bang, the author and illustrator, demonstrating how she uses simple shapes, colors, and the placement of objects to create alternating moods within the story *Little Red Riding Hood*. We walk participants through the book, then hand them four sheets of construction paper (one red, one black, one white, and one light purple) and ask them to create a scary picture within 5 minutes. At the end of the time we lay our pictures out, discuss what makes them scary or not so scary and what authors can do about it, and then take them back to finish the work. It is only at this point that authors can use glue. Similarly, in the video *Eric Carle, Picture Maker* (Philomel Books, 1993), the artist demonstrates his collage technique for making illustrations by first preparing "papers" and then cutting out shapes that form pictures. After seeing the video, participants are given tissue paper, tempera paint, newspapers, and are invited to try their hand using the same procedures as Carle, preparing their own "papers" on the first day of this project, and then cutting out shapes to make their own collages on a second day. Although Molly Bang and Eric Carle have been staples during this strand, we have used various books and engaged participants in such activities as Sketch to Stretch, Process Drama, Math Investigations, and Chunk Time (in which we put out a variety of curricular invitations and allow participants to work through as many as they can; see Short, Harste, with Burke, 1996 for details).

Demonstrations. Frank Smith (1981) defined a demonstration as a display of how something was done. He saw every act of literacy as full of demonstrations. Through engagement in literacy events we learn what topics are appropriate to talk about under what conditions, how to add humor to what we are saying, how we position ourselves to gain respect from our listeners, and so on. The notion of demonstration is why most of what we know about language is learned from being in the presence of other language learners. In similar regard, we see this strand as an opportunity to learn from demonstrations. Specifically, we focus this strand on methodologies that researchers have used to take a closer and more careful look at language and language learning. Although topics have changed over the years, we typically conduct sessions on miscue analysis (Goodman, Watson, & Burke, 1987) as well as study how the writing of children changes over time. We watch a videotape of a group of kindergarten children having a literature discussion and together create rubrics we can use in assessing and documenting what was going on (see Epstein segment in the videotape, *Literature Discussions*, NCTE, 1997). These techniques for looking closely reflect who we are and what we believe. We recommend that persons designing workshops based on our framework select techniques with which they are familiar and that they personally find powerful in terms of understanding reading, writing, and learning more generally.

The Reflexivity Strand. To introduce this strand we share reflective entries from our own professional journals. For example, Harste shares his sketch journal (for concrete examples of what is included in one of his journals see Harste & Vasquez, 1998) and talks about how he uses this journal to rethink teaching, record observations, plan conference presentations, take notes during presentations, and the like. Participants are then encouraged to start their own sketch journals. To this end and towards the end of each day, we ask students to write a reflection in which they focus on the connections they made between class engagements and their own. In similar regard, we ask them to pay particular attention to things that did not quite make sense, violated what they knew, or surprised them. We collect these entries at the end of each day and respond to students as our own form of homework. This strand allows us to make connections with each workshop participant and encourages participants to begin asking their own inquiry questions. Many participants keep these sketchbooks going long after the workshop is over.

New Curricular Engagements Strand. We end each day thinking concretely about curriculum. This strand provides opportunities for teachers to try out holistic strategies in a supportive environment. We have pilfered ideas for this strand from several colleagues. Pat Smith's strategy entails reading a familiar children's book like *Where the Wild Thing Are* (Sendak, 1988) and then charting what readers liked and disliked about the book as well as questions it raised and patterns it presented. Groups of three students fill out one form to insure collaboration, share their entries with the whole and then return to their triads to discuss what others had mentioned that they had never thought about. Literature Circles (Short, Harste, with Burke, 1996) is another strategy we introduce. Typically, we invite participants into this strategy by giving them a choice of short stories we have culled from Cynthia Rylant's *Every Living Thing* (1985). Participants form groups according to the story they selected and meet to discuss it. After 15 to 20 minutes of discussion time, we bring them back together and ask about what they observed happening in their groups, and how this experience compared to typical literature discussion groups with their students. In addition to living the curriculum, on alternate days we show videotapes of classrooms in action. While we change selections often, some of our favorites are *Voice & Choice, Alternate Sign Systems, Literature Guilds, Education as Inquiry,* as well as any of several other tapes in *The Authoring Cycle* and *Visions of Literacy* videotape series available from Heinemann (Harste & Jurewicz, 1988, 1990–1996). On Friday we typically show *An Amusement Park for Birds* (Forman & Gandini, 1995), a particularly suggestive video showing the Reggio Emilia program in action in preschool classrooms. Without fail, participants walk away with new visions of curriculum, which according to at least one participant, "keep me up all night."

Some Other Things You Need to Know

This course carries three graduate credits and is taken by teachers who are either actively pursuing a master's degree or updating this professional certification. By law in Indiana, teachers must take at least 6 credits of graduate work every 5 years. Teachers who are not enrolled in a master's program are more apt to take courses during the summer than during the academic year, and they tend to prefer the workshop format, which condenses the course into 5 or 6 long days and does not require them to do homework, as would a regular class taken at the university during the year. We have found that teachers prefer taking our workshop off-campus, at a local elementary school. During the 3 years that we have offered this workshop, we have identified schools in three different areas of our city to host this course. Principals like this idea because it makes it easy for their teachers to attend. We like it because we get lots of space to spread out and because we see a school as the most authentic environment for the course.

Issues We Have Grappled With

Tension, rather than consensus, drives the learning process in the education-as-inquiry model. All perspectives are not equal when we say up front that we value education that opens up rather than closes down the inquiry questions of all learners—ourselves as well as others. In many ways this workshop begins to build a diversity as opposed to a consensus model of education. Under these conditions we are never surprised when some participants inevitably share their feelings of discomfort. They want everyone to agree, plain and simple, and see no constructive value in achieving a state of tension. With these students, it's a constant effort to keep the conversation going.

With other participants, we have found it difficult (if not downright impossible) to move them out of their comfort zones. These are the ones who say, "Oh, I already do that," no matter how outrageous our suggestions become. With them, we sense that it will be "business as usual" when they get back to their classrooms at the end of the summer. While talking with several hard-to-move teachers during our second summer, Jerry finally gave up and said, "So, I guess you're going to do the same old crap when you get back to school next month ..." This assessment was not taken philosophically by these teachers, and the complaint appeared in several of their final course evaluations saying "He called our teaching crap!"

There are, of course, positive and negative aspects of meeting for 9 hours a day, five days in a row. First, on the positive side:

1. Total immersion. Often we have found we get further in five days than we do when we distribute the same content over a semester in three hour blocks of time once a week.
2. There are few distractions. Teachers have cleared their week and expect to devote full time to their learning. We tell them in a letter prior to coming to the first class to dispense of as many household duties as they can as there won't be time for both. We are often rewarded with amusing but pitiful tales of husbands who have had to run things and the catastrophes that their absence has caused.
3. The community that is built during the week is powerful. Often, teacher study groups have spontaneously formed and go on long after the workshop is over.

On the negative side:

1. The time element is exhausting for both participants and instructors. These are long days which we try to lighten with frequent coffee and bathroom breaks. As instructors we have a lot of materials to get prepared and hardly a moment between the end of one day and the beginning of the next.
2. Participants don't have time to reflect as deeply as we would like them to. While we push teachers to think about what kinds of mini-inquiries they might conduct in their classrooms to answer their new inquiry questions, there is no time for immediate follow through. Without doubt, the work-

shop would be improved if teachers could plan mini-inquiries based on their own questions, collect data from students in their own classroom, and bring this data and their results back to the group for discussion.

Despite difficulties such as these, we love teaching this workshop. Most participants grow by leaps and bounds and several have started their own inquiry-based classrooms. We know, because they work with us during the course of the normal year.

We started this article by asking you to think of the luxury of spending a whole day thinking about only just one topic. It doesn't happen often. Neither does having a sustained conversation with the same group of people over 5 weekdays. We see it as a model we can all learn from.

REFERENCES

Bang, M. (1991). *Picture this: Perception and composition.* Boston: Little, Brown.

Forman, G., & Gandini, L. (1995). *An amusement park for birds* (videotape). Amherst, MA: Performanetics.

Goodman, Y., Watson, D. J., & Burke, C. L. (1987). *Reading miscue inventory: Alternative procedures.* New York: Owens.

Harste, J. C. (Host & Developer), & Juerwicz, E. (Producer & Director). (1988). *The authoring cycle* (videotape series). Portsmouth, NH: Heinemann.

Harste, J. C. (Host & Developer), & Juerwicz, E. (Producer & Director). (1990–1996). *Visions of literacy* (videotape series). Portsmouth, NH: Heinemann.

Harste, J. C., & Vasquez, V. (1998). The work we do: Journal as audit trail. *Language Arts, 75*(4), 266–276.

Harste, J. C., Woodward, V. A., & Burke, C. L. (1984). *Language stories and literacy lessons.* Portsmouth, NH: Heinemann.

Kirby, D., & Kuykendall, C. (1991). *Mind matters.* Portmouth, NH: Boynton Cook.

Maxim, D., & Five, C. L. (1997). The teaching of reading strategies. *School Talk, 3*(1), 8 pages.

National Council of Teachers of English. (1995). *Literature discussions* (videotape). Urbana: NCTE.

Philomel Books, Inc. (1993). *Eric Carle, picture writer* (videotape). New York: Philomel Books and Scholastic.

Routman, R., & Butler, A. (1995). Why talk about phonics? *School Talk, 1*(2), 8 pages.

Routman, R., & Maxim, D. (1996). Invented spelling: What it is and what it isn't. *School Talk, 1*(4), 8 pages.

Routman, R. & Maxim, D. (1997). So you want to use portfolios: Perspectives, possibilities, and pitfalls. *School Talk, 2*(3), 8 pages.

Rylant, C. (1985). *Every living thing.* New York: Turtleback.

Sendak, M. (1988). *Where the wild things are.* New York: Turtleback.

Short, K. G., Harste, J. C., with Burke, C. L. (1996). *Creating classrooms for authors and inquirers* (2nd ed.). Portsmouth, NH: Heinemann.

Short, K. G. (1997). Inquiring into inquiry. *Learning, 97*(6), 55–57.

Smith, F. (1981). Demonstration, engagement, and sensitivity: The choice between people and programs. *Language Arts, 58*(1), 634–642.

Sample Syllabus
Creating Curricular Invitations: Reading, Writing, Inquiry

	Monday Reading Day	Tuesday Writing Day	Wednesday Sign Systems Day	Thursday Inquiry Day	Friday Evaluation Day
Composing Strand	Earliest Memories of Reading	Family Stories	Sign System Demonstrations	Sharing Our Best Learning Moments	Celebrating Authorship
Making Connections Strand	Why Talk About Phonics?	Invented Spelling: What It Is and Isn't	Mind Matters (2 chapters)	Inquiring into Inquiry	So You Want to Use Portfolios
Seminar Strand	What Do We Mean By "Education as Inquiry"?	Writing (guest author or teacher)	Sign Systems (guest author or teachers)	Inquiry (guest author or teachers)	Evaluation (guest author or teachers)
Research Strand	Sharing a Talent	Record Initial Hopes and Fears; Read	Conduct Interviews; Hands-on Lesson	Conduct Interviews; Hands-on Lesson	Share New Talents; Share New Insights into Inquiry from Experience
Multiple Sign Systems Strand	Children's Book: Record: 1 observation; 1 surprise; 1 connection; 1 question	Molly Bang Strategy	Eric Carle, Picture Writer	Process Drama	Sketch to Stretch Week's Workshop Experience
Demonstrations Strand	Miscue Analysis: Looking Closely at Reading	Kid Watching: Kammi	Using Sign Systems to Study Literature	Evluating Inquiry-Based Learning Using Rubrics	Portfolio Sharing as a Way to Evaluate This Workshop
Reflexivity Strand	Share Sketch Journal	Reflective Journal Writing Time	Reflective Journal Writing Time	Reflective Journal Writing Time	Reread Entries: Share Insights

35

History of American
Reading Instruction

James V. Hoffman
The University of Texas at Austin

Summer school is one of the few times during the year when there is room for some 'creative' course offerings at the graduate level. My experiences with the history of reading course grew out of chance discovery of a small, described to me as temporary, 'curriculum materials' library set apart physically from the main library but still on campus. I was doing some background research at the time on the uses of oral reading between the period 1880–1920. Several of the references I needed were from instructional materials popular during this time. Eventually, I found myself trudging over to a nondescript three-story building about six blocks from the college of education. It was clear to me upon entry that this building had not been designed as a library facility. The layout was awkward, the shelves temporary, and the lighting horrible. There was a central desk with a librarian, but I could not see anyone else in the building—staff or visitor. I gave the librarian the call numbers for the books I wanted. She appeared to be in mild shock that anyone had come into the building. The next thing I knew, she sent me on up to the third floor. I do not recall on that first visit if I located the texts I had come for. I was overwhelmed immediately with the vast (and I mean vast) collection of curriculum materials on the shelves. Row after row of reading curriculum materials. I first encountered books from the 1950s and 1960s—ones vaguely familiar to me from my own days in school. But as I worked my way through the collection I discovered books from the early 1900s, from the early 1800s, and even books from the 1700s. The books were not protected in any particular way. In fact, many of the books were crumbling. But just as many, including an original *New England Primer* were in mint condition. I stayed for hours. I came back again and again. Not only was I free to look around I could check out any of the books with no restrictions. The vast majority of the books had never been checked out before. A few had been checked out by someone in the early 1950s. (This was a pattern we were to find out later in connection to a Master's thesis on beginning reading instructional materials published in 1953.)

I made up my mind at that point that reading these books would be a wonderful context for exploring the history of reading. I scheduled the course for the summer. There were only eight students enrolled that first summer—all of them doctoral students in Language an Literacy Studies. I remember thinking all through that summer that this is what graduate seminars should be like—faculty and students on a joint inquiry. The person (a male this time, not a female) staffing the desk was a little concerned the first day of class when all nine of us showed up to visit the third floor. I could sense that he was wavering the next day on whether he should call someone to check on whether we should be allowed to enter the stacks. The students (all female) solved the problem the next day when they appeared at the library with fresh-baked cookies. They took turns bringing treats and smiling appropriately each day. No calls were made. The doors remained open to us. The treasure hunt was on.

The basic plan of attack for the course was to immerse ourselves in the materials from each of Nila B. Smith's periods. We looked at the books she looked at and we looked at books from the same period she does not mention. We compared her interpretations with our own. Issues arose but for the most part we gained a profound respect and regard for her scholarship. We read outside of these texts (philosophers mostly). We conducted abbreviated 'life histories' of key figures in the field. But the core experience was and has remained the reading of the books.

I have taught the course every other summer since the first year. Next summer will mark the fourth offering. Regrettably, the books were moved after the first year into a more remote library, in climate controlled conditions. We can't roam the stacks any more—a disappointment. But they show up for us at the main library with a one day notice. It has become almost a ritual to see the librarians carefully hand these fragile books from the late 1700s and early 1800s over to us to walk out the door. I suspect that sometime soon, someone will put a stop to this and the books will be restricted to room use only. This is probably the right thing to do … but I shall always miss the excitement of discovery that came with our first exploration.

REFERENCES

Austin, M., & Coleman, M. (1963). *The first R: The Harvard report on reading in American schools.* Cambridge, MA: Harvard University Press.

Chall, J. (1967). *Learning to read: The great debate.* New York: McGraw-Hill.

Flesch, R. (1981). *Why Johnny can't read: And what you can do about it.* New York: Harper & Row.

Huey, E. B. (1908). *Psychology and pedagogy of reading, with a review of the history of reading and writing and of methods, texts and hygiene in reading.* New York: Macmillan.

Manguel, A. (1997). A history of reading. London: Flamingo.

Olson, D. R. (1996). *The world on paper: The conceptual and cognitive implications of writing and reading.* Cambridge: Camridge University Press.

Smith, N. B. (1965). *American reading instruction.* Newark, DE: International Reading Association.

Sample Syllabus

Course Overview

The focus for this course will be an historical analysis of the methods and materials used in beginning reading instruction in American education. We will examine trends in curriculum and instruction as they relate to various sources of influence. This will be a "hands-on" course in the sense that we will spend a considerable amount of time examining materials that are part of the vast collection at The University of Texas at Austin. We will also identify and review specific contributions of prominent reading educators to research and practice.

For the most part, we will adopt a fairly traditional approach to historical research (as illustrated in our basic course text written by Nila Banton Smith). We will examine reading instruction as represented in primary and secondary sources (e.g., artifacts, reports), and then attempt to tease out the forces at work in producing changes in practice. Areas of primary interest will be: philosophical schools of thought (educational and otherwise), technological changes, societal issues, and research (educational research in particular). I would like to explore also some of the notions of the critical theorists related to history, in particular the focus on the treatment of race, class, and gender issues as revealed in the changes in reading instruction. One individual who has written from this perspective (with a particular focus on reading) is Patrick Shannon. You might want to seek out his book entitled Broken Promises as a supplementary text for this course.

Texts

Required:

American Reading Instruction. Nila Banton Smith, International Reading Association. 1965 (required). This book is out of print. I am exploring alternative publication routes. (Readings Packet IT Copy)

Why Johnny Can't Read, Rudolf Flesch; or *Learning to Read: The Great Debate*, Jeanne Chall; or *The First R: The Harvard Report on Reading in American Schools*, M. Austin & C. Morrisson.

Book Club Selections:

The World on Paper	David Olson
The Psychology and Pedagogy of Reading	Edmund Huey
Broken Promises	Patrick Shannon
History of Reading	Alberto Manguel

Primary Data Sources:

Textbooks/Materials (Teacher editions and Pupil's editions)

Research Reports/Monographs

Anecdotes—Literary

"Courses of Study"/State Guidelines

Method's Texts

Journal Articles and "Yearbooks"

Other Readings:

Other articles are also included in this course. (A listing of the additional sources can be found on the Web site accompanying this book.) Due dates for discussion and response will be negotiated.

Course Format

This course will be organized around a seminar format. We will rely on individual/group inquiry followed by presentations and class discussion. There will be no formal lectures. Most classes will begin with student presentations and discussion. These presentations will be followed by a discussion of readings from Smith's *American Reading Instruction*.

Requirements

1. Choose one instructional material/program from each of Smith's periods (after the Religious), or choose a book written during each of these periods that focuses on reading instruction. Write a two-three page summary of the material/program or book. Focus on philosophy, goals, activities and standards. An oral presentation will be required. These brief presentations will be scheduled throughout the session. There are a total of seven presentations/papers associated with this requirement. The oral presentations should last somewhere between 15 and 20 minutes.

For the instructional materials, focus your critical analysis on such areas as:

Explicit or Assumed Audience	Who would be using these materials?
Curricular Content	What is being taught?
Literary Content	What is the source? What is reflected?
Linguistic Form(s)	What about the language?

Organization	Levels, correlated materials, and so forth
Pedagogy	What teaching processes are encouraged?
Rhetoric	What appeals are made?
Roots/Influences	Cultural/Historical/Social? Religious? Economic? Philosopical? Research?
Authors	Who are they? What do we know about them?
Popularity	How widely were these materials used? Over what time frame?
Smith	How does the program/approach connect to Smith's descriptions?
Personal Reactions	Open-ended

For book analyses, you will need to adapt the framework to work for you. Most of the questions will still apply.

   2. Choose one of the following:

A.   Write a 5- to 10-page paper (maximum) describing some instructional material, approach, innovation and/or controversy associated with beginning reading instruction. You may choose to focus in very tightly on some aspect of one of Smith's periods (e.g., vocabulary control in readers; sexism in literature), or you may choose to approach the period in more general terms. Present an oral report of your research to the class. (*Note:* An example of a report from a previous semester can be found on the Web site accompanying this book.)

B.   Choose a prominent reading educator from one of Smith's periods. Write a 10-page paper (maximum) describing the intellectual history and major contributions of this individual to the field of reading education. Include a bibliography. You will present an oral report on the individual you have chosen to study. (*Note:* An example of a report from a previous semester can be found on the Web site accompanying this book.)

Note: All written assignments should be completed following APA guidelines for manuscript preparation.

3. Join a Book Club

A.   Form a group and read one of the books identified as optional.

B.   Pace yourself through the book so you will be prepared to report on your book to the class during the last week of the first summer session.

C.   Meet, a minimum, of three times during the session with your group to discuss the reading. Have a recorder take notes on your discussion. You will need to turn in your record of discussion at the end of the term.

D.   Your report back to the whole class can be creative or boring. Choose creative.

4. Read *Why Johnny Can't Read*. I will give you a completion date. Be prepared to discuss.

Extra Credit

You won't have time. But if you are interested, "Wanda K. Moore," we can talk about options.

Grading

All written reports and oral talks will be graded on an acceptable/not acceptable basis. Your major project will be graded on an A–F scale following University guidelines for grades: content, depth of research, elaboration of ideas, organization, insight, and form will be considered. I am willing to accept any assigned writing turned in before the final week of classes and give you feedback for revision purposes. Your report grade will be your final grade, assuming all of the short reports are acceptable. No final grade will be awarded until the short reports have reached the acceptable level. Class participation will be considered in borderline cases.

Getting Started

We will spend some of our early time in an orientation phase. We will visit the libraries and get some help in how to access information. I will suggest some readings to get you going. As soon as possible, start locating curriculum materials and begin your work. You may also want to start identifying some key figure that you would like to research.

I have ordered many of the curriculum materials from the earliest periods and they will be on reserve at the PCL library. You can check them out on a limited time basis. For the remaining periods, you will have to order the materials yourself and check them out directly. You need to plan ahead as the materials are not located at the PCL, but in a remote storage library. It may take a day or to get the books you order.

Dates/Schedule

This is a very rough outline of topics. It will certainly shift as we move through the course in a flexible manner. Each week we will look ahead at the schedule and make the necessary adjustments.

Sample Summer Schedule

Class #1   June 4   Wednesday

    Course Orientation

    Browse the IRA From Hornbook to Storybook publication in preparation for Class #2.

    Read Course Packet (#2) articles sections 3 and 4 as a follow up to class discussions.

Class #2   June 5   Thursday

    Class field trip to the HRC. Meet in our classroom and we will walk up together. Bring your #2 Packet from IT Copy.

    Locate one set of materials and examine it in detail.

    Prepare a brief presentation for Friday, June 6.

    No written report is required for this presentation.

    Read Smith: Chapters I and II (1650–1776) in preparation for the June 6th discussion.

Class #3   June 6   Friday

    Discussion of the materials reviewed from Thursday in relation to Smith's chapters I and II.

    Read Smith Chapter III

    Read and conduct analysis of the materials for The Nationalistic Moralistic Period (Report #1) to be presented on Wednesday.

Class #4   June 11   Wednesday

    Reports on Nationalistic and Moralistic Period. (Report #1)

    Read Smith Chapter IV for Friday.

    Read and conduct analysis of the materials for Intelligent Citizenship Period (Report #2) to be presented on Friday.

    For Thursday's class, read Literacy and the Common School Packet #2.

    UP CLOSE: Noah Webster

Class #5   June 12   Thursday

    Philosophical influences on education.

    Discuss Common School Movement and census data.

    UP CLOSE: Horace Mann

Class #6   June 13   Friday

Reports on Intelligent Citizenship (Report #2) and discussion of Smith's Chapter IV.

Read Smith Chapter V for Monday.

Read and conduct analyses of Materials for Cultural Asset Period for presentation on Monday (Report #3).

UP CLOSE: William McGuffy

Class #7   June 23   Monday

Reports on Cultural Asset Period. Report #3

Relate to Smith's chapter V.

Read Huey and Fries from Packet Materials for Tuesday.

Read Smith's Chapter VI for Wednesday.

Read and prepare reports (#4) for Wednesday.

Class #8   June 24   Tuesday

Discuss the Huey and Fries chapters.

Discuss the word and sentence methods.

Class #9   June 25   Wednesday

Materials presentations for the Scientific Investigations Period.

Report #4. Relate to Smith's chapter VI.

Read Smith's Chapter VII for Wednesday July 2 on Intensive Research and Application Report #5.

Prepare materials reports for July 2 class.

For Thursday Read Venezky's report on research.

UP CLOSE: William S. Gray

Class #10   June 26   Thursday

Discuss Venezky

Read Smith Chapter VIII for Thursday July 3

Prepare materials report for the International Conflict period to be presented on Thursday, July 3rd. Report #6.

UP CLOSE: John Dewey

Class #11   July 2   Wednesday

Present reports on Expansion and Application Period.

Discuss Smith Chapter VII. (Report #5).

Read Smith Chapter VIII for Monday July 7

Prepare materials report for the International Conflict period to be presented on Monday, July 7. (Report #7).

Class #12   July 3   Thursday

Report on Smith Chapter VIII. Report on materials from the International Conflict Period. Report #6

The Oral/Silent Reading Debate

Read Smith Chapter IX. Prepare report on materials from the Expanding Knowledge period. Report #7.

Read: *Why Johnny Can't Read*, or *Learning to Read the Great Debate*, or *The First R: The Harvard Report of Reading in American Schools*.

Class #13   July 7   Monday

Report on materials review for the Expanding Knowledge Period.

Report #7.

Relate to Smith's Chapter IX.

Discuss assigned readings.

Prepare for reports from book clubs for Tuesday, July 8.

Class #14   July 8   Tuesday

Book Club Reports

From 1965–1970   Hoffman's view ...

Prepare for Project Reports for Wednesday.

Class #15   July 9   Wednesday

From 1970–1990   Hoffman's view ...

Project Reports.

36

Negotiating a Syllabus for a Doctoral Course in the Psychology and Pedagogy of Literacy[1]

Richard E. Ferdig
P. David Pearson
Michigan State University

PSYCHOLOGY AND PEDAGOGY OF LITERACY AS SEEN THROUGH THE EYES OF THE INSTRUCTOR (OF RECORD)

I have been teaching college level courses in reading, language arts, and literacy since 1967, but it was not until the fall of 1998, some 31 years after I began my college teaching career, that I figured out how to engage students in the teaching-learning process. Fittingly, it was a course with a title that began, "The Psychology and Pedagogy …," that the epiphany came to me. Ironically, it was the size of the course (it had ballooned to initial enrollment of 20 because I had overlooked my responsibility to set enrollment limits) that paved the way for the discovery by forcing me to abandon my traditional seminar style, a highly teacher-centered Socratic dialogue, in favor of some other alternative means of organizing our encounters with the ideas, texts, and issues of the course.

---

[1] David Pearson was the instructor of record for the course described in this chapter. Rick Ferdig was a doctoral student who took the course and assumed a major role in setting up the Web-based environment that became the structural frame that allowed us to organize and document our experiences in the course. If we were really true to the collaborative spirit of the course, we would have listed 19 other coauthors of this article. They were, in a very real sense, equally responsible for authoring the course as we were. Rick and David, however, were the ones who set pen to paper. The organization of the chapter is as follows. First, David gives his reflections on the course, then Rick does likewise.

The fundamental question was how, in the face of such a large seminar enrollment, to achieve a high level of engagement, "floor time" (opportunity to shape the conversation), and opportunity to talk with the instructor. My first impulse was to do a lot of preplanning—to be very judicious in selecting the texts we would read and the formats (some combination of whole class and small group activities presented themselves to me). Then it occurred to me that if I did all that work up-front, I would be denying students, most of whom aspired to be professors themselves one day, an apprenticing opportunity. Why not have them participate in the process of selecting the readings and shaping the activities for our weekly sessions (the class had been scheduled for 4–7 on Thursday afternoons)?

I would set the broad topics, such as The Nature of the Reading Process, Early Literacy, Beginning Reading Instruction, Comprehension and Response to Literature, Remediation, and the Role of Research in Policy and Practice, and I would take responsibility for the first session and the last topic. Students would volunteer for one of the 5 topical teaching teams. Each team would meet outside of class time, initially with me and often on their own, to develop a reading list and a set of activities for each topic. In a sense, each group had the responsibility of building a syllabus for their topic. With an enrollment of 20, five groups of four worked out just fine.

In the initial meeting with each group, we would brainstorm the topic, trying to figure out how to deconstruct the topic and how we might ensure some rhetorical and methodological diversity among the pieces selected for each topic. Our first meeting usually ended with a provisional reading list and some assignments: Gina might read these three candidates for a research piece on phonemic awareness and pick one for all of us to read, or Dan might go on a search for a recent article on reader response pedagogy for secondary students that employed ethnographic methods).

Students also shaped the assignments and the activities, for which I was very grateful. Left to my own devices, I would have overrelied, I am sure, on whole class discussions just to make sure that everyone got to hear the same messages and insights from their peers. They knew, all too well, that the more we relied on whole class formats, the less opportunity they and their peers would have for active participation. So we spent most of our time in small group activities. I freely admit that I was initially very uncomfortable with this approach, mainly because I could not monitor and shape the quality and focus of the discussion in every group. I also freely admit that I came to understand and appreciate just how important small group opportunities are for doctoral students who are in the process of trying to figure out what and how they think about their future interests. So, I decided that instead of trying to get around to each of the small groups, I would make myself a real member of one group each week. Over the course of the semester, I tried to ensure that I was in a small group with each student at least twice.

The topical teaching groups really worked well. The students took the task seriously, worked tirelessly to find just the right set of pieces for their colleagues, and planned elaborately for activities that would engage everyone. They also expressed all the anxieties and frustrations associated with teaching—too much to cover, not enough time, clever activities that do not quite work, and puzzlements when their students did not find the pieces as scintillating as they did.

The other novel piece was the electronic component, organizing electronic forums and creating a Web site for the course—a public space in which we could share, at least with one another, the fruits of our labors. I wanted to try the forum approach as a way of increasing whole class dialogue. I knew that we would be working in small groups much of the time, and I worried, as I said earlier, that some of us might miss some of the insights that occurred in other groups. And this is where Rick, who had just become my advisee in the Educational Psychology doctoral program, came in. Rick was experienced in and very comfortable with a wide range of new technological developments, and he knew a lot about how to create them and how to shape them to achieve particular goals. As Rick's reflections on the course reveal, his colleagues had some initial concerns about the technology and the Web-based discussion, but after a few unnatural acts designed to get folks into the forum, we were able to create a vibrant, substantive, voluntary discussion forum.

Earlier, I alluded to the fact that I had been teaching for a long time and become comfortable, perhaps even complacent, with a particular structure and set of teacher-student relationships. This class was a watershed experience for me. First, it helped me realize how much opportunity for engagement and learning I had been squelching in the past by my insistence on the Socratic dialogue as the sole seminar model. Second, I learned how much students can contribute to the course, not only by their participation but also by their active engagement in shaping the readings and the activities. Third, I learned about the value added of the technology component, both the online forum discussion and the web as a home page to house our collective efforts and artifacts. Fourth, I learned that it is useful to regard the syllabus one hands out at the beginning of the course as a starting point, an invitation to begin the journey. The real syllabus can only be constructed along the way, as one fills out the pages in the journal that documents the journey. You never know what it looks like until you have arrived at your destination.

PSYCHOLOGY AND PEDAGOGY OF LITERACY AS SEEN THROUGH THE EYES OF A STUDENT (WITH TECHNOLOGY LENSES)

In the fall of 1998, I enrolled to take CEP 912: The Psychology and Pedagogy of Literacy, taught by P. David Pearson. I came into the course fascinated by technology, the role of narrative in learning, and the potential of technology in narrative-rich learning environments. I thought that taking the course would help ground the interest in narrative within the pedagogy of literacy. Further, I realized that taking the course from someone who has been a major contributor to the field of literacy over the last 30 years would offer a historical perspective and autobiography of where narrative had been prior to landing on my graduate doorstep.

The expectations of the semester were indeed high, and I am happy to say that many of my goals were realized. However, I also learned something valuable about pedagogy. The story I share has two parts reflecting the two roles I played during the course. First, I elaborate on the technology David and I attempted to introduce during the course and how that relates to the idea of a dynamic syllabus. Second, I share my experiences as a student during the integration of this dynamic system.

Technology Integration.   David's office is actually designed quite nicely for academia. It consists of a lobby area with space for administrative assistants and three rooms tied closely together. If a person wants to work alone, they need only retire to a room and close the door. However, when collaboration is called for, colleagues are in "talking" distance. It happened to be a late August "collaborative" day about a week before classes. David was in one office, Kara Lycke (another CEP912 student) was in the second, and I was hacking away in the third. I heard David call out, "What we need for this upcoming course is some type of collaborative tool that allows students to talk with one another outside of class.... We just don't have enough time in class to discuss all the things we need to."

With those words, we started thinking about how to incorporate technology into the course. We needed a place where we could disseminate information quickly and the creation of a Web site provided such a forum. It consisted of the following components:

- *Course Discussion*—The course discussion component was the interactive asynchronous tool that David had initially wanted. The discussion web was set-up as a Microsoft Frontpage Discussion web, which meant that students had the chance to post and reply to messages in a threaded manner. The messages were listed chronologically so students could return to previous discussions at any point during or after the course.
- *Course Information*—This area provided contextual comments about the course and potential perspectives to be encountered in the readings. It also described the assignments and related grading schemes. These assignments included a semester project, course readings, class participation, and web communication.
- *Course Notes*—At numerous times during David's course, graphs and charts were used to help clarify and organize major theoretical positions related to literacy and learning. The course notes section was a storage depot for those teaching aids.
- *Final Paper Abstracts*—As highlighted above, class participants were expected to complete a semester project which took the form of a major paper. Realizing that many papers might still be in draft form, the final paper nook was reserved for abstracts only. At the end of the semester, we left it up to the individual author as to whether they wanted their complete paper available to the general public.

- *Purpose of the Course*—A list of the goals and purposes of the course highlighted the home page of CEP912. It provided prospective and enrolled students with an idea of both the theoretical and philosophical foundations for the course.
- *Class List*—As one might expect, this area served as a contact/phone list for all of the participants in the course. During the first night's session, students were concerned (and rightly so) about putting their names and phone numbers on the Internet. Therefore, we created a "member" section of the Web site that was password protected. The class list became one of the first pages in the member section.
- *Schedule & Reading Lists*—One of the most important pieces of information to disseminate was of course the schedule and reading list. The web site became an important medium for this information because we knew the schedule and reading list would change and need to be updated occasionally.
- *Food and Group Lists*—Finally, the class was broken up into groups divided by areas of interest. Students also volunteered to bring food to class (it was a 4–7 dinner wrecker!). Both of these lists were added to the member section.

Many web pages consist of static information that is put on the web merely to disseminate information more easily. Initially, I would argue that we saw this as the main use of the Web site: a tool effective in posting pertinent information for potential or enrolled class participants.

However, when it came time for David and I to put the schedule/reading list and the discussion forum on the web, we started to realize that the web made the syllabus and the course a dynamic, living and breathing object. David had suggested that instead of taking sole responsibility for the readings, he would only suggest major content areas related to the psychology and pedagogy of literacy. For instance, we would want to discuss emergent literacy, beginning reading, and comprehension and response strategies. During the first class, we would form groups around areas of interest related to these major headings. Then, with the help of weekly group meetings with David, the groups would co-teach their interest area by selecting readings, leading discussions, and organizing activities. It was their responsibility then, to get the relevant information to the webmaster who could post the schedule and reading list to the web for immediate access.

This format of teaching not only highlighted a very social approach to learning and teaching, it also created a very dynamic class. Instead of having a static schedule that relied on the proverbial "sage on the stage," David was able to take a leadership role in helping the groups learn about their interest area of literacy, and, in turn, teach that to the rest of the class. However, because of David's experience and expertise, students were assured that they had freedom to explore without missing seminal pieces in the field. In this sense, the syllabus was always changing in large part due to the efforts of the class members.

The discussion component also added to the dynamic nature of the course. I believe David and I saw it as a valuable forum to continue conversations that time did not permit during the class sessions. However, it also became a place where students felt safe initiating their own discussions and conversations about certain readings, special topics in literacy, or problems/confusions that may have occurred during the week related to understanding the psychology and pedagogy of literacy.

In summary, we initially attempted to integrate technology into the course to provide efficient dissemination of information. However, as with most technological implementations, it afforded a conversation to start taking place between the students and the content of the course. In turn, the syllabus became a living object that changed as we journeyed towards learning about the pedagogy and psychology of literacy.

A Student's Perspective. As of this year, my 3rd year in the doctoral program at Michigan State University, I have spent the last 22 years either teaching or learning in a classroom setting. Over the course of those years, I have come to understand that a syllabus is to be seen as a roadmap with directions as follows:

- You are at X.
- You are taking this course to get to get to Y.
- Here's what to do to get there.

Needless to say, I was disoriented when David introduced the course by saying that we would make the syllabus as we went. Actually, excited is a better word. I knew the reasons why I was taking the course. I knew, as many students do on entering a course, that I was at X. However, I had always been told where Y was. Meaning, students are always told on entering a course, normally through the syllabus, where they are supposed to be and what they are supposed to learn by the end of the semester. However, I was told that Y would be decided as a class, in small groups, and as individuals. Maybe the disoriented part came when I was not sure about what to do in order to get there. We could not answer that question because we were not sure exactly where we were going.

There are three parts to my student perspective. This first part is a satisfied customer testimonial. This approach to teaching while learning about the psychology and pedagogy of literacy changed my perspective on teaching and learning and the achieved outcomes for the class. Again, in many classes, there is a prescribed outcome, where students feel like they have to take what they learn and apply it to their main area of interest. In this course, with this dynamic syllabus, I felt like what we learned was shaped by the interests and desires of the participants within the course.

The second component of this student perspective revolves around the issue of community. In classes I have taught, I always worry about the sense of trust and community. I have tried to build those things into the structure of the course. But, as teachers know, it is not something you can create artificially. In this course, I knew that I was responsible to a small group of members in learning about a specific topic.

However, I also knew that I was accountable to the large class in teaching them about my subject area. We grew to trust each other knowing that we were sharing our life goals (doctorally speaking, anyway) with each other. The class seemed to gel even though the class size was upwards of 20 students.

Finally, I speak as a student of technology. Technology people are generally the most critical of technological implementations, and David's class was no different for me. I was unsure, at first, if the technology would succeed. In other words, I needed to know what the value of the technology was. I wanted to be sure that the technology was really offering something that could not be done without the time and energy expense of technology. I was especially concerned when we started talking about requirements for web participation. Many chat rooms, listservs, and electronic communities are created and sustained because of a need within the group. Many do not succeed when the community is forced.

I knew that David was serious about the dynamic nature of this class when he cancelled mandatory web participation in the third or fourth week of the course. The comments and participation up until that time had been great. However, as Michael Pardales and other members of the class had noted, it seemed at times to be a bit forced. After the removal of the requirement, the web communication flourished. And, I began to see the value-added of the technology. Creating small groups opened up the floor to a variety of learning and teaching possibilities. However, having an optional discussion web site established a forum for discourse about where students wanted Y to be (where they wanted to go) and how to get there once Y was conceived. Potentially more importantly, the course web site began to grow as an archive of past discussion. It not only grounded us but also gave us direction and a sense of community membership.

There are many times when establishing a route from X to Y is a necessary and finite goal. For instance, my friends joke about a social teaching approach to learning morse code. However, establishing an authority as a guide and allowing students the opportunity to converse with the material brings them into the intellectual and discourse community surrounding literacy (or any topic for that matter). Further, the opportunity that technology affords in making syllabi more dynamic and interactive creates communities of learning—communities with a shared past and a socially constructed future.

THE SYLLABUS: A SNAPSHOT TAKEN
AT THE END OF THE COURSE

Space does not permit us to show you how the syllabus evolved, so we can only share what it looked like at the end of the course, after each group had put its signature on the syllabus by listing its readings and activities. We provide a brief synopsis of the final syllabus here. For a complete picture, the reader can visit the Web site accompanying this handbook.

Sample Syllabus

Purpose of the Course

This course is designed for doctoral students who want to grapple with key issues in reading—specifically an understanding of how individuals process written language and how they acquire competence in doing so. Within that broad scope, there are a number of enabling content goals. The course has a decided bias on the reading rather than the writing side of written language, a fact that, more than anything, reflects the interests and experiences of the instructor. With any luck, students who complete this course, should read about, understand, discuss, and/or critique:

- Major and competing theories of the psychology of the reading process,
- Key, and also competing, theories about the process of reading acquisition,
- The historical development of both sorts of theories,
- The role of research in the development and evaluation of these theories,
- Key relationships among reading, writing, and oral language,
- Some classic studies in the field of reading,
- Some important recent work, including exemplars of the key methodological traditions (experimental, correlational, synthetic, ethnographic, historical, philosophical, and critical),
- Key topics (reading before school, beginning reading instruction, comprehension processes, the role of text structure, metacognition and reading, remedial reading, and the like), and
- those phenomena (to use a word that avoids the associative link to positivism engendered by variable or factor) that impact the nature and quality of reading, with a decided emphasis on text, reader, and context.

Course Information

Some Contextual Comments About the Course.   This is not a course in post modern views of language, literacy, and learning. I say this only to make clear my perspective, as well as the perspectives you are likely to encounter in the bulk of the readings. This is not to say that we will not encounter post-modern thinking, research endeavors, or critiques. We will! But we will do so in the course of tracing out important developments in theory and research about reading and reading acquisition. If the course has a theoretical bias, it is probably the schema-based and strategicallyoriented views of learning that dominated the late the 1980s in the field of educational psychology and reading. This, at least in part, reflects my personal conviction that those views continue to provide compelling accounts of the nature of the reading process as well as the course of reading acquisition. It also reflects the fact that there are many other opportunities to encounter sociocultural and post-modern views of literacy and learning here on campus and in the college.

A Balancing Act.   To fully understand the psychology and pedagogy of reading and the other language arts (writing, speaking, listening) would require a working knowledge of many dimensions that we use as we study the research process: research paradigms (including assumptions about ontology and epistemology), research methods (especially experimental, ethnographic, and interpretive but also extending to other conceptual distinctions, such as qualitative–quantitative, correlational–experimental, empirical–interpretive, analytic–synthetic) the rhetorical conventions of academic prose, including the styles characteristic if different research traditions and historical periods. We will try to juggle all of these dimensions as we proceed through the course.

Assignments and Grading

I fully expect everyone in an advanced class such as this to attempt and earn either a 3.5 or a 4.0. To do so will require us to:

- Read a lot, sometimes critically and sometimes receptively.
- Write in response to the reading and share your responses, your questions, criticisms and puzzlements with the rest of us.
- Participate actively in classroom conversations, discussions (including electronic discussions), and presentations.
- Help organize and facilitate some of our class sessions (for each topical unit, I will ask a small group of students to work with me to organize the class sessions).
- Conduct some sort of special project that arises from the course content and meets your own needs and interests.
- Organize a set of artifacts that demonstrate that you have met the criteria/standards detailed below.
- Present work to your peers at the end of the course.

Although we will stop short of using a strict rubric in evaluating our work, we will use some consistent criteria to gauge our engagement with the ideas encountered in the class. My initial criteria (subject to negotiation) are completeness, complexity, and risk-taking. Completeness is met by engaging the broad array of the ideas encountered in the readings and discussions. Complexity is gauged by the number and depth of connections made with those ideas; connections can be personal, intratextual, and/or intertextual. Risk-taking refers to the extent to which

you are willing to take a critical stance toward these ideas, challenging their authority, the authority of their author(s), and even your own responses and interpretations
of the ideas. These are the lenses that I will try to keep uppermost in my thoughts as
I reflect on your contributions to our class. I hope you will learn to instantiate them
in a way that makes them meaningful to you.

The Special Project.   I want the special project to be an opportunity for individuals to pursue an issue, interest, question, or concern in more depth than is possible for the common topics. It can take many forms and foci. It could be a
conventional literature review, a critical analysis of a small set of important pieces of
research in the field, a small group replication of a classic work in the field, the expli-
cation of a new theory of reading, whatever. It can even be a rewrite of a paper that,
while started in another course, would benefit from a complete overhaul using the
perspectives and information encountered in this course.

Web-Based Communication.   To the extent that we are collectively and individually capable of entering into a virtual community, I would like to give it a shot this semester. With a little collaboration on our part, we can build a Web site that houses the
syllabus, the readings that would otherwise be handouts (assuming that we can get per-
missions), forums that can document (and shape) our responses to the readings and live
conversations in class, and sites in which we can share our ongoing work.

Deep Background Readings.   We will not be retreating to the beginnings of
literacy as we trace the development of theoretical accounts. Instead, we will begin
in the modern era of research, beginning just over 100 years ago. For those who have
not taken a course in the history of literacy, I want to recommend at least a perusal of
the following articles:

Venezky, R. L. (1984). The history of reading research. In P. D. Pearson, R. Barr, M. L.
    Kamil, & P. Mosenthal, (Eds.), *Handbook of reading research* (pp. 3–38). New York:
    Longman.
Olson, D. (1994). *The world on paper.* London: Cambridge University Press. The first cou-
    ple of chapters. Alternatively, there is an interesting interview with and introduction
    to Olson in one of the 1995 issues of *Written Communication.*

A chapter from somewhere on the history of teaching reading up to World War
II. I have a few in mind. See me if you feel the need for more background in this
area.

Issues/Topics Addressed.   Next, we have listed the issues/topics which were
addressed by the teaching groups. The readings and activities were the dynamic
part, the part that was negotiated as the course unfolded. For a complete picture of

the design of the course, the readings, and activities which were developed, see the Web site (http://reading.educ.msu.edu/courses/912/).

- The professional context of literacy research: How do scholars conceptualize research?
- The nature of the reading process: Current thinking
- Early literacy
- Beginning reading
- Comprehension and response
- Remediation
- The role of research in policy and practice.

37

Trends and Issues in Literacy:
A Focus on Balanced Instruction

Joyce E. Many
Georgia State University

I recognize that change is difficult and risky for most of us. Whatever we do for the first time, whether it is small-group guided reading, shared writing, integrating spelling, or holistic evaluation, we are bound to bungle it at the start. This is natural behavior for all new, comprehensive processes and procedures, and we need to be forgiving and patient with ourselves. The main thing is to begin, to give it a try.

—Routman (1991, p. 4)

A number of years ago, a teacher in one of my graduate classes brought in this quote to share. Since that time it has laced my speech and my teaching. Routman's words remain taped to my office door and the theme "be forgiving and be patient with yourself" weave in and out of my own self-talk and my words of support to other teachers. In the course I describe in this chapter, the teachers and I involved in the class were risk takers. Most of us were undertaking projects which were new, challenging, demanding, and exciting. The process was both exhilarating, stressful, and rewarding. We did bungle it at times, and we drew on each others' support and tried to be gentle with ourselves. But, overwhelmingly, we were glad we gave it a try.

At Georgia State University, we have a large selection of graduate literacy courses for masters, educational specialists, and doctoral level students. We have regularly scheduled courses related to literacy theories, research in various literacy fields, and pedagogy related to reading, writing, language arts, or literature. In addition, we also have a trends and issues course that can be used by faculty to focus on a specific topic or area of interest. We rotate this course around so that each of us has opportunity to teach a class relating to our particular area of expertise or to what we consider to be a burning issue.

In creating this rendition of our "trends course," I was inspired by my own changing interests over the last 5 years. I began my university work with a concentrated interest in children's literature, reader–response theory, and literature-based instruction. On accepting my position at Georgia State, I learned one focus of my new teaching responsibilities would be assessment of reading difficulties (an area in which I had previously not had extensive expertise). Consequently, I immersed myself in professional literature focusing on literacy assessment and instruction. As I reflected on the holistic, student-centered philosophy espoused in the works of theorists and researchers such as Carolyn Burke, Lynn Rhodes, Nancy Shanklin, and Marie Clay, I sharpened and expanded my understanding of the reading and learning process. Teaching assessment courses at GSU has also led me to consider new emphases within my orientation towards holistic literacy instruction. My involvement with teachers who work with struggling readers (and the tutoring I do with children in order to gain experience with the approaches we discuss in my classes) has increased my sense of the importance of explicit instruction within the context of literature-based instruction. Consequently, I have turned with interest to the scholarship of Michael Pressley, Penny Freppon, Steve Stall, and other proponents of a balanced approach to literacy and I have strived in my teaching to carefully articulate ways to provide for strategy instruction in the context of meaningful reading and writing tasks.

I began to design this trends and issues course as pre-registration for the course was underway. Enrollment grew from the expected 15 to 18 students to a total of 27 teachers. Reviewing the projected class list, I realized the participants ranged considerably in terms of the programs in which they were enrolled (master's degree students in reading and in English Education, EdS students in reading and middle childhood education, and PhD students in Language and Literacy), in areas of interest, and in grade level focus (early childhood through high school). I recruited a colleague, Mary Deming, to team teach the course with me and together we designed a course which provided an overview of balanced instruction while also allowing for focused study within particular areas of concentration (phonics, early reading instruction, writing, cognitive strategies instruction, and literature-based instruction).

Mary and I also decided to include a strong focus on technology within the course. Spurred on by a departmental hypertext demonstration, I had been motivated to integrate the creation of a CD-Rom into one of my courses. By having small groups collaborate on the creation of professional resources materials for inclusion on a CD-Rom, we realized we could create an atmosphere where our course work resulted in writing and producing materials for an authentic audience. Personally, we would also then be involved in exploring new forms of technology that we had not had time to learn.

From our point of view one of the most important things contributing to the success of the course was that we combined elements of choice along with an underlying framework of expectations. Consequently, although teachers were working on different areas of interest, minimum requirements regarding individual responsibilities and the group work were explicitly described. These detailed outlines provided a sense of clarity to the teachers' tasks and helped reduce the level of tension regarding what was expected.

In line with our course emphasis on balance, we realized we would need to provide opportunities to learn how to use technology as a tool without losing sight of our focus on exploring the literacy research, theories, and pedagogy related to balanced instruction. Consequently, as you will see in the sample syllabus which follows, we created three strands in the course. Each night we held discussions (breaking the large group into two smaller seminars) focusing on the overall trend to balanced instruction and then we broke into small content specific groups. The groups rotated between the computer lab time, a supper break, and a content-study discussion time. Using this framework for each week's 4-hour class session allowed us to work with smaller groups of individuals and guaranteed that we would have focused time to discuss content as well as to learn how to use the technology.

Personally, I found the course wonderfully demanding and informative, and at times stressful. I prefer to incorporate into my courses material that I have not read but I have long wanted to read. In this course, we followed that inclination. However, in addition to the common readings for the seminar discussions, as instructors we found ourselves needing to be familiar with the readings for eight different small groups. In addition, we needed to learn Dreamweaver, the software package that we were using to create our CD-Rom resource. As a coping mechanism, Mary and I decided to divide responsibilities. She would be the professor working with the small groups as they discussed their content, and I would be in the computer lab to work with the groups in creating their CD-Rom materials. This proved to be a helpful division of responsibilities, although it did mean that Mary did not get to learn as much about the technology and I did not get to read as much of the materials as we would have liked.

In working with the groups to create their CD-Rom materials, I was aided in my undertaking through a wonderful support system provided by our college's instructional technology center and I was comfortable learning the new technology. The difficult aspect for me was that, as a teacher, it was disconcerting to be working with groups and to come upon a problem that I might not have the knowledge or expertise to address. None of us had used this software previously and some in the class had never even worked with word processing software. I continually needed to reassure myself and the others in the class with Routman's words that I shared earlier, remembering that "we are bound to bungle it at the start" and that we need to be gentle with ourselves.

In retrospect, the course was an incredible learning experience for all of us. Luckily, Mary and I were naive regarding the complexity of the task we were undertaking, and therefore, we just charged on in. After you peruse the sample syllabus that follows, I encourage you to visit the web-based version of the Balanced Instruction Resource Material that the class participants created (http://msit.gsu.edu/balancedinstruction). We were amazed at the quality of the material that resulted from the class's efforts, and we were certainly pleased that, as Routman encourages, we did indeed give it a try.

REFERENCE

Routman, R. (1991). *Invitations: Changing as teachers and learners K–12.* Portsmouth, NH: Heinemann.

Sample Syllabus
Trends and Issues in Literacy

Catalogue Course Description

Analyzes current trends and issues in the field of literacy. The course features examination of the work of noted authorities and theorists, significant research, and current practices and direction.

Required Texts

McIntyre, E., & Pressley, M. (1996). *Balanced instruction: Strategies and skills in whole language.* Norwood, MA: Christopher Gordon.

Depending on the content study group chosen, teachers will also choose an additional text. Sample texts that may be considered for adoption by members of particular study groups are listed in the "Course Overview" section of this syllabus. Study groups may also choose other texts or additional texts.

Course Overview

This course addresses selected trends and issues in theory, research and pedagogy associated with literacy instruction. The focus this quarter is on the emerging national emphasis on balanced instruction. In addition to exploring the overall trend towards a balanced approach to literacy instruction, students will also explore how balanced instruction is reflected in current discussions regarding the following specific content areas: phonics, early reading instruction, writing, cognitive strategy instruction, and reader–response approaches to literature.

Each week our class will consist of three strands: (a) in-depth analyses of the national trend towards balanced instruction; (b) critical evaluation of theoretical writings, research articles, and practitioner articles related to a balanced approach in a specific content; and (c) creation of professional resource materials for literacy educators interested in balanced instruction. These focuses are outlined here:

Analyzing the Trend Toward Balanced Instruction: Seminar Discussions

Each week we will begin class with seminar discussions of the required text, *Balanced instruction: Strategies and skills in whole language* (McIntyre & Pressley, 1996) and other related articles. Because of the size of the class, two discussion groups will be formed (Masters and EdS/PhD). Each professor will facilitate one of the discussion groups and will involve participants in considering issues underlying the national trend towards balanced instruction.

Connecting Balanced Instruction to Classroom Practice: Content-Study Groups

Content-study groups will be formed to allow individuals to choose a topic of interest and to explore in-depth the theories, research, and pedagogy possible with balanced instruction within that content area. Groups will be formed around the topics listed here, and each group will select at least one book as a text. Sample texts are listed next, and other possibilities will also be shared the first evening of class.

- *Phonics*

Goodman, K. (1993). *Phonics phacts.* Portsmouth, NH: Heinemann.

- *Early Reading Instruction*

Fountas, I. C., & Pinnell, G. S. (1996). *Guided reading: Good first teaching for all children.* Portsmouth, NH: Heinemann.

- *Writing*

Fearn, L., & Farnan, N. (1998). *Writing effectively: Helping students master the conventions of writing in the elementary and middle school.* Needham Heights, MA: Allyn & Bacon.
Short, K., Harste, J., & Burke, C. (1995). *Creating classrooms for authors and inquirers.* Portsmouth, NH: Heinemann.

- *Cognitive Strategy Instruction*

Pressley, M., & Woloshyn, V. (1995). *Cognitive strategy instruction that really improves children's academic performance.* Cambridge, MA: Brookline Books.

- *Reader-response Approaches to Literature*

McMahon, S. I., Raphael, T. E., Goatley, V. J., & Pardo, L. S. (1997). *The book club connection: Literacy learning and classroom talk.* Newark, DE: International Reading Association.

Each week, group members will read and critically reflect on readings and will share information related to personal exploration of the topic. Group members will be responsible for establishing weekly goals, for determining reading assignments and discussion leader(s), and for scheduling when group members will share personal research information. Each group will have one of the professors as a mentor, and the mentor will serve as a resource for materials, will monitor the group's effectiveness, and will participate in group discussions.

Creation of Balanced Instruction Resource Materials for Literacy Educators: Content-Study Groups

Each content-study group will also work together to create professional resource materials for literacy educators interested in understanding a balanced approach to phonics, or early reading instruction, or writing, or cognitive strategy instruction, or reader-response approaches to literature. The professional resource materials developed by each group will be compiled into a CD-Rom (see the following table for an outline of the content of these resource materials). Each week, lab-time in the departmental computer lab will be provided to enable group members to learn appropriate software which can be used in creating professional materials (i.e. Dreamweaver) and to provide in-class opportunities for groups to design and create the cd-rom materials.

Outline for CD-Rom:
The Balanced Instruction Resource Materials

Title Page
- Picture of authors
- Author names

An Introduction to a Balanced Approach to Instruction Within This Content
- Description of content addressed and the "ends of the spectrum"
- Rationale for a balanced approach
- Description of relevant national standards and how this approach relates to teachers' ability to address these standards

Theoretical/Research Base
- Synthesis of theory and related research
- Annotated bibliography of related research
- Annotated bibliography of practitioner articles

Classroom Practice
- Sample teaching activities
- Video clips of classroom approaches
- Teachers' stories/reflections of classroom applications

Interviews with Literacy Educators
- Interviews with teacher educators, curriculum coordinators, and master teachers regarding this issue. Interview information can be shared on the CD in the form of a photograph and accompanying write-up on questions and answers or as an audio or videotaped segment.

Assessment

- Description of tools and/or approaches which would be most applicable
- Sample checklists, rubrics, or recommendations for artifacts for portfolios
- Sample student responses

In-service Activities

- Ideas and accompanying materials for use in in-service presentations

Resources

- References
- Related Web sites

Evaluation

Participation: (20%)

Each class session is considered vital to the student's understandings of the key concepts addressed in this course. Students are expected to have carefully thought about the assigned readings for the seminar and the content study group sessions and to actively participate in the discussions. Students are also expected to bring work related to the resource materials as assigned during the quarter to allow for in-class reflection and dialogue in the content study groups. In the case of absence, the student is responsible for negotiating with the instructor appropriate ways to document understanding of the material addressed during the missed class.

Work In Progress Folders (20%)

Each week students will update their work in progress folder. The folders will consist of the information listed below and provide an opportunity for the professors to be involved in on-going assessment of student progress. To receive a grade of "A" on the Work in Progress Folders component of this course, students will be expected to update the log on a weekly basis, to establish a contract outlining personal responsibilities and due dates within the first two weeks of the quarter, to complete all requirements within the due dates established, and to turn in high quality drafts of all work submitted to the content study group. Each of these areas are discussed in greater detail in the descriptions below:

Log. Each student will maintain a weekly log documenting activities completed and offering reflections on those activities. Forms for the log will be provided in student folders. (The reader can see the Web site accompanying this book for copies of these forms).

Contract outlining Personal Responsibilities and Due Dates.   An outline of requirements (see the following table) and a personal responsibilities contract form (see the Web site accompanying this book) will be provided to students on the first night of class. Using the contract outline, each student will determine her own plan of study to meet the course requirements. Where options are available, students are responsible for establishing which specific components they wish to have completed by the due dates provided.

Individual Responsibilities

Readings

- Read and annotate at least two research articles related to content under study

- Read and annotate at least two practitioner articles related to content under study

- Locate at least two Web sites/listserves related to content, write descriptions of the sites and a paragraph explaining the relation between the site and the theme of balanced instruction

Teaching Applications

- Create descriptions of at least two teaching activities which reflect the content under study

- At least one of following:
  - Videotape teaching episode demonstrating approach

  - Implement approach—and reflect on effectiveness

  - Administer assessment techniques—prepare description and sample student responses

Interviewing Literacy Professionals

- Participate in at least one interview with a literacy educator. Videotape or photograph the interviewee. Students may be the interviewer or the interviewee.

Serving as A Teacher-Leader in the Literacy Field

- Create one In-service Activity

Writing

- Choose at least one of the following activities (each of the following must be addressed by someone in your group):
  - Write Introduction—including description of content addressed, a description of the "ends of spectrum," and a rationale for using a balanced approach
  - Write component describing how this approach relates to National Standards

  - Write synthesis of theory/related research

  - Write description of assessment techniques with sample techniques

Editing

- Choose at least one of the following:
  Compile and edit Table of Contents

  Compile and edit Reference List

  Compile and edit Related Web sites

Completed Drafts of Work Submitted to the Content Study Group for the Professional Resource Materials.   Due dates for individual items will be determined by each student. It is the professional responsibility of each student to complete work on schedule and to turn in to her content study group carefully revised and edited drafts. Although groups may make editorial changes to the drafts after receiving all members' work, students should maintain a sense of professional integrity in the effort they put in to their construction on their original submissions.

Portfolio and Final Reflection Paper (60%)

At the end of the quarter, students will asked to compile a portfolio and to reflect on their learning across the quarter. The portfolio can include any artifacts the student chooses but must at least include all artifacts from the work in progress folders, a final reflection paper, and a copy of the CD-Rom. The final reflection paper will consist of a three part self-evaluation of work during the quarter using the guidelines below:

Evaluation of Individual Growth.   Using the free writes completed the first night of class, any reflections written during the quarter, and/or any artifacts in the portfolio, each student should reflect on how much she has personally learned across the quarter regarding balanced instruction in general and specifically in relation to the content area the student chose to study. Explicit references to portfolio artifacts should be used to compare a student's end of the quarter understanding of the theoretical, research and pedagogical implications of the trend towards balanced instruction with that student's knowledge and expertise regarding the topic at the beginning of the quarter. In addition to reflecting on this course content, students may also refer to any of the general competencies listed in the course objectives in which they feel they demonstrated substantial growth (see the Web site accompanying this chapter for a complete list of the course objectives associated with this course). The student should end by recommending a grade based on her evaluation of her personal growth.

Evaluation of the Individual in Comparison to Other Members in the Group.   Next, using artifacts in the portfolio, each student should reflect on how her contributions compared to the contributions of the other members of her group. Explicit references to portfolio artifacts should be used to evaluate not only the quantity but also the quality of the student's work as compared with the work of group members. Effort should be made to consider depth of theoretical, research, and pedagogical understanding as well as technological contributions or editing services. The student should end by recommending a grade based on her evaluation of her work as compared to the other graduate students with whom she has collaborated.

Evaluation of the Individual in Comparison to Established Criteria.
Finally, each individual should reflect on how her current knowledge and expertise relate to the following criteria:

- Understands the theoretical underpinnings, research support, and pedagogical implications for the current trend towards balanced instruction in the literacy field.
- Critically reflects on ways a balanced approach relates to instruction in a particular area.
- Utilizes cutting edge technology to produce professional resources for literacy educators.
- Is involved in independent learning and decision-making in the course of exploring literacy issues and then applying this information in constructive ways in classroom practices.

Author Index

AUTHOR INDEX 367

S

Sadker, D., 100, 101, 104
Sadker, M., 100, *101, 104*
Samway, K. D., 284, *286*
Santa, C., 185, 186, *188,* 313, *314, 315*
Sapphire, *110*
Scanlon, D., *34,* 37
Schaafsma, D., 107, 108, *109,* 115, 279, *282*
Schleslinger, A., 156
Schockley, B., 234, *238*
Schone, D. A., 234, *238*
Schrock, K., 89
Schroeder, J., 55, *60*
Schubert, W. H., 235, *238*
Schulman, L., 82
Scribner, S., *264*
Seale, D., *142, 147*
Sears, S., *264*
Sebesta, S. L., 3, 6
Sendak, M., 121, 123, *125,* 324, *326*
Shanklin, N., 352
Shannon, P., *60,* 100, *101,* 152, *157, 264,* 331
Short, K. G., 55, *60,* 100, *102,* 119, 120, *124, 125, 132, 134,* 139, *140,* 156, *157,* 185, 186, *186,* 313, *314, 315,* 318, 321, 322, 323, 324, *326, 355*
Siegel, M., 120, *125*
Simons, H., 31
Simons, R., 100, *102*
Sims Bishop, R., 130, *134, 142, 143, 147,* 149, 151, 152, *157*
Sipe, L., 47
Sloan, G., 150, *157*
Smagorinsky, P., 91, *96*
Smith, E., *313*
Smith, F., 323, *326*
Smith, K., 185, 186, 188, 313, *314, 315*
Smith, M. C., *264*
Smith, M. W., 96, 278, 280, *282*
Smith, N. B., *330, 331,* 332, 335
Smith, P., 324
Snow, C., 193
Snyder, S., 299
Soter, A., 130, *132, 134*
Soto, G., 223, *229*
Spears-Bunton, L., *143, 147*
Spillman, R. R., *264*

Stock, P., 108, *109, 110,* 111
Strickland, D. S., *60, 133, 264*
Stringer, E., 186, *188, 315*
Strudler, N., 224, *228*
Sulzby, E., 191, 192, 193
Sunstein, B. S., *56*

T

Tabachnik, B. R., 63, *64*
Takaki, R., 156
Tan, A., *46,* 334, *229*
Taxel, J., 142, *147*
Taylor, D., *264*
Taylor, M., *146*
Taylor, S., *101,* 104
Teberosky 192
Templeton, A., *299*
Templeton, S., 239
Tendero, J., 115
Tendero, T., 111, 115
Tenery, M. F., *264*
Tharp, R. G., 181, *182*
Todem, G. R., 181, *182*
Todorov, T., *34,* 37
Toulmin, S., *109*
Trathen, W., *34,* 37
Tripp, D., 237, *238*
Tse, L., 189, *196*
Tucker, E., 235, *238*
Turner, J. C., *34*

U

Unrau, N. J., *182*

V

Vacca, J. A. L., 204, 210, *212*
Vacca, R. T., 204, 210, *212*
Valerio, P. C., 224, *228*
Valencia, S. W., 41
Van Tassell, M., *313*
Vasquez, V., 323, *326*
Velasquez, G., 223, *229*
Venezky, R. L., *348*
Vinz, R., 108, *109*
Vygotsky, L., 15, *19,* 42, 191, 234, *238,* 245, 269, 270

Subject Index